Franz
BOAS

The Early Years,
1858-1906

Franz BOAS

The Early Years,
1858–1906

DOUGLAS COLE

DOUGLAS & MCINTYRE • *Vancouver/Toronto*

UNIVERSITY OF WASHINGTON PRESS • *Seattle and London*

TO CHRISTINE AND KATE

Published in the United States by the
UNIVERSITY OF WASHINGTON PRESS
PO Box 50096, Seattle, Washington
98145-5096

Published in Canada by
DOUGLAS & MCINTYRE
2323 Quebec Street, Suite 201,
Vancouver, British Columbia v5T 4s7

The paper used in this publication meets
the minimum requirements of American
National Standard for Information
Sciences—Permanence of Paper for Printed
Library Materials, ANSI z39.48-1984.

This book has been published with the help
of a grant from the Humanities and Social
Sciences Federation of Canada, using funds
provided by the Social Sciences and
Humanities Research Council of Canada.

Library of Congress Cataloging-in-
Publication Data

Cole, Douglas, 1938–1997
Franz Boas : the early years, 1859–1906 /
Douglas Cole
    p.   cm.
Includes bibliographical references (p.)
and index.
ISBN 0-295-97903-8 (alk. paper)
    1. Boas, Franz, 1858–1942.
2. Anthropologists—United States—
Biography. 3. Anthropologists—
Germany—Biography. I. Title

GN21.B56 C56 1999
301'.092
(B)   99-042589

Canadian Cataloguing in Publication Data

Cole Douglas, 1938–1997.
Franz Boas

Includes bibliographic references and index.
ISBN 1-55054-746-1

1. Boas, Franz, 1858–1942.
2. Anthropologists—United States—
    Biography.
I. Title.
GN21.B56C65 1999   301'.092
    C99-910820-4

Contents

Foreword

Douglas Cole began writing about the history of anthropology in the 1970s. The idea of writing a biography of anthropologist Franz Boas emerged around 1980 as part of Cole's research on the cultural history of the Northwest Coast of British Columbia. Boas was a pervasive and important figure in this history. His interests brought him to the region eight times in fifteen years, and his fieldwork and methodology influenced students of the local indigenous cultures for decades. Though Boas is widely regarded as the "father of modern North American anthropology," much of his personal and intellectual development remained obscure. Cole was impressed by the scope of Boas's scholarship, and even more by the character of the man. Two short biographies had been written about Boas, but neither had been based on his vast family and professional papers housed at the American Philosophical Society in Philadelphia. Over the next seventeen years, Cole conducted a meticulous study of this collection, supplementing it with further research in archives and institutions across Germany, America, Canada, and Great Britain. He articulated his findings in notes, drafts, and occasional articles that eventually formed the basis of this manuscript. In 1997, while making revisions to the final draft, Douglas Cole died suddenly at his North Vancouver home. The task fell to us as former collaborators to prepare the manuscript for publication.

It is a delicate matter editing a posthumous manuscript. The breadth of Cole's research and scholarship proved challenging. Our efforts were guided by a commitment to preserve the texture, voice, and style of the work. In doing so, we clarified the ideas and arguments of the text, occasionally adjusting the language where necessary. We also reviewed all of the citations and references. The published sources were verified, but not all of the unpublished material—especially the German sources—could be identified. Though the precise references may be lacking in these instances, the collection from which each is derived is usually apparent.

Cole originally intended this book to be the first of a two-volume biography. He unfortunately never wrote the second volume. In this work, he focuses on Boas's personal and intellectual development from his early childhood in Germany to 1906, when he left his post as curator at the American Museum of Natural History in New York. More than any other study, this biography profiles the character of Boas, exploring his ambitions, motivations, cultural roots, and personal struggles. The events and issues of Boas's later life—his teaching career at Columbia University, his views on race and immigration, his theories on language and culture, and his contributions to anthropological methodology—are not addressed here. They were meant for the second volume.

In the course of researching this book, Cole gathered an extensive collection of correspondence, notes, slides, photographs, and other materials. This collection has been donated to the Royal British Columbia Museum in Victoria, along with Cole's related files and versions of the manuscript, where they might assist researchers in further studies of Boas's life and career.

This biography was completed with the support of many individuals. The author intended to acknowledge their contributions in his own words, but was ultimately unable to finish the task. From the beginning, Franziska and Norman Boas provided advice, clarification, and personal assistance. Archivists and staff graciously assisted at numerous institutions in Germany, America, Canada, and Great Britain. Beth Carroll-Horrocks and Stephen Catlett, both formerly of the American Philosophical Society, patiently attended to numerous requests. Regna Darnell, Ralph Dexter, Leonard Glick, Ira Jacknis, William Koelsch, Igor Krupnik, Joan Mark, Ludger Müller-Wille, and Wendy Wickwire commented on various chapters and drafts. Wolfgang Bringmann, Richard Jantz, Konrad Colbow, Ralph Maud, Steve Ousley, Klaus Rieckhoff, Ronald Rohner, Peter Slater, and Marc Stevenson provided advice and information. Fred Deutsch reviewed the German spellings and translations. The research for this book was generously supported by an extended grant from the Social Science Humanities Research Council of Canada.

Ira Chaikin and Alex Long
Vancouver, British Columbia, 1999

Introduction

IN NOVEMBER 1905 Berthold Laufer, a young colleague of Franz Boas, called for contributions to a volume of essays to honor Boas on the twenty-fifth anniversary of his doctoral degree. The ostensible reason for Laufer's initiative, Boas's 1881 degree from Kiel, was not the only motive. The anniversary volume was very much a part of the fallout from Boas's angry resignation as curator of anthropology at New York's American Museum of Natural History. Laufer, a Boas recruit to American scholarship, initiated the volume as a protest against the tyrannical regime of the museum director, H. C. Bumpus. Boas himself believed that, if it were not for the disgraceful museum affair, there would have been no Festschrift.[1]

The appearance of the volume (belatedly published in 1907) symbolizes a turning point in Boas's career and forms an end to this biography, which explores the life and career of Franz Boas to the time of his resignation from the American Museum. In it, I take Franz Boas from his youth to about 1906. He was then in his forty-seventh year.

Born in Prussian Westphalia and educated at Heidelberg, Bonn, Kiel, and Berlin, he had come to the United States in part because of the opportunity it offered as a raw scientific field; but rawness carried, as he soon found, few professional prospects. After a series of false starts and bitter disappointments, his ambition, training, hard work, and sheer ability secured him a place at Columbia University and the American Museum of Natural History that he turned into an organizing center for American anthropology. Columbia (and Harvard) provided Boas with student apprentices, the American Museum supplied research funds for collections, and the Bureau of American Ethnology supported research in other areas. Private donors contributed additional money for students, research, even publications. Publishing outlets were available through the American Museum, the Bureau, the *American Anthropologist,* and the *Journal of American Folk-Lore,* all of which Boas affected.

1

In his first five years in New York Boas vaulted to a position of influence. He became a full professor at Columbia, launched the great Jesup North Pacific Expedition from the museum, placed students in the field to pursue research on the "vanishing Indians" of North America, sent Laufer to China as part of an ambitious East Asian program, and became responsible for the Bureau's Indian languages program. He was an officer in the newly created American Anthropological Association, co-owner of the *American Anthropologist,* and organizer of the 1902 International Congress of Americanists. All paths in American anthropology seemed to cross his threshold.

In as many years Boas lost much of that influence. His resignation from the American Museum meant the loss of a major part of his anthropological base. Even earlier, his position had been curtailed. The Bureau had fallen to individuals who, if not hostile, were certainly not as friendly as their predecessors. Harvard no longer sent students to Boas for ethnological and linguistic polishing. He was out of touch with the American Anthropological Association and disliked by a number of his professional colleagues. Now the museum too was gone.

He still had the American Ethnological Society and the American Folk-Lore Society (he would become journal editor for the latter in 1908), but he was largely restricted to initiatives he could launch from Columbia. His energy poured into university projects: a diplomatic and consular school based at Columbia and Yale, a school of ethnology and archaeology in Mexico to be sponsored by Columbia, Pennsylvania, Harvard, Paris, and Berlin, and, through his active secretaryship of the Germanistic Society of America, the promotion of German culture in the United States. He also retained his philologist position with the Bureau and was able to secure, for his prospective *Handbook of North American Languages* program, limited support for his students' work and some of his own.

This was a circumscribed base, but not a weak one. The Bureau's importance, as Boas had feared in 1902, was in decline. Museums, he recognized, had their limitations, and would have a declining role in American anthropology. The future lay with universities, especially those which, like Boas's Columbia department, provided strong training for graduates who would later fill university, museum, and Bureau vacancies.

Boas remained at the forefront of his field, respected, if sometimes grudgingly, for his amazing breadth and high standards of scholarship, and for his enormous activity and productivity. His practical influence, however, seemed severely restricted. As circumstances changed, he expanded his activities into public policy spheres, as a researcher on questions of immigration and race, and as a spokesman for ideals in which he strongly believed. Those activities would become considerably more significant in the second half of his life.

Franz Boas was an important presence in the North American world. He was, it has often been said, the "father of American anthropology." The paternity can be disputed, but his contribution to the discipline cannot be contested.[2] Besides his own prolific publications, he sponsored research in one way or another through the Jesup Expedition, the *Handbook of American Indian Languages,* the American Museum, the *American Anthropologist,* the journals devoted to folklore and linguistics, and the American Ethnological Society. As a "father" his influence remained with his student progeny: A. L. Kroeber, Clark Wissler, Edward Sapir, and Robert Lowie, among his earlier students; then Manuel Gamio, Paul Radin, Frank Speck, Alexander Goldenweiser, Ruth Benedict, Margaret Mead, and Melville J. Herskovits, just to mention a few. Others, like Elsie Clews Parsons, were collaborators. Remarkable, too, is that Boas, almost alone in his generation, spanned the "four fields" of the American discipline: ethnology, linguistics, physical anthropology, and archaeology. From this patriarchal position, he altered the course of American intellectual life by stressing the role of nurture rather than nature in the development of peoples, especially groups and races. His emphasis on the relativity of cultural values contributed enormously to the success of that idea in the forum of twentieth-century ideas. Recently Dinesh D'Souza has written, not entirely sympathetically, of how Boas and his students, as the founders of anti-racism and cultural relativism, brought the United States into a new era.[3] Those contributions, however, must be the subject for another study: here Franz Boas is the developing scholar, scarcely embarked on the battle of ideas outside his anthropological discipline.

His role even within the discipline has been criticized. He was not theoretical. He never completed much that he began, was never able even to write up his extensive ethnography of the Northwest Coast Kwakiutl. He saw only details, unable to grasp any big picture. His writing was hopelessly unstructured. His methods were critical rather than constructive. Even his fieldwork, for which he has sometimes been seen as an innovator, lacked length and participation. More recently, he has been seen as a narrow cultural determinist, dedicated to positions without any scientific basis. Moreover, he was, long before his death, passé. In America, innovators from British schools of social anthropology, Bronislaw Malinowski and

A. R. Radcliffe-Brown, had displaced much of his kind of anthropology.[4]

All this—and much more—is or may be true. But his importance remains. He is not dismissed, even by his critics. There have been scores of chapters and articles written on his ideas and on pivotal points of his career, some of it extraordinarily good, but, unlike Margaret Mead and Ruth Benedict, who have had more than a single biographer, the only books of which Boas is the sole subject are Melville J. Herskovits's *Franz Boas,* a slim volume published in 1953, and a 1979 dissertation, published virtually unrevised in 1990—neither of which used the voluminous Boas family papers.[5]

Verne F. Ray, reviewing Herskovits's book in the *American Anthropologist,* stated that he "writes of a man who was singularly difficult to know in a manner which would provide, in anecdote and expression, the material for an illuminating life story." Boas was "a man who helped his biographer very little by way of writings, public or private, which would add color to the portrait and cause to emanate from the brushmarks a sense of distinctive inner quality." Among Ray's remarks, favorable and unfavorable to Boas, this was the least true.[6] Boas and his wife left an enormous volume of correspondence that is quite personal and even anecdotal.

The Boas Papers, numbering more than 60,000 items, were deposited in the archives of the American Philosophical Society in Philadelphia shortly after his death. They contain box after box of correspondence, notes, photographs, and memorabilia. That a biography has never been written from this rich collection is partly because of its volume, and partly because so much of the personal correspondence is in German, a language no longer commonly commanded by North American scholars.

These papers form the nexus of this biography. The fact that they have been underexploited is the excuse for its length. While much has been written (and will continue to be written) on the basis of the large corpus of Boas's writings and the forty-odd reels of microfilmed "professional papers" held by the American Philosophical Society, this treatment is the first attempt to see the whole man.[7]

The untapped potential of the Boas Papers determined my decision to pursue a biography; they also determined, to a larger extent than I anticipated, the shape of its outcome. Their richness—an almost day-by-day account of his activity, ambitions, and concerns—means that this biography is more personal than I originally intended. This is not entirely regrettable. The development of Boas's thought has often been discussed, and much of that, notably the writings of George W. Stocking, Jr., I could not equal or surpass.[8] What has been missing is the personal context and a correction of much of the apocrypha that surrounds the man. Nevertheless, I hope that the tyranny of sources has not too severely limited its character as an account of Boas's intellectual development. This biography, then, is meant as a contribution to understanding the man and his career.

I have structured this volume conventionally as a chronological development of Boas's life. There is a pause at chapter 7, when he became an instructor at Clark University, to review and analyze some of his ideas to that point. Similarly, chapters 15 and 16 are concerned with intellectual ideas and themes. By 1906 Boas had developed an important graduate program, but its significance lay largely in the future. Alfred Kroeber, John Swanton, Clark Wissler, and Roland Dixon had already come under his influence, but, for thematic purposes, I have underplayed his Columbia career here, leaving that for subsequent treatment. I also have touched lightly on his linguistics work, which seems more appropriately set in the context of *The Handbook of North American Languages,* the first volume of which appeared in 1911.

A Note on Nomenclature

T HROUGHOUT THE BOOK, I have chosen to employ long-used and widely accepted terms for ethnic and linguistic groups, even though these are often inaccurate and not what the peoples concerned prefer to call themselves today. The Kwakiutl, for example, are more properly termed Kwagulth or Kwakw*aka*'wakw; the Bella Bella, Heiltsuk; the Bella Coola, Nuxalk; the Nootka, Nuu-cha-nulth; and the Thompson, Nlaka'pamux (or Nlha?kapmx). *Inuit* has replaced *Eskimo* in Canadian usage, though not universally. While it would be appropriate to use these names, I have preferred to follow the nomenclature used by Boas and his contemporaries, which, however inaccurate, has received a measure of sanction by long usage in English. Since usage varies, I have adopted that employed by the Smithsonian Institution's *Handbook of North American Indians* as a standard here.

I have also employed the older *Indian* or *Native*, in large part because *First Nation* or *First Nations people,* the now common Canadian usage, is unknown elsewhere, and *Native American,* the now common American usage, may not be appropriate to Canada's Indians. Alternatives, such as *Aborigine, Amerindian,* or *Indigene,* while having their merits, do not seem suitable in the context. I trust, as well, the reader's tolerant understanding if I occasionally slip into other older usages derived from the contemporary literature and if "primitive," "uncivilized," or similar anachronistic terms are not always used with quotation marks.

1 "My Old, Good Hometown"

MINDEN, WESTPHALIA

F RANZ BOAS was a sentimental man. Family and close friends meant much to him, and the associations of childhood and youth always remained a part of his consciousness. While it is now impossible to recapture much of the milieu of his formative younger years, it is important to try to put together an idea of those surroundings. Some features are so obvious that it might seem unnecessary to dwell upon them. He was born a German, indeed, a Prussian, and, though he might reject some features of that state and culture and even leave it for another, he was always some kind of German. Boas was also born a Jew. This, too, was ineradicable. Although his Jewish origin was a salient part of his consciousness only when forced upon him, his life was molded by the social and cultural values of emancipated German Jewry. He was reared and made his youthful way within a particular surrounding. In the search of the etiology of Franz Boas, we might start most properly with a look at his childhood city of Minden, then at his family, and finally at what can be reconstructed of his early life.

As the Weser River flows toward its union with the North Sea, it breaches Porta Westfalica, a narrow gap in the Westphalian Mountains which is its last barrier before the sea. On the west bank, a few kilometers downstream from the Porta defile, where roads met to ford the river, the settlement of Minden was formed in Saxon times. Charlemagne's conquest and subsequent conversion of its people in the late eighth century led to the establishment of a bishopric, which, after the breakdown of the Carolingian Empire, assumed temporal powers as a *Fürstbistum*. The great omanesque cathedral of the prince bishops became the center of Minden, though later churches—St. Mauritius, St. Simeon, the Petrikirche, and St. Marien—built on the terrace above the lower city, captured the skyline with their higher towers. The Peace of Westphalia in 1648 ended the rule of the bishops and awarded the region to the Mark

Brandenburg and thus destined it to become Prussian. The city later became a part of Napoleon's short-lived Kingdom of Westphalia, but the Congress of Vienna reinstalled Hohenzollern rule. Minden remained a part of Prussia's province of Westphalia until the dissolution of Prussia after World War II.

The nineteenth-century town, with its maze of small, irregular streets and courtyards, was typical of German cities with medieval roots. The major mercantile area ran from the Weser Bridge westward down Bäckerstrasse to a square called the Poos, then along the Scharn- and Höhenstrasse, to the market square before the Rathaus. The fifteenth-century Rathaus commanded the entrance to the smaller cathedral square and, across it, to the cathedral's doors. Atypical of most cities, however, the imprint of the military was greater than that of the civil and sacred.

After 1815 Prussia turned Minden into a fortress city. It was surrounded in stone bastions and walled fortifications while massive military buildings were built within its walls. Barracks, hospitals, provision depots, and headquarter buildings lined the cityscape. The fortifications, directed as much against Hanover as France, not only surrounded the city but flanked both ends of the Weser bridge and guarded the mid-century railway station on the east side of the river. A free-fire zone created an unoccupied aureole around the walls. More than two thousand men formed the Minden garrison in 1859, over three thousand in 1869. The Stadt Minden was dominated by the Festung Minden.

The city remained small. It was an administrative and military center that was important as a commercial hub for only its local area and retained but a share in the commerce of the Weser. It had no great advantages in the second half of the nineteenth century, and the fortress girdle hampered its growth. The rapid increase of the linen industry at Bielefeld, sixty kilometers to the southwest, reduced Minden's significance, a decline compounded by the transfer of administrative offices to that increasingly prominent city. In 1858 the population was reckoned at 12,252. It grew to 16,512 by 1873 and reached 24,314 by 1900. Mindeners were almost 85 percent Protestant; Catholics, who had retained the cathedral, accounted for another 13 percent.

The Minden Jewish community was small, though it grew continuously in the nineteenth century as part of the general movement of rural Jews to the cities. At mid-century they numbered about two hundred. There was no ghetto area or even a Judengasse, but the city's Jews did form a somewhat separate community with its own social and economic networks. Most Jews in the city were merchants, a few were bankers, with a sprinkling of artisans and professionals. Compared with Jews in other German cities, Minden Jews were prosperous, and most belonged, socially and politically, to the middle and upper class. Only a few households lived at the margin of existence.[1]

The favorable economic position of the Jews caused some disaffection. There was a short-lived anti-Semitic flurry in 1843 when a regimental auditor named Marcard carried on a placard campaign against their prominent position in commerce. A petition to similar effect secured 144 signatories, predominantly merchants and artisans. This middle and lower class agitation met with upper class opposition. Bürgermeister Kleine insisted that "if any city is without cause to complain about the Jews, it is certainly this one." In a debate in the Prussian Landtag in 1847, the Minden representative spoke in favor of complete emancipation.[2]

Although the Prussian government did not extend official recognition to Jewish community organizations until 1847, the Minden Jews had, since at least 1814, been assessing themselves for religious and educational expenses. In 1840 the synagogue was formally organized under its own statutes, occupying premises on Videbullenstrasse. A new building on the Kampstrasse was dedicated in March 1865 and remained the community's religious center until its fiery destruction in the "Reichs Kristallnacht" of 1938.

Franz Uri Boas was born into the Jewish community of this Westphalian garrison city on July 9, 1858. His parents, Meier Boas and Sophie, neé Meyer, lived then in house 143, a few doors from the Rathaus on the east side of Scharnstrasse, one of the twin streets that formed a boulevard between the Poos and the Market. The house is gone now, supplanted by modern stores in the general rebuilding of the street after the bombings in 1944 and 1945 that also damaged the cathedral and the Rathaus.

The young Franz would have had little memory of living on the Scharn. The Boases soon moved to Kampstrasse in the upper city. There they shared the ground floor with Meier's older brother Aron. In 1861 they moved again, this time into Sophie Boas's family home, situated opposite the military Hauptwache on the Market. This old Westphalian half-timbered house was Franz's boyhood home. By Minden standards it was a large lot. The house fronted on the Market; behind it lay a tiny courtyard and a Hinterhaus, used for the grain trade. That building rose four stories

9

to front on Opferstrasse in the upper city. Stairs ran from top to bottom, allowing the boy access to both upper and lower towns. House 166/167—both buildings still exist, one constantly altered by changing facades on the Market, the other fallen into dilapidation—was the same house in which Sophie had lived almost all her life. Her father, Jonas Meyer, had bought it in 1820, and on his death it passed to his six children, with Abraham, the eldest son remaining in Minden, eventually extinguishing the interests of the other siblings. Abraham Meyer—"Onkel Hampster"—and his family shared the house with Sophie, Meier, and their family. Meier Boas paid rent to Abraham, but held a partial mortgage on the building for many years.

Franz Boas's childhood was surrounded by family, by the Meyers and Boases, more distantly by another generation of Menkes and Maases. There is nothing quite so tedious as other people's genealogy, but kinship was always very important to Franz Boas, both in personal attachments and in his career. His antecedents are helpful in placing his youth in context.

Jewish family records are hard to trace in Germany. Jews tended to move frequently; before the nineteenth century they rarely had formal religious centers that recorded life-cycle events, and only in the early nineteenth century did they begin, under government compulsion, to use inherited surnames. The earliest traceable Boas paternal ancestor was Aron Heinemann Levi, a man who settled in Werther, a small town near Bielefeld, in the early eighteenth century.[3] Of him and his son, Feibes Aron Levi, we know little. The son of Feibes, Bendix Feibes Aron, moved to nearby Lübbecke, receiving permission to settle there as a protected Jew (a "Schutzjude") at the time of his 1793 marriage to Schönchen Joel of that town. It was Bendix, a cloth merchant, who, following the 1808 emancipation of the Jews in the Kingdom of Westphalia and the concomitant requirement that Jews assume permanent family names, chose the name Boas, after the kind man of Bethlehem who married Ruth and became the great-grandfather of David.[4]

Feibes Boas, born December 4, 1798, to Bendix, was Franz Boas's grandfather. He studied at Münster's university, but seems to have stayed only a single semester.[5] In August 1821, he married Caroline Frank, the only child of Joseph Meyer Frank, a Minden merchant of south German origin, who in 1808 had purchased House 146b Kleiner Domhof, an ancient dwelling that backed on the Rathaus.

Feibes Boas settled in Minden and continued his father's trade in textiles by operating a store on the Obermarkt, a street running southward off the Market. Here he and Caroline had five children, the second being Meier Boas, born in 1823, and father of Franz. Feibes died of tuberculosis in 1836 at the age of thirty-nine. Caroline announced her loss and her intention of carrying on the business in a newspaper notice:

> It has pleased the benevolent Creator, in His unfathomable decree, to free last night from this earthly life my beloved husband and tender father of 5 children not yet of age.
>
> I bring to the many friends and acquaintances knowledge of this great loss to me and, with this notice, pledge that I will continue unaltered the business that has operated for several years and ask that the trust they gave to him who is now eternal be kindly transferred to me.[6]

Meier was then twelve. Caroline's parents, prosperously in business on the Kleiner Domhof, would have been able to help their sole heir and probably did. The children's education continued as before, under the guidance of Jewish tutors and rabbi-teachers. The boys finished their study at the city's Gymnasium. Meier enrolled in grade ten in 1836, after having been a trade apprentice in Bonn. He then transferred to the new, more practical *Realschule,* or secondary school, for his final year, graduating in 1839 at the advanced age of twenty-five. All the Boas boys entered commerce: Meier and Aron in Minden, Max in Paris, and Salomon in Berlin.

Caroline Boas continued to operate the firm of F. Boas on the Obermarktstrasse, but moved with her store to her father's house on the Kl. Domhof in 1851 after his death at the age of ninety-five. At some time Meier opened his own clothing and textile store, perhaps in rented premises on Ritterstrasse and then on Scharnstrasse where he lived after marrying Sophie Meyer in 1851. A few years later he moved his business premises to Jonas Meyer's house on the Market. According to a family source, the F. Boas store catered to farmers and simple Bürgers, while Meier Boas's, on the Market, was "elegant" and "*the* store where one bought in Minden."[7]

The antecedents of Franz's mother, Sophie Meyer, were also mercantile. Jonas Meyer, her father, came from Petershagen near Minden. Settling in Minden, he bought the large house on the Market where he established a retail store for *Kolonialwaren*—material imported from the colonies—

and a grain trade in the outbuilding. Jonas, according to his granddaughter, had a "complete" German education for his time, presumably some secondary-level schooling. His wife could write German, but only in Hebrew script.[8]

The Meyers kept "a good, *bürgerliches* Haus," in which the virtues of "a simple, healthy life were highly valued." But there were also constant tragedies. There were eleven children: four died before their majority, another during her first childbirth, one was mentally retarded, and yet another epileptic. The children who survived all received a good education. The boys attended the Gymnasium after earlier private and religious schooling, and the three daughters, Berthe, Sophie, and Fanny, were sent to the Minden Töchterschule, a fine secondary school.[9]

Franz's grandparents were moderately prosperous merchants. The Meyers, Franks, and Boases were not among the wealthiest in the city, but they were well off. The 1849 voters list, compiled on the three-class Prussian system by which each category represented one-third of the taxes paid, tells a little. Jonas Meyer, whose taxes totaled 73 thaler, 18 silbergroschen and 11 pfennige, belonged to the sixty-five voters in Class 1, whose taxes ranged from 57.2 thaler to a city high of 202 thaler. Caroline Boas's position is unrecorded—women were not allowed to vote—but probably approximated Meyer's. Joseph Meyer Frank's taxes were 30 thaler, 20 silbergroschen, 3 pfennige, placing him among the 207 electors in Class 2 (between 18.2 and 57 thaler taxes). The remaining Minden males over twenty-four years who paid 18 thaler or less were in Class 3. Aron and Meier Boas are included among the 1,610 voters on the list, but paid no taxes probably because they were not yet independent of their mother's income.[10]

The generation of Franz Boas's grandparents, Jonas and Henriette Meyer and Feibes and Caroline Boas, were pious Jews. The Meyer household lived religiously, "moved by a genuine piety on the mother's side, perhaps more from tradition, custom, and an overwhelming sense of duty on the father's." Jewish dietary regulations were followed and the Sabbath was strictly observed: no meals were cooked (enough food from Friday's mid-day meal was left in the fire's ashes to provide warm meals on Saturday), and no candles were lit unless by a Christian servant. Caroline Boas's house was similarly observant and her children were raised amid ritual and in piety. The next generation lost much of the religion and ceremony. Meier's drift from tradition, according to his daughter, began during his apprenticeship in Bonn where his faith was shaken when he saw his master, behind closed shop doors, selling on a Saturday. It suffered further erosion when, in a Bonn restaurant, he did not eat kosher and found that "heaven did not fall to earth nor did his mother suddenly appear threateningly before him." He thereafter "dared to sin more often."[11] Neither Meier nor his wife remained religious. He did his turn as the Jewish community executive and retained an emotional affection for the ceremonies of his parental home, but the family largely ignored customary laws and holidays. They celebrated, in a secular way, Christmas and the other holidays of the Protestant society around them. Their children received religious schooling, but were raised within a free-thinking environment.

Franz's mother, Sophie Meyer Boas, emerges much more clearly from the historical record than does his father. Meier is the matter-of-fact merchant who leaves behind only official records of school registration and property deeds, who goes about his business without other involvements, the paterfamilias who delegates letters to his wife. Even in the fragmentary reminiscences of their children, Sophie emerges as the more real and arresting personality. By all evidence she was an earnest, compassionate girl and woman. She, like her siblings, was raised according to strict Jewish principles. The foundations of their education came from Rabbi Elkin's classes, but all were given the benefits of instruction at the higher schools of Minden, the Gymnasium and Realgymnasium for the boys and the Töchterschule for the girls. Tradition and secular education did not always go comfortably together. Berthe, at the Töchterschule from 1834 to 1836, demonstrated conspicuous talent, but her religious curiosity impelled her parents to withdraw her from the school. Only when Sophie was fifteen, in 1843–44, was she sent to join the final grade of the Töchterschule. Her school report is exceptional in its praise for her character: she was a model student, among the best the school ever had, and her departure left the staff with deep sadness and an earnest wish that her future would be as blessed as it deserved.[12]

The Meyer family shared many of the characteristics—and the dilemmas—common to German Jewry of their time. Tradition was highly valued by the parents, but it was jeopardized and, in Sophie's generation, eroded by the strong desire for advancement and acceptance in the larger society. The process of "Verbürgerlichung," of integration into German society, had been proceeding since the late eighteenth century. German and Minden Jews were already deeply assimilated into economic life, if less so into German culture and society. To the emerging generation, full emancipation and assimilation did not necessarily mean an end to their Jewishness, but it certainly meant a decline in its significance. Moreover, like other German Jews of their age, education was embraced as a means of advancement and integration.

"Bildung," mental cultivation, was a German ideal, one particularly identified with Wilhelm von Humboldt and the German Enlightenment, but German Jews adopted it particularly as their own. "Assimilation through *Bildung*," states Herzig, "was obviously among the Jewish *Bürgers* of Minden, an unquestioned principle."[13] The Boas and Meyer households, despite the ambivalences and dilemmas that Bildung might bring to their tradition, did not often question the principle. Sophie and her brothers and sisters shared in this integrating and secularizing process. As their emotional concerns departed from tradition and faith, they turned to the pursuit of intellectual understanding and social and political reform. The revolutionary upheavals of the 1848–51 period have left a few shreds of evidence of the concerns of Sophie and her circle. Most come from her friendship with Abraham Jacobi, a youth from the neighboring village of Hartum who would become a lasting presence in the life of Franz Boas.

Jacobi's father was a friend of Jonas Meyer, and when the son came to Minden to study at the Gymnasium he spent most of his time at the Meyers'. Abraham Meyer was his age, and Jacobi gave lessons to a younger Meyer, Jacob, then eleven, and perhaps ten-year-old Fanny. The Minden Gymnasium in which Jacobi and the Meyer brothers studied had among its teachers several men of advanced political views. Even Minden, lulled by its heavily military and bureaucratic elements into a politically sleepy town, had its democrats and radical thinkers. The liberal and democratic ideas of one of these, Gymnasium teacher Theodor Herzberg, found fertile ground in Jacobi, and the young student remained in touch with Herzberg and the younger Meyers after he left Minden to study medicine. Jacobi was at Greifswald when the 1848 revolution broke out. On moving to Göttingen later that year, he joined a democratic "Turnverein," or club, and befriended revolutionaries Wilhelm Pieper and Johannes Miquel. Back in Minden in the summer holiday of 1849, he joined with Herzberg in a group, primarily Jewish, which discussed science and politics. Among them was the twenty-one-year old Louis Kugelmann, also the son of a Westphalian village Jew, who had fled to Minden from his revolutionary activity in Düsseldorf. Sophie Meyer and her younger sister, Fanny, formed part of "this revolutionary-democratic, intellectually exciting circle in Minden."[14]

Jacobi left at the end of the summer, but stayed in touch with Sophie, Fanny, and others from their circle of fellow revolutionaries in Minden, and continued his political involvement, tending more and more toward revolutionary socialism, even as political reaction in Germany increased. He visited Minden in the late summer, where he renewed his discussions with Herzberg and the Meyer sisters. Over the winter of 1850–51, he began to work with the Cologne-based Communist Bund. He maintained an intense correspondence with Sophie and her younger sister. In October he asked Fanny to distribute some lottery tickets for the benefit of German exiles in Switzerland, enclosing a list of sympathetic friends, including Meier and Aron Boas. In February he sent Fanny and Sophie a copy of the *Communist Manifesto,* though he warned that it was not meant "for the streets and market." Little is known of Sophie's involvement in this, only that she had traveled to Stuttgart in January where she met Kugelmann.[15] Early the next month her mother died. Her one surviving letter, written soon after, suggests not only support for the failed revolution, but, in its almost bitter statement of the realities of feminine existence, a certain disappointment and frustration. From it we capture something of the strength of Franz's mother and of the restrictions that confined that strength.

The letter begins with an expression of sympathy for the political exiles and deep regret at the powerlessness of the revolutionaries. "The consciousness of our impotence, our inability to do even the smallest thing, would completely defeat us if we did hold up the hope for a better future." She then went on to write of how practical she must be, now that her mother was gone. This was not meant, she said, as a complaint. "What I do now, I do gladly; it makes me happy, as is fitting to any girl, to be busy, but it does often make me terribly sad that I must sacrifice so much of my previous intellectual life." When she resumed the letter the next day, Sophie gave Jacobi a little lecture on the revolutionaries' neglect of women. "Sometime, perhaps after centuries, when all humanity is recognized as human, even the yoke under which women are burdened will be broken. They too will lift themselves up, elevated by circumstances and the times, and rise to the place that is their due. Believe me, my friend, that then and only then will you all be able to be happy." The apparent vanity, sensuality, and coquetry of women were merely the consequence of their upbringing. "Do not leave us so alone," she admonished; "we too have strength."[16]

Two months later Jacobi was in Berlin, ostensibly for his state medical examination, but very probably to establish a new branch of the Communist Bund. Here he was arrested "by a dozen irresistible courteous constables"[17] and charged with high treason. Because he was carrying letters from Sophie and Fanny, the Minden police launched a search of the Meyer household for further evidence. None was found, and the women were left alone, regarded as young and harmless.

Jacobi was acquitted of the treason charge, but immediately imprisoned in Minden for *lèse majesté*. He was released two years later. Fearing yet another arrest, he fled to England, but found no opportunity to practice medicine. After visiting Marx in London and staying as Engels' guest in Manchester, he left for America. Once established in what became a very successful New York career, he was joined by Fanny Meyer, whom he married. Fanny died during childbirth in 1856, but Onkel Jacobi remained a close friend of Sophie and became an important element of Franz's life.

Not long after Jacobi's arrest in August 1851, Sophie married Meier Boas. She had just passed her twenty-third birthday; he was slightly five years older. In the circumstances of a small town, where Jewish families formed a still smaller network of relationships, they would have known each other for years and shared many of the same friends and associations. The death of her mother may have hastened her into matrimony. Her father was probably also in ill health, as he died less than two months later.

Sophie and Meier Boas established residence on Ritterstrasse in the upper city. Their first child, Helene, was born in June 1852, followed by another daughter, Antonie, in July 1853. That same year, perhaps to meet the needs of their growing family, they moved to Scharnstrasse in the lower city. Meier dedicated himself to business. He did not participate actively in the community, though he fulfilled, as did his brother Aron and his brother-in-law Abraham Meyer, his duty as a member of the synagogue council. In 1857 Helene died, a loss that was partly, but never wholly, assuaged by the birth of Franz in July 1858. In 1862 the family moved into the Meyer house on the Market, Meier moving his business there as well. In 1865, however, he withdrew from the retail business to become the German representative for the fancy goods import firm operated by Sophie's younger brother, Jacob Meyer, in New York. This required him to be frequently away from home on buying trips to Bielefeld, Berlin, and other cities.[18]

This was the context, then, for Franz Boas's formative years: an assimilated Jewish family in a small Prussian city that had its progressive, even revolutionary, element. Minden remained a bastion of liberalism into the 1870s and 1880s. More importantly, the ideals of 1848 lived on in Sophie and Meier's home.

2 "What Claim Can Someone Like Me Have Upon Fame?"

THE BOYHOOD YEARS

"I SPENT MY EARLY childhood happily with my sisters in my parents' house." So wrote the nineteen-year-old Boas in a long autobiographical exercise compulsory on the occasion of his graduation from the Minden Gymnasium. This curriculum vitae is a precious document, and for these early years must become, in part, youthful autobiography.

Boas's graduation memoir speaks only too slightly of his pre-school years. There is his older sister, Antonie, called Toni, and a two-year old cousin taken into the household by his parents for nine years "whom we were accustomed to consider as a sister." At this sibling level there is another presence that strongly affected the boy. "When I was three years old another son was born, who lived only four months. I have only very dim recollections of him, but through his death a brother was taken from me forever." The boy was Ernst Boas, born in 1860 and dead from whooping cough the same year. Franz felt the absence of a brother in his life: "my life became very different from what it would have been, as I was always thrown more on my own resources." Without quite stating or perhaps yet realizing it, Franz was now and forever the only son of Meier and Sophie. He wore a heavy mantle of parental expectation and filial responsibility.[1]

There were sisters born later, Hedwig in 1863 and Aenne in 1867, but they were too young to be companions. With Toni, however, Franz formed a strong bond, despite her long absences from the household. Five years older, she was his confidante and patroness; he was her shining protégé who would accomplish things that she, as a girl and woman, could never expect for herself. There were also the Meyer children who shared the large house on the Market. Theodor and Julius were older and Adele younger, but Willy was a frequent, almost constant, companion. Yet the two boys, born within days of each other, were too different for the personal intimacy that Boas felt deprived of by the loss of Ernst.

Franz's mother was the dominant presence. Sophie Boas, he remembered late in life, was "the chief influence" upon his childhood. Through her Boas acquired very early the love of nature that was the most consuming of his boyhood passions. She "liked to read to us things from the children's books by Hermann Wagner which dealt with our immediate environment, the phenomena which meet the child in the room, the yard, the woods, and with animals and plants." These were memorable times for the boy. "I always very eagerly drank in the contents and was as happy as a king with these hours of reading aloud."[2]

It was not only at home that Boas received from Sophie an initiation into the wonders of the natural world. His mother had been influential in the creation of a Froebel Kindergarten in 1860, on premises provided by the apothecary Faber on the Poos. Sophie thought the room, with its large adjacent garden, "more beautiful than any other place where I have ever seen a kindergarten." The institution was watched over by a teacher and an assistant, with Sophie taking an active part. By 1861–62 it had enrolled thirty-eight children, among them Franz, Toni, and probably some of the Meyer cousins. "There we were entertained with little games and talks, which at the same time were directed toward awakening our minds, especially our interest in nature by games which imitated animal life, and by keeping our own flower beds which we had to sow, water, and care for."[3] As early as these kindergarten days, then, Boas began his intense interest in natural phenomenon. The naturalist interest was reinforced when Franz spent the summers of his fifth and sixth years at Clus, a lovely forest and field setting about four kilometers east of Minden. Accompanied by Wagner's nature books, he explored the woodlands, occupying himself with the pursuit of nature.

The reason behind the Clus summers was not so idyllic. Franz's health was delicate. Mid-century medicine could diagnose no cause for his illness, which resulted in severe headaches, and it possessed no cure except the open air. These headaches carried the blessing of summer escape from the cramped city, but they also caused him to miss months of school and thus contributed to his uneven student record.

When Franz was about six, he left the kindergarten for private lessons, shared with Willy Meyer, from Herr Pemeier.[4] The next year they were admitted into the fourth class of the Bürgerschule, a grade appropriate to the seven-year-old cousins. The Minden Bürgerschule, the elementary school built in 1834, still stands on the Ritterstrasse. A handsome structure of neo-classical restraint, it is two stories high with additional rooms under the four-gabled roof. Like most Prussian elementary schools, it was co-educational, although already, in Franz's grade 4, curriculum streaming was evident. Franz and Willy attended the school for two years, from 1865 to 1867.

"Of all the books that I read," Franz wrote of his Bürgerschule years, "*Robinson [Crusoe]* made the greatest impression upon me." From it he received "a great longing to see and become acquainted with foreign countries," a desire, which the nineteen-year-old graduate retained. "At that time my desire was always directed toward Africa, chiefly to the tropics, and I still remember very well that I ate as much as possible of certain foods I did not like in order to accustom myself to deprivations in Africa." He seems, too, to have had the Arctic in mind. A childhood friend remembered him depriving himself of food in preparation for the demands of polar travel,[5] and he wrote his uncle in 1868 that he had run for two hours in the snow and rain "for America."[6] At about the same time the boy's romantic sensibility was captivated by Grimm's fairy tales. His favorites were "Sleeping Beauty" and "The Seven Ravens."

When he was almost nine, Franz moved from the Bürgerschule to the all-male Gymnasium, the oldest Protestant secondary school in Westphalia. Under Dr. Siegmund Imanuel, a converted Jew from Hamburg and the school's director from 1822 until his death in 1847, the Gymnasium's prestige had grown as its curriculum was reformed, its staff strengthened, and a more practical Realgymnasia program added.[7] By Franz's time the school had lost many of the progressive qualities Imanuel had given it, though its teachers were competent, usually conscientious, and sometimes extraordinarily helpful toward the interested student. By then, too, the building was overcrowded and "almost derelict."[8] Boas was among the last students on the old premises.

Minden's Gymnasium was organized along standard Prussian principles. After two years, students opted either for the academic program or for the vocational Realgymnasia curriculum. Subjects in the academic stream included history, geography, German literature, science, and mathematics, but there was a very strong emphasis upon languages. At the end of another seven years of rigorous instruction was the leaving examination, the dreaded "Abiturprüfung." Attrition was high. Of the 330 or so students enrolled in the academic stream, only a handful completed their last year and sat the Abitur.

Under the influence of Gymnasium lessons, Franz's naturalist interests moved from plants to animals. While he kept his moss and flower herbarium, begun while in the Bürgerschule, he turned almost entirely to zoology. "Our natural history lessons have now turned to the mammals," he wrote, "and I want to prepare the heads of ducks, geese and pigeons (I cannot get other animals) and to compare them."[9] Even his zoological interest was for a time subordinated to a continuation of the Crusoe inclination. He preferred, he later wrote, lessons in geography, at least those in physical geography, to all others.

The Gymnasium also meant a new adventure into languages, first Latin, then French and Greek. Latin was taught in every year of the Gymnasium, with French added in the second year and Greek in the third. He was initially enthralled by Latin, writing letters to his Uncle Jacobi in tortured schoolboy Latin and sending translations of Horace to Toni. English was not taught, but Boas began learning the language privately while in his fifth year at the Gymnasium.[10]

Headaches continued to plague him in these early years as a Gymnasium student. His mother took him to Ruhme for six weeks in the summer of 1867. The cure was only partly successful, however, and in Quinta during 1868–69 his health again became precarious. Dr. Hermann Cramer,[11] the family physician, warned against strain, and Boas was compelled to miss half a year of school. Sophie took him north to the sea, where they spent two months at Heligoland, the British rock island in the North Sea. He was captivated by the sea and by its wealth of animals and plants.

Young Franz returned to find his interests broadened by the rocks he had collected. The eleven-year-old's new enthusiasm was reinforced by the gift of a mineral collection and a handbook on geology and mineralogy. He turned immediately to a serious study of these, gaining, "in a very rough outline, the history of the development of the earth up to the present." At the same time, the popular books of A. D. Bernstein introduced him to astronomy.[12]

Despite the intense intellectual interests of the boy, he did not perform as well in the classroom as he should have. He had done well initially, finishing the first year as third in his class and with marks of "very good" in his academic subjects. Penmanship, a lifelong Boas deficiency, rated merely "satisfactory." The following year, perhaps only because of poor health, he began to falter. His February 1869 marks slipped to merely "good" or "generally good," but only a borderline "satisfactory" in, of all things, natural history. To everyone's relief his September report restored him to third in his class.[13]

His first year in Tertia, 1870–71, was marked by a number of important events. The outbreak of the Franco-Prussian war occurred in the summer as Franz was again holidaying with his mother and sisters at the Clus. From their balcony they watched Prussian soldiers, accompanied by martial music and song, marching toward France.[14] The garrison city of Minden was greatly affected by the conflict. By July 29, ten days after war had begun, eight thousand troops were quartered among the townspeople. A lazaret and a bandage and refreshment stand were set up at the railway station, and Sophie worked, as she had during the 1866 war, with the Red Cross volunteers. The astonishing capture of Napoleon III and the entire army of Marshal MacMahon at Sedan on the first day of September caused the city's church bells to peal and flags to sprout from every building. The first French prisoners of war arrived in the city ten days later. When General Bézaine surrendered in late October, another six thousand arrived. Meier had a pass to the camp, and the general public could purchase visiting tickets for a few groschen, the proceeds going to military charity.[15]

Sedan, Metz, the Commune, the proclamation of the new German Empire, all these were exciting events for a boy of twelve and thirteen. The war, Boas recalled, "gripped us Tertianer and we dreamed of all kinds of splendid deeds of war which we would have wanted to perform if we had been big." The brilliant success of the German forces made a great impression upon the youth, and "the newly acquired unity of the German Reich inspired us and increased our love for our fatherland and awoke our pride in it." He remembered having received his first knowledge of political parties on the occasion of the Commune, an event "which moved me no less than the war."[16]

The years 1870 and 1871 were stirring, but they were difficult ones for the Boas family. In September, as the German armies were besieging Metz and the French emperor sat humiliated in Sedan, Sophie accompanied Toni to Jena where she was enrolled in a girls' pension run by the family Weichardt. It was a common and fashionable procedure for the daughters of well-to-do German families to spend a year at such a "Mädchenpension," a kind of minor finishing school. Toni received English lessons from Lisbeth Weichardt and private instruction in Latin and drawing. More important, she was able to advance her study of the piano, the instrument which had become her first love.

Toni was happy at the Weichardts', but by the end of October she began to suffer from what was diagnosed as rheumatism in her left hand and wrist. She wrote that Mama was not to worry, that the camellia baths and wristlet had already improved her condition and that she was back to the piano. But the ailment worsened, with the inflammation affecting her hip. The doctor would not allow the girl to return home to Minden and placed her in a sanatorium. Sophie now had to split her time between the ill Toni in Jena and the rest of the family in Minden. Franz, at twelve, was relatively responsible, but Hedwig, affectionately called "Hete," was only seven and Aenne just over three. Meier's travels, necessitated by his agency work for Jacob Meyer's New York firm, did not make the situation easier. The Meyers next door could be of help, but they had their own four children to look after.

As the winter of 1870–71 set records for its severity, Franz's marks at Christmas were scarcely encouraging to his already harassed parents. He had slipped to sixth in his class, with his mathematics mark, a "quite good," the brightest spot. At Easter he was duly promoted to Obertertia, but scarcely had the new class begun after the Whitsun holidays when he was struck by a recurrence of severe headaches. "My headaches came back yesterday during Greek Extemporary," he wrote Toni, "so I have to leave school."[17] He was sent to the Porta countryside, but the next month, with both Toni and Franz in need of their mother's care, Sophie took all the children to Jena.

Franz must have been moved by the associations of this old Saxe-Weimar town. Napoleon had routed the Prussians there, and the place was full of memories of Goethe, Fichte, Schelling, and Schiller. The ancient university and the modern Zeiss optical works should have competed for his attention, but in his vitae Boas mentions only the botanical garden. He somehow became acquainted with Dr. Johann Dietrich, the custodian of the university herbarium, who gave him free rein of the grounds and tutored him in botany, teaching him something of plant physiology and anatomy, and introduced him to the science of cryptogams—mosses, fungi, and ferns.[18]

He enjoyed an almost carefree life, taking walks and excursions with Hete and Aenne, but he was a little lonely, since he knew no boys. His health improved enough that by October he was able again to take regular classes. Jena possessed no Gymnasium, so Sophie sent him instead to Zenkersches Institut, a boys' day and boarding school run by Professor Zenker. He found that the school lagged behind the Minden Gymnasium, so he did not greatly amend his losses, mostly reviewing what he had already learned. The outcome, so far as the young boy knew (or acknowledged), was that "my parents saw that I was getting too far behind" and so decided "to send me back to Minden."[19] This was not quite the whole story.

From letters that passed from his mother to his father in Minden, it is clear that Sophie was indeed concerned about Zenker's school, but less with its educational standards than with something more serious. Though her letter that raised the need to remove Franz from Zenker's institute has not survived, Meier's resigned reply suggests that it touched upon the question of Franz's Jewishness. "The Zenker episode," the elder Boas wrote, "probably does not have the bad character to it that you think. Such crudities unfortunately happen everywhere and from them, alas, our children cannot be shielded. They must endure it as their parents have."[20]

Meier was not entirely happy at Sophie's decision to return the boy to Minden. She had suggested sending Franz to board with Ludwig Finsterbusch, director of the Minden Töchterschule. Finsterbusch occupied quarters at the school and, being a bachelor, had rooms to let. The prospect of having to place Franz outside the family disturbed Meier. He planned no long trips away. "I can take care of his physical and mental welfare as well as strangers and will give it my best."[21]

The idea of lodging with Finsterbusch appealed even less to Franz. Already back with his father in Minden, he wrote his mother that "I do not want, for all the world, to go to Finsterbusch." He would be isolated, the only boy on the premises. Finsterbusch would restrict his outings, and none of his friends would come to the girls' school. The Meyers, he implored, could take him in, an invitation underscored in a note added to the letter by cousin Willy. The two boys hoped that Finsterbusch would have no room available, something that was almost true.[22]

Finsterbusch had rented his spare rooms to officer recruits, but Fräulein Schoën, a permanent lodger, agreed to free one of her rooms for Franz's use. Meier had a bed sent over, and the boy took up residence, though he was often able to eat with Grandmother Caroline Boas at her house on the Kleiner Domhof or with the Meyers. Franz, though he "never felt really at home at Mr. Finsterbusch's house," reluctantly accommodated himself to the arrangement.[23] He returned to his Obertertia class and resumed piano lessons with Fräulein Jahn and religious instruction with Rabbi Edler.

He was badly behind in his courses. He had missed a year of regular classes, and the Zenkersches Institut had been a poor substitute. Mathematics was not a serious problem, since the same course had been given at Jena, but he was behind in Greek and missed "the security in the use of Latin which one gains in the Tertia." Despite strenuous work, he could not catch up with the others. Homesickness, anxiety about Toni's condition, and an unsympathetic teacher did not help. This was, he wrote, "almost the worst period of my life."[24]

Toni improved enough for Sophie and the girls to return to Minden at Easter. Franz, back in his parents' home, was happier, but "the great gaps" in his schooling had not closed and his health would not permit the strain of additional tutoring. He gained promotion to Secunda, but in September even his best marks, in history and geography, were no better than "generally good." His German and Latin were "generally satisfactory," but his Greek was not. Perhaps as shocking was the weakness on the scientific side—the marks in mathematics and physics were merely "satisfactory."[25]

His grades were a consequence not simply of being behind in Latin and Greek, but also of a mood of apathy. His diligence failed, and he did only as much schoolwork as was necessary.[26] His graduation memoir gives just one cause: the disagreeable difficulty of being unsuccessful in school and the feeling that his teachers had little sympathy or understanding for his problem. Instead of redoubling his efforts at school, he found refuge in subjects that hitherto had been of little interest to him. In the summer of 1872, in a shift of "great significance," he used the free time from his "laziness in school" to pursue a general education, "allgemeine Bildung." While the sciences still remained a preference, he felt "a pressing need" to read German literature.

He plunged first into Schiller's dramas. "I could hardly tear myself away," he wrote; "the stormy fire which swept through them carried me with it so that these plays became almost my daily reading." From the dramas he went on to Schiller's histories of the Thirty Years War and the Dutch Revolution, until he "knew much of it perfectly."[27] Poetry followed, including the lyric work of Uhland and the ballads of Chamisso.[28] The *Nibelungenlied* and *Gudrun,* read as part of the Secunda curriculum, made little impression upon him, but Goethe's *Egmont* and *Götz von Berlichingen,* read on his own, did. To the nineteen-year-old graduate, this abrupt alteration of his interests was seen as a profound break. "Approximately here I can make a division in my life, since my development now followed along different lines."[29]

This adventure into literature did not bolster his flagging performance in school. Not even his German marks improved, and his "great gaps" in Latin and Greek remained. At Easter he was held back from promotion to the next year of Secunda, though the decision was later reversed and at the end of the summer of 1873 he rejoined his comrades in Obersecunda. Gradually his diligence returned "and soon I bent all my strength" to schoolwork.[30] The effort was unsuccessful.

His father had long held doubts about his son's development and felt, along with some of the boy's teachers, that Franz was not ready for Prima, the final two-year class of the Gymnasium. His parents were also concerned that his health could not sustain the demands of preparation for the Abitur examination. Early in 1874, Meier conferred with Director Grauthoff. The principal was frank. Unless it was expressly against Meier's wishes, the boy would have to be kept back. Franz protested, but to no avail. "That is all very nice, but it will drive me to despair if I have to chew through all that boring stuff again."[31]

The boy's failure should be kept in perspective. While Franz was the only one in his class to "sitzenzubleiben," such a thing was far from unusual. In that year, 78 of 337 students in the school were not promoted. In the following year, five of his twelve Secunda classmates failed to pass into Unterprima, and in 1876 three more were kept back from Oberprima. The Prussian Gymnasia were demanding schools.

As a consolation, Franz was given a holiday devoted to travel and natural history. After an April visit to relatives in Elberfeld and a trip to Cologne, Bonn, Bad Godesberg, and the Drachenfels in April, he rejoined his family at their rented cottage at the Porta Westfalica. He went with his school class on a three-day hike through the Deister Hills, then was off to Norderney, one of the East Frisian islands, where cousin Willy Meyer and his family were holidaying. There he learned to swim, while assuring his mother that he was "terribly careful" and never entered water above his chest.[32] The White Dunes on the island's north shore provided a happy hunting ground for gulls' nests and other specimens.

Back in Porta Westfalica, he continued with nature studies. He began in June by resuming some of the interests awakened more than two years before by Dr. Dietrich in the Jena botanical garden. Dietrich, he later wrote, had introduced him to the world that lay beyond descriptive botany by teaching him the rudiments of the physiology and anatomy of plants. "It became clear to me that true science consists not in describing single plants, but in a knowledge of their structure and life and in the comparison of all classes of plants with one another." He concentrated chiefly upon cryptogams which, "because of their peculiar life phenomena" (they reproduced by spores rather than seeds), had become his favorite botanical field. A microscope enabled him to "penetrate into the structure of the more deeply rooted cryptogams" and, aided by Oskar Brefeld's publications on minute fungi, he was able to understand their structure more clearly.[33]

The influence of Dietrich's tuition extended further during this free summer. The Jena botanist had also taught the boy something about the determinants of plant growth, and Boas traced the geographic distribution of plants in the Minden region, entering the different species on a map. Something quite new was an attempt to establish plant classifications other than those of the Linnean system. He had, he wrote proudly to Toni, "contrived a system quite on my own." He found it difficult to explain to his sister, but it involved differentiation by root, side, and top growth.[34]

This nature study was self-directed. Some friends shared his interests, yet the relative adventurousness and sophistication of his endeavor remain striking. He was already dissatisfied with "simple learning," wishing to penetrate into the "fundamentals of things." He sought insight from the works of Alexander von Humboldt, reading "with respectful awe" *Die Ansichten der Natur,* "then dared, though fearfully," to dip into that "sublime work," *Kosmos.*[35]

Literature continued to be a substantial part of Franz's reading. Goethe dominated it, followed by Schiller, Lessing, and Kleist. He also read popular books and historical novels on the medieval period and Herder's collection of German folk songs. His English was sufficient for him to read part of Henry Hallam's *The Middle Ages,* Byron's poetry, *The Vicar of Wakefield,* and a little Shakespeare.

At Easter, 1875, Boas was "finally" promoted to Prima, the two-year final level of the Gymnasial program and, letting "all my side studies lie," dedicated himself almost totally to the classroom.[36] Mathematics and science, now including physics, remained his favorite subjects, but he liked history, and his passion for the German classics endured.

He spent the 1876 summer holiday at Norderney, happily back on the dunes and sea, but nursing a badly burnt nose. In October he began his final year of the Gymnasium. "Now the good time ends and the work begins." Ahead was the Abitur, and it stood before him "like the Alps." Greek grammar with Egyptian and Persian history ran through his head, chasing out all other thoughts. "I cannot tell you what I am doing besides reviewing, because I do absolutely nothing else." Despite a slot in his study plan for a weekly report to Toni, the letters dropped off as the preparations closed in around him. A month before the exam he had a badly inflamed throat. Sophie feared that his body would not be able to sustain the strain of the final weeks, but Franz, though he looked like "a walking corpse," held on for the long examination ordeal.[37]

The five candidates began the process on Saturday, January 20, 1877 with a Latin dictation. More Latin followed on Monday. Tuesday was taken up with religion, so Franz had the day off. Then, day by day, came French, mathematics, German and history, and Greek. Two weeks later the results arrived. All had passed, but none well enough to be excused from the oral examination.

On the morning of February 12, the five students were brought before the examining board. They first had to translate from Cicero's *Tuscan Disputations.* Shifting to mathematics, Franz was asked to explain Archimedes's principles and other axioms. Greek came after lunch—a passage from the *Iliad,* frightful "because it had always been very hard"—and, finally, history. Franz had to recite Lycurgus' legal contribution and compare it with the laws of the Roman decemvirs and Moses, then present a narrative of the Vandal invasions and the Crusades, and recapitulate the phases of the French Revolution. At 5:30 the ordeal ended. The board, after conferring just two minutes, announced that all had passed.

Franz ran straight home. "How I ran down the stairs or up them, I don't know, but faster than ever before." His father, arms outstretched, awaited him. The noise brought the Meyers up from below, but Franz was despatched to tell Grandmother Boas and Aunt Emilie (Aron's widow), while Meier hurried to telegraph the good news to Toni. Franz characteristically marked the date. "I will never forget Darwin's birthday," he wrote, "the day of our examination." Now came the party. With the class below them, the Unterprima, as host, the "Abiturienten-Sauferei" continued until three in the morning. A long walk helped heal the next day's hangover.[38]

Franz had passed the examination, but his results were uneven. In the history essay his phraseology and expression was somewhat awkward and the conceptions often strayed from the main line, but the work was satisfactory. His written Latin was also satisfactory, but he emerged weak in both Greek and French. In neither language was his paper good enough to be considered satisfactory, but the examiners allowed his class work to count toward an overall passing mark. Only in mathematics, the single scientific subject in the examination, did he achieve an outstanding mark. The high grade was based in part upon his handling of a special project dealing with the tetrahedron and triangle. His results were partly negative, yet exemplary in a correct formulation of the theorems and an elegant demonstration of proof.[39]

His overall marks, reported in his diploma, reflected both the examination results and his classroom performance. He had satisfactory marks in German and the three languages, though his failings in the Greek and French examinations were noted. He received "goods" in geography, history, and physics, and again an outstanding grade in mathematics. His excellence in gymnastics was commended, but his handwriting was condemned as "ugly and untrained."[40]

Sophie took a mother's pride in the success of her son. "We are," she wrote Jacobi, "congratulated from all sides." She reported Banning's pleasure at Franz's mathematical exercise and that the entire teaching staff thought his mathematical knowledge far outstripped the normal graduate, that he had a genius for the subject, and that he must become a university teacher.[41] Grauthoff had called on Meier and strongly urged that the boy be sent on to university.

These opinions were important for determining Franz's future. Meier had long before abandoned his dream of Franz climbing the ladder of commercial success. He now accepted Sophie's ambition of university training for their son, but was unconvinced that the boy should be free to study any subject he fancied. The practical Meier wanted the boy to take up medicine, not a scientific subject less certain of financial and professional security. Director Grauthoff's visit strengthened the hand of Sophie and Franz. She was sure that Meier would bend and "allow him his choice, allow him to follow his heart."[42]

Meier did not defer easily. There were the three daughters to think of. They had no livelihood and there was no certainty that they would marry. "Parents become older, they do not live forever." He would prefer to see his son as a merchant because if he was industrious, he could more easily reach a position to support his sisters. If Franz must go to university, his studies should be directed toward the secure and remunerative profession of medicine.[43]

Franz had long been concerned with his future and by this time was almost dead set against a medical career. That had been his goal when he was twelve, but within a few years medicine had lost its attraction. He regarded it as essentially routine, at most a descriptive branch of science and, as such, intellectually unsatisfying and a field in which he would be unable to rise to distinction.

This matter of distinction is a key element in the boy's ambition. He was determined, even at fifteen, to "rise above others." "If I do not become really famous," he confided to Toni, "I do not know what I will do. It would be terrible if I had to spend my life unknown and unregarded." He feared that such would be the case—after all, "what claim can someone like me have upon fame?"—but he was intent upon doing his utmost toward success even though he was conscious of the danger of an overweening ambition.[44]

As he faced "that fateful corner of life, 'what will you become,'" he wanted to stay in science, to devote his life to botany. Yet that would mean he might end up in a teaching post where "I would have to kill my precious time with dumb schoolboys and never rise even a little above the crowd." By his last year in Prima, he had somewhat tempered his expectations. His goal, he told Toni, should be like her own in music. He should exploit his talents as far as they could be stretched and then be satisfied. But Franz remained determined to do what he wanted, to trust that his ability would match his hopes and "to work until I have reached that goal." Like Ulrich von Hutten, he had to dare to do what he wanted to do.[45] (Hutten, the much romanticized warrior for freedom, the Reformation, and a united Germany, was a hero of his at the time.)

The intentions of the fifteen- and sixteen-year-old Franz Boas remained fixed, altered only by the appeal of the mathematics and physics he studied in Secunda and Prima. In his last year of school he was still convinced that medicine was not the right field for him, partly because it would leave him hungry for knowledge and understanding and partly because he could not rise to distinction.[46] "From youth on," he explained in his curriculum vitae,

> my favorite desire has been to study natural science and, when I learned mathematics and physics, it was these which attracted me the most. But I cannot carry out these dreams because my father believes that they would not be *Brotstudium*. So I have decided, even without inclination, to take up medicine, the subject closest to my interests. Chiefly because my favorite sciences are the comparative ones and medicine has little to do with these, I have no real desire for medicine.[47]

Though he wrote resignedly about following medicine, he had not given up hope of pursuing his real interests.

By March Franz was fairly certain that his father would relent. "I am now quite sure, though Papa has not directly said it," he wrote Toni, "that he will leave in my hands what I will be." He waited almost a fortnight before making "a last assault on Papa," then was put off for an expected letter from Uncle Jacobi. The New York letter decided the issue. "Papa said that I can decide," Franz wrote joyously to his sister. "Now the whole future lies in my hands. We will hope that it works." Then Franz echoed Hutten's "Ich hab's gewagt" motto: "I have dared!"[48]

While this debate raged over Franz's future field of study, a simultaneous discussion emerged about where he would pursue it. Franz weighed the advantages of three universities—Bonn, Heidelberg, and Strassburg. Bonn traditionally attracted a large number of Westphalians. Willy Meyer was at this Rhineland university, completing his first year in medicine, and some of his classmates, like Alf Vogeler, were planning to matriculate there in the fall. But Franz was much more attracted to Heidelberg and Strassburg, largely because they were close to Toni in Stuttgart. The Alsatian university soon had to be ruled out, however, because its first year mathematics course would not be offered in 1877. For a short while Franz inclined toward Bonn, but by the time he secured his father's consent to a free hand in his choice of subjects, he had settled on Heidelberg.[49]

All was now decided and the future stood before him, uncertain but free. He chronicled it all in an effusive letter written to Toni from "seventh heaven."

> Now my school time is closed. The ideas which have moved me until now are finished and new ones will pull upon my life. . . . What does the future hold for me? I don't worry about that right now. I have no more wishes. All have been fulfilled. The examination is happily past. I can become what I want. What more can a heart desire?[50]

Less than a month later, the young man left for Heidelberg.

Who was this Franz Boas now on his way to the lecture halls of Heidelberg? His education and intellectual interests are clear, his character and personality more elusive. The nineteen-year-old Boas was the product of the Prussian Gymnasia, perhaps the best educational system in Europe. Its curriculum, essentially unreformed since 1815, preserved the humanistic and classical emphasis that Wilhelm von Humboldt had stamped upon it. Over half of the courses were in Latin and Greek. Franz never achieved mastery of these languages and their literature, but his knowledge of the classics was probably about normal for an Abiturient. Among such works his preference had run to the historical writers: Homer, Herodotus, Thucidides, and Tacitus.

German language and literature occupied a prominent place in the curriculum, but Franz's knowledge of German literature rested, as his diploma citation noted, "largely upon comprehensive and thorough private reading." He was deeply affected by it. *The Sufferings of Young Werther,* for example, made such an impression that "I could not leave this book until it had taken hold of all my thoughts." *Faust* at first left him untouched, but seeing a performance of it so moved him that "day and night I thought about almost nothing but *Faust.*" His reading concentrated on the classics. "I have never had a great desire to read novels," wrote the matter-of-fact youth, "and so I am almost totally unacquainted with this type of literature."[51]

Franz pursued some of his literary interests with Reinhard Krüer, with whom he became close during Secunda. Krüer, son of the secretary of the Minden Handelskammer, the local chamber of commerce, was a year behind him in school, but Franz found him a helpful associate for complementing and expanding his own interests. They arranged to spend one evening a week reading German literature.

Krüer exposed him to the kind of new ideas which he felt were so hard to find in Minden. His friend, he wrote Toni, "reads quite a lot and likes the classics. I like to talk with him about such things, for example, about the things we read in school—Cicero, Horace, Homer, what we think of Cicero's views, how and why we like Homer and Horace." Aside from their school readings, the two boys read various plays by Kleist, *Don Carlos* by Schiller, Goethe's *Egmont, Iphigenie,* and *Tasso,* and Lessing's *Nathan der Weise* and *Emilia Galotti.* Reading something together was "better than if we had read it alone." Only when Oberprima began, with its intensive preparation for the Abitur exam, did he drop these weekly readings—though not his close friendship—with Reinhard.[52]

Franz's education in other areas of culture was not entirely undeveloped. He had been provoked by Goethe's essay on the Strassburg cathedral to investigate its Minden counterpart. From the upper floor of both his own and his grandmother's house, he sketched the facade, using a telescope to examine the capitals. He wished he had a book to help orient him to architectural styles, for he noted the difference between the Gothic front tower and the Romanesque character of the rest of the cathedral. With Carl Droege and Reinhard Krüer, he explored, too, the architecture and monuments of the Gothic churches in the upper city.[53]

His knowledge of art was thin. From his lessons in ancient Middle Eastern history, he gained some sense of its art which was fortified by that of classical antiquity, but more recent art was a near blank to him. Minden had no gallery, and his taste was formed almost entirely by the "big selection of the prettiest pictures and beautiful statues" that were in his parents' home. Indeed, he convinced himself that painting was not an essential part of Bildung.[54]

Music was. It formed an important part of his life. He had begun to learn the piano early, and his enjoyment of Haydn, Mozart, Beethoven, and Bach increased as he grew older. Beethoven was his favorite, with Bach close behind. He never developed a taste for more contemporary composers, though he did learn to like Schumann. While he enjoyed the piano, he persevered not so much to play the instrument well, but as a way to better appreciate the music when he heard it performed by others. "I want to learn only in order to understand and, of course, to listen. I want to learn the playing of music only in so far as it allows me to appreciate it."[55] Even a mediocre performance of something like Beethoven's Fifth Symphony could powerfully affect him. "It made a gigantic impression upon me, and the melodies swirled around in my head for days." Minden was too small to often attract really fine artists, but a performance by the superb Florentine Quartet sent him spinning. He had never heard such playing, and he was so "completely enthralled" that he was unable to find words to describe it.[56]

Much of Franz's Bildung—in literature, architecture, music—was formed outside the school curriculum, the result of his own intellectual and emotional curiosity. "A burning desire to see everything that I heard or read about dominated my youth."[57] The Gymnasium was never more than the formal aspect of his education, and its curriculum formed the skeleton but not the flesh of his education. This was particularly true of the natural sciences, which were always the consuming passion of his boyhood and youth.

Botany had been his earliest enthusiasm, but his passions were seldom steadfast and he was easily captivated by an introduction to a new area. Zoology, geology, mineralogy, astronomy, chemistry, and finally mathematics and physics fascinated him, and he pursued all to the extent of his resources. He received only a small satisfaction from these enthusiasms within the Gymnasium. Science was not strongly emphasized there. Only eight hours were given to biology, all in the early levels; physics received an equal share in Secunda and Prima. No chemistry was offered, although twenty-two hours were devoted to mathematics in three upper classes. Most of Boas's knowledge of the natural world came from his own work.

By the end of his Gymnasium career he had acquired an exceptional background in the life sciences and, partly because of Banning's lessons, in mathematics and physics. His knowledge of chemistry, geology, and astronomy was less developed, but not inferior to that of other Gymnasium graduates.

The sciences had been his first and enduring love, but they did not monopolize his roving and eclectic interests. Besides literature and music, he was absorbed by geography and history, and these often competed with science for his attention. Geography was initially his favorite Gymnasium subject and, though his interest waxed and waned, he also "liked history very much."[58] He did well in both subjects and emerged from the Gymnasium with a good grasp of physical geography and of Western and German history. Again, some of this was pursued on his own, by browsing in a world atlas and reading in F. C. Schlosser's general world history.

Franz's intellectual curiosity and his earnest dedication to Bildung were permitted—doubtless indulged and encouraged—by his family. Franz's world of learning seemed so much his own that he scarcely mentions his parents' participation in it. But certainly his family gave free rein to his curiosity and encouraged it with gifts suitable to his sometimes capricious interests. His Christmas and birthday gifts from parents and family included Wagner's cryptogam herbarium (a sampling of mosses, mushrooms, and ferns), atlases, and naturalist and history books.

Something must also be attributed to the social and cultural ambitions of assimilated German Jewry. Franz's youthful intellectual enthusiasm, the desire for knowledge and Bildung, the intense curiosity and self-propelled learning, were probably not exceptional for one of his background. While not typical of German youth, Franz did represent a German schoolboy type, even more, a German Jewish schoolboy type.

The curriculum vitae and letters provide only fragmentary comments that might reveal Boas's political consciousness. His father cast his ballot for the National Liberals, but took no active part in political life and seems not to have discussed such matters at home. Sophie was the more crucial influence; she made the Boas home one "in which the ideals of the revolution of 1848 were a living force."[59] Franz, awakened by the Commune to the role of political parties, lost interest once the "great events" had passed. His extracurricular reading tells us a little more about the biases that guided his thoughts. Hallam's *Middle Ages* was Whiggish; Schlosser's world history was infused with the principles of the Enlightenment and liberalism, and Freytag's "pictures from the German past" with democratic radicalism. David Friedrich Strauss, the author of the controversial life of Jesus, provided biographies of Hutten and Voltaire, two libertarian, iconoclastic heroes in the fight against political, religious, and intellectual tyranny. The memoirs of Malwida von Meysenburg, an associate of a number of leading revolutionaries of 1848 and an advocate of the rights of labor and women, made a strong impact upon the youth.[60]

Physically, the young man who emerged from Minden's Ratsgymnasium early in 1877 was healthy and athletic. The delicacy of his boyhood health seems to have stemmed from nervous strain, not from bodily weakness. He was an above average gymnast in school and participated in the strenuous three- or four-day hikes taken by his school class. He spent much of his free time outdoors and wandered the Porta Mountains almost effortlessly in the summer. He swam when he was on the North Sea and skated on the Weser-flooded fields in the winter. While always small for his age, he was strong and agile.

On the other hand, he had lagged behind his classmates in maturity. This, as much as his health, was the cause for his father's decision to keep him back from Prima. Franz, his father had written, remained a very immature Knabe, a youngster rather than the Jüngling (youth), which, at fifteen, he ought to have been. In the end, Franz came to accept the wisdom of the decision. "I have noticed," he wrote in 1877, "that this last year has significantly strengthened my physical and mental development."[61] Boas still lacked social self-confidence. He did not mix easily with strangers, feeling self-consious, shy, and unable to bring himself easily to conversation. Social occasions were a great trial for him, and he avoided them when he could.[62]

His friendships were those normal for a boy of his age. Willy Meyer was a close associate, especially in things to do with natural sciences, but the boys drifted apart a little, especially after Franz was left behind in Obersekunda. His closest friends then and in Prima were Carl Droege, the son of an apothecary, Alf Vogeler, and, most especially, Reinhard Krüer.

His friendship with Reinhard was entirely a personal and literary one. Krüer had absolutely no interest in natural history or mathematics and did not even want to hear of Franz's. Boas regretted this, but felt that Krüer's literary subjects so consumed his attention that he had nothing left for other things. "A year and a half ago, I too had almost no interest aside from nature; that changed only with time." Boas was himself amazed that "we share almost no interests and no viewpoints, yet he is my best friend." The friendship had an almost inexplicable intensity and, while speculation is dangerous, there is a possibility that the relationship possessed the elements of the usual schoolboy "crush." Boas could later write, quite unself-consciously, of how, reading together in the evenings, "he would lean his head on mine and I could feel his soft hair." On the other hand, Boas later recalled that he actually had a crush on Reinhard's elder sister, Aenni, and was happy whenever he could skate with her.[63] The close friendship with Reinhard formed early in 1876, when Franz was seventeen, at an age of adolescence when there is a deep need for friendship and conversation. Reinhard provided one outlet, his sister another.

Franz had long looked to his own elder sister, Toni, for advice and guidance, as someone with whom he could discuss family matters that could not be raised directly with his parents. She had been away from home much of his life, briefly in Jena, a year in New York, and now at music school in Stuttgart, but "we have been bound together this summer more than ever before." For Franz there was a particularly magical moment when the two sat together awaiting his departure for Norderney. That hour "on the suitcases," he insisted, would always remain in his memory as one in which "we poured out our souls." It mattered little to his view of the relationship that Toni was again in Stuttgart in autumn. Excepting special moments like that "on the suitcases," he found it much easier to write his thoughts and feelings than to speak them. "When I want to tell you something," he wrote, "no word comes off the tongue, but in a letter I can say it easily." To this summer, perhaps, belonged the long-remembered conversations with Toni, "to whom my materialistic world seemed unendurable."[64]

With Toni, Droege, Vogeler, and Krüer, Franz could talk about most subjects, though probably nothing deeply personal. With all four, however, he did discuss religion. Franz had received religious instruction from Rabbi Edler more or less regularly until he entered Prima. He was confirmed when he was about thirteen. His parents, even if they sent their children for instruction, had themselves "broken through the shackles of dogma," and Franz "was spared the struggle against religious dogma that besets the lives of so many young people." He was amazed at how Carl Droege "swallowed the whole soup" of the Bible. Their conversation made a lasting impression: in 1938 he recalled that "the shock that this outright abandonment of freedom of thought gave me is one of the unforgettable moments of my life."[65]

An indication of his religious scepticism comes from his report of a conversation with Vogeler in their final year of Prima. Vogeler was a conventional Lutheran, but Franz, it seems, had somehow given the boy's faith a severe blow. "I am sorry to have brought him into this struggle between faith and reason," Franz wrote Toni. "I would of course be happy if he let go of his faith, but I think it is better for a person to give up his old ideas himself rather than for it to come from outside." He would not bring up the subject with Alf again: "I do not want to persuade him to lose his faith."[66]

How much of the man is in the boy? Hindsight is dangerous. Used facilely, it can destroy the historian's work; used deftly, it can lift it to explanation. So a biographer must sometimes yield to the temptation of teleological research, seeking in the mind of the boy the seeds of the man who bore the same name.

Early on, Franz showed an interest in history. Of the ancient literature that was read in Tertia, he especially liked Caesar's *The Conquest of Gaul.* The appeal lay not in military exploits, but in the description and history of the vanquished. "So in Caesar the history of the Celts interested me, and what was said of their cultural position and of their religion, rather than their wars against Caesar."[67] His affinity for the Celts may have awakened a proclivity for history which seized him during that decisive period of self-development. Cultural history, "Kulturgeschichte," claimed his chief interest, he wrote, but it was scarcely treated within the school curriculum. He learned something of ancient cultural history from the classics, but little about recent history. He resorted to Schlosser and Gustav Freyberg to learn what he could of the recent past.

A similar portent of the man lay in the boy's fascination with legend and folklore. As a child he was very much captivated by fairy tales. Like his adolescent interest in the Nordic and Germanic sagas, in Gudrun and the Nibelungen cycles, this can be regarded as no more than what would interest other German students exposed to the Gymnasium curriculum. Yet his mentioning them, along with other examples of myths, legends, and ballads—Walther von der Vogelweide, Adelbert von Chamisso's medieval ballads, Ludwig Uhland's collection of folk songs, and Johann Gottfried von Herder's *Stimmen der Völker in Liedern*—is enough to lead even a cautious biographer to wonder if it might not be the seed of later concern for mythology and folklore among quite different peoples.

One might find some irony in Boas's incorporation of music rather than art in his Bildung. Certainly his later writings were much more concerned with "primitive" art than with music, but he did much more than is sometimes realized. The deficiencies of his handling of art might be traceable in part to his youthful innocence.

Franz took the train toward Heidelberg on Sunday, April 15, 1877. "I looked for a long time at my old, good hometown—until the tower of the Marienkirche disappeared behind the Porta Mountains. And then I watched the mountains, through which I had so often roamed." He broke his journey at Elberfeld with his Kaufmann relations and in Bonn with Willy Meyer and Alf Vogeler. He arrived at Heidelberg late in the evening. The station was in the new city so he entered into his university career in luxury by hiring a carriage and having a hot dinner at the hotel Pfälzer Hof.

3 "One Learns to Be Content"

THE UNIVERSITY YEARS

H EIDELBERG IN THE 1870s was more than a university, more than a city. It was an idea, a dream, an unreal moment from another time. "Everything around me," remembered Friedrich Meinecke, "looked like poetry." The city was small, squeezed between the Königstuhl hill and the Neckar at the point where the river flows from the charms of the Odenwald forest onto the broad Rhine River plain. Crowded under the ruins of the castle of the Counts Palatinate, the old town retained the oddities and landmarks of a picture "that happens only once in the world and only here."[1] In 1693 the city had shared in the destruction of the castle by the French, but it had been rebuilt in baroque style, the red sandstone buildings of its streets and alleys lying in elegant irregularity and its house doors decorated with a rich assortment of madonnas, coats of arms, and gilded ornaments.

The university consumed the life of the city as much as the castle dominated the view. Students overflowed into the streets with their cerevis hats and colored breast bands and filled the Bierstuben and wine cellars with the songs and idle banter of the Burschenschaften. The Ruperto-Carola University, dating back to 1386, was the oldest in Germany. Heidelberg's fame rested as much upon its professorate as on its romantic tone and landscape. Perhaps the most glittering, in an age that bestowed its high honor to men of science, were the chemists and physicists whose names became synonyms of epochal discoveries in thermodynamics, spectroscopy, and electricity. Gustav Kirchhoff, Hermann von Helmholtz, and Robert Bunsen had given Heidelberg a distinction in the physical sciences that few universities—certainly no other small one—could match.

Franz, on his first day, climbed the hill to the castle, the most magnificent edifice he had ever seen. The view from its parapets unleashed from him a romanticism inspired by Sturm-und-Drang literature.

The surrounding walls, in which princes once wandered, the trees, rooted in the collapsed walls, made the rugged forms of the ruined walls wilder and gave the dead ruins a new life. As I sat on the balcony of the castle and looked out toward the lovely Neckar valley, I saw in spirit the wild malaise. I saw the destroyed fields, the burning city, the poor inhabitants driven from their homes. The movement of such gloomy thoughts was matched by a thick fog that lay over the broad Rhine plain.[2]

Other excursions and vistas awaited him in the next few weeks as he explored the Philosopher's Trail on the hill opposite the city and castle, the Odenwald to the north and east, and the row of castle ruins up the river valley.

The tedium of class registration—it took four hours to pay fees and secure all the necessary signatures—did not break the spell. He enrolled in Immanuel Fuchs's calculus and Moritz Cantor's analytic geometry courses. Then he met Robert Bunsen, "the first scientific giant whom I have seen with my own eyes." This was the man who had invented the Bunsen burner, created the modern science of spectroscopy, and made a dozen other discoveries that helped revolutionize the physical sciences. Though aged, hard of hearing, and blind in one eye, he retained a magnetic presence at the lectern. Franz and the other students greeted him at their first lecture with foot-stomping applause. The freshman's rapture remained: the feeling he had of "sitting at the feet of such a master and hearing his words" was ineffable.[3]

Heidelberg's romantic past and present greatness deeply moved the young Boas, but there were also disappointments. He had no friends and could find none. No fellow students from Minden were at the Baden university, so he knew no one. His own lodgings, on Grosse Mandelgasse in the old city, were home to about a dozen other students, but only Alfred Polis, a chemistry student, was friendly, and he was a year ahead in his studies and terribly hard-working. His first acquaintances were all "loud-mouthed Jews"[4]—"a quite unbearable circle" with whom he decided he wanted nothing to do. He remained so "very much alone" that when he visited Toni at Whitsun in May, he found himself so unaccustomed to using the familiar "du" that he almost addressed her with the formal "Sie." Now that he was "rather in despair at being still without friends," he regretted his promise to his father that he would not join a fraternity.[5]

It was not only that he could find no real friends, he assured his parents, but because the other students were so morally degraded, so "steeped in vulgarity," that one could find safety only within the small, closed, and orderly circle of a Burschenschaft. Boas was rather a prig, yet his impression was somewhat accurate. Few restrictions were imposed upon students, and, after the regimentation of the Gymnasium years, the almost total freedom of the university could breed irresponsibility— loafing, drinking, and sexual liaisons with barmaids or prostitutes. The Burschenschaften did offer a social support that protected against loneliness and, because they stressed an honorable and moral life, a protection against the excesses of freedom.[6]

Boas's terrible loneliness was resolved in June when he finally made two friends. He had met Hermann Ambronn at the mathematics club. Ambronn also had an interest in botany, "so we have lots in common."[7] Rudolf Bartelstein, a schoolfriend of Ambronn's, was studying law. Now, he wrote home, "my whole life here is absolutely different." The three young students took walks up the Neckar valley and over the Königstuhl. They fenced together in the afternoons, ate dinner, and then spent evenings playing chess or listening to music in a locale. The seal of the friendship came on June 24 when they drank a "Schmales," that is, they agreed to address one another with the "du."[8]

This formality of student life sounds strange to the modern reader. Jackets and ties were proper street and class dress, Boas taking off his coat only in his room even during the June heat wave. Students did not reach a first name basis until they had agreed to "sich zu dutzen" their friendship. In this case, with Ambronn and Bartenstein, the process required about three weeks.

The new friendships made Boas's personal life easier. There are other indications that he was accommodating more easily to life as a university student. He had become active in the mathematics club, though he thought members formal and standoffish, and signed up for lessons from the university fencing master, Friedrich Schulze. This step, expensive though it was—not only for the lessons at some 24 marks but also for the purchase of the gear—proved a wise investment. Late in June Boas received a challenge.

The incident illustrates the extremes to which student society perverted personal prestige into concepts of honor. Boas had rented a piano for his room. An acquaintance asked to use it, and Boas agreed. The borrower turned out to be a terrible pounder, and some of the other students in the narrow, three-story house complained about the noise. Boas offered to buy out the pianist's remaining time and, when this was refused, attempted to adjust the problem by changing his renter's practice time. The alteration did not appease his discontented neighbors. On June 26 several students in the courtyard began mocking the piano playing, though they knew that Boas was home.

> I was furious and yelled that they should come to my room to play their kiddies' symphony. They immediately sent me a challenger who demanded that I take back the remark. I said I would if they would say that their noise was not meant as an insult to me. They replied that I could take it as I pleased. I accepted their card.

Boas was now involved in a formal "Mensur," a duel to be fought with the aim of wounding the opponent's face. "The horrible part," he wrote Reinhard, "is that my opponent is an old and skilled fencer." He was certain to be cut.[9] What would his parents say?

The duel occurred in the Kirschgasse a month later. The athletic Boas, his fencing skills quickly developed by Fechtlehrer Schulze and daily practice with Ambronn and Bartelstein, surprised himself by winning. True, he received a large wound to the front of his head, a piece of scalp four centimeters by half a centimeter was cut clean away, but his opposite came off much worse: "3 cuts from ear to nose required 8 stitches." Boas was out of the house the next day, but his antagonist had to remain at home for three days.[10]

Victory was not entirely sweet. The holidays were only a few days off and he had to go home with an obvious, unhealed wound. He had breathed nothing of the challenge to his family, writing even Reinhard only after he had left for the vacation. It was six days before he could screw up the courage to confess to his parents the secret that "lay like a stone on my heart." He explained the affair, begging them not to be angry. He had done what he had to do. "I believed that my duty to myself was higher than my duty to you and so I did it."[11]

His duel was not his only transgression. He had also been arrested for mischief. It had begun innocently enough when members of the mathematics club had adjourned to a beer cellar and enjoyed themselves until two in the morning. "None of us, as we climbed up from the cellar, was quite sober. We staggered awfully, but went cheerily down the street." Reaching the square, they decided on the old prank of putting out a few gas lamps. Boas was "the poor fellow who got caught." He had to tell his parents—only a week before they were to receive the duel confession— and ask them not to be angry at his silly conduct. "A stupid thing can hap- pen to anyone," he wrote. "I am otherwise just as good and solid as before."[12]

The lantern escapade and the duel were severe blows to his parents. "The recent news of your first semester is not of the most pleasant kind," wrote his father. (It was one of those occasions that called for a paternal letter.) The lantern high-jinks he had regarded as merely youthful excess, but the duel worried him more. "You have, of course, not injured our love, but we now follow your life and deeds with much greater concern than we had thought necessary."[13]

And how were his studies? Of these no judgment can be made. German universities gave no grades, and his letters discuss classes and professors only in general terms. They give the impression—and they cer- tainly gave his mother the idea—that he spent much of his time in cafés and taverns ("Kneipen") and tramping the woods. He did spend many hours in class, though, between fifteen and sixteen a week, meaning that almost every morning was fully occupied. He had no written assignments, so, if he caught on to the mathematics quickly and kept up in his labora- tory work, the program need not have been heavily taxing on his time. He claimed, at least, to have been working very hard.

He enjoyed experimental chemistry far more than mathematics. Bunsen had much to do with this. To generations of Heidelberg students, the great chemist "passed among us as one of the last living heroes of a sublime past." His lectures were simply "famous," as "beautiful and clear" as anyone could want.[14] Moritz Cantor's analytical geometry lectures were interesting, even if sometimes hard to understand. Immanuel Fuchs's cal- culus lectures were boring and difficult, but, by reading a textbook, the subject became clear. Kuno Fischer's course in aesthetics was quite a different matter. The philosopher's lectures were so famous that tourists came to his classroom, and Boas, though he found it difficult to follow the abstractions of aesthetics, thought Fischer absolutely brilliant.[15]

He clearly enjoyed this world of enquiry. He did not regret rejecting medicine. "My studies are the most beautiful thing conceivable," he told his parents. "Do you know anything more beautiful than to learn about the laws of all appearances, the causes of all things around us and, yet more beautiful, to investigate them?" The immensity of what was to be learned astonished him. "Every day I see better, frightfully better, how large the field is that I want to learn, but I nevertheless hope to learn all that I have put ahead of me as my goal."[16]

The semester closed with a large celebration to honor Bunsen's twenty-fifth year at the university. The following day, Boas had an appointment with the university police about the gas lanterns. He received a three-day sentence to be served in the "Kazer," the student jail, at an undetermined time. He left Heidelberg, the sentence unserved, and his scalp wound unhealed, on August 3, 1877.

It was not a happy holiday. He had to undergo a lengthy conversation with his mother and father about his conduct. That was expected, but a tragedy which occurred three weeks after his arrival was not. Shortly after noon on August 24, Reinhard Krüer drowned while swimming in the Weser. Struck by severe cramps, he was unable to reach the shore. Rescue attempts failed, and he was gone. Franz joined in the melancholy search for the body, which was found four days later. Reinhard was an unusually esteemed young man, and his death struck the city hard. "He was the best student of his class, full of freshness and life, a respected youth, enthusiastic about all that was good and beautiful."[17] The funeral was on August 29, and the entire Gymnasium and many from the city walked behind the bier to the cemetery.

That evening Franz was on board a train to Berlin, despatched by his parents in an attempt to distract him from the loss of his closest friend. He stopped with his uncle Mons, who took him on a holiday to Denmark and kept him busy in a whirl of visits to friends, relations, and the sights of the city. He came home on September 20, and dabbled in a review of calculus with a student from Bonn. A month later he was off to that university himself.

Boas had never intended to stay at Heidelberg for more than his first semester. He had gone there largely to be close to Toni, who was now in Berlin studying under Theodor Kullak. Franz had grown fond of Heidelberg, but Ambronn and Bartelstein were leaving, and he did not think he could find there the teaching he wanted in physics and organic chemistry. Physiology, his first love, would take too many years of study, so he had decided on physics, "the discipline that most attracts me."[18] There was hardly anywhere better to study that subject than under Rudolf Clausius at Bonn.

Bonn's setting was very different from Heidelberg's, but it too was a small city. Its most notable building was the Romanesque church, but much of the city's fame rested upon Beethoven, its greatest son. The

43

university was much newer than Heidelberg's: the electors' academy had been elevated to university status only in 1784 and lasted but thirteen years before it closed its doors under French occupation. Prussia, succeeding to the electorate in 1814, had reestablished a seat of learning, now named, like its older sister in Berlin, after Friedrich Wilhelm.

The university occupied the former residences of the electors, with the central facilities in the three-story palace on the southern edge of the city and the scientific laboratories in the nearby Poppelsdorfer Schloss. On the third Saturday of October 1877, Franz Boas, still depressed by the loss of Reinhard, arrived in Bonn to begin the winter semester, the first of four semesters he would spend in this Rhineland city. Willy Meyer put him up for the night; the next day he located furnished rooms at Belderbergstrasse 16. He rented a piano and again hung his photographs on the wall, now adding Reinhard's between those of his mother and father.

He put himself down for a heavy schedule of integral calculus, experimental physics, electrical theory, crystallography, and geography, with additional seminars in mathematics and physics. As important, perhaps, was his decision that day to join the fraternal organization Burschenschaft Alemannia. Behind the decision lay his overwhelming fear of loneliness, now increased by the loss of Reinhard. "I cannot be alone," he wrote Toni. "If I were, I would think too much about the past, about what cannot be altered."[19]

The Alemannia was a natural choice. There were also the Korps, but they were conservative and aristocratic; he would not have sought their association and none would have accepted his overtures. He had no affinity with any of the Catholic groups or with the Protestant Wingolfs. Only the three Burschenschaften were possibilities, and with the Alemannia he already had close associations. It traditionally recruited from Westphalia; Willy had been a member for three semesters and had already introduced Franz to the group. Also influential was a new friend, Karl Bertelsmann, a young student from Bielefeld whom he had met on the train from Minden. Before the two had exchanged more than a few words, the mutual camaraderie was apparent, and they were soon tramping the Kreuzberg together. "It is laughable," he confided to Toni, "so to like a complete stranger, but I cannot help it." For a time he was jealous of anyone else who befriended Bertelsmann.[20]

The German Burschenschaften dated back to the early nineteenth century and had been notable for their dedication to the unification of Germany on liberal and constitutional principles. This was particularly true of the Burschenschaft Alemannia, whose colors, black-red-gold, remained those of the liberal revolution. Its roots lay in the Prussian reform and the Vormärz era, and it remained essentially liberal, based as its membership was in the Rhineland, Westphalia, and the Hanseatic cities. It freely accepted Jews like Boas, Meyer, and a young law student of Boas's "Fuchs," or pledge semester, Eduard Springorum. Only later, in the 1890s, did the Alemmania join the general trend of the Burschenschaften to exclude new Jewish members.

These fraternal university organizations were close knit. Members usually lunched together, the Alemannia in Boas's time normally meeting at Löllgen's on Wilhelmstrasse where a warm meal could be had for 90 pfennige, and then at their own premises on the Rhine bank. They usually gathered together again in the evening, compulsory on Wednesdays, at a beer Kneipe. Friendships with nonmembers were discouraged.

Boas was caught up in this close life of the Alemannia. His letters are full of references to the Burschenschaft, his initiation or "Eintrittscommerz," the annual founding celebration with Old Boys, or "älte Herren," the weekly Kneipe nights and fencing practice at the Fechtboden, and business meetings or the "Convents." For one semester he served as secretary; the only surviving minute book is in his handwriting and cites a reprimand received when Gustav Öhlert and Franz Boas came "betrunken zur Kneipe."[21] The bond among the members strongly impressed Boas. "I would never have thought such close ties between the whole group were at all possible. We are 21, constantly together. You would think there would be cliques formed, and certainly one is closer to some than to others, but we stand all for one and one for all."[22]

Student life at Bonn was typical of small German universities. Close to a thousand students attended the Rheinisch Friedrich-Wilhelms Universität at this time. More than half were from the Rhine provinces around Bonn, Westphalia providing the next largest number—some 115 of 895 in the winter semester of 1877–78. Only a minority, perhaps less than a tenth, were members of the Korps, the Burschenschaften, or the Landsmannschaften, all of which demanded that their adherents defend their honor through "unconditional satisfaction," that is, by a duel with sabers. Catholics made up a slight majority of the Bonn students and were forbidden by the church from dueling. Some formed their own Catholic corporations along lines similar to the Burschenschaften. The remainder of Bonn students were, as Boas had been at Heidelberg, independents, "Finkenstudenten."

Duels were illegal, but this was ignored by the student organizations. The university authorities remained tolerant except when serious injuries forced them to take action. Like other groups, the Alemannen held their Mensuren more or less safe from university police—in summer in the Kottenforst woods, in winter in some suburban locale. The technique changed over the years. The deft and artful parrying of mid-century had given way by the 1870s to an emphasis upon a static fighting pose in which a contestant stood firmly in place, seeking to overcome his opponent largely by the strength of his blows. As a consequence, wounds became larger, a dozen stitches no longer being unusual.[23]

Boas was already a veteran of the Mensur, and membership in the dueling Alemannia only increased the likelihood of such encounters. His letters record one in January 1878 when he received an "elenden Blutigen"—a miserable cut—which required him to stay home for a day. No more are reported until his final Bonn semester, when he fought Walther Langen, a Korps student sometimes considered the best swordsman in Bonn and Göttingen. Boas was "very happy" when "I did more to him than he did to me." The cut across Boas's mouth, necessitated only a day in his room (such seems the measure of severity). "My duels are over," he wrote home after that one, but this was not the case. Langen's Korps decided that their match had not been satisfactory, a calculated insult which forced Boas to demand an immediate settlement. "If you knew student relationships better," he explained, "you would understand how severe this insult was."[24] The outcome is unrecorded.

While the Alemannia dominated much of his life outside the classroom, it did not monopolize it. Music continued as an important element. He formed a trio with Bertelsmann and Springorum that performed for the group's founders' day celebrations, and he found satisfaction in the rich musical culture of Bonn. He joined the choir, which allowed him better (and cheaper) access to concerts at Beethoven Hall. He heard, one after another, some of the great performers of the age: Max Bruch conducting one of his concerti, with Pablo de Sarasate as soloist; Joseph Joachim, the most famous violinist of his day; and Clara Schumann playing Mozart, Chopin, and Schumann. Some pieces he had never heard before. Despite his long devotion to Beethoven, he had never heard a performance of *Egmont* or the Ninth Symphony. The march from the former enraptured him; the latter sent music careening around his head the whole night. Even Bonn could not support opera, but Cologne was near enough that he could attend a performance of *Die Walküre*, his first experience with Wagner. He was impressed by the power of the musical drama, by Wagner's knitting of music and poetry into a moving unity. He left puzzled at the attacks upon the composer.

There were other diversions, though only in May did he cross the Rhine for his first hike in the Siebengebirge. He enrolled in a dancing class and in February attended his first ball. The Lenten carnivals of Catholic Rhineland were new to him. Everyone abandoned all normal inhibitions, "dutzening" each other and playing the fool. He left Bonn's frolics at 3:00 A.M., "not quite sober," to rise early to travel to Cologne. He missed the train back and had to sleep rough. A third night's ball adjourned at 2:00 A.M. to Hagemann's tavern. The result was "ein grosser Kater," a monstrous hangover. He had been "quite crazy the whole time," celebrating as foolishly as any one. "It's good that it only comes once, but I really had fun."[25]

Boas, in his first semester at Bonn, still owed one responsibility to his former university—the unserved term in the student jail. A gentle reminder came from his father: "the nemesis for your Heidelberg student pranks had come knocking" in the form of a police enquiry.[26] The Bonn university court had no information about his case, but the paperwork finally caught up with the condemned, and on Friday morning, November 30, Franz was locked up in the student jail until the following Monday. The stay was terribly boring and the air foul; any longer and "I would certainly have become sick." The warder bent the rules to allow a visit from Willy.[27]

Such activities did not necessarily impede his study, which by December "possessed me like a demon." In the summer semester of 1878 he scheduled himself for a daunting twenty-six hours of classes. He enjoyed the work, especially the botany class which allowed him to get out into "fresh, free nature." Much of the botanizing was with Franz Richarz, a younger member of the Alemannia who shared many of his interests and who, as a native of suburban Endenich, already knew the local plants.[28] Together they went to the Lachensee in the Eifel, a volcanic region new to Boas. Richarz and Hermann Blendermann, a medical student from Bremen, now succeeded Bertelsmann as his closest friends. Willy, studying for his doctoral examination, moved to the periphery of Boas's circle and then left for military service at Erlangen.

In the winter semester, Franz moved into the same house as Blendermann on the Bergstrasse. There were the normal run of student events: the February Alemannia founders' night at Hagemann's (and a hangover afterwards), a May trip to Marburg as part of an Alemannen delegation to visit the Burschenschaft Armenia, and an outing to the Ahr valley with Richarz. The Commerz in June for the Kaiser's wedding anniversary was politically repellent, but Boas, as treasurer of the students' association, felt obliged to participate. Finally, there was a doctoral jubilee for astronomy professor Eduard Schönfeld, with Boas selected to deliver the student address. There was an unfortunate aftermath: a street fight involving members of the Korps, other students, and townspeople. The scuffle made the newspapers, including mention of a wounded Alemanne. "That was me," he wrote his parents. He suffered cuts to the arm and forehead, but assured them that, immediately stitched, both wounds were healed.[29]

Student life and student honor made heavy demands upon the young man, but during these two Bonn years he also settled into the satisfying role of a scholar. Boas was, despite the drinking and dueling, a more serious student at Bonn than he had been at Heidelberg. His commitment to the sciences had been made; he worked very hard at them, and he foresaw a future for himself as a university teacher.

He took most of his classroom work in mathematics and physics, his chosen disciplines. Hermann Kortum's calculus was a continuation of the course begun at Heidelberg, and he progressed to probability calculus and algebraic elements from Rudolf Lipschitz. Physics at Bonn meant Rudolf Clausius. Boas took the physicist's basic course, dealing with acoustics, optics, magnetism, and electricity, as well as advanced courses in elasticity theory, the mechanical theory of heat, and electrical theory. Clausius's lectures were clear and unpretentious. Moreover, he was among the most advanced thinkers in theoretical physics. He had restated the second law of thermodynamics and introduced the concept of entropy; he advanced the kinetic theory of gases and formulated a theory of electrolysis, a field in which he was particularly active while Boas sat in his seminars. For Clausius, he had a "gigantic respect"; the physicist was "certainly a man such as one seldom meets."[30]

Boas hardly pursued chemistry at Bonn. He registered in a laboratory under Friedrich Kekulé, but the course is so absent from his letters that he probably dropped it. His dedication was to mathematical physics and, when he sought diversion, he found it in those subjects that had captivated his boyhood and Gymnasium enthusiasms. With Richarz he took Johannes von Hanstein's botanical microscopy and botanical seminar. He sat in on some geology classes and several of Schönfeld's astronomy courses. He would have liked to have taken zoology, but could fit in only a semester's course in comparative anatomy.

To some of his student friends, Boas was being quixotically indulgent in taking or auditing such courses. To their sentiment that "we do not need them for the exam," he scornfully retorted, "as if one studied for that reason." The challenge of allgemeine Bildung was still with him. "I often want to devote myself exclusively to mathematical physics," he wrote, "but there is more to learn than one thing. I constantly remind myself that there is a great danger of becoming one-sided, but it takes so much to finish my studies that I do not know where to steal time for general learning." He wished he could take a whole semester for private tutoring in his own field so he could register only for arts courses at the university.[31] In January 1878 he began attending Bona Meyer's history of philosophy lectures.

Boas also took several courses in geography, yet another subject that related more to his boyhood interests than to his mathematical physics vocation. In his first Bonn semester he signed up for a two-hour lecture course in the geography of America and Australia, taught by the youthful docent, Theobald Fischer. At their first meeting, Boas found Fischer surprisingly friendly, even willing to change his lecture hours to accommodate Boas's conflicts. Fischer's cooperative response stemmed in part from his desire to attract science students to geography, even more from himself being an Old Boy of Burschenschaften in Heidelberg and Halle. While Boas did not formally register for any more geography courses, he did audit several of Fischer's other offerings, including one on hydrography, meteorology, and methodology, and another dealing with the history of polar research. Fischer was the single instructor at Bonn with whom Boas had a social rather than merely academic relationship. This was largely because of the Burschenschaft connection, though Fischer established at Bonn a lifelong practice of inviting students to his home. Boas's interest in geography and friendship with Fischer were to have an important influence on his career.

There is a final experience, or rather there are two, that need to be added before we can allow Boas to take his departure from Bonn. In February 1879 Bonn's new synagogue was dedicated. Boas received invitations to a dinner and ball. He saw no reason to go, he wrote as an excuse, because he thought that he would not know anyone there. But he did join Springorum to attend the inaugural service on Saturday morning. The building, Boas found, was splendidly decorated, the cantor had a good voice, and Rabbi Dr. Emmanuel Schreiter gave a very progressive sermon. Noticing other celebrants at the service, however, turned Boas's emotion to anger. "I got mad at myself for not having accepted the invitation because I saw what I had already half-thought—that one of the girls in our dance class of last winter, Fräulein Hirth, was a Jewess and naturally had gone to last night's celebration. If I had known that, I would certainly have gone."[32] This was not the end of his unhappiness over Fräulein Hirth, the first girl, aside from Aenni Krüer, of whom Boas recorded any interest.

The synagogue dedication had been in February; in July Boas was writing of the painful state of his soul, of how he was suffering from a passion that robbed him of tranquillity for study. The ache was Fräulein Hirth—or rather his inability even to meet her under favorable circumstances. "Dumb pride and fear" had prevented him from attending the ball; "you cannot imagine how much I now wish I had gone." The visit to the synagogue had not been at Springorum's initiative, but because he had hoped to see Fräulein Hirth there. Boas's letter continues, as do such confessions of pain by a young man in the throes of infatuation. He vows to try to pull himself together, to be as rational as possible, but there are some days when he is half crazy and has to get out into loud company, other days when he would rather quietly withdraw into himself. "I am unsatisfied with myself and with the world," he wrote in August. He considered himself "a mental invalid," requiring solitude to restore his rationality.[33]

The sickness in Boas's soul was not merely from unrequited, even unacknowledged, love. Summer also brought depressing memories. Boas carefully cherished anniversaries. August was the month of Reinhard's death: "I think about that a lot." He asked his parents to send a wreath to the cemetery. "You know what a favor that will be to me."[34]

His concern for Toni hardly helped. She was seriously ill and had been for some time. She had, it will be remembered, fallen victim to some kind of bone or joint ailment in Jena as a girl. Something similar seems to have developed during Franz's first semester at Bonn and, at the Christmas break, he had traveled with her to Kiel for an examination by Dr. Friedrich Esmarch, the famous specialist. Toni was well enough to meet Franz in Düsseldorf for the musical festival that June, but he canceled a summer's tramp with Richarz so he could accompany her on a holiday to Heligoland. The illness, which had again begun in the wrists and then spread to the hip, became worse in the winter. By January she was under Dr. Esmarch's care in Kiel where Franz visited her during his semester break. She remained there, with Franz anxiously enquiring as to what was wrong. "Poor Toni, first one thing, then another," and now so far from home.[35]

In September 1879 Franz left Bonn for the last time. He loved the place and his life there, but Clausius was almost purely a theoretical physicist, and Bonn's laboratories were inadequate for the kind of advanced work that Boas needed for a doctoral dissertation. He planned to move to Berlin for the winter semester to work under Hermann von Helmholtz, the most towering German figure in the physical sciences. Toni's condition altered that.

Sophie could not leave the teenage Hete and Aenne. Franz decided to abandon his Berlin plans in order to be with his sister. "I can," he wrote his mother, "learn enough in Kiel next semester."[36] Franz arrived in the Holstein city late in October. He was up early his first morning for a look around the university, then went to see Toni at Johannes Baasch's hospital, a private institution operated in association with Esmarch. She was in traction, enduring great pain and a high fever. Though she was suffering from frequent vomiting, her headaches and faintness had receded. "I found her," he reported, "looking better than I had feared."[37] Toni's improvement was short-lived. She suffered a severe relapse in December. Esmarch, who earlier had suspected her ailment was due to "nervousness," altered his diagnosis and operated on her hip, removing several pieces of loose bone. She was soon able to sit in a chair and to walk a little on crutches. In March she was well enough for Franz to accompany her home to Minden. She would have a limp for the rest of her life.

Meanwhile, Franz recommenced his studies. He was not without a friend at the Christian-Albrecht University. Theobald Fischer, the geography docent at Bonn who had invited the Alemanne Franz to his home, had accepted a professorship at Kiel. Boas found him "*very* friendly," offering support in every way. Fischer's presence (which probably influenced Boas's decision to forsake Berlin) provided "a very pleasant outlook" for his future at a university where he was otherwise unknown and without friends.

His connection to Fischer reestablished, Boas went more confidently to call upon the director of the Physics Institute. Gustav Karsten received him cordially and agreed to allow free access to the institute's labs. In addition to his laboratory practicum, he decided to hear lectures in mathematics, biology, and Fischer's geography. He found a place to live, only a single room, but with a good piano, at Brunswiekerstrasse 27,[38] and settled into a routine of hospital visits and laboratory work, at first merely learning basic measuring techniques in preparation for his doctoral research. He gradually made a few student friends, with Wilhelm Giesbrecht, a biology student from West Prussia, becoming his closest companion. In January he affiliated with the Teutonia, occasionally eating with the group and accompanying them on outings. Most of his time, however, was dedicated to study and research.

He was disappointed in his choice of a dissertation topic. Initially he had wanted to deal with the "Fehlergesetz," C. F. Gauss's law of the normal distribution of errors. While mathematical and theoretical, the problem affected a broad range of sciences from astronomy to statistics. The origin of Boas's interest in this theme is unclear: he would have come across the problem of random error in any number of his mathematics or science courses. Gauss had developed his principle partly in collaboration with astronomer Friedrich Wilhelm Bessel, who may be a key to Boas's particular interest. Franz had grown up near the house on Kampstrasse that bore a plaque denoting it as the birthplace of Minden's greatest son of science. For the 1884 centennial of Bessel's birth, the younger Minden scientist would go to some length, both in the city newspaper and with the city fathers, in urging suitable commemoration to the century's most distinguished German astronomer.[39]

Boas converted Karsten's assistant, Leonhard Weber, to the viability of the topic, but Karsten himself did not share their enthusiasm. Reluctantly, Boas decided that it was best to follow his supervisor's choice, research dealing with the optical properties of water.[40]

He restricted himself to the questions of water's absorption of light and the polarization of light reflected from water. This caused him to spend time in a boat on Kiel's harbor, sinking zinc tubes with attached mirrors or porcelain plates into the sea, but most of his work was in Karsten's laboratory, passing both sunlight and artificial light through tubes of distilled water. His major problems were keeping his samples uncontaminated, his light sources constant, and finding photometric instruments sufficiently sensitive to yield satisfactory results. None of this was easy, and he struggled week after week with his apparatus.

The most difficult obstacle was ensuring that his water was pure. "The slightest impurity, impossible to see, changes the transparency of the water enormously." He had to take great precautions, double-distilling the water and changing his samples frequently. He also had trouble finding suitable tubes. Zinc cylinders altered the absorbency of the water within minutes, and no method of blackening their interior prevented this. He ended up using a pewter tube, its inside coated with nitrate of saltpeter oxide. Until he perfected his water and containers, errors crept into his work. In June he realized that all his measurements were wrong, and everything that had been done since February must be thrown out. Only in October did he find a way to solve the purity problem. "If only I had had the right tubes from the beginning, who knows how long it would have taken." A new photometer, the third, but this one his own contrivance and three times more sensitive, eased his last major problem. From here it was all downhill, a matter of careful measurement, logarithmic calculations, a survey of relevant literature, and writing up the results. "Now," he wrote in March 1881, "I will doubtless get a result on the refraction of light that will, after all, be of interest, even if I have not solved the whole problem."[41] Finally, at the end of May, after discovering that Kiel's library was as inadequate as its laboratory, the text and tables were finished.

Completion brought relief but scarcely exaltation. He had done what could be done, but the subject was a troublesome one. Water, despite its ubiquity, is a difficult fluid for research, and Boas's pewter tubes, sodium light, jerry-rigged photometers, and double distillation flasks, were not quite up to the problems presented.[42] The dissertation was passable, but he knew it was "nothing special." "If someone had told me a few semesters ago that I would submit such a dissertation, I would have laughed at him. But one learns to be content."[43]

The frustration and disappointment of the dissertation research had already led Boas to reevaluate his career plans. The evidence is not complete, and his course was probably haphazard and even accidental, but he was clearly drifting away from physics. One symptom of the drift was a new interest in psychophysics, an area first developed by Gustav Fechner a quarter century earlier and to which Helmholtz and others had contributed. Although owing much of its development to physicists, the problems it sought to solve were essentially those of experimental psychology and, because of their relevance to epistemology, often interested philosophers. The immediate genesis of Boas's interest seems to have come from issues raised in his research, but it is also likely that he was encouraged by Kiel university philosopher Benno Erdmann.

Erdmann, only seven years older than Boas, was primarily a Kantian scholar, but his interests ranged widely. Refusing to exclude psychology from philosophy, he continued to consider sensory perception as part of the theory of knowledge. He followed Helmholtz, one of his Berlin mentors, into psychophysics, and another mentor, Heymann Steinthal, into the Herbartian area of apperception. In May 1880, when Franz enrolled in Erdmann's seminar, he was surprised to find that Erdmann already "knew my whole studies and my plans." What happened subsequently can only be speculation, but it seems most probable that Erdmann's concern with problems of perception made Boas more attentive to aspects of those which arose in the course of his work with reflected light. Thus, when Boas came across some "photometric difficulties which led me to psychological problems," he turned to Erdmann for advice about whether the material was worth pursuing. Erdmann not only encouraged him to follow up the matter, but helped place the resulting article, Boas's first scholarly publication.[44]

Boas was seduced by psychophysics and its concern for the relationship between physical sensation and psychological perception. In November 1880, when he had overcome most of his laboratory problems and could see the end of his dissertation research, he entertained the idea of spending the next summer at Helmholtz's Berlin laboratory. There he could do some work that touched only indirectly on his dissertation subject, but for which there was no apparatus in Kiel.[45] He doubtless meant to do something with psychophysics. Significantly, Uncle Mons's Christmas gift was a copy of Wilhelm Wundt's *Physiologische Psychologie,* the standard text in the field.

The Helmholtz plan did not materialize. Though Boas devoted much of his summer to reading and writing up more psychophysics investigations, this seductive field was not his main interest. He was unqualified in any other area of psychology, and it was a dubious area of physics, despite Helmholtz's forays into it. He had decided that his future lay in geography.[46]

This was a major shift, and the record behind it is not entirely clear. Certainly his physics research had not gone well. His thesis was satisfactory, but not brilliant, and Boas must have realized that even his magna cum laude degree from Kiel was not a promising card with which to launch a career in German physics.

Boas's plans had been along the best lines: a thorough grounding in mathematics from Fuchs, Kortum, and Lipschitz and four semesters of theoretical physics under Clausius, followed by laboratory research with Helmholtz at the great Friedrich-Wilhelm University in Berlin. But personal considerations, Toni's illness, intervened. Instead of doing research in the best laboratory in the country and earning a doctorate under

Imperial Germany's most eminent and influential physicists, he went to Kiel, a small, undistinguished university with inadequate and rudimentary laboratories and whose single physicist had no great reputation.

This point needs emphasis. The German scientific world was brilliant, but Gustav Karsten's "dark and ancient" Physics Institute shared in none of the glow. Kiel was remote from the centers of German physics, and it suffered neglect by a Prussian ministry whose main attention was devoted to Berlin; "with Karsten as its director, the Kiel physics institute was almost devoid of significance for experimental research for a half century." Heinrich Hertz, who became a docent there two years after Boas had left, commented scornfully on its isolation and poor facilities. "It lacks all kinds of things, and Kiel is not an easy place to get them. God only knows how long it takes to run down a piece of suitable platinum wire or a glass tube."[47] Karsten had little influence and, indeed, stood in opposition to the Berlin scientific establishment. Kiel would soon get Hertz, then Max Planck, in theoretical physics, but they were in the future, and it could keep neither, settling for the mediocre Leonhard Weber, Karsten's son-in-law, as their successor. No doubt Boas realized much of this, though he made few complaints. He was gratified that he could study at Kiel at all and that Karsten offered him use of the Institute's facilities.

During his entire time in Kiel, he was forced from studying Gauss's distribution of errors as his topic to Karsten's color of water. His research proceeded slowly and even badly, and Boas was spending a great deal of time in Theobald Fischer's geography seminars. Fischer was not happy at Kiel. He thought the place small, confining, and socially desolate. He was hurt that his first year's lectures had not been announced, and he was offended that Karsten, "who is at home in any saddle," insisted on teaching physical geography. The two "freshmen" from Bonn were pushed closer together when Boas turned out to be the only student enrolled in Fischer's seminar. Under the circumstances, he may be excused for writing of his only student as the one "who followed me" from Bonn, though he knew that Toni Boas had been the primary cause.[48]

Throughout the long months of discouraging experiments, Boas was a frequent guest at the Fischer home and found satisfaction in painstaking work on a map compiling data on the world's volcanoes for Fischer's seminar. During his four Kiel semesters, he sat in on Fischer's courses on vulcanism and earthquakes, the history of geography, the geography of Asia, and a geographical practicum, work that was more fulfilling than what he was doing in his principal subject of physics. By March 1880, he was as concerned with geography as he was with physics, concentrating upon plant geography and the general application of physics to geography (meteorology and geomagnetism). He was, as well, looking toward some future expeditionary work.[49]

Something more might be said about Fischer. He had begun as a historian, but, influenced by youthful travels, he habilitated at Bonn in geography. His specialty was the Mediterranean area, particularly southern Europe and northern Africa, but his interests ranged widely, with an emphasis upon physical geography, especially geology. Affable, respected, and very active within the discipline, he was a useful patron. Although he was not Boas's dissertation supervisor, he did look upon him as his student.[50]

A renewed interest in geography under the friendly Fischer and disappointment in physics were two important factors behind Boas's shift from physics to geography. Another influence, perhaps more basic, lay behind his change in career goals.

Boas had pursued science under the assumption of what he called a "materialistic Weltanschauung," one "very understandable for a physicist."[51] Scientific materialism and Comtean positivism were natural assumptions for a scientist and freethinker, but they were philosophies with which he was probably becoming increasingly uncomfortable. Erdmann's influence shattered the shell of materialism.

Erdmann was at the center of Kantian scholarship, part of the wave of renewed interest in the Königsberg philosopher that became dominant in German philosophy in the last quarter of the nineteenth century. Kant already had an impact upon Boas, but it was Erdmann's recommendation of F. A. Lange that was immediate. Boas's encounter with Lange's *History of Materialism,* published in the 1870s, was one of those instances of a book that comes at just the right moment and marks a kind of sudden enlightenment, an epiphany, which clarifies inchoate ideas and guides thoughts in directions they were already seeking. The book surveyed the great systematizers of materialism, allowed their correctness from the scientific view, and then, by showing how the physicist's world was situated in the sensibility and reason of a thinking man, demonstrated the impossibility of remaining within this standpoint. Friedrich Paulson, a friend of Erdmann's, wrote of how Lange "came as if called to my need," and Boas seemed similarly affected. He read Lange's *History* in Kiel, then reread it in Berlin. Together, Erdmann and Lange convinced Boas "that my previous materialistic Weltanschauung" was no longer tenable.[52]

This sounds a sea change in Boas's thinking. Psychophysics and philosophy combined to call attention to the relations between the objective physical world and the subjective realm, toward a concern as George W. Stocking has noted, "with the *relationship* of the external and the internal, the physical and the psychic, the inorganic and the organic." At about the same time, Boas might have concluded that geography was a broad enough field to explore this concern while employing much of his natural science background and interest. The Gymnasium and the university student who had roved over botany, zoology, mineralogy, geology, astronomy, chemistry, physics, philosophy, folklore, and cultural history may have now, in his disillusionment with experimental physics, embraced geography because of its interdisciplinary character. Within geography all the sciences he had pursued in his boyhood and student years could find practical application. In a sense it was a return to a boyhood interest. "After long years of infidelity," Toni wrote, "my brother was reconquered by geography, the first love of his boyhood."[53]

Boas's career brings out some of the fortuitous factors that influenced his formative years. In a sense Toni's hip was Cleopatra's nose. Her ailment took him to Kiel, and there his disappointing research into a subject that had never been his first choice, in a laboratory he never otherwise would have chosen, bred a disenchantment that spread to physics itself, and even to the materialistic philosophy that dominated much of scientific thought. Almost as fortuitous was Fischer's presence at Kiel and his continued friendship and patronage of his Bonn student. These were accidents, but they determined Boas's life.

One other aspect of Boas's experiences at Kiel must be mentioned. From his time in this city on the Baltic Sea comes the earliest record of Boas's encounter with the ugliness of anti-Semitism. If something to do with his Jewishness had been responsible for his mother's withdrawing him from Zenker's school at Jena, he was probably unaware of it. One childhood letter does contain a shocked account of being pointed out as a Jew in a Minden shop, compounded by the remark that "Jewish faces are hard to tell apart,"[54] but the Minden of his boyhood and youth seems to have been almost free of overt anti-Semitic incident.[55] Similarly, there is no record of Boas encountering prejudice at Heidelberg or Bonn, though he was sensitive to the issue. Indeed, Boas had some views of his own about "lauter Juden" with whom he did not want to mix.

His experience at Kiel was different. For one thing, Kiel was a rapidly growing Prussian naval and shipbuilding city, strongly Protestant and nationalistic, with none of the influences of Baden's liberalism that affected Heidelberg nor the Rhenish and Catholic character of Bonn. Moreover, 1879–82 were significant years in the history of Germans and German Jews.

The Jewish question emerged as a political issue after 1875 for a number of complicated reasons, including the prominence of Jewish speculators in the scandals of the "Gründerzeit" of the early 1870s, the depression which reached its depth in 1879–80, the disproportionate number of Jews in many professions (especially their dominance of the Berlin press), and, as much as anything, because of Bismarck's realignment with the Christian-conservative forces at the expense of the weakened and divided National Liberals. Germany's Jews were predominantly Liberals. The government no longer needed the support of either.

In January 1878 Adolf Stoecker, a cleric in the court of Wilhelm II and founder of a Christian Socialist Workers' Party which had failed to attract working-class support from the Social Democrats, took up the theme of anti-Semitism. Stoecker's initiative had an extraordinary impact upon the capital city. Until Stoecker, German anti-Semites had been largely obscure journalists and politicians, usually considered eccentrics and demagogues. Under the court preacher, anti-Semitism became a force capable of unifying many small and otherwise insignificant groups into a political movement. He preached a hodgepodge of Social Christian, conservative, and state socialist ideas in which anti-Semitism was often the central issue. Bismarck, concerned with crushing both social democracy and liberalism, found the movement a useful ally in fighting "Jewish liberalism." While Stoecker and Wilhelm Marr, who founded the Anti-Semite League and the *Anti-semitische Hefte* at this time, attracted the attention of artisans, petty officials, and small businessmen, Berlin university historian Heinrich von Treitschke made anti-Semitism intellectually respectable in several statements, beginning in November 1879.

The Berlin Movement, as it came to be called, shocked and confused Jews by its sudden and extraordinary strength. Jewish community leaders had assumed that their emancipation had been achieved and that prejudice and discrimination would continue to decline. Their dominant reaction, one adopted also by Meier Boas, was to avoid confrontation, counsel patience, and encourage community self-criticism.

In the meantime, in the fall of 1880, Bernhard Förster and others began collecting signatures for a petition to present to the chancellor which demanded restrictions on Jewish immigration from the East and on Jewish participation in the judiciary and in school and university teaching, and introduced other measures that would "emancipate the German people from a kind of foreign domination." In October, after the anti-Semite petition had begun to circulate, a Leipzig law student conceived of a student petition along similar lines.[56] At Bonn and Heidelberg there was no response, but elsewhere, especially in the north, committees were formed to circulate the petition among local students. In Kiel it was taken up by law and theology students, who held meetings demanding "that the destructive influence of corrupting Jewish ideas must be suppressed and defeated through Germanic-Christian ideals."[57] Boas noted the agitation in a letter to his parents, but emphasized student opposition. A leader of the anti-Semite movement was in one of his classes, but was ostracized by the others. Kiel students were talking of nothing else, but "I don't bother at all with the thing."[58]

His father was very concerned, not so much because he had heard about anything in Kiel, but because the Jewish question was so much discussed in the capital and elsewhere and because he had read about student provocations leading to duels, one in Tübingen having ended fatally, so reports went. Meier Boas was worried about "young hotheads who think that they must answer every provocation and revenge every insult with weapons." In case this was not pointed enough, he became personal about it.

> I know that you are very sensitive on this point, and it is easy for an attack to be made on you that you think you cannot avoid. I warn you, my dear son, to avoid such things. Ignore provocation, do not believe that you can improve the position of the Jews through your personal intervention. Always remember that we have only one son and do not let yourself into anything whose outcome you cannot foresee.[59]

Franz replied immediately. There was no need to worry; he had only a few acquaintances and mixed little with other students. He had discussed the matter with his closest friends and found them unconcerned; with strangers he avoided political or religious conversation. When some students had brought the Anti-Semitic League petition, he had not intervened except to have his friend Giesbrecht circulate "a stinging declaration" against "Jew haters" that had gathered forty signatures. Then came a little Burschenschaft bravado that could hardly have reassured his father: "I remain unmolested since every student here knows that I would not be shy to defend my affairs with the sword." He would, however, avoid unpleasantness. "I promise again to remain distant from all occasions in which, as a Jew, I would be exposed to insult."[60]

Avoiding such occasions was not easy. In January he and Giesbrecht were sitting in a tavern when one of the anti-Semitic leaders asked to join an acquaintance at the same table. Boas immediately took his beer to a neighboring table, declaring that he could not share a table with this "gentleman." "All got up and left the boor coldly sitting," he wrote. "I think that the good young man will think twice before again becoming the 'leader of a political movement.'" Boas regretted only that it had not been another of the petition instigators, a student he had known well and who still solicitously greeted him when they met. "Of course I never look at him, even when he walks by so closely that I could touch him."[61]

Franz, his promises notwithstanding, could not avoid the anti-Semites. "Unfortunately," he wrote his family before he returned to Minden in April 1881, "I bring home again—for the last time—a few cuts, even one on the nose. I hope you won't concern yourself too much about it, but with the cursed Jewish situation this winter, one could not come through without quarrel and strife."[62]

The agitation, condemned by the university rector, died down, but only after the petition had gathered eighty signatures from among the approximately three hundred Kiel students.[63] The gigantic petition, signed by a quarter of a million people, including some four thousand students (about a quarter of all German university students), was delivered to Bismarck in April 1881. The student movement then became institutionalized with the founding of the nationalistic and anti-Semitic Verein deutscher Studenten (Union of German Students), which became a strong feature in most northern German universities but particularly in Berlin where the prominence of Jewish students, upward of one-third in law and medicine, provided a focus for resentments.

The Berlin Movement and its repercussions in Kiel left their mark upon Boas in more ways than the added scars to his face. As significant as his challenge to antagonists to back their prejudices with their sabers was his weighing the option of conversion to Christianity. We have no record of this from Boas himself, only a reference in a later Fischer letter of their having discussed the matter. Fischer did not recommend conversion, and Boas, for reasons that we can only guess, decided against it.[64] Even if the

Stoecker agitation burned out, Boas would be conscious of the continuing prejudice against Jews and the discrimination, in the public service and elsewhere, against even those who, like himself, were otherwise fully assimilated into German society and culture.

By 1882 Boas had a Ph.D. degree in physics, a field in which he did not intend to make his career. In his university years, he had experienced a great deal. The four years had also been very expensive for his father's purse. The cost of a university education was between 4,000 and 8,000 marks, roughly the wages of an unskilled laborer.[65] Boas existed on a monthly stipend from his father, which never seemed to go far enough—and often had to be supplemented after appeals.

He also had a scarred face, the result of at least five university duels. He later would joke with his children that he got them from a polar bear on Baffin Island, but he did not hide the truth. Most photographs show him from the right side (the protected side of the face) or are retouched, but we know from an 1891 journalist's account that Boas was "a battle scarred veteran."

> On one side of his forehead, near the temple, are three scars, each over an inch in length, crossing in something the shape of a six pointed star. Diagonally across his nose is the scar of what must have been a terrible slash that laid open that member and somewhat altered its elevation. Then from one corner of his mouth, reaching back to the ear, is the longest and most conspicuous scar of all. Docent Boas must have got a slash that laid his mouth open clear to the ear, necessitating the kind attention of a surgeon.[66]

On his way to Baffin Island, Boas wrote about his student years. "I must now wonder how I could for four years be in the midst of that wild and irresponsible life, which would now sicken me in a day." It may be stretching analogies to write that Boas's first experience among a tradition-bound tribe occurred at Heidelberg, Bonn, and Kiel, where he experienced ritual scarring as significant as Kwakiutl Hamatsa bites or Eskimo tattooing, and where concepts of honor and retribution were as strong as in any clan group on the Northwest Coast. Certainly the deep hold that the duel, the elevated conception of honor, and similar student customs had upon his own life were as traditional and as taboo-bound as those of any "primitive" group. At university Boas was caught up in—and embraced—the convention of caste distinction and solidarity, of protection of status and prestige, that must have sat uncomfortably with his own social and political beliefs and certainly violated those of his family.

Boas realized something of this. Sitting in an igloo in Anarnitung on Cumberland Sound late in 1883, he wrote that the more he saw of the customs of the Eskimos, the more he realized "that we have no right to look down on them. . . . We 'highly educated people' are much worse, relatively speaking. The fear of tradition and of old customs is deeply implanted in mankind, and in the same way as it regulates life here, it halts all progress for us." A man sensitive, even in boyhood, to what he later called the shackles of tradition and custom, learned something from his years as a participant in the tribal sub-culture of German student life. Later, in discussing taboo and magic, he reflected that as a student he would have fought a duel with anyone who had damaged a photograph of himself.[67]

At the same time, the student years reveal a bit of youthful naiveté, even intolerance. On his trip to Copenhagen, his first visit abroad, he was astonished to hear an unknown language. More striking, he was scandalized by the Catholic Corpus Christi celebrations of the Rhineland. The first procession he saw, made up of thousands, was "totally incomprehensible." A year later, he was even more scornful:

> Certainly such a procession looks beautiful, but it made a very unpleasant impression on me to see so many people walk completely without thought. I am convinced that among the 3000 participants, scarcely any would be found who actually know why they go or be able to conceive what significance such a procession *could* have and I wonder about the power of the church and customs which permits such a crowd to follow them.[68]

Here too was a concern about the shackles of tradition, though one untouched by an appreciation for the relativity of values. Yet Boas attributed much to his training in the German university system. Once students had found their place, they stood on firm ground. His own independence of thought and action was owed, he felt, to that system.[69]

4 "I Belong to the Men of Anarnitung"

BAFFIN ISLAND

F RANZ BOAS, the newly minted *doctor philosophiae* now had to weigh his career alternatives. His degree qualified him for few positions; it was more like a current North American master's degree than a doctorate. He could take the state teachers' examination, a course urged on him by his parents, but the Gymnasium had never attracted him. Moreover, the examination would take up months of "useless cramming"[1] and then, with his specializations, the most he could hope for was a certificate to teach only as high as the Secunda level. Even then, he would have to serve an unpaid probationary year and then face possible anti-Semitic biases for a permanent position in a crowded field.

A university position presented more obstacles. He would need yet another degree, the "Habilitation," and that would require at least a year, depending upon the university and his ability to produce publications acceptable toward the degree. Habilitation would qualify him only as a Privatdozent, a teaching position that would bring little or no income. Docents often waited years before being called to a salaried professorship.

Before he could embark on either option, however, he still had his military obligation. Fortunately, the Prussian system allowed those with six or more years of Gymnasium the privilege of serving as an "Einjährig-Freiwilliger," a one-year "volunteer," rather than as a three-year conscript. Within limits, the Einjährige could choose when and where to serve. Boas considered doing his service in Göttingen, where he could work with the geographer Hermann Wagner, but his parents insisted that he serve with a Minden regiment. This he decided to do. He did not look forward to a year as a soldier, but it would give him breathing space, time to review his options and pick up some unfinished threads of his scholarship. He had hoped for a fellowship at Baltimore's new Johns Hopkins University, but that application failed. In the interlude between his July doctoral examination and his October military service Franz spent a few days in the Harz mountains, then spent most of September in Berlin, reading geography and psychophysical literature, and writing up some psychophysics research.

He arrived in Minden on September 29, 1881. Two days later he presented himself to the garrison adjutant, picked up his kit and weapon, and had his hair cut to regulation. As an Einjährige he was permitted to live at home and wear civilian dress when off duty. Moreover, he was able to change his posting from the Ninth Fusiliers, based at the railway station barracks, to the First Battalion headquartered at the Marienwell Kaserne, mere steps from the Boas home. Doctor Franz Boas became Gefreiter Boas of the Third Company, Prince Friedrich of the Netherlands (Second Westphalian No. 15) Infantry Regiment.

A number of things had altered in the four years since Franz had lived in Minden. Hete and Aenne were now young ladies, at eighteen and fourteen respectively, and he enjoyed "getting to know his sisters properly."[2] The biggest change, however, was the new house Meier had built at the northern edge of the old city.

Minden's walled fortifications had been torn down in 1874–75. Though most of the land was preserved as parkland, the demolition opened the city's borders to new residential development. Meier bought a lot and in 1878 began to erect a large two-story house. Franz had followed the building plans from Bonn, luxuriating in the thought of "my nice quiet study, the fine music room," and the location—"almost in the city!" "Villa Boas" was finished late the next summer. Franz had helped with the move from the Market to Marienstrasse 19, but was hardly settled into his new room when he left for Kiel. His visits were so infrequent during his dissertation research that the new house and its garden remained strange and, as he had written his family, "in my imagination I often see you on the Market."[3]

The regiment claimed at least six or seven hours of his day and robbed him of much of his scholarly concentration, yet he was able to do a surprising amount of work. The military had its requirements, but Franz worked very hard in his spare hours. Fischer, learning of what he had done in the first half of the year, concluded that service in Minden must be less strenuous than elsewhere, but Franz's productivity was more a result of dedication than an easy life in the 15th Regiment. Franz, his mother wrote at Christmas, "sits in his room and allows *nothing* to disturb him. . . . I have never seen anyone (except Jacobi) work so much. The whole world disappears from him; only science exists."[4]

Psychophysics occupied his free time during the first six months of his service year. Most of his work was concerned with a review of the concept of "the just noticeable difference," one of the most basic principles of psychophysics. In some projects he resorted to introspective research, and one required the assistance of Hete and Aenne. Hete remembered "how we young girls sat there blindfolded with little boxes of shot on our index fingers and, while he put in or took out shot, we research subjects had to say what we felt." This translated into print: "research has convinced me that sudden elevations of stress on a finger through increases of weight bring quite comparable differences of perceptible sensation," part of a demonstration that the method of mean gradation had broader utility than believed. He "cleaned up" his psychophysics by March and prepared to "concentrate my powers entirely upon geography." He worked on a study of isotherms, but his real interest was the relationship between people and their natural environment through an investigation of the "quite special and simple case" of "the dependence of contemporary migrating Eskimos upon the configuration and physical relationships of the land."[5]

The Eskimo, he later wrote, were the best case of "a people living in a wide area of uniform character" and thus suitable for investigating "the fundamental question" of the extent of environmental influence. Yet his choice of the Eskimo was likely in part a personal one, its roots lying far back in Boas's youth. As early as 1870, when he was a boy of twelve, he had written his sister of undertaking an expedition to the north or south pole after completing university. That had been at a time of active German polar explorations. Sailing into the Arctic in 1883 he would describe the trip as the realization of his dream of fifteen years before.[6] The childhood fascination was doubtless reinforced by the polar research course he had taken under Fischer at Bonn, at a time when preparations for the First International Polar Year of 1882–83 were beginning.

Having decided to study the Eskimos and their environment, Boas, once free from military service, moved to Berlin to prepare himself. He had no means of undertaking an expedition—no sponsor, no transportation, no equipment, no destination. But there were a dozen institutes and foundations to which he could apply for assistance, and, meanwhile, he could acquire the knowledge necessary to be an arctic explorer.

After staying with the Lehmanns, old family friends, he found a third-floor room in a typical, old "Berliner" house on Puttkammerstrasse. Even before his room was ready, he was busy reading at the library and making important contacts. Fräulein Hennig, a family acquaintance, worked for Dr. Johann Wilhelm Reiss, vice president of the Berlin Geographical

Society, and she arranged for Boas to meet her employer. Reiss received him cordially on October 18 and quickly became the key that opened doors to Berlin's geographical and anthropological communities. Within days Boas was taking cartographic lessons, had an introduction to W. J. Förster of the Berlin Observatory for training in astronomical and meteorological measurements, and was impressing his plans upon Adolf Bastian of the Berlin Museum of Ethnology. Bastian, the reigning patriarch of German ethnology, showed him the Royal Museum's Eskimo collection and continued "to respond with great kindness to all my efforts." Reiss, with an "unending concern to introduce me everywhere," remained the greatest help.[7]

The old South American traveler took him to the Geographical Society's November meeting, where he heard the North Pacific explorer Aurel Krause and met Dr. Moritz Lindeman. Lindeman was the guiding spirit of Bremen's Geographical Society and former secretary of the 1869–70 Second German Northern Polar Expedition. Although Lindeman suggested that he travel with the German Polar Commission's ship, which would be departing in June to return to its scientific party on Baffin Island, Boas wrote that there was still "absolutely no outlook for my taking a trip."[8] By January, the Polar Commission prospects had improved. Bastian recommended him to Georg von Neumayer, director of the Imperial Seewarte (marine observatory) and chairman of the Commission. At about the same time, after exhausting all possibility of funding from foundations, Boas boldly addressed a letter to Rudolf Mosse, proprietor of the *Berliner Tageblatt,* a major Berlin daily.

Citing Stanley's connection to the *New York Herald,* Boas outlined his plans and described how exciting it would be to have reports on the exploration of yet unknown parts of arctic America. Boas found himself telling Mosse of the scientists interested in his expedition ("all the people with all their titles obviously impressed him") and providing testimonials from Fischer, Erdmann, and Karsten. (A letter from the Lehmanns' doctor, a friend of editor Arthur Levysohn, may have helped.) An arrangement was made: he would receive an advance of 2,500 marks against fifteen promised articles.[9] "I acted as if I was, all in all, very important, and that I would give them my reports as a pure act of grace and mercy. That the trip depends upon their providing the means, I did not allow them to think for a moment." His parents gave a cool response to the *Tageblatt* triumph: they had never been enthusiastic about his expeditionary plans. "It sounds as if you are not pleased that I succeeded with the money," he wrote. Papa, he thought, should at least be happy that he could achieve practical success, and he assured them that "where I am going there are Europeans, namely a Scottish sealer who lives there the whole year."[10]

On February 1, 1883, he was in Hamburg to meet Neumayer, who "offered much more than I had thought," not only passage, but complete outfitting: instruments, weapons, furs, and provisions. His expedition was thus secured. The support of the Polar Commission determined that his work would be on Baffin Island and not, as he seemed at first to intend, in northern Alaska. He would travel with the *Germania,* despatched to pick up Dr. Wilhelm Giese's scientific party of eleven men at Kingua in the upper reaches of Cumberland Sound. The captains of the Second German Northern Polar Expedition promised to help outfit him with a stock of appropriate provisions—guns, ammunition, sled, dory, and trade goods, principally tobacco, saws, knives, needles, and ammunition.

While these arrangements were proceeding, Boas worked hard at learning all that was necessary for the scientific traveler and arctic explorer. He spent two mornings a week with his cartography and studied astronomical determination under Ernst Becker at the Berlin Observatory, learned anthropological measurement with Rudolf Virchow, and acquired photographic skills from H. W. Vogel of the Technische Hochschule. In his own time he examined the arctic collections at the museum and worked on the Danish, English, and Eskimo languages. "I am busy," he wrote home, "and live one day like the last, drawing, reading, observing the sun, and visiting the Lehmanns."[11]

He kept most evenings free for time with his uncles Mons and Emil Meyer and the Lehmanns, whose home they had said to regard as his own. Rudolf Lehmann remained his fast friend and companion. Together they discussed philosophy or visited Berlin's theaters and concert halls. Cultural life in the capital was rich beyond Boas's experience, and he reveled in seeing and hearing Beethoven's Ninth and Wagner's Nibelungen tetralogy. He left *Götterdämmerung* "*absolutely* in shock."[12]

By mid-February his plans were firm. He would use the Polar Commission's Kingua hut as a base, but he also obtained a letter from the owner of the Scottish whaling station at Kekerten Island, asking the resident master for his cooperation should that seem a preferable base. His father had agreed ("insisted" may be a better word) that he take servant Wilhelm Weike, a young Mindener ten months Boas's junior, who had been with the family since October 1879.

Preparations were frantic during March and April. He made trips to Gotha, Weimar, and Jena, to Frankfurt and Stuttgart, again to Gotha and Weimar, then to Hamburg and Bremen. He settled for a while in Minden, then was off to Berlin to pick up his theodolite and photographic apparatus.

Boas's arctic research strategy developed from his rapid mastery of arctic literature and several contributions he made to it during his preparatory year. The most important article, ostensibly about the homeland of the Netsilik Eskimo of Boothia Peninsula, partly described and partly postulated extensive travel and trade routes between Eskimo groups of the central and eastern Arctic.[13] According to Boas, these well-established routes extended from Ugulik, a settlement at the western tip of King William Island, through Iglulik on Fury and Hecla Strait, south from there to Wager Bay and north to Pond Inlet at the northern end of Baffin Island, with a connecting link east to Cumberland Sound.

He fitted these interests and postulates into a plan for a one-year investigation based at Cumberland Sound. Aside from cartographic and meteorological work, his intention was to investigate the relationships between the size of groups, the range of their migrations, and the configuration of the land and its food supplies. This, coupled with a study of migration, hunting areas, trade routes, and the connections of one group to another, would provide the context of the geographical and environmental determination of routes and relationships.[14]

He planned to travel in the summer and fall of 1883 with Weike and some Cumberland Sound Eskimos to Lake Kennedy (Lake Nettilling), a large inland sheet of fresh water, and from there attempt to reach the west coast of Baffin Island and follow it north to Fury and Hecla Strait, the home of the Iglulik Eskimos. He would then return to winter in Cumberland Sound. While awaiting spring, he would collect ethnographic material and make a thorough study of the language, customs, and habits of the Eskimos. In the spring he would take the shortest route back to Iglulik and then, by the route postulated in his article, travel north to Pond Inlet to investigate the Eskimos of that region. He would return to Kingua in July, if possible along a northern, Baffin Bay–Davis Strait route, and would sail home in the fall aboard a Cumberland Sound whaler.[15]

This ambitious itinerary and the tenacity with which Boas held to a trip along the west coast of Baffin Island, despite overwhelming setbacks, indicates he was exceedingly intent upon demonstrating the routes he had postulated in his article on the Netsilik Eskimo. There was more to it than proving Eskimo routes. The western shore of the island was almost completely unexplored. An overland trip from Cumberland Sound would bring Boas to the west coast, one of the largest unknown regions of the Arctic and onto an apparently easy route north to Iglulik and Pond Inlet. It would be a significant piece of geographic discovery.

Boas's plan was extraordinary for its time, breaking with almost all practices of previous polar expeditions in its emphasis upon a detailed study of a limited region over an entire year and in its reliance upon a small, virtually one-man expedition living largely off the land. Boas's model was C. F. Hall, "the first one to prove how much one could achieve in arctic areas by adopting completely the Eskimo mode of life,"[16] and to whose arctic endeavors he devoted one of his articles for the *Berliner Tageblatt.*

Boas actually hoped to extend his itinerary at the end of his expedition. Knowing that vessels traded along Davis Strait in the summer, he hoped to be picked up by an American whaler and sail south to the United States. There he could investigate professional possibilities and visit Marie Krackowizer whom he had come to know well on his post-doctoral Harz holiday the previous July.

Marie Krackowizer was the daughter of Dr. Ernst Krackowizer, an Austrian emigré of 1848 who became a prominent New York doctor before his death in 1875.[17] The remaining family retained a close friendship with physician and German Forty-Eighter Abraham Jacobi, Boas's uncle by marriage. In the summer of 1881, Marie visited Germany with Jacobi and her mother, Emilie, and sister Alice. In July they met with Sophie, Hete, and Aenne Boas for a Harz mountain holiday. A few days later, fresh from his doctoral examination, Boas joined them, meeting the holidayers as they returned from a visit to the Ilsenstein. The remaining three days were very pleasant. He discussed his career plans with Jacobi, but seems to have spent most of his time with Marie. They were together almost constantly, walking in the park at Wernigerode, looking from the cliff of the Regenstein, climbing in the dark cavern of the Baumannshöhle, and they had an unforgettable early morning in the wild and picturesque Bodethal before all left for Minden. The Krackowizer party spent two days there as the Boases' guests before leaving for Austria.

As a souvenir of the Harz, Franz sent Marie a fifteen-page notebook recalling the holiday in cut-out caricatures and humorous verse. From

Austria came a polite thanks "from your enthusiastic (?) botany student." The Krackowizers settled in Stuttgart, where Marie and her sister enrolled in a girls school, and kept in touch with the Minden Boases. Franz would have heard reports of them from his mother and sisters, but his own relationship with Marie lay dormant during his military service and his arctic preparation. With his expedition definite, he felt compelled to renew the connection. Attending the Geographical Congress at Frankfurt in March 1883, he feigned an appointment in nearby Stuttgart as an excuse to call upon Miss Krackowizer. "I could not bring myself to begin this trip," he wrote Jacobi, "without again having spoken to her." That April 1 afternoon, a beautiful spring Sunday, they walked the city's woods together, stood under the old Schiller Oak, "and told one another everything except what we really thought." He would not go further than that. Marie had been in his thoughts since the Harz holiday, but it would be wrong to speak frankly of his affection. Before him lay a dangerous trip and an insecure future: "I cannot know how long it will be before I can begin my own home."[18] While he shared his feelings with Jacobi, Toni, and his mother, to Marie he went no further than to send a photograph and the plan of his trip.

Such restraint eroded as his June departure neared. "Liebes Fräulein," he wrote, on May 28, "I cannot leave here without telling you how much I love you, how constantly you are in my thoughts, how you are the substance of all my dreams and desires." He needed to know if his affection was returned, if she could "give me the right to think, amid snow and ice, of the hope for a happy future."[19] The answer came before his confession had been posted. Toni had seized the initiative and, unknown to him, written to Stuttgart. In the quiet of the garden arbor, Toni read him Marie's response. It left him mute, "so happy, so blessed." He rushed to his room to compose a new letter, this one addressed to his "Liebe Marie" and flowing with the joy of love and the end of tortured doubt. Now he knew what he wanted in life.[20]

Three weeks of intense correspondence ended in a quiet engagement. When he left for Hamburg on June 17, he carried with him a black-white-red Imperial flag emblazoned with "Marie" and two less tangible mementos. One was the melody of Schumann's *Nachtstück,* made "their song" by his having played it for her in Stuttgart. He played it again, just before he left, the better to hear it "gently and blissfully in distant lands."[21] The other was a wish he attributed to Brünhilde that love be blessed, whether in joy or sorrow.[22] His voyage now had additional inspiration: "Believe me, I *will* come back and provide us with a future." En route to Hamburg he told her that she was "my strength and my courage, my hope, my life, my everything!"[23]

Boas, accompanied by his father and Weike, arrived at Hamburg harbor on June 18, 1883. Two days later the *Germania* slipped from the dock. As the schooner sailed into the North Sea, Franz read Marie's final farewell. "Vorwärts! Ich warte auf Dich!", she wrote. "Onward, I wait for you!"[24] "Vorwärts," along with Brünhilde's words of love, were slogans repeated time and again by Boas to himself as he pursued his labors in the lonely barrens of Baffin Island.

The expedition meant a difficult separation for two such recently declared lovers. For twelve or more months any communication between them would be impossible. Under the circumstances, they both kept diaries of unpostable letters. What did it matter if they could not be answered or even read for months? In Boas's collection, his cramped hand mixes affectionate effusions with descriptions of life on board, of his small and smelly cabin, of how he tried to give Weike lessons in English ("he has a terribly thick head"), and how, by July 5, life had become "very monotonous." On his birthday, July 9, when the ship passed Greenland into the Arctic Ocean, he was so seasick that only in the afternoon could he look at the letters and presents Weike had kept for him.

On July 15, Cape Mercy, the outermost point of Baffin Island's Cumberland Peninsula, came into sight, but further progress was impossible. "All we can see, looking landwards, is a desert of ice, shoal after shoal, field upon field."[25] Already he was forced to revise his plans since it was doubtful that they could break through the dense pack ice and into the Sound before the middle of August. He gave up his plan for a fall trip to Iglulik, and by August 7, after they had been amidst the pack ice for four weeks, he worried that his whole project might have to be abandoned. The morning of August 28 brought a dramatic change. The wind rose, the ice and fog cleared. Sails were quickly hoisted, and by noon Kekerten was in sight. The *Germania,* towed the last mile by Eskimo whaleboats, was soon at anchor off the Scottish whaling station.

The season was now too late for Boas's western expedition to Lake Nettilling and beyond. Indeed, the ice lay so thick in the upper reaches of the Sound that it was impossible to sail to the Kingua station. Boas volunteered to take a whaleboat and Eskimo crew to tell the isolated Germans that they must make their way back to Kekerten. Borrowing a

71

caribou-skin Eskimo suit, he left on September 5. Progress was slow, and the ice sometimes hazardous, but he and his crew made their way safely to the *Lizzie P. Simmonds,* an American whaler under Captain John Roach caught in the ice, and to the Polar Commission station nearby. For the worried scientists, Boas's appearance was cause for celebration; for him it was the first arctic adventure.

Because of the ice conditions, it was impossible for Boas to move his supplies to the Commission's hut and, in any case, it was too isolated from Eskimo settlements to serve his purpose. Boas and Weike instead established themselves at the Scottish station, the much-modified building brought originally to the island by William Penny in 1857 and now the residence of James Mutch, a whaler from Aberdeen. The quarters consisted of one large room for living and sleeping, and smaller storage and service rooms. Boas soon had his pictures mounted on the wall: Marie's photograph joined those of his mother and father.

Boas found it impossible to engage a whaleboat crew: many of the Eskimo were hunting caribou in the interior and almost all those at the station were fully employed in unloading and loading the station's own brig. Thus his hope for an immediate start on major exploratory work was crushed. From Captain Roach, however, he was able to hire Signa, one of the Eskimos who had taken him to Kingua and back. Born on Davis Strait but resident in the Sound since he was a boy, Signa was about fifty. He was, Boas wrote, reliable and "a good soul" who does "what I tell him without objecting and does not drink."[26] The secondment was sealed by the presentation of a Mauser rifle; in addition, Signa received bread, molasses, and tobacco according to his needs. He served Boas during his entire stay in Cumberland Sound.

Nevertheless, until he could engage a full boat crew, Boas had to confine himself to examining the immediate vicinity of Kekerten Island. The first excursion was a trip up Kingnait Fjord by Boas, Signa, and Wilhelm, much of it strenuous walking along the irregular coast. On a trip up Pangnirtung Fjord, he first tasted raw seal liver ("it didn't taste badly once I overcame a certain resistance").[27] A survey of the east coast of the Sound was interrupted by the return of the caribou hunters, from whom Boas was anxious to purchase enough skins to make suits and sleeping bags for himself and Weike.

While none of these trips satisfied his urge for exploration, he did accomplish some useful coastal surveying and, even when sheltering from fog, snow, and wind, he sat with Signa learning Eskimo games. Late in

October, ice began to form on the Sound, confining him to Kekerten Island until the ice became strong enough to bear a sled. His diary for this seven-week period is sparse—only ten entries—but it is clear from this and other accounts that he was busy. He pitched a tent on the ice near the American station so he could measure the tides, charted the island and its surroundings, and, "greatly helped by Mr. Mutch," pursued his study of the Eskimo, particularly their geographical knowledge. He spent every night with the natives, who told him in pidgin English about the lay of the land and their travels over it. "Almost the whole of Kekerten is drawing maps for me so that I can find clues to new problems." He listened to stories and songs and watched them playing the games "with which they shorten the long, dark winter nights."[28]

Still hoping for a major western trip, Boas was again disappointed once the Sound had iced over in December. His mobility was restricted because it was impossible to buy sled dogs. In the fall a devastating canine disease, apparently brought to the island from Greenland by early whaler ships and now endemic, struck every settlement, killing about half the dogs in the Sound by December.[29] Mutch lent Boas his own team for short periods, and he clung to the hope that he could get dogs from Davis Strait. In February he almost accompanied two Kekerten families across the Peninsula to Padli, a region free of the dogs' disease, but the snow was so thin and the ice so rough and rocky, that he gave up. It was yet another setback. His plans for a western trip to Lake Nettilling and beyond was now hopeless: if the Padli dogs came at all they could not arrive before the end of March, too late for a proper trip to the west coast.

He persisted, nevertheless, in the hope that he could yet get as far as Igluling and even Pond Inlet. This, he later realized, was a chimera; he should have foresworn the trip and turned to research on the west coast of Cumberland Sound for the rest of the winter. "It was so very hard, however, for me completely to abandon a plan which I had long nurtured and cherished and worked for; so, as long as a spark of hope remained, I staked everything on reaching the longed-for Foxe Basin." Holding firmly to the small hope that he could still find a team, he went to Anarnitung to hunt seal meat for the expected dogs. Even here he was disappointed. The hunting was unsuccessful, due partly to an unusual paucity of seals at the water holes and partly to terrible weather. "The only thing I shot was pulled under the ice by the current."[30]

Poor sealing and bad weather contributed to the frustration of his exploration plans, but most of all it was the lack of dogs. By March he had given up the last hope for a trip to the shores of Foxe Basin. To the absent Marie he confided the nadir of his disappointment. "I must find comfort in you from the troubles and cares that worry me day and night. It's easy to say that one should keep one's head up, but that's really very hard with this wretched dog disease that endangers even my Padli trip."[31] He feared that he would not be able to travel even to Davis Strait where he could catch a whaler to the United States. He faced the "unbearable" prospect of having to wait until the fall Scottish schooner came to Kekerten.

From the depth of his despair, new hope arose. Two men from the tip of Cumberland Peninsula reported an abundance of dogs in their settlements. This was the happiest news since his arrival. "After the endless misfortune of the previous months, I awoke to the new hope for a turn for the better, toward a new enterprise."[32] After a difficult trip, he was able to buy ten dogs. On his return to Kekerten, he found that Mutch had been able to buy five dogs from visiting Padli Eskimos. He now had the means to leave Cumberland Sound, but it was the end of March, far too late for his great western plan.

On March 28 Boas left Kekerten for an abbreviated version of his original trip. It was more a homage to his abandoned dreams than a serious exploration, but he "wanted at least to see the longed-for Lake Nettilling and to catch a glimpse of the form of the land west of the Sound." He reached the lake on April 1 and, always extraordinarily conscious of anniversaries, noticed the coincidence of this warm and sunny day with that memorable day in Stuttgart a year earlier. He was sad rather than exultant; "I turn around here, right where I thought I would really begin."[33]

The emphasis that Boas placed upon travel, in the interests of his cartographic survey, in his urgency to correct the British Admiralty map, and with his concern to learn of Eskimo communications, exposed him to hardship, privation, and danger. The most perilous occasion, caused in part by careless preparation, came on his first major sled trip. Fresh snow caused him, Signa, and Weike to miss a rendezvous with a supply sled from Kekerten, and they soon found their provisions depleted. Signa broke one of his guns, had only a single cartridge for the Mauser, and their lamp oil was exhausted. Leaving their equipment behind, they decamped by foot for Anarnitung, the nearest settlement, a distance of fifteen kilometers, in extreme cold, fog, and deep snow. They wandered for hours in fog and darkness, stumbling and crawling over soft snow that covered thick, jutting sheets of ice. "I don't know," groaned Weike, "how often I went down face first." Their two dogs "declared a holiday," forcing the three men to leave still more supplies behind.[34]

When they finally found the coast, the disoriented Signa had no idea where they were. They found a sheltered place where they waited, hungry and cold, for the moon to rise. Afraid of being overcome by sleep, they tramped in circles, jostling each other awake. Then, finding the sled track to and from Anarnitung, they followed it in the wrong direction. Only when they reached the Sarbukdjuak seal holes did they realize their mistake. They turned back and, after twenty-six hours with little food and no water, the three men at last reached Anarnitung. Signa's nose and Boas's nose and fingers were frostbitten, and poor Weike's feet were so severely affected that he sat out the next three months at Kekerten. "The last day was really taxing," Boas wrote in his diary, "to walk without stopping for 26 hours with the thermometer at [minus 45 C] so that I could not keep my fingers and nose from freezing, with nothing to eat and nothing to drink and no assurance that we would ever find our goal."[35]

Boas had scarcely recovered from this crisis when another emerged, one that threatened any success for his expedition. Diphtheria, previously unknown on the Sound, had appeared at Kekerten in October. Boas's journal recorded that on the 23rd a woman, very ill with fever and inflamed lungs, had asked him for help. He provided turpentine for her chest, quinine to combat the fever, ammonia to relieve her respiration, and opium against her cough, but he could do nothing more. Her death two days later marked the beginning of a large number of fatalities throughout the region. "It is terrible how diphtheria and pneumonia are now prevalent among the poor Eskimo," he wrote the next week. The sick turned to him, to the "Docteraluk" or "big doctor," but there was little he could do. One November morning he was called to the deathbed of a small boy. "There the mother and I sat in that small, cold hut, the boy between us wrapped in covers. The mother, with frightened looks, asked me again and again if 'the pikanini was pinker,' and I saw only that the little limbs grew colder and colder, his grasping for breath harder and harder. Then it was over."[36]

The disease spread throughout the Sound, leaving the Eskimos "deeply shaken by the devastation of the epidemic among the children and by the quick and deadly course of individual cases." Given the coincidence of Boas's arrival with the outbreak of the disease and his frequent if unavailing ministrations, it is not surprising that "an extraordinarily unpleasant ill-will formed among the Eskimo against me." The center of the hostility was at Imigen on the west side of the Sound, where the primary antagonist lived, an "angakuk" or shaman named Napekin or Tyson. "It was declared that no one was to have anything to do with me; above all, no one was to allow me into their huts or lend me their dogs."[37]

Boas, feeling that the hostility must be dealt with quickly, traveled immediately to Imigen. Fortunately for Boas, Napekin also intended spending the summer on Davis Strait. There Boas would be his only source for ammunition. Boas assembled the men and told Napekin that "all intercourse between us would cease until he invited me into his hut." Since the man had only a poor gun and little ammunition and would be dependent upon Boas on Davis Strait, the threat carried weight. "I let him know that he would get nothing from me, even if I saw him starving before my eyes, if he did not first come to me and ask me into my igloo."[38] A man immediately invited him into his igloo for the night, and the others gave no signs of mistrust.

Boas thought that his resolute action had been both appropriate and effective. Nevertheless, he was afterward made frequently aware that many of the Eskimos, though hesitant to be openly hostile, were unwilling to deal with him or to lend him their dogs. In March, about six weeks later, Napekin came to Kekerten especially to reconcile Boas with gifts of seal pelts and an offer of service in the spring. Once Napekin made his peace, "the incident closed and from then on nothing disturbed the relations between the natives and me."[39] Indeed Napekin served as a loyal assistant and companion in some of his summer work on Davis Strait.

On May 6, 1884, Boas and Weike with Signa and several other Eskimos left Kekerten Island by dog sled for Davis Strait. Boas had spent the previous month finishing his Cumberland Sound map and settlement census and making preparations for this trip. He had packed much of his material to be sent to Germany with the Scottish steamer that would come again in August and carefully selected whatever was necessary for the remainder of his time on Baffin Island. From now on he would be isolated from the station and its provisions and would have to depend on what little he carried on his sled and what he could hunt.

The journey was arduous. The ice, pressed together into great blocks, made travel very difficult on Kingnait Fjord, and the overland portion required heavy hauling over a series of steep terraces. The work was "so unspeakably difficult" that he was forced to leave the bulk of his baggage in Tornateling Canyon. "If my provisions had already been trifling, the little I now took with me could only be regarded as emergency supplies to supplement poor hunting."[40] After eleven days of heavy packing, they reached the head of Padli Fjord and, on May 22, Padloping, the settlement at its mouth. The spring sun's brightness afflicted him with painful snow blindness, and for several days he was unable even to write.

With Sanguja, a Padli Eskimo who was hired as companion and guide on Davis Strait, Boas and Weike moved northwest along the Strait as Signa returned to Kekerten. Boas wanted to survey the coast as far as Cape Henry Kater. The next month, to and from Siorartijung, his most northerly point, was an extremely difficult time. Travel conditions were terrible in the thawing snow, and at times they resorted to night travel when the surface was firm. Heavy fog, spring snowstorms, a face-swelling toothache, snow blindness, and days without food for men and dogs were some of the sufferings and deprivations of the journey. At the end of June they were forced to sleep on their sled, were out of bread and so short of provisions that they were at the point of killing a dog to provide meat for the rest. "I do not think I shall ever in my life forget horrible Home Bay!" he wrote on July 1. It was the worst time of his entire year. "You cannot imagine how happy I will be no longer to have to sit on a sled," he wrote in anticipation of the end of his travel.[41] Both he and Weike were increasingly preoccupied with thoughts of home, food, and the arrival of Scottish or American whalers.

They settled at Idjuniving, on a harbor frequented by trading vessels, where Boas worked on his ethnological material while they anxiously awaited the coming of a ship. On August 19 a Dundee whaler was seen, then lost in the fog before it could be reached. A week later, two ships were seen. The dogs were harnessed and, after traveling several hours over the difficult ice, they reached the ships, both Dundee vessels. One carried welcome mail from Germany and America.

The captains of both ships offered passage, but the next day the *Wolf*, under Captain John Burnett, arrived. Since she was sailing to St. John's almost immediately, Boas unhesitatingly chose her. He reached the Newfoundland port on September 7 and immediately wired Minden and New York. "Gott sei Dank!" he wrote from St. John's, "the time of tribulation is past."[42] The voyage to Halifax and New York was frustratingly slow, but the two arctic travelers, wearing clothes borrowed from Captain Burnett, at last arrived there on September 21.

Willy Meyer, having recently arrived in New York to establish a medical practice, met them at the pier and took them to breakfast at the home of Jacob Meyer, Sophie's brother, and his wife Phips. Other relatives of Franz and Marie came to greet them, but Marie herself was with her sister Helene upstate at Lake George. Franz, impatient to see her, left for the resort area as soon as he had called on Jacobi and bought some clothes. From Lake George he asked his parents to announce their engagement, the card backdated to May 30, 1883.

Boas had been on Baffin Island for almost exactly a year. Of his 364 days on the island, 209 were spent in tupiks or igloos, usually in travel but often in outlying settlements. Even when based at Kekerten, he spent a third of his nights away from the station or ships. At Kekerten Island the eighty-odd Eskimos far outnumbered the Whites: Mutch, Rasmussan of the American station, and Boas and Weike. This meant that Boas joined in much of the daily activity of the Eskimos. During his Anarnitung stay, he wrote proudly of seal hunting "just like an Eskimo. I sat beside the water just as patiently as they do." Inside the snow house, he shared their food and, as far as he could understand it, their talk.

> Their hands are usually folded over their bellies, their heads usually bent sideways. They talk, laugh, and sing. Once in a while someone seizes a knife and cuts off a large piece of seal meat, which he devours. If it is frozen, it is chopped up and eaten by all, including myself, with the greatest enjoyment.

> I am now a true Eskimo. I live as they do, hunt with them, and belong to the men of Anarnitung.[43]

In most of this, Boas remained much more an observer than a participant. Weike, responsible for the daily chores, probably mixed more (he certainly had a female companion). It was the need for seal meat for his dogs, more than a desire to indulge in Eskimo ways, that drove Boas to sit all day at the Sarbukdjuak seal holes—"something that bores me dreadfully."[44] He shot his first caribou, needed as dog food, in May 1884. When not pressed in this way, he let Signa, Weike, or others do the hunting. Before this trip, Boas had been abroad only twice—brief trips to Denmark—so he had very little experience with foreigners, even other Europeans. Now, plunged amidst the world of "primitive" people, he did not turn away in disgust.

True, his first impression of the Eskimo had been of repulsive ugliness and repellent stench. Closer contact, however, changed his mind; soon he was sharing their huts and cooking kettles ("though I usually took care to use my own kettle"). "I must say," he wrote in January, "that I am well satisfied with the character of the 'savage' Eskimo."[45]

In Oxaitung's igloo in Anarnitung, he ruminated at length on the customs of his hosts. Seals had been scarce at the breathing holes, but those caught were scrupulously shared. Was it not, Boas asked, "a beautiful custom among these 'savages,' that they bear all deprivation in common?"

> I often ask myself what advantages our "good society" possesses over that of the "savages" and find, the more I see of their customs, that we have no right to look down upon them. Where among our people could you find such true hospitality as here? Where are people so willing, without the least complaint, to perform *every* task demanded of them? We have no right to blame them for their forms and superstitions which may seem ridiculous to us. We "highly educated people," relatively speaking, are much worse.[46]

As he sat eating raw seal liver with his Anarnitung friends, he wrote of the "real meaning" of his expedition. The experience had strengthened his view of the relativity of virtue among peoples. The kindness and sensitivity of the Eskimos, the sympathetic tact that they demonstrated in their personal relationships, gave proof that inner character, their *Herzensbildung*, was far more significant than the gloss of civilization and learning. "The evil as well as the value of a person lies in *Herzensbildung*, which I find or find lacking here just as much as among us."[47]

Boas's deep respect for his native hosts did not diminish the one great gap in his Baffin Island life. If there is any one outstanding theme to his diary, it is of intense loneliness. He had little in common with Weike, his Scot host, or the Eskimos, and he found hardest to bear "not having anyone to whom I can speak a sensible word, no one to whom I am in any way close." Again and again he expressed his longing for intelligent conversation. "When a person lives like I have, here in a solitary wilderness—for is Wilhelm company?—he will understand the need to communicate, the need to see people around him with whom he can *live*."[48] His family need not fear, he assured them, that he would return reticent and self-contained. The Arctic had taught him the value of company.

Judged in terms of Boas's original intentions, the expedition had been a failure. "Fortune has favored me but little," he wrote as he left Cumberland Sound; "none of the hopes I had when I arrived here have been fulfilled." His late arrival was an initial, if not entirely unexpected, setback; both weather and hunting were exceptionally bad all winter; above all, the death of so many dogs denied him access to the only means of winter transportation. Despite these reversals, he was reasonably satisfied with the results. He had made an accurate survey of most of Cumberland Sound and much of Davis Strait, all previously imprecisely rendered. Only able to survey Lake Nettilling sketchily and the rest of the interior not at all, he nevertheless secured sufficient information to draw a close approximation of the actual outline of the interior lakes and the entire coast and to conclude that Foxe Channel was a basin. He spent night after night learning about native knowledge of the land and their travels. A primary tool in his research on Eskimo geographical knowledge was informant-drawn maps, for the Eskimos had long been respected for the accuracy of their line maps.[49]

His travel and enquiries provided information on his main research intention which was to determine Eskimo distribution and mobility, routes of interchange and communication, and the related questions of origin and migration history. By the end of 1883 he felt that he had already attained much of this purpose. "I know very accurately about the migration of the Eskimos and the routes they take, how they travel back and forth, and their relationships to neighboring tribes."[50] What he found seemed to confirm the routes he had set forth in his Netsilik article. Although he discovered that few Cumberland Sound natives traveled to or even knew of the western coast, he was pleased to find on Davis Strait a man from Iglulik who had often traveled the coast of Foxe Basin to Nettilling. This was a welcome confirmation of his travel route thesis.

Boas remained convinced that the west coast provided a link between Nettilling, Iglulik, and Pond Inlet. As late as 1907 he was still publishing evidence to support his theory, and he continued to regret that he had not been able to prove it by personal travel. This conviction, which lay behind Boas's detailed advice to Bernhard Hantzsch in 1908, may have contributed to the Dresden ornithologist's death in 1911 along the barren and deserted shore of Foxe Basin. Such an overland passage would have been an achievement comparable to Shackleton's conquest of the Antarctic plateau, but "not very probable of accomplishment."[51]

Boas's ethnographic results, though completed by April 1886, were not published until 1888 as *The Central Eskimo*. The monograph reflected his ethnological data-gathering in its emphasis upon human geography, the description of subsistence activities and material culture, and recording of traditions and songs. He gave almost no attention to social structure and only a little to ceremonial and religious life. His work in linguistics was not published until 1894 and was, by his own account, "defective and incomplete"; having assumed that missionaries had already given a sufficient picture of the language, he was "not clearly conscious of the importance of linguistic studies during the entire trip." Nevertheless, within its scope and context, his ethnography was sophisticated. He later judged *The Central Eskimo* to be "a description based on intimate knowledge of the daily life of the people, with bad gaps, due to my ignorance of problems."[52]

Retrospectively, of course, the most significant aspect of Boas's experience in Baffin Island was his ethnographic immersion among the Eskimos. His life and reputation were to be made in anthropology and this was his initiation, his *Jünglingsreise*. A shift of interest was already evident by the end of the Cumberland Sound trip: "My work among the Eskimo satisfies me more than my travels."[53] Participation in the life of the Eskimos also sharpened his social sense and his belief in the equality of virtue among peoples. Their *Herzensbildung* was far more significant than the veneer of civilization and learning. All the more regrettable, he believed, was the inevitable destruction of the Cumberland Sound Eskimo. Already they had shrunk in number from thousands to hundreds. It was important "to save what can yet be saved" of their tales and customs. While Boas did not cease being a geographer, he began to see ethnology as "more pressing."[54]

Franz Boas never returned to the Arctic. Later, in Berlin, he sought various means for further expeditions. A plan for a three-year exploration from Labrador to the Pacific Coast failed to secure Bastian's endorsement, and the Bureau of Ethnology in Washington, D.C., was no more helpful. His proposal to the Geological Survey of Canada for a season in Hudson's Bay brought an offer of transportation but no provision for salary. While his attentions were increasingly drawn to the Northwest Coast Indians, he never lost interest in the Eskimos. He later gathered ethnological collections for the American Museum of Natural History and the Museum of the American Indian through whaler George Comer and his old Cumberland host, James Mutch. He advised Russel W. Porter on his Baffin Island expeditions and Bernhard Hantzsch on his tragic attempt to traverse the route Boas had abandoned. Later, as a Bureau of American Ethnology philologist, he guided William Thalbitzer's linguistic work for the *Handbook of American Indian Languages*. He kept in touch with members of the Fifth Thule Expedition, Kaj Birket-Smith and Therkel Mathiassen. Boas continued to publish articles, even books, on the Eskimos for twenty-five years after his field work, but these were based entirely on reports by others. Still *Baffin-Land* and *The Central Eskimo* are the major results of his personal arctic work and stand as his foremost contributions to northern and Eskimo studies.

5 "How Depressing It Is"

BETWEEN GERMANY AND AMERICA

IN LATE SUMMER OF 1884, Franz holidayed for a week at Lake George in upstate New York. He felt a compulsion to return to his unfinished work and, even more, to seek a way out of the pressing problem of his uncertain future. He returned briefly to stay with Uncle Kobus and Aunt Phips in New York, then went to Washington. Because of the Smithsonian Institution and other government agencies, the federal city was a major center of nineteenth-century American science.

Boas had two immediate objectives. One was to begin writing up his expedition results. He finished off his *Tageblatt* obligation and wrote a number of repetitious pieces for the New York *Staats-Zeitung,* the American Geographical Society's journal, and other periodicals. He traveled to New England to gather information from arctic whalers and in Washington, D.C., met with the American arctic explorers Frederick Schwatka, Lucien Turner, John Murdoch, and Emil Bessels, chief scientist with C. F. Hall's tragic *Polaris* expedition. There he also reached an agreement with Major John Wesley Powell of the Bureau of Ethnology to publish his ethnological results. More important, Powell might provide a solution to his second, overriding objective: the securing of a position.

Powell, geological explorer turned director of the government's Bureau of Ethnology, was the leading American anthropologist of his generation. A self-taught ethnologist and devotee of Louis Henry Morgan and Herbert Spencer, Powell single-handedly developed the research focus of Washington anthropology. His Bureau was the major center of American ethnology and linguistics, and its annual reports, contributions, and bulletins were a major outlet for publications.[1]

Establishing contact with Powell and the Bureau of Ethnology was important, but it did not solve the question of Boas's future. He desperately wanted a job that would allow him to pursue his science and provide a home for Marie. His thoughts focused on their marrying as soon as possible, but he had no prospects, no idea even where he could find a position.[2] Could he attain a satisfactory place in America or must he return to Germany?

He leaned strongly toward an American future. His reasons were in good measure political. There was both a push and a pull. Bismarck's Germany had become increasingly repellent. To live outside "our government and its impoverished policies" was a happy thought. Boas's attitude reflected the falling fortune of German liberalism and, with it, German Jews. The chancellor's break with the Liberals and the construction of the conservative, Christian-national coalition of agrarian and heavy industrial interests meant the end of any hope for a continued liberalization of the state and diminished expectations for a more open society, where merit not status earned rewards. The change had come while Boas was a student, but became more apparent to him on his return from abroad. Illiberal tendencies, associated with prejudice and discrimination against Jews, pushed Boas away from his native county.[3]

America, in contrast, seemed a land of opportunity, with a political system that, while hardly perfect, was based on liberal and constitutional principles. There "a willing man has the opportunity to work according to his powers." Boas nurtured, moreover, a desire to do something in the public sphere, a course "as good as closed" to him in Germany. Although a thousand threads drew him back to home and homeland, he did not cherish career prospects there. A professorship was difficult to obtain and unattractive. He would have to habilitate, then wait for an open chair. Anti-Semitic biases might enter into the selection process and, even under the most favorable circumstances, it would be three years before he could achieve a paying professorship. Fischer, who accused him of seeing things through "Yankee spectacles" and strongly denied any anti-Semitic element in academic selection, nonetheless had to concede that a long wait was inevitable in a field where all chairs were held by younger men. Seldom could a professor marry before his early thirties; should Boas wish to marry sooner, he would have to look to institutions outside the university.[4]

More factors than the uncertain wait and fears of anti-Semitic prejudice made a German university unattractive. A "snobbish aristocracy" ruled the academy, placing obstacles in the way of younger men and scorning modern geographical and ethnological work. Even with a professorship, Boas felt that it would be several years before he could have his own classes, and these would claim most of his time. The geographical field was filled, its possibilities restricted, its limits established. In America "everything in our science is in the raw," open and unformed, waiting to be created. "Here I see a possibility of success; at home in Germany, I see none at all."[5]

Boas's ambition, like the potential in America, was almost unlimited: to be no less than the instrument for the creation of a scientific geography in the United States. "If only I can create a geographical science and places in which it can be nurtured, I would consider myself happy," he declared. "I consider that alone to be a worthy task." More precisely, he hoped to reawaken the American government's interest in polar research and establish an association which, with relatively modest means, could undertake systematic arctic research. This might, he admitted to Jacobi, sound beyond his power, but he was confident of his ability. "I know what I am worth and what I can do," he wrote yet more boldly to Marie. "So I feel the duty to do what I can, even if it is difficult."[6] The difficulty was partly that this raw land for science had no place for him and partly that he felt the pressure to return home.

His parents had not seen their only son for well over a year. They wanted him back in Germany, wanted him to become a professor, and feared that he would throw this away for an early marriage and an inferior position. More than anything, they feared that he might want to establish his future in America. That, wrote Sophie, "would be so hard a fate as I cannot express, and I do not know how I could stand it." Her letters drove Franz "almost to despair." "You cannot imagine how badly I feel," he confessed to Marie, "about the many admonitions from home."[7]

He tried to explain his position, arguing that they misjudged him badly if they thought he would sacrifice his goal as a man and a scientist for a quick marriage and a mediocre position. He would not, he promised, take any binding step before he returned to Germany to survey the situation there, but he refused to concede more than that. He knew what he wanted and would do everything to accomplish it, even if it involved deep pain to his dearest relatives.[8]

Boas bowed to his parents' wishes—at least temporarily. There were no openings for him in Washington or New York. The appropriation from Powell's Bureau of Ethnology was inadequate. A library position in New York and a possible place with the meteorological division of the Signal Corps evaporated. Johns Hopkins University had no openings. The Smithsonian was not hiring. He had made his qualifications known everywhere, and while people would publish his articles and monographs, none was willing or able to hire him.

His English may have been a factor. He worked hard to improve his facility in the language, but he spoke mostly German with Marie and his relatives. His writing capability improved, and he soon found that Marie and Jacobi needed to correct his drafts only a little. Nevertheless he had to rely on the secretary to read his paper for him at the November meeting of the Washington Anthropological Society and, though he struggled fairly well in fielding questions, he had difficulty following the discussion. Late in February he gave two lectures at Columbia College. The first was such a disaster that few returned for the second.

The Columbia catastrophe was a depressing exit to his American sojourn. On March 14, 1885, after almost six months in America, Boas took passage on the *Donau* back to Germany, leaving behind Marie and a basketful of disappointments.

His mother was waiting for him in Bremerhaven. Franz insisted on traveling immediately to Minden where, at three in the morning, the tired pair were met by Toni, Hete, and Aenne. The Marienstrasse house had been decorated with wreaths and garlands to celebrate the prodigal's return. The clock turned five before Franz escaped to bed. Meier arrived that evening from Paris to greet his son with a warm embrace and tearful eyes. Franz was overcome by this demonstration of his father's affection, but retained his usual dry-eyed reserve.

After a week with his family, he went to Hamburg for the annual congress of German geographers. On the way, he received a survey of prospects from Fischer in Marburg. His mentor still favored the academic route—possibilities of habilitation at Halle, Giessen, and Berlin were weighed—but Franz was more interested in publishers or institutes. The Hydrographic Office, Perthes Institute, and Bastian's new Ethnology Museum were possibilities.

Fischer had arranged a place for Boas on the geographical congress program. His paper, presented Saturday morning on "The Eskimos of Baffin Island,"[9] was received with lively applause from the full hall. The successful lecture highlighted the difference between "the whole fruitless American story" and the reception he was surprised to receive among German scholars. His Columbia lecture disaster still hurt, and the Hamburg applause was the more gratifying because of it. Even more pleasing was the respect accorded him from all sides. To his astonishment, "everyone knew where I've been and what I'm doing," and he found geographers whose work he admired coming to introduce themselves, enquire after his plans, and wish him well. After all the depressing failures of America, this was a strong tonic, "moral support for my intentions when people here, whom I admire scientifically, attach importance to my personal opinions and aims." Alfred Kirchhoff asked him to habilitate at Halle, and he received invitations to lecture before the Anthropological Society in Berlin and geographical societies in Frankfurt, Berlin, Halle, and Strassburg. "Here I am in quite a different position than in America," he wrote Marie. "There no one works for me while here I am known everywhere."[10]

The Hamburg congress was intoxicating. On the other side was the political situation he discovered on his return. Liberalism, a splintered and declining force, had suffered defeat in the 1884 election. At the same time, Bismarck took a colonial turn, declaring protectorates in New Guinea and in East, West, and Southwest Africa. Conservative nationalism was in the ascent, liberalism was wounded, and Boas did not like it.

Everyone in Germany seemed bewitched by Bismarck and the new surge of nationalist policies. "All Germany lies in the dust before the brutal power of Bismarck," Boas wrote, "and one hears nothing but the splendor of the German Empire and the advancement of national interests." The sentiment that "thank God, we have overcome our old idealism and now strive for practical ideas," shocked him. "The German nation" seemed to have suppressed all other aspirations. No one appeared concerned with social questions, only with unending talk about Empire. Fischer was full of it, wrapped up in colonial, naval, and Germanic causes, laboring away for a national union of the "ältere Herren" of the Burschenschaften. Everywhere an exaggerated national sentiment reigned, and Boas felt alienated from it all. Humanness, "Menschlichkeit," was no longer on peoples' lips; all the talk was of Germanness, "Deutschtum."[11]

Such disagreeable political impressions were offset by his scholarly reception. Perthes confirmed its desire to publish his expedition report as a supplementary volume to the geographical journal, *Petermanns Mitteilungen*. It was to come out in the fall, so he would have to "wear out his trousers" to get it finished. Between lectures in Berlin, Frankfurt, and Halle, and a long session in Copenhagen with Heinrich (Henrik) Rink, an Eskimo language and legends scholar, he worked away at the manuscript. The writing went rapidly—by early June it was half drafted—but he was depressed. "What good is it," he asked Marie, "to sit in a room and write the whole day on a book that, at best, only 4 or 5 people will read?" He was missing her terribly and longed to be back in "our parlor and our chair."[12]

The disappointments of America were repeating themselves in Germany. Hamburg had been illusory. Lecture invitations were not job offers. There were no openings at Perthes. Boas let himself put high hopes on a position with Vienna's Hölzel Institute, even asking Marie if she would enjoy returning to her father's Vienna, but the expected letter never came. Berlin's Geographical Society was looking for a director, but then decided not to establish the post. "Do you know how depressing it is, here as over there, to feel so superfluous?"[13]

His "blues"—he had picked up the word from Marie—were only deepened by the spring and summer wedding season. In April Willy Meyer had married Lilly Maass in New York, and their happy nuptials had made him wish for a little of Willy's luck. Hete's own wedding preparations were in progress, while he and Marie had to wait in tortured separation for their bit of future.

Hete's engagement had come as a surprise when he learned of it in New York. Her betrothed was none other than Rudolf Lehmann, Franz's close Berlin friend. While this should have pleased him, he received the news with reservations that only deepened upon his return to Minden. Toni had always nurtured an attachment to Rudolf, and now she had been spurned for a younger, prettier sister. Franz had consoled her from New York, insisting that the relationship would never have worked and encouraging her to seek her happiness elsewhere. Her mood, however, remained contrary, even bitter. "She tortures herself half to death," he now wrote Marie, "because, as she says, no one needs her love." Her situation hurt him terribly, but he did not know how to help.[14]

The Lehmann-Boas ceremony was at the registry office, with Franz appearing among the witnesses. The celebration followed at Marienstrasse where over one hundred friends and relatives gathered for the festivity. Franz put on an air of happiness, joining in the entertainment at the piano, mimicking a tree and, of course, an Eskimo, and in the more serious business of presenting a toast. The last was particularly painful. "You can't imagine what I endured; you know how hard it is for me to speak in public." But he overcame both shyness and blues to act "terribly amiably."[15]

As the Lehmanns left for an Alpine honeymoon, Franz decided that habilitation was his only option. This reluctant decision was made after the prospect at the Berlin Geographical Society had completely collapsed. He still preferred an immediate nonacademic position, hoping that something might yet open up in Germany or, even better, in America, but for the moment he had no alternative but to pursue the university option. On

The F. Boas store on the Kleiner Domhof, owned by Feibes Boas and then his widow, Caroline Frank Boas, the grandparents of Franz. It no longer stands. Photographed in Minden by J. Hülsenbeck. APS B/B61/NO. 19/N.B. #33

Markt zu Minden. Bahnhof zu Minden. Eisenhütte zu Porta. Bahnhof zu Porta.

Porta Westfalica.

TOP LEFT: A view of Porta Westfalica, just south of Minden, the gate in the Westphalian Mountains through which the Weser River flows.
KOMMUNALARCHIV MINDEN

ABOVE: Boas's Quarta Gymnasium class, 1869–70, with the teacher, Dr. Frommann. Franz stands at the upper right. APS NEG. #915

BOTTOM LEFT: Members of the Burschenschaft Alemannia, summer semester, 1878. Boas stands at the lower left behind the Bierfass, Alf Vogeler is beside him holding a sword, and Franz Richarz sits tapping the keg. APS NEG. #922

NEAR LEFT: Boas wearing his black-red-gold Alemannia ribbon, in summer semester, 1878.
BURSCHENSCHAFT ALEMANNIA, BONN

TOP LEFT: Boas at Kiel. APS B/B61/N.B. #52

TOP MIDDLE: Willy Meyer. His Burschenschaft photo at Bonn, winter semester, 1877–78. BURSCHENSCHAFT ALEMANNIA, BONN

TOP RIGHT: Theobald Fischer, Boas's geography teacher at Bonn and at Kiel, as portrayed later as a professor at Marburg. UNIVERSITÄTSMUSEUM FÜR KUNST UND KULTURGESCHICHTE, MARBURG

LEFT: The Prussian infantryman Franz Boas stands at the extreme left (behind the Pickelhaube helmet) among officers and his fellow trainees at the end of his service in the Prince Friedrich of the Netherlands Regiment (Second Westphalian No. 15). APS B/B61/NO. 32/DS

ABOVE: The Boas family, without one daughter, in Villa Boas, during Franz's military service year. Left to right are Franz, Sophie, Meier, Toni, and probably Aenne. APS NEG. #917

LEFT: Villa Boas, the Boas residence of Marienstrasse, soon after its 1879 completion. COURTESY NORMAN BOAS

the advice of Fischer and Kirchhoff, he decided on Berlin University.

Geography was a new discipline to universities and, though Germany led other countries in its academic development, weak departments existed, most strikingly in southern Germany and, surprisingly, at Berlin. Preeminent in so many areas of learning, the senior Prussian university had only one professor of geography, the sixty-seven-year-old Heinrich Kiepert. Successor to Karl Ritter, Kiepert followed his master's historical geography to a fault. To the aging *Ordinarius,* geography "was nothing more than a piece of history." Aside from a strong cartographic concern, his interests never went beyond the lands of classical antiquity, and he remained unaffected, even disapproving, of new trends within the field. His narrow obsolescence was not offset by other talents. Notoriously unpleasant, he attracted few students. Blunt to the point of rudeness, unapproachable to the point of being forbidding, and critical to the point of bitterness, Kiepert caused even his sympathetic memorialist to apologize for his unfortunate temperament. The circumstances made Berlin seem a splendid opportunity for a promising young man. Kiepert's unbearable lectures left room for a younger teacher, and the growing interest in geography meant that Berlin would soon have to increase its faculty. On the other hand, Fischer and Kirchhoff had made it clear that Kiepert might prove disagreeable. Boas, as he left Minden for the capital, wondered "if old Kiepert will put difficulties in my way."[16]

Franz's interview went as feared. "The dumb ass seemed to want to be contrary. He declared that he would not be able to criticize the work I would present because he was a historical geographer and knew nothing of the modern, natural-historical tendencies." Boas would have to see Helmholtz or Bastian. Franz was firm. "I am a geographer and intend to present my expedition results," he replied, restraining himself to gentle "flute tones." Kiepert barely listened. His time, he said, was fully committed until October; there were others who should take on the supervision, and, in any case, Boas could not expect to have students for years. The meeting would have been comic (and Boas wrote of it almost that way) if so much did not hang upon his habilitating in Berlin. Kirchhoff, who got on well with Kiepert, had already written on the young man's behalf, but that had not moved the dyspeptic professor. If Boas's "well-inclined patrons"—Kirchhoff and Fischer—could not intervene successfully and Kiepert's resistance could not be sidestepped, then he was sure to fail.[17]

He considered fleeing to Halle, but both Kirchhoff and Fischer, seconded by Wagner in Göttingen, counseled him to stay in Berlin.

Kiepert alone could not block his way. Boas could trust in the good sense of the faculty to see that "this nonsense" did not hinder his habilitation. An important discipline at the country's largest university, Fischer assured him, could not be left to drift because it suited one old man. He should discreetly work through professors in allied disciplines while his friends outside used their influence wherever they could exercise it. Bastian, Reiss, and Förster promised their support, and Neumayer introduced him to Wilhelm von Bezold, the university's new meteorologist, who reacted sympathetically. Since he would not formally apply for the habilitation until the appearance of his Perthes book, his major qualifying piece, there was time to let these influences work in his favor.

Apprehensive and insecure, Boas settled into a room at 26a Kanonierstrasse, near Unter den Linden and Friedrichstrasse. He did not look forward to the Berlin stay. "The old, lonely bachelor life won't be to my taste."[18] He returned to his manuscript, finishing the text by August and turning to the maps and tables while printing began. An order to report to his regiment for fall maneuvers threw him into a panic; five weeks of service would be fatal to the publication schedule. Against all expectations, his application for exemption succeeded. He was able to complete the proofs and maps so that the book appeared a week before Christmas. In September, just as his final *Baffin-Land* corrections had been sent off, Bastian offered him a temporary assistantship at the museum. Franz was gratified: it demonstrated Bastian's interest in him, and for once he could be, even on 150 marks a month, reasonably self-sufficient.

He avoided beginning serious work on the Central Eskimo manuscript for Powell, preferring to sort out some ideas for a book on geographical methodology. He drafted a first chapter, then decided he had better get started on the Eskimo ethnology. He was well into the new book by November, but there were problems. He had begun to write it in English, with Marie correcting his slips. The process was slow, the bundles taking two weeks to reach her in New York, then two weeks back for rewriting, before again crossing the Atlantic to Washington. Worse was that so much was wrong with his English. He knew he had problems, but had not expected them to be so serious. He feared that he had overreached himself by trying to write in a foreign language; he might reluctantly have to revert to a translation of German drafts. Indeed, he resorted to translating large chunks from his Perthes manuscript, but continued to draft largely in English. The Central Eskimo manuscript was going better by Christmas when the first copies of *Baffin-Land* reached him.[19]

The book, a one-hundred-page supplementary volume to *Petermanns Mitteilungen,* gave him renewed courage. It would both serve as a habilitation thesis and promote his employability. He wrote all his professional friends—Fischer, Kirchhoff, Gerland, Reiss, and Bessels—asking them to review it. He felt a bit monstrous in such self-promotion, but he had to do it. The moment would not return, and he was determined to "set all means and all personalities in motion in order to advance myself."[20]

He faced the new year with more optimism. The book notices were kind, especially Gerland's, which termed it among "the most distinguished geographical works of recent years." With the book out, he could now apply for habilitation. His prospects for a job were no better, but at least he was enlarging his reputation and his contacts. With a little luck, these eventually had to turn into something. America remained attractive, especially with his deepening dislike of German university life, but six months in the United States had brought nothing, and he could not hope for better results. He had not given up: "I try to keep up every connection with America."[21]

The habilitation issue remained unsettling. Kiepert, he heard, had told a faculty meeting that Boas had proved himself an inexperienced traveler and that his book contained nothing of scientific value. The faculty dean, philologist Wilhelm Scherer, suggested that the old man would continue to put a spoke in every wheel. The faculty, too, realized that Kiepert was being selfishly obstructionist. While wanting to push the young man through, they were reluctant to tread upon Kiepert's professorial prerogatives. They knew, Boas reported, that Kiepert's "vulgar jealousy" about losing his few students to a competitor had been successful in deterring other aspiring candidates, but "no one wanted his fingers burned." The whole thing was simply scandalous. Kiepert kept insisting that Boas's publications were outside his own field. "I have absolutely no judgment over the entire discipline to which your work belongs," he had written Boas, "so, should the task be assigned to me by the faculty, I must decline to judge your habilitation thesis and turn it over to specialists—the new meteorologist von Bezold and, for the ethnological portion, Bastian." Kiepert's abdication permitted a February faculty meeting to name von Bezold as Boas's major examiner and reduce Kiepert to subsidiary examiner. Although Franz remained sceptical, refusing to believe all he was told, the decision "lifted a stone from my heart." Kiepert might still oppose, but Scherer assured him that, having declared himself incompetent in Boas's work, Kiepert's opinion would carry little weight among faculty.[22]

Setbacks continued. Boas missed an opening at the Dietrich Reimer publishing house, and Bastian treated him badly over his proposal for a four-season expedition through arctic and subarctic America. Such reversals easily plunged him back into depression. "How happy I would be if I could turn my back on Germany and come to you!" he wrote his beloved. "Blues" understated his feelings. It was almost a year since he had left his "Schatz," Marie, and the separation was becoming unbearable. If he could not go to New York in the summer, then she must come to him. "I cannot hold out."[23] At the dimmest glimmer, however, his hopes would soar. He lectured Marie that they should not build "Luftschlösser," castles in the air, but contact with Robert Bell of the Geological Survey of Canada made him think that there could be a place for him in Ottawa. Where there was no opening, he sought to create one, hatching a plan for an exchange between the United States National Museum and Bastian's Berlin Museum. An arrangement would benefit both institutions' collections; most of all it would take him to America without breaking his Berlin connection. Though his father had offered to pay for Marie's travel to Germany, Franz preferred to return to New York to refresh his contacts. His Berlin lectures would not begin until October—if, that is, he succeeded in his habilitation struggle.

By April that battle seemed almost won. Kiepert mounted a rear-guard skirmish over Franz's suggestion of three examination topics. Boas, wishing to be agreeable, made a list of alternatives. Kiepert, seeming to want to push the applicant into historical geography, rejected them all. Boas remained adamant. He would compromise, but "I will not be forced." At a second test of wills, Franz again proposed "Ice Conditions in the Arctic Ocean," but added "Temperature Conditions of Inland Seas" and "Trade Routes of the Northwest Coast Indians." Kiepert objected that two were physical; Boas answered that both were geographical. Kiepert argued that Boas alone was the authority on trade routes and no one could comment upon it. Boas answered that the faculty could judge the scientific value of his treatment. In the end, Kiepert conceded that the topics had to come from Boas's own fields and Franz was all the more convinced that Kiepert betrayed a fear of competition.[24]

From then on the process went smoothly. Bezold reported to the faculty that *Baffin-Land* was acceptable as a habilitation thesis, and Kiepert reluctantly approved it. The monograph, read Kiepert's letter, dealt with a restricted area far from general interest, and its treatment scarcely rose above those of practical seamen describing the same regions. Neither the publication nor Boas's proposed colloquium topics were proof of the candidate's comprehensive knowledge of the field. The old man's reservations had little impact. On the evening of May 27, Boas presented a forty-five-minute lecture on arctic ice to the faculty colloquium. Helmholtz, Wilhelm Dilthey, Heinrich von Treitschke, Theodor Mommsen, and other "big guns" were among the thirty or so professors present. At the end of the lecture, Boas fielded Bezold's question about icebergs, and discussion turned to Greenland's climate, the movement of pack ice, and warm-water currents, after which the examinee was excused. The faculty discussion, dominated by Helmholtz's emphatic judgment of his satisfaction at Boas's clear separation of fact from theory, took only minutes.[25]

The inaugural address was mere formality. On May 5 Dean Scherer, twenty students, and a proud Onkel Mons, learned about "The Canyon Area of the Colorado." Boas would have preferred either of his other suggestions, "The History of the Search for Franklin" or "The Northwest Coast Indians," but the faculty, perhaps in costless deference to Kiepert, chose the more orthodox theme. Boas was now a privatdozent. The ordeal was over. He hoped "never again to hear the word Kiepert!"[26]

The difficult year had solved little. He could now lecture at the university, but only for student fees. Kiepert would be his colleague, but the whole situation was changed by the decision to call Ferdinand von Richthofen to a new chair. The eminent physical geographer of Asia would give strength to the discipline and, Boas spitefully thought, put Kiepert in his place. On the other hand, Richthofen's presence might block his own succession to Kiepert's chair and open the way to Alfred Hettner, an up-and-coming young man whom he had known as a student in Fischer's Bonn seminar. Hettner had been Richthofen's student at Leipzig, conducted field research in South America, and might be preferred as well because he came from an academic family.[27]

Richthofen and Hettner were future concerns. For now Boas made his plans for the winter semester. He submitted his course topics and arranged to supplement his income from a teaching position at the Humboldt Academy, a popular education institute, and persuaded Bastian to assure another temporary museum assistantship. Three incomes would free him from his father's purse, but would be insufficient for marriage.

Despite small gains, he was still separated from Marie, still had no secure position, and still could not marry. Boas was in the midst of the structural "crisis of overcrowding" that affected the employment market for university-trained young men in general and the academic field in particular.[28] There were no jobs; Boas's only course was to accept a docent's position at the university and hope that he could, within a reasonable time, secure a permanent, salaried position.

The year, moreover, had confirmed his opinion of German academic life and strengthened his desire to be free of its deadening influence. He had, it is true, received strong and sympathetic support from the professorate—from Fischer and Kirchhoff outside and from Bezold, Scherer, Förster and others within—but that did not alter his view. He somewhat resented being forced to call upon friends to pull his chestnuts from the fire. He hated the whole system, "the noble guild of professors" who protected their group prerogatives and placed such "an unbearable yoke" upon younger scholars. His own intention to write on methodological questions had been put down, even by one otherwise friendly to him, with the comment that such matters were not the concern of the young. Such experiences strengthened his desire "to be away from here," to again try his prospects in America, and "never to return to this unhappy university!"[29] Other thoughts darkened his outlook. Toni remained wrapped in loveless melancholia. Death, too, had touched him again.

Hermann Blendermann, in some ways his closest friend from Bonn, had drowned in the Rhine in July 1884. He and Franz had exchanged letters just as Boas was leaving for the Arctic, and the news of the death, heard at the end of that trip, cut deeply. "You cannot imagine how painful the thought is, that this man, whom I treasured and loved above so many, is now gone." Blendermann's drowning was made more poignant by Franz's remembrance of having pulled him from the Rhine during their student days. The tragedy, so similar to Reinhard's, stirred painful memories. Now, a year and a half later, came the report of Karl Bertelsmann's death. The man had been very sick, so the end was not surprising, but Franz had not expected it so quickly. The memory of this friendship also took him back to Reinhard. They had met, he recalled, right after Reinhard's death and became friends very quickly. "With Bertelsmann and Blendermann my Bonn life is dead. These two were far and away my closest friends there."[30]

Lost in Boas's disappointments and sorrow was a significant movement in the young man's interest. The Berlin winter, discouraging in so many ways, was, in fact, pivotal to his future. Partly by inclination, but partly also by chance and opportunity, Boas was increasingly becoming an anthropologist.

Geography had been a compromise, a means of melding his eclectic interests under the umbrella of a single discipline. There his scientific interests could mix with his boyhood historical and geographical inclinations. His Baffin Island project had been conventional human geography—the interplay between people and their physical environment—but even while preparing for it, he had wondered "whether I should let myself be taken up by the anthropologists."[31] His concerns had remained largely geographic—cartographic surveys, meteorological observation, place names, and travel and trade routes—but he had devoted almost as much time to the Eskimo themselves, to their seasonal cycle, material life, language, myths, and songs.

He had returned from the north realizing that it was urgent to salvage knowledge from these doomed people. Other things helped tilt him increasingly toward the ethnological side. Probably the most significant factor was that, just as he was beginning to settle down to work on his anthropological monograph for Washington's Bureau of Ethnology, Adolf Bastian took him on temporarily at the Royal Ethnological Museum.

The museum was a difficult place to work. Bastian was disorganized and unpredictable, erratically changing work patterns and constantly alternating between cordiality and rudeness. "It is no fun to work for Bastian," wrote Boas. On the other hand, Bastian and Rudolf Virchow, who was responsible for the physical anthropology section of the museum, were the leading men in their fields. Their prestige, together with the richness of the collections, "attracted anthropologists from all parts of the world, bringing us younger students into enviable contact with men of the most varied experience and opinions." Bastian possessed wide experience and broad erudition, and, despite his dense, confusing, and prolix style, had established himself as German ethnology's leading theoretician.[32]

Adolf Bastian was of that breed of prodigious scholars and organizers whose accomplishments leave one in awe. He studied law, then medicine, traveled as a ship's surgeon to Oceania, South America, Asia, and West Africa. The experience turned him to ethnology, and he published his accounts almost immediately upon his return to Germany. Thereafter, frequent publications alternated with frequent travel, yet Bastian found time to launch the journal *Zeitschrift für Ethnologie,* help organize the Berlin Society for Anthropology, Ethnology, and Prehistory, and establish the Museum für Völkerkunde as a separate division of the Prussian state museums and oversee the move to its new building in December 1886. As a theoretician, he was identified with the concepts of "elementary ideas," the basic strata of human thought shared by all peoples, which were elaborated as distinct and multiformed "ethnic thoughts" in the various geographical provinces of the world. As an ethnologist and museum man, he was obsessed with the urgency of collecting objects and information from the primitive cultures of the world which were everywhere being buried by advancing civilization. Once these peoples' cultures were gone, they could never be reconstructed.[33]

Bastian had an eye for bright and promising men. Boas was but one of a small constellation of assistants, some permanent, some, like him, struggling to find permanency. "It was my good fortune," Boas wrote years later, "to work in the inspiring surroundings of the Royal Ethnographical Museum of Berlin" and "in close friendship" with Albert Grünwedel, Wilhelm Grube, and Felix von Luschan. The three were roughly his age and, though from diverse backgrounds and specialties, were also trying to make sense of the new science of anthropology.

The twenty-nine year old Grünwedel, an East Indian specialist, was already bringing his philological and archaeological training and his artistic temperament to the area's problems. His "painstaking care in elucidating the historical relations of ethnographical phenomena" left a lasting impression on Boas. The Austrian polymath, Luschan, four years Boas's senior, was a medical doctor "whose versatile genius embraces all sides of anthropological study with equal ardor." Wilhelm Grube, a St. Petersburg native, was a year younger than Luschan. He had studied philology and Sinology in Russia and Leipzig before settling in Berlin, "where his studies of Chinese culture were carried on with a fine appreciation of their ethnographical basis."[34]

Boas entered this anthropological hothouse in September 1885. He worked with some of the African accessions and catalogued a new Peruvian collection, but his major task was cataloguing and installing the extensive collections from Alaska and British Columbia gathered by J. Adrian Jacobsen from 1881 to 1883. The Eskimo material was interesting for its comparability to the central Eskimo material he already knew. The Northwest Coast area was new, familiar to him only through Aurel and Arthur Krause, the Berlin Gymnasium teachers who had wintered in 1881–82 among the Chilkat Tlingit. "I am now working in the museum here among Jacobsen's highly interesting collections," he wrote Major Powell in Washington, D.C. The dance masks were the most intriguing part of the collection: "I find in them very encouraging material, and become more and more convinced of the importance of the study of the traditions of that region." He wrote years later, "My fancy was first struck by the flight of imagination exhibited in the works of art of the British Columbians as compared to the severe sobriety of the eastern Eskimo." From Jacobsen's fragmentary collection notes, he "divined what a wealth of thought lay hidden behind the grotesque masks and the elaborately decorated utensils of these tribes." A study of these and other neighbors of the Eskimo would, as he wrote at the time, bring important "psychological results," and he considered that "almost the most important problem of ethnology."[35]

In January, Jacobsen and his brother Fillip brought to Berlin a touring group of nine Bella Coola Indians from British Columbia, giving Boas an opportunity "to cast a brief glance behind the veil that covered the life of those people." The Bella Coolas performed and lived at the Kroll'sche Etablissement hall near the Reichstag. Boas spent all his free time with them during the group's short January and March visits. Their ceremonial dances revealed the use of those fanciful masks and rattles that, even as museum specimens, had struck his imagination and hinted at the richness of the religious and artistic elements of this "remarkable" tribe. He recorded some songs, but concentrated on their language, "a terrible headache," but completely unknown. He was a little bored with his "eternal Eskimo" and was overjoyed at being able to work on something new. He hoped for material enough for "a pretty little essay." There was also another element in his enthusiasm and energy: he wanted to demonstrate to American scholars that he possessed an expertise beyond the Eskimo. "I will do everything," he wrote Marie, "to force the people over there to recognize me." In February, when his "dear Indians" were leaving for Breslau, he posted an article on their language to the New York journal *Science*. He put great store on the short piece. "Who knows if this work will be decisive for America!"[36]

By a particular blend of opportunities and enticements, Boas was drawn to the Northwest Coast at the same time as he was concentrating increasingly upon anthropological problems. Bastian and his corps of assistants had an important role, but Jacobsen's collections, the visiting Bella Coola, and fascinating conversations with Aurel and Arthur Krause provided an invitation into a new ethnological field, exciting in itself, while also offering an opportunity to expand his breadth as an Americanist and thus make him more marketable in the new world.

He went home for a few days in late April. The same old disagreements about his future insured that the stay was not pleasant. "Believe me," he wrote Marie, "the conversation this morning was very hard, but I could not give in and put our outlook into jeopardy." Things were difficult for him. "I have such loving and good parents and my aspirations and hopes are so contrary to theirs." His mother could not understand what moved him, what drew him to America. "Since it goes so against their heart," he was unable to shake them from the belief that Germany was better than America.[37]

Back in Berlin, Boas was even more determined to go his own way and sick of trying to make it clear what pulled him to America, what could be done there that was impossible in Germany. Scholarly accomplishment was not all that was on his mind; people could not understand that he was moved by ideals other than a freedom to pursue his own work. "I want to bring something out of my work," he declared. "Whether I write a thick book or whether the students sleep in my class or someone else's is unimportant." The meaning is a little vague, but he felt that America offered broader possibilities, not just in science, but "in many other things": the possibility "to plant a seed which will grow according to one's spirit and work." That was what he admired in German emigrés like Jacobi and Felix Adler.[38]

Boas decided to revisit America before starting his courses in October. He wanted to again survey the American scene, and could return to his Berlin teaching and museum posts. Toni, he hoped, would come with him. She needed to be shaken from the morose mood in which she seemed determined to wallow. He would go by way of London. He placed great store on a possible opening with the Canadian Geological Survey. Robert Bell in Ottawa encouraged him, even securing passage of a resolution at the Royal Society of Canada meetings urging support for his work.[39] Alfred Selwyn, the Survey's director, would be in Britain for the Colonial and Imperial Exposition where Boas, armed with Neumayer's letter of introduction, could speak with him.

The London visit was another disappointment. The exposition was magnificent, unlike anything he had ever seen. India had the most beautiful display, though his own interests drew him to the South African and Canadian exhibits. A few minutes with Selwyn, however, made it clear that Canadian prospects were hopeless. Selwyn knew nothing of the Royal Society resolution and dismissed it as valueless. Moreover, Selwyn had no interest in ethnology. Franz joined Toni on the *Eider* at Southampton.

Toni, though seasick, seemed in good spirits. He had not seen her laugh so much for a long time.[40]

The liner reached New York on the morning of July 27, 1886, and Franz left Toni with Phips and Kobus while he ran to 60th Street to find Marie. Unfortunately, with all her relatives away from the city, she was forced to stay most of the time in Lake George with her sister. In the ensuing days, Franz's own imperatives kept him in New York or sent him south to Washington. He had to renew his contacts, wanted to study the collections at the American Museum, and needed to look after the corrections to his Central Eskimo monograph.

In mid-August, at Jacobi's insistence, he went to Buffalo for the annual meeting of the American Association for the Advancement of Science. He might make some worthwhile acquaintances there, but he feared being a stranger at the edge of the crowd. To his surprise, he was received cordially, more well-known than he thought. He had a two-hour talk with Canadian philologist and ethnologist Horatio Hale, was greeted warmly by Frederic Ward Putnam, permanent secretary of the Association, and was even asked to read a paper. This he refused, fearful of his English and unwilling to test it without full preparation.

He returned with renewed enthusiasm for America as a worthy field for scientific work. "I see such a wide and free field of labor before my eyes that the mere thought excites me." The excitement came partly from the possibility that New York's American Museum of Natural History might want an anthropology curator. The position would be ideal: visits to Germany would complement his duties, and he could have relative freedom in his research. It would "fulfill all my hopes" and ensure "success in all my plans."[41] Albert Bickmore was responsible for the department, but his duties as museum director and in developing public instruction left little time for anthropology. Unfortunately, Bickmore was abroad, so Boas could do little except, against his better judgment, build another castle in the air. He hoped that his New York contacts—Jacobi and the latter's close friend, fellow Forty-Eighter Carl Schurz, who had risen to national prominence as a Union general, a U.S. Senator, and the Secretary of the Interior—would sway the museum trustees.

Meanwhile, Boas made plans for a fall research trip to British Columbia. The idea had been in his mind before he left Germany. The region fascinated him, partly because so little was known about it, partly because of its inherent interest. Moreover, the situation was "extremely pressing"; the construction of the new Canadian Pacific Railway meant "that within a few years everything will be obliterated." Schurz arranged for a Northern Pacific pass and transportation from Chicago to St. Paul. Jacobi offered to lend $500, a sum which Boas calculated could be repaid by collecting artifacts cheaply in British Columbia and selling dearly to Bastian or the American Museum. He hesitated at putting himself in his uncle's debt, mostly because he knew his mother would dislike it, but, with Schurz's coaxing, did so.[42] Having decided to make the trip, he canceled his announced Berlin lectures.

He left Penn Station on September 11, 1886, arriving in Victoria five days later. Walking the streets that afternoon, he was surprised to see his pictures everywhere. An Indian trader, it turned out, had reproduced the photos, and he discovered that, though the troupe had been back a month, two men were still in town. He sought out Alkinous and Itlakuani, astonishing their friends "when they heard me talk their language."[43]

He spent three weeks in Victoria, a British colonial city of about 13,000 souls. Founded forty years earlier, it was a peculiar place, mixing elements of British and Hudson's Bay Company gentility with frontier roughness. Perhaps two thousand Indians lived in the city, often transitorily, the men working on the wharves and steamers, as carpenters, or selling fish and fur, while the women performed domestic duties or worked as prostitutes. The Indians lived on the harbor reserve or on the outskirts of the city, usually in shanties, sheds, or canvas tents that were, despite their filthiness, "frequently places of merriment and joy." Here, in one location, he could learn from Tlingit, Tsimshian, Haida, Bella Coola, Kwakiutl, and Salish something of their languages and myths. Still "sick and tired of my Eskimos," he was happy to be working on something new and worthwhile, but the confusion of dialects and languages made his task difficult. Native social and religious life, he quickly discovered, were so complicated that he feared he could not get far. Every day brought surprises. The material threatened to overwhelm him. He hardly knew where to begin.[44]

He could have profitably stayed in Victoria, but he wanted to get north to collect artifacts, cheaper there than in the city. On October 4, accompanying a returning Indian, he took a steamer to the remote Kwakiutl village of Newitti, where he had been told a series of feasts were to be held. He spent eleven days observing dances, potlatches, and a shaman healing, but primarily gathering stories and buying pieces for his collection. From Newitti he traveled to Alert Bay by sailboat and canoe, a dangerous choice since a storm almost broke the canoe against the shore. After returning south for a break in Victoria, he stayed five weeks at Quamichan, Comox, and Nanaimo, accumulating linguistic and mythological material from the Salish and and their Lekwiltok Kwakiutl neighbors. He again returned to Victoria in December to fill in gaps and make a quick trip across the strait to Vancouver, the new terminal city of the Canadian Pacific Railway, where he secured information on the Squamish Salish. He left such a mass of material unexplored that he half wished he could stay longer, but he had been counting the days until his reunion with Marie. His passes expired on January 1, 1887, and that decided any conflicting attractions between the Indians and his fiancée.

Boas's concerns were largely with language and myth. He wanted to learn enough of the languages to map the distribution of the Vancouver Island tribes and their linguistic relationships. He collected vocabularies and texts, and sought to penetrate at least the essentials of the grammar of the several languages and numerous dialects. Mythology was an instrument to explore some of the same questions. After two weeks, he was convinced that using mythology was a sound method to distinguish and judge the relationships of the groups. He collected as many stories as he could, not only in pursuit of relationships, but also because they contributed useful information about religion and society. The myths and stories, moreover, were often related to the masks, rattles, and other artifacts of Native culture. He had brought photographs and drawings of New York, London, and Berlin museum pieces, and he found these an excellent way to prompt some of his informants into story telling. The Indians, however, rarely recognized the masks because they belonged to individual families, and only they could give a full explanation. Moreover, the meaning of articles belonging to secret society dances was known only to the initiated.[45]

In all this he worked extremely hard, begrudging every unproductive moment. It was always difficult to find the right informants and then to keep them available and talking. The Songhees were often too drunk, a valuable Tsmishian proved unreliable, an old Somenos man clammed up when laughed at by younger men, a Comox woman tried to fool him with an invented narrative, and the Quamichan were almost intractably suspicious, uncooperative, and covetous. Potlatches, dances, and feasts were intriguing parts of the culture, but they kept people from telling him stories. Except for a little Bella Coola, he could not hope to use the native languages and had to do almost all his work in English or Chinook, the simple, rudimentary trade jargon of the coast, which he had to learn.

The tribal divisions among the Salish were so complicated that he feared he might have to give up his map.

Amidst the complications, compensations abounded. He discovered an unknown Salish language, Pentlatch, spoken only by two or three families among the Comox, and this raised his spirits. Though the amount of material was awesome, his notes running over 300 pages, he kept it under control by diligently sifting and recopying every night. By the time he left for New York late in December, he had collected well over one hundred myths and stories, some of which added to the value of the museum pieces and all of which helped to elucidate the culture and the relationships of the diverse groups occupying Vancouver Island and the adjacent mainland. From this and his linguistic work, he felt that the names and ethnological relationships of over seventy groups, previously almost unknown, were now clear.[46]

Boas was also intent upon acquiring an artifact collection of his own, one that he could resell for a sum large enough to offset the credit extended by his uncle. The task occupied his mind from his arrival in Victoria until he had expended all the money he could spare for the purpose. He avoided buying anything in Victoria, correctly anticipating lower prices and better goods further north. His first purchases were at Newitti, by which time he knew "exactly what I want to buy and assemble into a very compact collection."[47]

He began cautiously. He broached the subject of buying only on the seventh day, spending the first six in intensive ethnological work— recording stories, sketching poles, observing shaman healings, watching dances and potlatches. On the fourth evening he gave his own potlatch to pay for a dance he had asked to be performed for him. His respectful patience secured the confidence of the villagers. The Newitti chief praised him for his kindness and for the potlatch; he was "not like the other whites who have come to us." Should Boas want anything, "we shall do our best to do what he asks." Boas was thus well established to begin to buy, and he was remarkably successful. He bought some of the best masks and many other good pieces, and he also put two women to work weaving mats and blankets for him. It was "a quite splendid collection." He added to it, more indiscriminately, in Alert Bay so that he judged its worth to be at least $250, though he had laid out only $70. He scoured an old graveyard in Quamichan where he picked up two well-preserved deformed skulls and more from middens at Comox. The entire collection, now some 140 pieces (not counting the skulls), went off ahead of him to

New York. He intended offering first refusal to the American Museum, where he still hoped it might be a useful instrument in his pursuit of a curatorial position.[48]

The museum possibility had obsessed him during his entire British Columbia trip. "I think every day about the museum and again about the museum," he wrote from Victoria. He knew that he should avoid the obsession, but the offer just had to come because he was so perfectly suited for it. "If only other people would realize that." He hoped the influence of Jacobi and Schurz would bring the director and trustees around, but it did not. Devastated in October by Jacobi's report that Bickmore considered six to eight departments had more urgent needs than anthropology, he refused to abandon hope. He would bring back such a valuable collection that the museum could refuse neither it nor his services. As a last resort, he would offer to catalogue and reorganize the existing collection; "*perhaps* something more would come of that," Boas thought. "I won't quit until all is lost."[49]

The news on his arrival in New York was discouraging. The museum simply did not want a curator for anthropology. He made a last effort to avoid returning to Berlin, writing letters to every American friend and acquaintance he knew. "I have resolved," he wrote F. W. Putnam at Harvard, "to make a strong effort to stay in America." His research was here, and if he returned to Germany he would be so distant that he would have to abandon it for another field. He offered other reasons for his resolve. In Germany "chauvinism and servility are so much the features of our age that I should feel relieved if I could live in the wholesome and refreshing air of American liberty." He could no longer be content "with the way in which our people are scorned by their own government and, even more, I am disgusted with the way in which they stand it and even pride themselves on it." Mixed with political repulsion for Germany were positive feelings for America. "I see myself working here, collecting a scattered manpower to a scientific focal point and, even more, working in my small way for the German idealism which lies within me and is the propelling force in this drive for effectiveness." Germany offered no opportunity for that kind of effort, no possibility of speaking out from a public position. "I am and remain," he told Toni, "an unregenerate idealist—and for that you and I have our mother to thank."[50]

One other element made the desire to stay in America urgent. The Easter deadline for his return to his Berlin courses was less pressing than the threat of European war. Warmed by Bismarck, the Balkan situation was threatening, with Russia forcing Prince Alexander of Bulgaria to abdicate in August and then, in what seemed a prelude to invasion, breaking off Bulgarian relations three months later. Russian action would force an Austro-Hungarian response with support from Britain. All Europe might be drawn into a Balkan war just at the time when General Boulanger was riding a tide of French patriotic zeal that provoked a responding surge in Germany. Boas worried about the prospect, fearing that he might suddenly find himself ordered back to active service with his Prussian regiment.

All this pushed him in his work. His ethnographic map of southwest British Columbia was finished and sent to *Petermanns Mitteilungen,* with a preliminary report on his excursion's results. Then he took an article on "The Study of Geography" to the offices of *Science.* Editor N.D.C. Hodges, hoping to recruit a Berlin correspondent, took him to dinner. Learning of Boas's desire to stay in America, Hodges changed his request to an offer as assistant editor in New York, with special responsibility for geography. Quickly, unexpectedly, Boas's search for a position was over. On January 24 he signed the two-year contract, at a salary of $150 a month, and immediately dispatched a cable to Minden: "made contract with science declare my emigration at mayors and military office instantly."[51]

The ambivalence between Germany and America was over. Boas was now committed to an American career. Years later, he remembered that the main reason for looking outside Germany was probably that "I saw no future there and wanted to marry." But behind that lay much else: "The anti-Semitic agitation in my student years, the intrigues in Berlin while I wanted to habilitate, and the idea that America was a politically ideal country, seem to be the major factors." His military status, he thought, probably also had something to do with it.[52]

6 "The Whole Field Lies Before Me"

LAUNCHING AN AMERICAN CAREER

THE BOAS-KRACKOWIZER wedding was set for Thursday, March 10, 1887, in time for Toni to attend before her return to Germany. Franz's *Science* salary would be enough to live on. They needed only a little money to start them off. "For the last time," he asked his father for help, enough "to make a beginning." Meier, as usual, opened his pocketbook, though Jacobi and Kobus answered the need first with a combined gift of $700 toward furnishings. One thousand dollars, half from Papa and half from Uncle Mons, went into the bank. Marie, with help from her mother and Toni, found a third-floor apartment at 196 Third Avenue, between Seventeenth and Eighteenth streets in New York City. Newly built, with both steam heat and a fireplace, the two-bedroom flat (one for Franz's study) rented for $35 a month.

The wedding ceremony was simple. Mrs. Krackowizer hosted the magistrate at her East Sixteenth Street apartment. Jacobi gave the address at the small reception afterwards for the family and a few friends. Franz took Friday and Saturday off work for a brief honeymoon with his bride at her family home in the Hudson River summer community of Sing Sing.

Toni had been the single sour note at the wedding. She had not had a happy time in New York. Aunt Phips had died in January following an agonizing illness that spoiled any possibility of the American holiday pulling Toni from her dejection. She was now, at thirty-two, making the difficult transition into mature spinsterhood. She disliked America, both for what it was and for stealing her brother and his talents. She "closes her eyes to all that is good here," he wrote, "and sees only a dreadful heartless mass of mankind." Franz realized that she had suffered much, "but she must also recognize the good." He wanted her to celebrate his marriage, but instead she was morose, "as if someone had thrown a bucket of cold water over her."[1]

Franz worried that Toni's jaundiced views would infect his parents. "You must not believe Toni's most dreadful descriptions," he warned; they should not "see my present work and position through her eyes." She could not realize that *Science* was not a theft of time, but what he had always wanted most. It provided "an opportunity to awaken here an interest in my field." The journal could become, he insisted, the hub of geographical work in America. Where in Germany could he have found such an area for expansive work? "The field which stands before me is large," he wrote, one to which he was committed heart and soul. Like Goethe's Wilhelm Meister, he had "the urge to be a useful, serviceable person who contributes his might to the general good and, while working for himself, also works for all."[2]

To Toni he was wasting his time in an inferior position in an inferior country. Looking at the modest twelve-page weekly of general scientific news and notes, mostly extracted from other journals, she could not see things his way. *Science* did have its limitations. Only four years old, it remained a financial incubus for editor and publisher N. D. C. Hodges, costing him something like $4000 a year. Virtually unknown abroad and still struggling to find its role in relating the broad range of scientific advances to the developing American learned community, it promised more potential than it had yet realized.

That promise was what caught Boas's enthusiasm. An editorial position on the journal gave him a mere toehold in American science, but he had ambitious plans to expand the paper and his role within it. His own ambitions and the publication's were, in Boas's view, interchangeable. "If I can awaken interest in my science and make our paper a central place for geography, I will have accomplished something," he wrote in February, but at the same time he saw himself becoming "the pivot for all geography and related endeavors and so, in two years, I can hold a certain power." His department of *Science* would become the American *Petermanns*. His maps would be designed to form later a popular atlas and, by securing outside map work, he could hire a draftsman. "That would be the beginning of my geographical institute." After two years he hoped to be independent of Hodges. He was confident "that my plans, which are not small, will come true with time and patience."[3]

His ambitions were not exercised just at *Science*'s Lafayette Square office. He joined the American Geographical Society, hoping to convert it into "something significant." He volunteered to supervise a new book review section in its *Bulletin,* the first step in his intention to become the publication's editor.[4] Yet a third springboard was the founding of an ethnological society.

The idea for such a society had been with him from the beginning of his work for *Science,* but only in November did he find the means to move the pieces into place. His plan was for Jacobi and Schurz to interest a number of New York notables and form them into a sponsoring committee, and then circularize for a general membership. He secured the written endorsement of the country's leading anthropologists—F. W. Putnam, Daniel G. Brinton, and J. W. Powell—and sought the support of Judge C. P. Daly of the American Geographical Society, J. S. Newberry of the New York Academy of Science, and Albert Bickmore of the American Museum. Here, too, Boas's plans were "not small," nothing less than an organization with resources sufficient to sponsor courses through both the geographical society and the museum and to launch arctic and antarctic expeditions within two years. "Don't laugh at me," he wrote home, "but I have the will and the audacity at least to try my chances." The first meeting of his co-opted committee was promising, but the project collapsed at the second. The society, "the center of my thoughts" in November, all but dissolved a month later.[5]

So it was with most of Boas's plans during this first year. A few map contracts came, but not enough to hire a draftsman and launch his institute. His plan for a series of geographical textbooks elicited interest from two publishers, but could never be pushed further. The American Geographical Society and its journal remained amateur.

Boas did not lack for work. *Science* kept him busy at the office five and a half days a week, and he brought more work home. Each week he wrote about four pages, a third of the journal. Most were unsigned pieces made up of reports and excerpts drawn from American and foreign journals. He started off with a fairly regular column of "Geographical Notes," later recaptioned "Exploration and Travel," and often added an "Ethnological Notes" column. Almost every month *Science* carried a map he prepared: arctic America, Central Asia, Pacific railways, Congo explorations. He reviewed books and contributed articles on diverse themes within his interests: Native music, Gulf Indians, the orthography of geographical names, a critique of psychophysical methods. For the most part, the articles were descriptive, reporting and commenting on new discoveries and papers. *Science* was not a scholarly journal but a scientific newspaper. Almost all his serious work was sent back to Germany, to *Globus, Petermanns,* or the Berlin Anthropological Society's publications. America, he found, had few outlets for his kind of scientific papers.[6]

Other work crowded his days and evenings. He agreed in August to assume responsibility for the North American section of the *Geographisches Jahrbuch,* edited by Hermann Wagner, and with the 1888 founding of the American Folk-Lore Society and its journal, edited by William Wells Newell, took charge of its American Indian section. The new *Internationales Archiv für Ethnographie* asked him to be its North American co-editor. In April he began cataloguing the Powell-Bishop Northwest Coast collection at the American Museum.

The Powell-Bishop contract was something of a consolation prize. He had been obsessed the previous fall with a possible curatorship at the museum, but there was no opening. Heber Bishop, a wealthy contributor to the museum, agreed to pay $300 for a catalogue and labels for the Northwest Coast pieces that British Columbia Indian Superintendent I.W. Powell had recently collected on his behalf for the American Museum. With Marie's help, Boas finished the job by August. Another remnant from his fall trip was his collection. Since the American Museum was uninterested, he sent the bulk of it to Berlin. "The interest of the Berlin Museum really lies in my heart," he wrote Bastian, but it was the American Museum's indifference and Bastian's promise of $500 that sealed the bargain.[7]

Between all the projects and plans, the collections and the cataloguing, was his own Northwest Coast work. He published a number of small pieces, but his fall trip to British Columbia had left him with a huge collection of linguistic and mythological material. He had floated the idea of a book to Powell at the Bureau of Ethnology and then to several German publishers. None was enthusiastic. Kiepert, his old Berlin antagonist, agreed to take installments for *Globus,* the geography journal he edited. Some went to the Berlin Anthropological Society's *Proceedings.* With all this on his plate, it is little wonder that he wrote that he had taken on too much for the winter.[8]

At home the new couple were happily settling in. "I don't find it at all hard to get used to my new life," he wrote days after their marriage. Aside from being without a maid for the last months of the year, domestic life soon became pleasantly routine. "We live very calmly and quietly," he wrote. With Marie helping with some of his drawing or merely sitting next to him as he worked at his desk, he found a wife to be "a very useful and pleasant institution." She too was happy as a helpmate: "How lovely it is to be able to sit next to him and sometimes hear a word or catch a kiss and to share in his work." They saw Uncle Kobus often. He was at loose ends now that Phips was gone. Often he and Franz went out for a beer

(Marie insisted that it was more like five) at Görwitz, a German Kneipe.[9] They saw Jacobi less often, and Willy and Lilly Meyer infrequently. Marie kept up with her circle of friends, mostly New Yorkers of German and German-Jewish origin. Franz as yet had few non-family friends. Most often mentioned in his letters was an acquaintance of his relatives, Felix Adler, founder of the Ethical Culture Society. The German-born Adler, son of a well-known rabbi and one who had himself preached as a rabbi, was too rationalistic to accept Judaism in any traditional sense. He secularized and humanized his religion into a moralist movement directed at the welfare of the poor and young. Boas attended a few meetings of the Ethical Culture Society, and Adler later put Boas on the board of his Workingman's School. The social life otherwise centered largely around the Deutscher Gesellig-Wissenschaftlicher Verein, the major German-American cultural organization in the city and sponsor of musical and lecture evenings.

Boas was hardly a lonely immigrant. He joined a large German-language community in New York, some of whom were, like his uncle Jacobi, his wife's parents, and his uncle's closest friend, Carl Schurz, Forty-Eighters who had made successful careers in their adopted country. Other Germans had followed, as much for economic as for political reasons, including Onkel Kobus and Willy Meyer. This community had its own differentiations, by religious and regional origin and by social and economic class. Among the more educated and well-to-do, there was a great deal of integration into the larger metropolitan New York society.[10]

Franz and Marie's first Christmas together was celebrated over dinner with the "whole Meyers"—there were seven in New York. The remainder of the holiday was spent rearranging the apartment. They had not had any time to put it completely right, especially after his Minden belongings were shipped over by Sophie and Meier on their own move from Minden to Berlin.

After long debate and many hesitations, his parents had decided to leave Minden. (It was at Meier's insistence; Sophie would have greatly preferred to stay.) The Marienstrasse villa had been sold in February, and Franz sent instructions about the disposition of his things. Marie's Baffinland flag, the walrus tusk, his Alemannen "Commersbuch," his Humboldt statue, and Reinhard's photograph and lock of hair were important to him. The herbarium could go to the Minden Gymnasium and the mineral collection sold, but he needed almost all his books, notes, and scientific instruments.

The new year brought changes. "I want to tell you something beautiful," began a February 1888 letter to Berlin. "In the autumn we—or rather Marie—will promote you to grandparents." The baby's name was already settled: Ernst if a boy, Helene if a girl." This happy news was mixed with promising professional prospects. A letter from Canada had asked if he could undertake a trip to British Columbia on behalf of the British Association for the Advancement of Science (BAAS).

The BAAS had met in Montreal four years earlier, and its anthropological section, anticipating the completion of the Canadian Pacific Railway, had established a committee on the northwestern tribes of Canada. "Soon afterward, it determined that an effort should be made to record as perfectly as possible the characteristics and conditions of the native tribes" before their "racial peculiarities" became indistinct through absorption, and their arts, customs, and beliefs were obliterated by settlement.[12] The chair was vested in Oxford's Edward Burnett Tylor, the leading anthropologist in the United Kingdom, but actual direction was in the hands of the three Canadian members, George Mercer Dawson of the Geological Survey, Sir Daniel Wilson of the University of Toronto, and especially Horatio Hale, the philologist and ethnologist from Clinton, Ontario.

The committee had accomplished little since its inception. Hale, a septuagenarian who had hoped to return to the fieldwork he had last performed with the U.S. Exploring Expedition to Oceania and Oregon in 1842, came to realize that he could do no more than correspond and direct. In January 1888 he wrote Boas, whom he had met at Buffalo two years before, of the committee's desire to secure a full report on British Columbia tribes, complete with an ethnological map. Would Boas undertake the work?[13]

Boas was more than willing. Another field season would fill the gaps in his book of British Columbia myths. Hodges consented to a two-month leave from *Science,* and Hale promised $120, plus expenses, for his services. Boas's only reservation was leaving a pregnant Marie, but he "couldn't turn down this offer."[14] She could spend most of the time at Lake George with Helene; Jacobi had assured them that, with the baby not due until September, he had no need to worry.

Boas left for the Canadian West on May 25, 1888, traveling through Montreal to use the committee's pass on the Canadian Pacific Railway. Except for a view of Kicking Horse Pass from the engine, the trip to Vancouver was uneventful. He spent two weeks in Victoria, then caught a boat north to Port Essington on the Skeena River for work among the

Tsimshian. On July 3 he was back in Victoria, where he remained for eight days, when he left for the province's interior, spending a few days among the Interior Salish at Lytton before going on to Golden for the long trip by Columbia River steamer to Windemere. Here, in the narrow valley between the Purcell and Rocky mountains, he was among the Plateau Kootenay. "Tall and eagle-nosed," wearing moccasins and braided hair, they were "the first real Indians I have seen." Yet he could not warm to work among these people who were unrelated to the Salish or coastal Indians. He was impatient to return to Marie and stayed only long enough to get what he needed.[15]

His instructions had been to prepare a general outline of all British Columbia linguistic stocks, based on his own research and published material. Hale particularly emphasized the need for an ethnological map of the province and attention to physical anthropology. Boas's report also had to include comparative vocabularies and a detailed outline of one grammar from each linguistic stock. Information, both Boas's own and from others, was lacking on the Interior Salish and the Kootenay, and they should receive attention. Aside from these special concerns, Hale left things to Boas's experience.

Boas had already prepared two ethnological maps of the southern British Columbia coast—a rough one for *Science* and a more detailed one for *Petermanns*—so he worried little about that portion of his instructions. The Port Essington trip more accurately delineated the north coast stocks and contributed to the comprehensiveness of both his mythological and linguistic material. He learned something in Victoria of the Nootka from Father J. Nicolai of Kyoquot and from some Natives there and in New Westminster, but spent most of his time with Haida, Tlingit, and Tsimshian informants.

Boas had previously neglected physical anthropology. He seems never to have used his measuring instruments on Baffin Island, and, though he was tempted by the Eskimos' shallow burial grounds, he made no effort to procure physical remains. He had left the anthropometrics of the visiting Bella Coolas to Virchow and, though he pilfered skulls, did no work of that kind on his trip to British Columbia in 1886. Now, under Hale's instructions, he took up both measurements and serious osteological collecting. The mayor gave permission to measure any Indians in Victoria's jail, but there were only seven. He refrained from attempting measurements in the field, fearing to arouse distrust. What he missed among living Indians, he made up for from the dead.

Taking bones from a grave was "repugnant work" and even prompted horrid dreams, but "someone has to do it"—and skeletons were "worth money." He dug several times in burial grounds near Victoria, in Port Essington (while a photographer distracted the Indians), in Saanich, and, on his way home, at Lytton. He collected only a dozen or so skulls himself and about the same number of skeletons, but he heard of a collection of about 75 skulls that had been gathered for the American phrenological market. When he received assurance from the Army Medical Museum in Washington that there was a market for such remains, he bought the entire collection, bringing his British Columbia total to some 85 skulls and 14 complete skeletons, and left an order for more. Distasteful as bone collecting might be, he was pleased with the results. His physical anthropology might be "the most valuable results of my whole trip."[16]

He was less happy with the overall results. His instruction to survey the entire province had compelled him to spend too much time in travel and scattered his efforts among too many groups. He had accomplished "only about one quarter of what I did last time." Yet, two discoveries excited him. Early in June he concluded that Haida and Tlingit belonged to the same linguistic family and, a day later, his frantic measurements of the skull collection led him to the unexpected conclusion that skulls even from individual tribes that spoke the same language varied considerably.[17]

Boas arrived, tanned and a little fatter, at Alma Farm on Lake George on July 27. He was back at *Science* on August 1, only to receive six-months' notice. Hodges assured him that the contract cancellation was not from any dissatisfaction—"my respect for you has constantly grown since our acquaintance began"—but simply from the need to limit expenses. Boas's feelings were mixed. By now, after a year and a half, the job had lost much of its attraction. His dream of turning the journal into the American *Petermanns* and his office into a Perthes Institute were not materializing. *Science* remained a respectable newsletter, but little more. "My office work, whatever it may be," Boas had written in March, "is certainly of no great scientific value."[18] Boas's goal of being independent of Hodges in two years was now too true. About to become a family man, he again had to worry about a position and an income.

Fortunately the American Association for the Advancement of Science (AAAS) was meeting on August 15, and that offered an opportunity to renew contacts and scout prospects. His own contribution at the Cleveland meeting, the first he had dared to present before the AAAS, went well enough, and even "though English is still a very considerable hin-drance," he also participated in the discussion. He took satisfaction in his election as a Fellow and in the Association's adoption of two of his pet projects—a catalogue of American ethnological collections and the estab-lishment of a committee to improve geographical education in the schools. He left Cleveland "with the pleasant consciousness" that his two-year apprenticeship in America had been well spent and that he was now as well known there as he was in Germany.[19]

There were some hopes for the future. Otis Mason spoke of the possi-bility of a temporary position at the U.S. National Museum. He and Hale discussed future BAAS research. Boas proposed a further three seasons of work, and Hale, who must have been thinking along similar lines, sug-gested that he communicate his ideas to Tylor.

Boas drafted a letter in Cleveland outlining his plans. His contract with *Science*, he told Tylor, would end in the spring, and "I should gladly avail myself of this opportunity to devote my time more fully than I have done so far to ethnology and to carry on my researches on the Canadian tribes in a systematic way." His preliminary report had already underscored the necessity of doing this work quickly. Only among a few groups could the customs of the Natives be studied uninfluenced by Whites, and mission-aries were already at work among them. Languages were disappearing, their elaborate grammars forgotten; physical features were dissolving through intermarriage; settlement was destroying valuable cairns and burial sites. "After ten years it will be impossible in this region to obtain any reliable information regarding the customs of the Natives in pre-Christian times."[20] He asked Tylor for three years to study British Columbia in reasonable detail, spending three months or so for each lin-guistic stock at a cost of $700 to $900 annually.

The bid was successful. The committee's grant was renewed, allowing Hale to promise $600 for 1889. The committee was then able to secure a supplementary grant from the Canadian government that raised to $1000 the amount available to Boas. Hale, appreciating the effort involved in the initial report, had already rewarded him with an extra $100.[21]

By this time, Boas had been able to piece together other sources of sup-port. Hodges agreed to continue his connection with *Science:* for three columns on geography and ethnology, Boas would receive $50 a month, more for drawings, large maps, or longer articles. In January he was elected secretary of the Gesellig-Wissenschaftlicher Verein, a position that paid $400 a year, compensation for editing the society's published reports and lectures. Moreover, Powell of the Bureau of Ethnology agreed to his proposal to work up his linguistic material, putting him temporarily on the Bureau payroll at $150 a month.[22]

The instability of these part-time and temporary arrangements was bothersome, but Boas was content: "If I wanted only a government position, it would of course be more advantageous, but if I really want to accomplish something, I must take the risk, and I'm not afraid to do so." He assured his parents that his two years in America had established his reputation. He was satisfied with his work and his prospects.[23]

In the meantime, Boas toiled away at the *Science* office during the day and worked on writing his BAAS report. He expected the report to "advance me very significantly." He wanted it to be a good summary of British Columbia's anthropology, something that would more than satisfy Hale and the committee and allow future work to concentrate on intensive studies of individual tribes.[24] Even this major effort, however, had to defer to the joys and responsibilities of fatherhood.

The baby had been expected after September 20, but on Sunday evening, September 9, Marie began to feel contractions. At two the next morning Boas rushed to fetch the doctor. Jacobi was away, but his assistant, Dr. Julius Rudisch, attended. At 5:30 Boas woke Emilie Krackowizer. Then, for several hours he searched frantically for a nurse (they had booked one, but she was away, not being scheduled until the 20th), finding one only at 8:30 A.M. Jacobi came later in the morning. By 2:30 in the afternoon, Jacobi decided that Marie had suffered enough. She was anesthetized, and using his instruments, Jacobi brought a baby girl into the world. Within the hour Franz had cabled Berlin that "helene and marie well." He wrote more fully the next day, "what a feeling it was when I first heard the tiny thing cry and then saw it and poor Marie there, not moving from the chloroform, and then she woke and also heard the little thing crying!" Jacobi's forceps had distended the baby's face a little, but otherwise she was "smooth and as red as a little crab." Franz was awestruck: "It is such a funny feeling to see such a little creature lie there and to know that it is our little worm."[25]

The next weeks' letters home were filled with news of the baby and Marie's convalescence. He worried when Helene would not feed and again when she and Marie came down with fever and rash. Otherwise, the "worm"—his usual term, though it competed with "pikinini" and "little monkey"—was normal.[26] She kept them awake, of course, and there would be few concerts or plays now. He did break his domestic routine with occasional lectures—to the Verein, to the Academy of Natural Sciences in Philadelphia, and, in his first essay in extempory English, at the New York Academy of Science. He finished the Canadian report by the end of February and launched immediately into his linguistic work for Powell.

By then he had formulated his summer plans. He would travel to British Columbia in July, but they would visit Germany before his western journey. They had long been saving for a trip, and now the time seemed right. Franz's *Science* work and BAAS proofreading could be done in Berlin, and he could renew old contacts and restudy Berlin's collections. He would have to come back in late June, but Marie and the baby could stay on. They would be more comfortable in Berlin than in New York's summer heat. Not least, by giving up their apartment and living cheaply with his parents, they could make the trip affordable.

Accompanied by Marie's younger sister, Alice, a teacher interested in German schools, the Boases boarded the Hamburg-America Company's *Rugia* on May 2. On the evening of their eighth day out, when the steamer had passed the halfway point in the Atlantic, flames burst from the ventilator of the afterhold. Sparked by spontaneous combustion in bales of cotton and fed by lard destined for Hamburg, the fire roared out of control. Franz and Marie, with Helene and Alice, assembled on deck with the 182 other passengers, the lower cabins flooded in the crew's effort to douse the flames beneath. With the fire blazing uncontrollably, the boats were lowered. Some attempted to abandon ship, but Captain Karlowa, using his revolver for authority, retained control. After almost five hours, and with hope of saving the ship almost gone, it occurred to Karlowa to try steam instead of water. This proved successful and the "terrifying night" was over. Although most passengers had to remain on deck for forty-eight hours, the ship was safe. The *Rugia* arrived in Plymouth on May 11, proceeding later to Cherbourg and Hamburg.[27]

Once settled at his parents' flat on Grossbeerenstrasse in Berlin, Franz studied the museum's collection, read his proofs, surveyed geography texts, and accumulated slips for his myth book. He left Berlin late in June for New York, traveling by way of London to meet with E. B. Tylor in Oxford. After arriving in New York, he remained long enough to collect his mail before taking the train to Montreal and the West. Awaiting him in Victoria were Hale's latest letters, including instructions which forced him drastically to revise his field plans. Boas was furious at Hale's intrusion and his last-minute alteration of well-laid plans.

Boas had tried to avoid just this kind of disruption. A year earlier he thought it was agreed that he should study the Kootenay and the mainland and Interior Salish. But Hale, after realizing that Boas's 1886 research had not encompassed all the coast tribes, asked at the last moment that he include the Tlingit, Tsimshian, and Nootka in his report. Boas read this as explicit instructions and altered his plans to include study of the Tlingit and Nootka in Victoria and a time-consuming trip to Port Essington. Hale's late letter had taken away "two-thirds of the joy of the trip." To avoid repeating the loss of field time to travel, Boas had asked to spend the summer of 1889 entirely on the central and north coast, making Alert Bay and Bella Bella his bases. His Oxford visit had been expressly to persuade the committee's nominal chairman to free him from Hale's disruptions to his field plans. Tylor, he hoped, might be able "to see that in the future I am left in peace."[28]

The attempts to free himself from Hale did not succeed. If Tylor wrote Hale, it would serve only to anger the man, and Dawson refused to intervene. Hale did not like Boas going behind his back. "I may say," he wrote to Victoria, "that since I have been placed in charge of this enquiry, no member of the committee, either here or in England, has interfered in it in any way whatever, except when I have directly requested an opinion. I regret very much that you should have sought to bring about such an interference." He ordered his field man to follow instructions and rebuked him for previous lapses. He was told to study the Kwakiutl, Salish, and, particularly, the Nootka, and a reinforcing telegram ordered him to visit the west coast of Vancouver Island for Nootka research.[29]

Boas could only steam and curse. He had worked in Berlin, both at his desk and at the museum, in preparation for his Kwakiutl and north coast research. Now Hale had rendered all this in vain. "The good man has again changed his mind," he wrote Marie; "you can imagine how angry I am that I have to alter all my plans." He would have to go to the west coast, where results would be negligible; "I'll scarcely meet an Indian there." He condemned Hale's latest whim as childish and useless, contradicting both Dawson's wishes and Hale's previous letters. "The old man is simply so forgetful that he doesn't remember from letter to letter what he said before and then accuses me of not having followed his instructions." Hale knew "nothing of general ethnology," but his vanity, pedantry, and sensitivity were the basic problem. Boas drafted letters of complaint to Tylor and Dawson, then tore them up, fearful that people might think he was, indeed, intriguing behind Hale's back.[30]

The Hale-Boas conflict is a little hard to evaluate. Part of the problem lay in the great gap in age: Boas was just entering his thirties; Hale was over seventy. The Canadian, with his decades of experience in anthropology, assumed a naturally superior and mentorial attitude. Boas, while willing to flatter Hale's vanity to a point, would not unhesitatingly defer to the old man's self-esteem. More important, perhaps, was Boas's determined independence. His earlier field trips to the Arctic and the Northwest Coast had been self-propelled expeditions, and his previous experience with superiors had not all been happy ones. Hodges seemed to give free reign, but Boas clashed on occasion with Bastian at the Berlin museum, and struggled continuously and bitterly with Kiepert. Unhappy with subordination, he had expressed his discontent from the beginning. "It is a very uncomfortable feeling always to have to follow instructions," he had written a year earlier. Hale, on the other hand, insisted that he was "the person entitled in this matter to instruct you."[31]

Hale did bear some responsibility in the matter. His instructions were sometimes contradictory and, in their lateness, capricious. He was stubborn, vain, and, in the days before carbon paper, a little forgetful of what he had written from one letter to another. Yet his intention had always been clear. From the beginning, he had put priority on a general survey of the province. That was what the committee and the association wanted; further work, if funding permitted, could enter into "monographic" treatments of individual stocks. Boas's 1888 report, while admirable in many ways, had, by neglecting Kwakiutl, Salish, and Nootkan linguistics, accomplished only part of the task. Hale insisted again on the "primary importance that you should first complete your general 'synopsis'" before embarking on detailed work. Boas's plans of devoting himself to single stocks was fine for the future, but for now "the general survey is the paramount object." Boas later came around to the usefulness of the approach. His BAAS work was fragmentary, he would write in 1891, but "the opportunity which I have had to become acquainted with so many different tribes was very welcome."[32]

Hale, as Jacob Gruber has pointed out, remained tied to his own experience with the Wilkes expedition of fifty years earlier. He had given a comprehensive outline of Polynesian and Oregon linguistics, and he wanted Boas to repeat that treatment including an ethnographic map complementary to his Oregon one. Hale, as Gruber sympathetically concluded, "involved himself vicariously in Boas's work" and "saw the activities of the younger man as an extension of his own work which had begun, but was never finished, a half-century earlier." Boas was his successor, and he conducted the relationship as "master to student, almost as father to son."[33]

The clash, it must be noted, was over research strategy, not over anthropological ideas. Hale's views had been formed in the pre-Darwinian period of American anthropology. He was sceptical of racial categories, and his own hierarchy of peoples was based upon linguistic, not evolutionary, principles. Although his ideas were somewhat rigid and occasionally eccentric, they did not clash with Boas's.[34]

Boas succumbed to Hale's imperious direction. He had been tempted to quit, but knew that would destroy everything just as he had begun to work out some of the complex coastal relationships. He caught a steamer for Port Alberni, but found little that he wanted. The Nootka were "remarkably uninteresting" and "without any trace of originality," everything being borrowed from the Kwakiutl. After sixteen days, he left Alberni for Qualicum, taking a difficult, seldom-used trail. His Nootka guide lost the way, and they stumbled through the bush and over rocks in pouring rain for hours before finding it again. Darkness had fallen by the time the soaked pair reached Qualicum Tom's hostel. He woke stiff in the shoulders and legs from a trek that could not have been less than forty kilometers.[35]

He was now free to resume his Kwakiutl work at Alert Bay. This was his third visit to this Kwakiutl center, and he was among old friends. Stephen A. Spencer put him up again, and he was able to use Reverend Alfred J. Hall's study as a workroom despite the bitter animosity between the canneryman and the missionary. He learned more about the winter dances, the language, and, most important, he discovered that the Nootka and Kwakiutl languages were closely related. His work went even better when George Hunt, Spencer's brother-in-law, whom he had used as an informant the year before in Victoria, arrived from Fort Rupert. Working with Hunt almost constantly over the weekend, Boas "pumped so much out of him," he wrote, "that the results of my stay are very satisfying."[36] He left for Victoria on September 1, and then started back east, staying briefly in Harrison, longer in Kamloops and the Okanagan. He reached New York on September 28.

Marie had arrived from Germany a month before and was staying with her mother. She had not moved back into the Third Avenue flat because she knew they would be leaving New York for Massachusetts and a position at Clark University. Franz, on his arrival in Victoria from Alberni, had found a letter offering a position at the university in Worcester. The offer, while unexpected, was not totally a surprise. For over a year he had been in touch with psychologist G. Stanley Hall, the president of the newly established university, and had met him on the way to the Cleveland AAAS meetings. The prospect of employment must have come up then; certainly Boas entertained the idea because he asked Marie what she thought of moving to Worcester.[37] He had kept in contact, sending Hall offprints and asking advice about bringing anthropology closer to psychology.

Franz hesitated only a little. The salary was very low, only $1,000 a year, but he regarded the position as an honor and the pay not unfair, considering his lack of teaching experience. If he could continue his BAAS and Bureau of Ethnology work, they could get by the first year and hope for better later. He was more concerned that Hall's letter had not specified whether the appointment would be in geography or anthropology. He and Hall had corresponded more about the former, but his American reputation was as an ethnologist. He accepted the offer, hoping, he wrote (as ambiguously as Hall), "to further that department of science to which I have devoted myself." His conditions were that he be free to carry on his Northwest Coast work in summers and that he begin only in November.[38]

October was hectic, with trips to Worcester about housing and arrangements and to Washington to settle matters with Powell, with lecture planning and book lists for the embryonic Clark library, and, of course, with packing their belongings, stored variously at *Science*, Jacobi's, and Mrs. Krackowizer's. The Clark University position was in anthropology. In November, Boas began the life of a university teacher, a career previously spurned at Berlin's great university.

All of Boas's aspiration during these first years in America had proven abortive. He had not secured the coveted curatorship at the American Museum, his atlas and geography textbook proposals never found publishers, and his grand dreams of New York simulacra of Perthes and the Berlin Anthropological Society fell by the wayside. His ambitions overreached what was realizable for a young newcomer. Geography and anthropology were, as Boas thought, open fields, but they were not ones capable of being organized and directed by an outsider possessing only a few publications, only recent acquaintances and associations, and no institutional base beyond an assistant editorship of a struggling new journal. Jacobi and Schurz were influential figures within their own circles, but they could offer little assistance in those that he aspired to organize. His own initiatives failed, but what kept him going, what advanced him in the open field before him, was his usefulness to the initiatives of others. Wagner and Schmeltz needed an American contributor to their journals, W. W. Newell counted on Boas for the Native side of American folklore, Horatio Hale needed an experienced ethnologist to carry out fieldwork, and G. Stanley Hall wanted a good, but inexpensive, anthropologist for his new university—all the better, one with a strong psychological interest. Boas was not in a position to seize initiative or direction in his areas of American science, but American science was prepared to offer opportunities for apprenticeship to a qualified and industrious European. A little wiser after two years in New York, Boas recognized the situation: "Only through my activities in *Science* and in the West was I chosen for the *Folk-Lore Journal,* the *Internationales Archiv* and probably by the Canadians."[39] His American career was being built upon his ability and accomplishments, but not yet at his own direction.

7 "An Ardent Desire to Remove Obscurity"

HISTORIAN AND COSMOGRAPHER

Franz Boas began working at Clark University in the fall of 1889. He remained there for the next three years with his research shifting strongly toward anthropometric investigations. For two summers, in 1890 and 1891, he worked again on the Northwest Coast, this time largely among the Salish and Chinook Indians of Washington and Oregon. Otherwise his Northwest Coast studies took a back seat to anthropometrics, teaching, and university concerns. Before continuing with the personal and professional narrative, it is well to pause to examine some of Boas's ideas and concerns as they had evolved to the Clark years.

He still straddled two fields, geography and anthropology, never quite willing to forsake the former while being increasingly drawn, by interest and circumstance, toward the latter. The division was far from neat. Many German geographers, notably Friedrich Ratzel, Otto Peschel, and Georg Gerland, spread their concerns over both physical geography and ethnology. Boas felt at home with geography, had increased his skills as a cartographic draftsman, and had even refined what he considered to be a superior method of map projection. He still nurtured ambitions of a good atlas for the American market, using German maps but concentrating on North America, and he had become very interested in improving geographical instruction in American schools. His most important change was not a move from geography to anthropology, but a decisive shift in his basic approach to both fields.

When Boas left physics for geography, he had attempted to continue within a scientific framework. Motivated in part by his psychophysical research, he sought to explain human behavior in terms of geographical environment. His concerns, influenced by Karl Ritter, emphasized geography as a determinant of human life. Boas's subsequent attempt on Baffin Island to establish links between the external world and internal behavior ended, however, in "a thorough disillusionment." He had established "only a few, quite general facts"—that the distribution of seals and caribou determined settlement and migration patterns, that the smoothness of sea ice affected population density—but these "could not be regarded as fruitful results." Although he recognized human dependence upon the environment, he ceased to be in any way an environmental determinist. Geographical influences were, as he later phrased it, "patent" and "so shallow that they did not throw any light on the driving forces that mold behavior."[1] Ethnology, essentially concerned with the mental life—the psychology—of primitive groups, was not an environmental science.

This collapse of his posited connection between the external world and human behavior threatened his sense of purpose. At the conclusion of his Eskimo research, Boas was thrown into a personal intellectual crisis. The exact sciences, spectacularly successful in their discovery of natural laws, possessed an unquestioned significance and prestige. He had left that secure area for geography, what he called a "half-historical" field, and his thin results cast doubt on its value. He wondered whether it was "worth it," whether his move had not placed him in "an inferior scholarly position." Boas, after a period of "tortured" thought and "severe mental struggles,"[2] resolved his problem while in Berlin in 1885. His solution was to go the whole way, to personally repudiate the scientific approach by making his new field of geography an entirely "historical" discipline possessing a legitimacy equal to the sciences. This conclusion was intended to be the basis of a book on geographical methodology. He got only so far as a fragment, "The Study of Geography," published in 1887, the same article that occasioned his meeting with N. D. C. Hodges and his first American job. In writing it, Boas worked out the solution to his personal crisis.

The physical scientist, Boas wrote, was concerned with compiling similar facts in order to isolate a general principle common to them all. Single facts were unimportant; the stress was upon their accumulation to demonstrate a general law. To the historian, however, the facts themselves were interesting and important. Newton, for example, was uninterested in the action of any two bodies upon each other once he formulated the general law of gravity. This law, however, was but preliminary to Kant's question of why each heavenly body existed where it did. Comte viewed any single phenomenon as insignificant except for its exemplification of a law or its service in finding a new one. Humboldt, on the other hand, considered "every phenomenon as worthy of being studied for its own sake," its mere existence entitling it to a full share of attention, no matter what its relationship might be to general laws.[3]

These divergent approaches arose, Boas believed, from two different desires within the human mind. The physical scientist's search for a regularity of process and a clear arrangement of phenomena stemmed from an aesthetic aspect of the mind that sought a logical ordering of the universe. The historian, moved by an emotional or "affective" impulse, found each individual fact interesting and important in its own right. While Boas ranked the two tendencies as equally natural and equally legitimate, his own emotional preference lay with the historian or "cosmographer" who investigates the single phenomenon and "lovingly tries to penetrate into its secrets until every feature is plain and clear." The "truth of every phenomenon" was enough for the historian to wish to study it.[4]

Two striking points here require investigation: first, the background to Boas's distinction between the methods of science and history (or, as he almost preferred, "cosmography"); and, second, his decision, after years in the physical sciences, to reject much of their methods and values.

There is a critical element of originality in Boas's essay on the generalizing method of the physicist and the individualizing method of the historian/cosmographer. Boas's conclusion, that the same subject of enquiry could be studied from either standpoint, probably went back to Erdmann's seminar at Kiel. It was refined and confirmed in his own mind during the fall of 1885 through discussions with Rudolf Lehmann, who was trained in philosophy, and Ludwig Haller, a young philosopher in Berlin's Charlottenburg district. By the end of 1885, Boas was convinced that his view, because it rested on philosophical foundations, was correct.[5]

The analysis, while apparently his own, was very much a reflection of current German philosophical concerns, part of a widespread reevaluation of the relationship of the natural sciences (*Naturwissenschaften*) and the human sciences (*Geisteswissenschaften*). Erdmann had dealt with the subject in an 1878 essay, and Wilhelm Windelband and Wilhelm Dilthey published contributions to it in 1883.[6] The distinction between the historical and the scientific was itself an old one, going back at least to Leibnitz, Kant, and Schopenhauer, though for the latter two the distinction had been invidious to history. Genuine knowledge must be universal, necessary, and eternal, not individual, contingent, and temporal. By the late nineteenth century, this apparent inferiority of history was being eroded by philosophers who sought to explain how historical thought could be "wissenschaftlich" and yet have individual facts for its study.[7] The most important in these attempts included on the one hand, Dilthey's continuing concern to separate and legitimize historical thought, and, on the other hand, Windelband's precise 1894 distinction between the general, law-positing approach of scientific enquiry (his "nomethetic" method) and the detailed description of individual historical facts (his "idiographic" method).[8] Boas's position, which dealt with different approaches to the same subject matter, was much closer to Windelband (and Heinrich Rickert) than to Dilthey, who stressed the division as subject matter.[9]

In Boas's own field, a debate had raged for more than a decade over whether geography was primarily a natural science or a historical discipline, with almost every distinguished practicer, as Boas noted, feeling it necessary to express a view on the method, aim, and scope of his field. Most came down somewhere in the middle, but some argued strongly that geography was much nearer to history than to science and that individuality was its special concern.[10] This controversy over the nature of scientific thought and the distinctions of the mental and the natural sciences was part of Boas's own intellectual environment—one to which he was forced, in his own personal crisis, to pay close attention. His distinction, a kind of independent invention seven or so years before Windelband's 1894 address, was built upon the general climate of opinion that produced the remembered giants: Windelband, Dilthey, and Rickert.

More striking than the background to Boas's distinction between science and history is that he opted for history. He made it clear that his "affective" impulse led him toward a study of the individual phenomenon of nature and not to the aesthetic pleasure of an orderly row of facts useful for defining laws. His choice of cosmography over physical science was dictated by his own temperament. Cosmography's appeal to him, his very use of the term, stemmed from Alexander von Humboldt and "the personal feeling of man toward the world, toward the phenomena surrounding him." Every fact, wrote Boas, quoting Goethe, "is the really interesting object . . . because it is true." Its mere occurrence "claims the full attention of our mind."[11] The student of the history of mankind, Boas later stated, is directed principally by "a personal love for the particular question and from an ardent desire to see its obscurity removed."[12]

He had come to learning through nature, through a fascination with the natural surroundings of his youth. He had worshipped Goethe and read Humboldt with awe. Boas's approach, Alexander Lesser insisted, was "as a naturalist, as a student of natural history." Indeed, amidst the chemistry and physics courses of his university studies, were almost as many in geography, geology, anatomy, and zoology. Even as he labored in Karsten's physics laboratory, he participated actively in Kiel's Biology Society.[13]

Briefly seduced by Comte, then put straight by Lange, he left the abstractions of scientific clarity to return to an approach that would more fully gratify his "love for the country we inhabit, and the nature that surrounds us."[14] Geography, because of its affective appeal, its long concern with the explication of the individual, and its aim to instruct in the beauty and unity of nature, belonged with the human sciences. That was the subjective, the cosmographer's position.[15]

As a cosmographer, Boas would find no laws, but he might be able to keep alive the interest in individual phenomena and their mutual interdependence, "to bring home the grand truth of the unity of nature." This was, he declared, the ultimate aim of geography: to stimulate the imagination and to experience the grandeur of nature. In 1936 he glossed his concerns as "the affective appeal of a phenomenon that impresses us as a unit, although its elements may be irreducible to a common cause. In other words the problem that attracted me primarily was the intelligent understanding of a complex phenomenon."[16]

Boas, it is plain, was as much the son of Goethe, Humboldt, and the German Enlightenment as of Comte and the scientific age. Small wonder that Boas thought himself as an Idealist, that Humboldt's statue stood in his study, that he wrote that Kant was "a powerful means of guarding students from falling into a shallow materialism or positivism." Boas was a cosmographer because he loved the particular more than the general. He declared himself a historian not only on this basis, but also because he was concerned with the past of the particular. "The thorough study," he asserted, "must refer to the history and development of the individual form."[17]

This concern with the past was also part of Boas's age. The century of his birth was dominated as much by a historical consciousness as by a scientific one. History had become "the leading cultural force" by the time of Boas's birth, and historical consciousness one of the highest forms of culture. Boas dated the impact of the historical idea only to Darwin; but, even in science, it predated *The Origin of Species* and, as he recognized, had an impact far beyond biology. The progress of science, wrote Edward Richter, "has been through learning to conceive of nature as the result of a history."[18] The historical aspects of nature, as Boas later wrote, had taken hold of investigations in the whole of science, gradually revolutionizing the methods of both the natural and human sciences.[19] Boas accepted the implications for the study of human as well as natural phenomena. As he had earlier embraced environmental determinism, now he took up an equally thorough historical determinism. "Every living being," he contended, "is considered as the result of a historical development."[20]

Boas had not moved to the historian's position quickly. He had been concerned, of course, with the history of the Eskimos and had found traces of their past in their myths and language, especially in the ritualistic language of the shaman. But his full-fledged adoption of the historical principle came gradually. His ambitious 1885 proposal to study people throughout the entire Arctic and North Pacific Coast was still governed, at least in part, by anthropogeographic considerations. By 1887, at the end of his first trip to British Columbia, however, he was convinced that, at least for the Northwest Coast, "historical factors are of greater influence than the surroundings." "The longer I studied," he told Major J. W. Powell of the Bureau of Ethnology that June, "the more convinced I became that customs, traditions and migrations are far too complex in their origin to enable us to study their psychological causes without a thorough knowledge of their history." He was now persuaded, ostensibly by the principles of evolutionary biological theory, that "no event in the life of a people passes without leaving its effect upon later generations."[21]

A thoroughgoing historicism had become Boas's leading principle. It emphasized that "the physiological and psychological state of an organism at a certain moment is a function of its whole history"; that the character of biological man and his cultural expressions—in language, inventions, beliefs, and customs—were not determined by their appearance, or as he put it, not "by the state in which it *is,* but by its whole history." This sense of a temporal depth created for Boas, as for much of German thought, "a whole different conception of the world."[22]

Boas's historicism—consistent with the view that "the history of anything is a sufficient explanation of it, that the values of anything can be accounted for through the discovery of its origins, that the nature of anything is entirely comprehended in its development"—discarded any teleological ingredient. Histories were so different and complex that no single aim or plan could be envisaged. Boas's position put emphasis upon complexity: upon how "complicated" the elements were affecting the human mind, upon the "intricacy" of the causes that lay behind ethnological phenomena, upon the "extreme complexity" of the elements behind the character of a people.[23] His position challenged the assumptions of a simple teleological plan. This eradication of plan was characteristic of both the natural and the human sciences, part of a general reaction to the earlier concern for "natural" principles behind everything. Even Kiepert, Ritter's successor, had dispensed with his geographic teleology in Boas's own field, and Lange had spent pages blasting its rudiments in philosophy. But teleological strands remained strongly embedded in evolutionary thought, both biological and social, and in the idea of progress, strands that Boas continued ambivalently to accept.

Boas's matured historicist conviction led him into his first controversy in America. In 1887, shortly after returning from his first British Columbia trip, he had gone to Washington, D.C., to study its Northwest Coast collections. He found them scattered in a dozen different sections of the National Museum, arranged according to type and use rather than displayed together as aspects of one cultural area.[24] Using the forum provided by his new *Science* position, he criticized the museum's exhibition methods and the assumptions of Otis T. Mason, whose ideas they represented.

The hypothesis behind Mason's method, Boas wrote, was that similar ethnological phenomena were caused either by a common source of ideas or by independent invention in response to similar circumstances. While this was true as far as it went, Boas's point was that the hypothesis overlooked another possibility so important that it overthrew the assumption of comparability between apparently similar phenomena. The similarity might be accidental, the result of quite different causes. A rattle from one area might look like a rattle from another, but one might represent a religious conception, the other simply the pleasure children get from noise. They might appear identical, but the chain of events—their historical causes—were quite different. Contrary to Mason's argument, like effects did not necessarily mean like causes.

Boas's logic had already been portrayed in German geography where Ritter had been criticized on just this point. Given the diversity and inexactitude of human thought, wrote Peschel, "those who wish to discover laws must demonstrate that similar causes always have similar results." Gerland had pointed out that identical developments could arise from very different environments, just as identical environments could produce very different phenomena. The determinants rested on character and history more than on geography. Boas had already made the point in a review of W. H. Dall's study of Northwest Coast and South Sea masks. Dall assumed that the similarity of masks from such separate areas were the result of similar ideas; yet, as Boas pointed out, the mythologies connected with the masks showed scarcely any relationship. This was a point he would dwell upon later: masks might be used to hide from evil spirits, they might be used to represent a spirit personified by the wearer, they might commemorate a dead person, or they might be merely theatrical.[25] The concept of "mask" covered so broad a range of psychological origins and purposes that no common cause could confidently be ascribed to a similar appearance.

The character of an artifact was expressed not merely by its present appearance, but by its past; phenomena might appear identical even though they actually owed their origin to different causes. To study masks on museum shelves was deceptive: "We have to study each ethnological specimen individually in its history and in its medium." By removing a single implement from the surroundings of the people to whom it belonged, by viewing it outside other phenomena affecting that people and their productions, Mason's museum arrangement deprived it of its meaning. It lost its context when placed among other different historically determined phenomena.[26]

Mason's method, Boas wrote, was comparative and deductive: to compare phenomena and draw conclusions by analogy. Mason was classifying objects a priori, and, while analogy might be suggestive, it was "not fit for scientific researches." Privately, Boas raised another important point. Environmental similarities, he wrote Mason, would lead to a supposition that the Ingalik, an Alaskan Athapaskan group, would not use a child's cradle. Yet they did. To Boas this was proof that an a priori environmental consideration was insufficient to explain the occurrence of similar phenomena, and that such a priori theories ought not to be used in ethnology.[27] This iterated the point that every theoretical deduction needed to be scrutinized by empirical induction, yet it was, at the same time, a criticism of environmental determinism.

Boas's doctrine of individualistic historical concern was not, in 1887, an attack on evolutionary theory, as some have assumed. Boas still subscribed to many evolutionary assumptions. He was not quarreling with that so much as insisting on the inductive method. His point was methodological, not theoretical. A researcher could be either a historian or a physicist, but both must use empirical induction, the only proper scientific method for either approach. This was a dogma of nineteenth-century German scholarship and philosophy (though influenced by John Stuart Mill). Induction was "the dominant scientific consciousness" of German research, whether in Helmholtz's physics or Bastian's ethnology. Science, to Boas, was not content with deduction and arguments from analogy; it demanded inductive methods of drawing conclusions from facts, not seeking facts to support a conclusion.[28]

Boas's criticism of Mason's method stirred controversy. He hoped soundly to defeat the Washingtonian, but, when others sided with Mason—first Dall, then Powell—Boas began to feel uncomfortable. Bastian wrote personally to support Boas's position, but his characteristically untranslatable German was useless. Boas wished he had Rudolf Lehmann at his side: the Mason affair now gave him a headache, he wrote his parents, and it would be nice to be able to discuss it with a rational friend. The debate, however, trailed off, neither side convincingly the winner, but Boas would return to the theme of empirical induction, so basic to his framework, again and again.[29]

Boas's conversion to the historical and the individual did not mean that he rejected any search for generalizing principles or for social and psychological laws. His objection was to Mason's method, to a priori deductions expressed in a classificatory arrangement that assumed a common origin before it was empirically demonstrated. Boas demanded that the origins be known before accepting the posited commonality. Only historical investigation of particular phenomena could provide trustworthy material for "the laws of development." Historical research, then, furnished the inductive building blocks which were preliminary to a second "and indeed more important goal": the discovery of some general laws that governed human development. At this second stage there was room for the comparative method based on careful correlation of phenomena observed among a great number of tribes. "The purely historical method without a comparative study will be incomplete."[30] Again, he was discussing method—attacking deduction—not evolutionary theory itself.

Some general phenomena—that there were no people without religion, without body decoration and art, without social organization— were already clear, doubtless the result of the mental characteristics of all mankind. This concept was a version of Bastian's elementary ideas and Lazarus and Steinthal's folk-psychology: traits that appeared everywhere with monotonous regularity and formed the common psychological foundations for the similarities among peoples. Secondary to these, however, were "laws of development," the search for which preoccupied anthropologists of the day. In the search for such laws, the historical method gave way to the comparative method, to the analysis of similarities and differences between people. Ethnology remained in too preliminary a state to ascertain such general laws with any certainty, but Boas was persuaded that comparative scholarship had helped to illuminate the development of the family. Research had brought an understanding of the progression from communal marriages to age classes, to wife purchase with matriarchy, and finally to the purchase of the child by the husband, the final stage that formed the family. Such fundamental features, despite endless variation, repeated themselves everywhere, thus allowing the assumption that development was basically the same among peoples. In spite of this acceptance of the fruitful results of comparative methods (one he would later withdraw), Boas insisted upon caution, upon the realization of the extreme complexity of the origins of ethnic phenomena and a careful analysis of what had originated with a tribe and what was borrowed.[31]

Independent invention versus borrowing, or diffusion, was one of the great questions in ethnology by the 1880s. Boas was very attentive to the question. The ethnologist always had to distinguish between phenomena from a common origin or spread by diffusion and those arising independently of each other. He believed "there is no people whose customs and usages have developed uninfluenced by neighbors, that have not acquired arts and ideas which it has then developed further in its own way." But when the same custom or idea occurred among people for whom no historical connection could be established, then it showed that "the human mind develops everywhere according to the same laws."[32]

Boas's scorn, however, was for different theorists. While he criticized the facile application of biological evolution as a methodological vagary, he was more concerned with those who inferred, from superficial similarities, extravagant theories about America being populated by lost tribes of Israel or remnants of sunken Atlantis. More significantly, he dismissed adherents of "so-called anthropogeography," another wide-ranging theory built upon weak foundations and capable only of negative generalities.[33] In rejecting geographical determinism and embracing historicism, he reacted against his former model, but less against social evolutionists, who were, after all, historical in their own way.

Boas's essays, partly in *Science* and partly delivered in lectures before his Clark students or the Gesellig-Wissenschaftlicher Verein, became outlets for his methodological concerns. His ambitions to write on such questions had been dismissed in Germany as a matter reserved for the professorate. Boas would not be so restrained. One piece, "On Alternating Sounds," appeared in the *American Anthropologist*, welcomed by Otis Mason as "just the paper we want." The article drew together Boas's work in psychophysics, philology, the laboratory at Kiel, and his fieldwork in

Baffin Island and British Columbia. Boas had read an article in the *American Journal of Psychology* on how children misheard certain sounds, especially in unfamiliar words. From that he examined sound perception and its apperception by means of similar sounds, and then psychophysical concepts of the differential threshold, reviewing some of his own experiments to demonstrate that "a new sensation is apperceived by means of similiar sensations that form part of our knowledge." The phenomenon, he wrote, was better observed in the field notes of philologists than in the schools: "the study of their misspellings cannot fail to be instructive." Heinrich Rink had shown that the nationality of even well-trained observers was recognizable in the Eskimo vocabularies they collected. Boas noted that his own field notes revealed the misspellings of a single collector on hearing the same word at different times. The problem was that the sounds heard were different from, and often intermediate to, sounds familiar to the hearer. His variants *Kaímut* and *Kaívun* occurred because the Eskimo *v* was very similar to the English *v* and *m*, and so he heard it initially "by means of these sounds." Some writers, notably Max Müller, George von der Gabelentz, and Daniel Brinton, had written of his "synthetic" or "alternating sounds" phenomenon as a sign of the primitiveness of the speech of tribes. This, Boas wrote, was quite wrong: the so-called alternating or synthetic sounds "are in reality alternating apperceptions of one and the same sound." They did not show a deficiency in "primitive" speakers, but in the ear of "civilized" perceivers. Boas's demonstration has been called an exercise that "sets the keen critical edge of his rigorously empirical mind hard against a widely prevailing set of culture-bound assumptions which affirmed in a specific respect the evolutionary inferiority of non-European man," though this seems a little exaggerated.[34]

The idea of alternating sounds was not a particularly widespread or significant concept. The mishearing of words by children or persons learning a second language was a widely observed phenomenon. Indeed, Boas's conclusions had been anticipated some years earlier by Horatio Hale, who shared many of Boas's concerns with what Hale called the "Aryocentric fallacy." Boas, of course, drew on the concept of "apperception," something from his Kiel experience, as much from Erdmann's seminar as from his laboratory work. The essay demonstrated his concern with methodology, emphasizing empirical induction, objectivity, and the relativism of the perceiver.[35]

Relativism was something that Boas had long considered, and his recent historicist conception only fortified it. Cultural relativism was an idea that could be traced to the Enlightenment and certainly to Herder, but historicism brought it to the fore. All ages, Ranke said, "are equally near to God," all were to be treated in terms of their own values and points of view, and grasped as centered on themselves. Boas's discussions with Lehmann, whose own writing was highly conscious of the importance of historical context, of "Zeitgeist," would have influenced him. If all knowledge was historically determined, then the judgments establishing this knowledge were themselves subject to the historical conditions under which they were made. To many this was a liberating conception, opening the mind to possibilities, dispensing with dogmatism, overthrowing tradition, and enlarging the freedom of will. Such relativity of historical periods went hand in hand with a relativity of ethnic groups, and Boas, certainly by the time of his debate with Mason, had accepted the idea and championed it. For Boas it could even be the main aim of ethnology, to disseminate "the fact that civilization is not something absolute, but that it is relative, and that our ideas and conceptions are true only so far as our civilization goes." "To make conclusions about human development," he argued, "we must shake off these influences by immersing ourselves in the spirit of primitive peoples whose outlook and development have nothing in common with our own."[36]

This relativism—an appreciation of the contingent position of Western civilization and values—became a refrain whenever Boas turned to expressing the purpose or value of anthropological study. His point, however, was not merely the appreciation of the relative position of other peoples, but the subjectivity of Western society. Indeed, he more often turned his relativism toward his own culture than to that of the Eskimo or the Kwakiutl. "We learn from the data of ethnology," he wrote in 1889, "that not only our ability and knowledge but also the manner and ways of our feeling and thinking is the result of our upbringing as individuals and our history as a people." From there it was merely a step to assert that ethnology "opens to us the possibility of judging our own culture objectively," and the conclusion that "only in this way can our intellect, instructed and formed under the influences of our culture, attain a correct judgment of this same culture."[37] Ethnology thus became, not so much a field for a knowledge of others, but a means of self-knowledge, a self-knowledge that should instill humility. In examining the shackles of tradition in other cultures, ethnology could serve to break the shackles of one's own.

This was, no doubt, a broad humanistic belief, part of his German background and the liberal tradition of the Enlightenment. It can be found, more specifically, in his boyhood reaction to Carl Droege's declaration of his belief in the authority of religious tradition and his refusal to doubt it, a conception shockingly foreign even to Boas's fifteen-year-old mind. "My whole outlook," Boas remarked in 1938, "is determined by the question: how can we recognize the shackles that tradition has laid upon us." Once recognized, they could be broken.[38] This historical and cultural relativism, with its liberating potential, was, like Boas's affective disposition toward the treatment of individuality, a temperamental one. It lay perhaps in his own nurture: in his family's varying rejection and acceptance of Jewish tradition, in the free-thinking character of his home, in the life of an assimilated yet non-Christian youth surrounded by boys of a Protestant outlook. The iconoclastic tendency could only have been fortified by his youthful studies—of Herder, D. F. Strauss, Darwin, Lange, and the Enlightenment authors whom he read—and then by his year-long immersion in Eskimo life and the lesson that *Herzensbildung* existed among them, perhaps more than among his fellow Germans, and that raw seal liver could be the culinary equal of "Rindsrouladen." This deep relativism and the liberating value he ascribed to it distinguished Boas's thought from his American contemporaries as much as his historicism and emphasis upon the inductive method.

Boas's historical, individualistic, and relativistic approach was a general framework, a method but not a research strategy. In his British Columbia fieldwork, he tested and refined a strategy aimed at the fundamental question of the origin of Northwest Coast peoples.[39] In this, he practiced three approaches—a study of physical characteristics, of language, and of ethnology—to reach the anthropologist's aim of reconstructing the past. Since all were the result of the history of a people, they could be used to discover that history.

Only on Boas's second Northwest Coast trip, and only reluctantly at the urging of Hale, had he taken up physical anthropology. This was the beginning of his anthropometric measurements of native peoples. His attention to physical anthropology for the BAAS brought home the historical significance of bodily form. As he saw it, the first task was to find the characteristics of each area. Physical features, especially head forms, were a permanent inheritance that "opens vistas into remote periods inaccessible by any other method."[40] His British Columbia measurements were just a start, too crude to be taken seriously. Without proper instruments, he had had to use a T-square equipped with a movable arm. He accepted the basic lines set down by predecessors like Broca, Topinard, Quetelet, and Virchow, but he was soon pointing his Clark students toward the recent statistical methods of Francis Galton. Some preliminary conclusions, especially on mixed groups, appeared in 1891, but only in 1897 was he prepared to make significant conclusions about Northwest Coast population history.

While anatomical features were valuable because of their permanence, language had a special importance to research because its constant change reflected the history of its speakers. Philological research, by tracing the alteration of language, enabled a reconstruction of the history of the culture of a people and, in part, its admixtures and migrations. Boas, coming from German scholarship that had made a specialty of Indo-European philology, was only adopting tried methods to the historical reconstruction of other language families.

The final method of enquiry into the history of uncivilized peoples was a study of customs and beliefs. No people had developed uninfluenced by their neighbors, yet all were remarkably conservative in retaining customs and beliefs even when their cultures underwent radical changes. Pottery shapes might preserve their preceding basketry forms; traditions, especially those in verse or melody, were maintained with great tenacity even if, as with Eskimo shamans, they became unintelligible. His initial British Columbia research placed special emphasis upon myth or folklore. This instrument was "of great importance, as it reveals customs which easily escape notice" and was the best means of tracing the history of tribes by revealing traces of the past when each group possessed its own independent culture. The most trifling features of social life were important because they were expressions of historical happenings.[41]

In the winter of 1887–88, Boas began systematic work on his corpus of Northwest Coast myths, customs, and traditions. He saw this as a "statistical method" in which he built up, for example, a card catalogue of myth "elements," discreet portions of American Indian myths arranged systematically to reveal the occurrence and absence of such elements among various peoples across the continent. This was an attempt at understanding "the growth of myths and their migrations" and answering the question, as he envisioned it by 1891, of how foreign material, when taken up by a people, was modified by preexisting ideas and customs. This was, then, an investigation into the "psychology of dissemination and amalgamation," of diffusion and "acculturation" of ideas.[42] It was, in a way, directed against the idea of independent invention, a supposition on which Boas was becoming increasingly critical. Similarly, he had cards of "all characteristic peculiarities of a tribe" which, when tabulated, showed that certain phenomena were always coexistent. These must have originally belonged together, while newly developed or introduced phenomena appeared isolated or unvaried.

The results of his three British Columbia trips seemed to vindicate his methods. Culture on the coast seemed uniform, but careful analysis brought out important differences. Different sources had contributed elements to the growth of a common civilization through exchange and borrowing. There were a great number of languages and dialects, but he distinguished three broad groupings on the basis of grammar: the Salish, Kwakiutl, and Nootka on the southern coast, the Tsimshian on the central coast, and the Tlingit and Haida to the north. The stock of legends showed a general uniformity, but with notable differences. By arranging the myths according to their "elements", he grouped them by regions, which did correspond with their linguistic divisions. Each group had eroded the differences, but had not eliminated them. The Raven myth, for example, was dominant in the north, the Sun myth in the south, with the central group characterized by a mixture of Raven, Sun, and Mink myths. The northern, central, and southern Kwakiutl, whose language was almost uniform, possessed almost entirely different myths.[43]

The diversity of cultural origins was most clearly shown in the distinct division of social organization. Matrilineal institutions were particular to the northern groups, patrilineal descent was found in the south, but the Kwakiutl, it appeared to him in 1888, possessed a mixed organization that seemed originally to have been patriarchal but modified by the influence of their northern neighbors. He could not, however, quite make up his mind on the Kwakiutl. They seemed transitional, a very complicated case; the next year he revised his thought to have them moving from matriarchy to patriarchy.[44]

Boas, in all this, was searching for methods while practicing research strategies. He was still in transition, both methodologically and in his research practices. Even his goals were ambiguous. When he spoke of ultimate aims to anthropology, he sometimes emphasized only the quest for knowledge. In 1887 Boas had described the great goal of anthropology as outlining the early history of mankind and working out the psychology of nations. Two years later he defined the anthropologist's ultimate aim as "the description of the history of mankind . . . beginning from the first traces we find buried deep under the surface, up to the present time and in all parts of the globe." To accomplish this it was necessary "to trace the history and distribution of every single phenomenon relating to the social life of man and to the physical appearance of tribes." Or, on a different level, the aim might be, as we have seen, to disseminate "the fact that civilization is not something absolute, but that it is relative, and that our ideas and conceptions are true only so far as our civilization goes."[45]

In the next twelve years he would develop his views on method, discard many ambiguities, and pursue more firmly the "Boasian" agenda.[46] But for the present, he was immersed in the day-to-day establishment of the new Clark University.

8 "The Idea Is Better than the Execution"

CLARK DOCENT

LARK UNIVERSITY had begun its first classes almost a month before Boas arrived in Worcester in 1889. The university was the dream of Jonas G. Clark, a childless native of nearby Hubbardston who decided to devote his wealth to founding an institution of learning that would perpetuate his name. Unschooled, but with a high respect for learning, he followed the precedents of Leland Stanford, Johns Hopkins, and Ezra Cornell. The brilliant Johns Hopkins psychologist, G. Stanley Hall, was chosen as its first president. But Hall was uninterested in heading yet another small New England college and persuaded Clark and his board of trustees to begin with a research-oriented postgraduate university.[1]

Clark's initial benefaction had the hallmarks of late nineteenth-century philanthropic generosity. He donated a site on the southern outskirts of Worcester with two ample buildings, which he personally designed, as well as an endowment of $700,000. And he promised more. Only Johns Hopkins and Rockefeller's University of Chicago began with more promise.

The munificence of the benefactor and the promise of a research-oriented institution allowed President Hall to attract a faculty of established and promising scientists. The university began with only five departments, though these were broadly conceived. In psychology, neurology, and pathology, he recruited Henry H. Donaldson, Warren P. Lombard, Edmond C. Sanford, and Franklin P. Mall, all from Hopkins. The privately wealthy chemist Arthur Michaels came from Tufts on the prospect of research opportunities for both himself and his wife, Helen. C. O. Whitman, head of the Woods Hole marine laboratory, was attracted to the biology department by similar research possibilities. Albert A. Michelson, a future Nobel Prize winner, left Case to head the physics department. Mathematicians William Story and Oskar Bolza were both Hopkins men. Clark's initial ten faculty were outstanding. Donaldson, whose career included service at Johns Hopkins, Chicago, and the Wistar Institute, felt that "I never had such choice colleagues."[2]

After these men, Hall hired Boas and seven others as "docents," the German term which he used to describe "men whose work has already marked a distinct advance beyond the Doctorate and wish to engage in research." The dividing line between these one-year appointees and their seniors, Hall admitted, "may not always distinguish greater age, attainment, ability or salary."[3] Nor, he added, was there to be any clearly marked line between this teaching staff and the thirty-seven postgraduate students admitted for the university's first year, most of whom were on fellowships or scholarships.

Despite the potential of the Clark foundation, Boas did not leave for Worcester with exaggerated expectations. Jacobi thought it promising, but Boas was more reserved. The place was "well worth a trial" he told his parents, but "we shall see how it works out."[4] He knew that he was underpaid. He also had personal reservations. He had never taught before and knew absolutely nothing about American universities, neither what would be expected nor what he should expect himself.

Boas's first lecture on November 4, 1889, was an inauspicious beginning. The lecture room was so dim he could not read his meticulously prepared notes, and he suffered from the worst "Lampenfieber," stage fright, of his life. He thought there were about eight in his audience, but anxiety prevented him from even making a count. "I lectured badly," was his summary of the debut.[5]

The next few weeks were difficult. He felt strange and insecure in an American university, and he was lecturing four hours a week, twice the Clark norm, on North American ethnology and on anthropological methods. He began his American course with the familiar Eskimo, but, because of his insecurity and Lampenfieber, he overprepared. His English, certainly spoken with a strong accent, may still have been a problem. The library was, of course, completely inadequate, and he found that his most urgently needed books had not been ordered. His physical anthropology laboratory, begun in December in two small rooms on the second floor of the main building lacked any instruments but his own.

The opportunity to "learn again" was gratifying compensation. He audited courses on brain anatomy under Donaldson and experimental psychology under Sanford. Hall's ideal of a community of scholars was working. Two of Boas's students were fellow docents, and in March he, Donaldson, Lombard, and Hall held an interdisciplinary seminar on shamanism.[6]

Henry Donaldson quickly became his closest friend. Donaldson and his wife, Julia, were close to Franz and Marie in age and lived only a block away. The Boases, meeting the Donaldsons at a gala reception at Jonas Clark's home in November, took an instant liking to the couple, and the fact that their son John was almost the same age as Helene sealed the friendship. The Clark teaching staff was filled with Germans or German-trained men, and Bolza and Henry Taber, both German-born mathematicians, also became close friends of the Boases.

Domestic life soon became as routine as his lecture preparation allowed. The Boas home, a four-roomed lower floor of a house at 210 Beacon Street, was close to the university. Franz had supervised the repainting, and they furnished it sparsely but comfortably. His study was at the front, separated by pocket doors from the living room where he hung portraits of Mozart and Beethoven. In December he discovered that they could rent a piano for only twelve dollars a quarter, and it gave them great pleasure the rest of the year. They shared the bedroom with Helene, now called "Bubbi" by Franz.

During this first year, the Boases had little to do with the city of Worcester. Marie had spent some time there as a girl and still retained at least one friend, but the university was just over a mile from the city's center (though the horse-car made the trip easier). Worcester, although Massachusetts's second largest city, had a population of only eighty thousand, far less than Boston, which lay an hour away by rail. It was an industrial city, but the presence of the American Antiquarian Society, a polytechnic institute, a state normal school, and Holy Cross College gave it some pretensions to learning even before Clark's gift of a university. The setting, in the undulating hills, lakes, and fields of south-central Massachusetts, was pleasant. There was, however, little time during that first teaching year for the Boases to explore the city or the countryside. Bubbi and the piano provided their few amusements.

Franz's lectures and his physical anthropology practicum took up a great deal of time, but he also had his own work to do. The BAAS report had to be readied for the annual meeting, and he finished off his long manuscript of British Columbia myths. He made a frantic trip in February to New York for library material for a survey of new North American geographical literature for Wagner's *Geographisches Jahrbuch*. He was active in Newell's American Folk-Lore Society, traveling to Philadelphia for its November meetings, and wrote a paper on the diffusion of North American tales for its journal. In April he decided to accept another summer's engagement with the BAAS as well as with the

Bureau of Ethnology. He took the position partly because he wanted to do more work on the Coast Salish, but more because he had to supplement his income.

President Hall had offered Boas a promotion to faculty status, but at an annual salary of only $1,500. That was a considerable raise, but far less than he wanted as a faculty member. After rejections and new offers, Boas decided instead to accept a one-year reappointment as docent at $1,500. He was not happy with it or with the negotiations, but expected a further raise the next year.

There was no question of his leaving Clark, though his ambivalence about the university intensified. "It seems to me," he had written at Christmas, "that the idea is at the moment better than the execution." Things took so long to be decided, and his unfilled library orders were particularly annoying. "So many mistakes" continued to be made, and the contract renewal, where "a distinct lack of candor reigned," had been unpleasant. Yet mistakes and unfilled expectations had to be tolerated in the first year. Time should make things better. "I only wish," he wrote at year's end, "that I could have greater faith in the university." Hall, he thought, was both a bad businessman and a bad politician.[7]

He did want to stay because Clark was "so attractive in many ways." If only it would "put itself in order, then I will remain." Major Powell, without making any definite offer, said he wanted him at the Bureau of Ethnology in Washington, D.C. A position there, however, would curtail his independent scholarship much more than would his post at Clark and also would not pay well. "The more I think about it," he wrote Marie, "the less I am inclined to go to Washington." If only Clark would fulfill its promise! He was learning from his lecture preparations and they would get easier. He hoped to attract some students—one from Toronto seemed certain for the next year. In any case he was happy that his future was decided for the year. Washington could wait.[8]

After a summer's fieldwork in the West, Boas returned with the expectation that things would be better at Clark. Hall had modified requisition procedures, and Boas was jubilant that he could now order according to his immediate needs. Moreover, he had much larger rooms for his physical anthropology laboratory, and he had attracted his first students: A. F. Chamberlain had come from Toronto and Gerald West from Columbia College. "I have never been," Boas wrote as the term began, "in such ideal circumstances."[9]

The two students added to his work. Boas was disappointed at Chamberlain's anthropological naiveté and lack of scientific training. West seemed more satisfactory, but, coming late to fill a vacant fellowship, he required extra effort. The fall term, though hectic, was satisfying. Above all, Boas was learning, both from his own teaching and from that of others. During the year he sat in on Spanish and comparative osteology classes. "I have it very good here," he wrote at Christmas, "and hope it will become better and better."[10]

Domestic life ran more tranquilly. Dissatisfied at how busy things had been the previous winter, "when we often had scarcely a decent conversation," they hired a second maid to help Marie with child care and housekeeping. Helene still occupied most of their leisure, but that fall they regularly read aloud for an hour or two in the evening, beginning with *Macbeth,* in both the original and Schiller's translation, and going on to *Twelfth Night.* The piano remained a source of pleasure, with Boas's preference turning more and more toward eighteenth-century music, especially Mozart, whose sonatas he played from beginning to end.[11]

In February their second baby arrived, and the house was again plunged into the irregularities of infant care. To Franz's great joy it was a boy. Helene, who greeted him with a polite "How do you do Ernst Philip!" was ecstatic at the idea of a new playmate. Although the delivery had been easy, the doctor insisted that Marie stay in bed for three weeks. By then she was insisting that the shrieking Ernst must be the reincarnated Raven of Boas's folklore.[12]

There were disappointments with Boas's own work. The publication of his collection of British Columbia myths fell through. While in Europe in 1889 he had succeeded in placing it with a Leiden firm. He had sent off his final version at the end of 1890, but received no response. At the end of the summer he learned that the Dutch publisher had issued a circular asking for one hundred American subscriptions before printing commenced. Boas was not pleased, and when by Christmas he had received only a single chapter in proof, he demanded the return of his manuscript. He recovered quickly. The editor of the journal of the Berlin Anthropological Society agreed to publish installments over three years, then provide 150 offprints which Boas could sell as bound separates.[13]

Although he launched a lecture course on African ethnology, his teaching and research concentrated increasingly on physical anthropology. The difficulties were great, not least because he had to learn almost all the material from scratch. Georg Bauer, a Munich Ph.D. who worked in paleontology and osteology, and Walter Channing, a Boston neurologist who collaborated with Boas and Donaldson, were of some assistance. The bulk of his research was in anthropometrics, the statistics of bodily measurement, and took two directions: as a guide to the history of racial groups and in measuring the growth of children.

At the end of the 1890 school year Boas had begun to measure Worcester children, starting with a local boys' club. He also measured Indians in the West whenever he had a chance. Now, in January 1891, he began his plan for the extensive measurement of children in the city's schools. His application to the Worcester school board was approved in early March, a decision that brought a tempest to the city, to Boas, and to his relations with President Hall.

Boas's proposal was to perform a series of measurements—mainly of height, head, and chest—and to test eyesight and hearing. Individual physical defects would be pointed out to school authorities. The project offered practical value to the schools and satisfied Boas's scientific interests, which intended to chart the differential rates of children's growth and any relationship to mental development. He secured the support of Superintendent A. P. Marble and Normal School Principal E. H. Russell. The school board went along with their recommendation, despite strenuous opposition from Clark Jillson, a former mayor of Worcester. Boas's proposal was pounced upon by the *Worcester Daily Telegraph,* a sensationalist paper that had already made Clark and his university a target of its columns. The animosity between the newspaper and the university stemmed partly from Clark's reticence and partly from others on the faculty who had shunned the paper's prying reporters. In 1890 the *Telegraph* had launched a bombastic antivivisectionist campaign against animal experimentation in the university's laboratories. Now it targeted Boas's proposal to measure the thighs of Worcester schoolgirls. Taxpayers must not remain silent, screamed the newspaper,

> while their children at school have their anatomies felt of and the various portions of their bodies measured for no reason established in science, and by a man unknown to Worcester, either personally or by established reputation, except as the representative of an institution UNDER A BLOOD RED CLOUD.[14]

The paper's attacks were intensely personal. Boas, who had "fooled around with the top knot of medicine men and toyed with THE WAR

PAINT of bloodthirsty Indians," would be feeling their children's heads and bodies. Boas, the paper said,

> must have been a scraper from way back. He has scars on his face and head that would make a jailbird turn green with envy. His scalp is scared with saber cuts, and slashes over his eye, on his nose, and on one cheek, extending FROM MOUTH TO EAR, give his countenance an appearance which is not generally considered au fait, outside the society of the criminal classes.[15]

Boas's support held fast, with the schoolboard confirming its permission. With four assistants, led by Gerald West, he began the work in the third week of April. By minimizing the number of measurements per pupil, the team was able to measure at a rate of one child every three minutes. Boas was pleased that he secured permission from 80 percent of the parents, but the whole affair had been a strenuous ordeal. By the time he began, he had already become "fed up with the whole thing."[16]

His anger was directed not only at the *Telegraph* and small-city politicians, but also at President Hall, who, instead of extending support, had discouraged the work. "I was hindered at every step," he wrote in disgust. "I was told again and again that the university would not support me, but that it was my own affair." Once the board reiterated its approval, Hall reversed himself, offering full endorsement, but Boas thought that it was done only to control the research and "of course, I politely declined."[17]

In the school controversy, Hall may have been caught between faculty and founder. The president claimed that Boas had not told him of his plans in advance, and both this and the controversy displeased Jonas Clark, who wrote angrily of Boas "taking the bitts [*sic*] in his own mouth." The staff, he felt, must be prepared to follow Hall's lead. Having acted independently, Boas "should look to some other source for his salary." Hall did not accept that position, perhaps because Boas had *not* acted so independently as Hall led Clark to believe.[18]

This incident represented Hall's position within the university. He was committed to the institution that he had in large part conceived. Its existence, however, depended upon Clark's purse, and its entire future was mortgaged to his capricious will. Hall could not afford to alienate Clark lest the whole dream—*his* whole dream—evaporate. Hall's commitment led to deviousness with both Clark and the faculty. He had made, for example, extravagant promises to faculty members and was unable to fulfill many of them, but covered his tracks by blaming Clark for the failures. Hall's version paints himself as shielding Clark by assuming responsibility for the old man's imperious whims. "This was most humiliating to my honor and even to my conscience," Hall wrote in retrospect, "but the situation demanded nothing less, for the entire future of the institution seemed to hang upon this." In just the first year, Hall fired chemist Arthur Michaels when he clashed with Clark over laboratory alterations and insisted upon his wife's presence in the lab, as Hall had promised. "You cannot get along with Mr. Clark and we cannot afford to incur his displeasure."[19] When the chips were down, Jonas Clark was indispensable; individual faculty members were not.

The controversy over Boas's school measurements put Hall in a similar position. He was able to keep Boas, but Clark was convinced that "we must let quite a number of our men go where they can have what freedom they want if they can find such a place. The remainder must be more considerate not expecting there is freedom to dictate or controle [*sic*] the University." If Clark was disillusioned, so was Boas. The university was in a "miserable state" and, though he wanted to remain, he would go elsewhere if things did not improve.[20]

Finances compounded the friction between Hall and Boas. The president offered to renew Boas for a third year, but only at his present $1,500 salary, a sum far from what the young man had anticipated. Boas refused the offer, then accepted it on the condition that he teach only a single lecture course.[21] Boas looked toward this upcoming year at Worcester without hope. He did not wish to start again elsewhere, "but why should I give all my energy and labor to a lost cause? With Clark and Hall, nothing in Worcester can improve." Marie, even more distrustful of Hall, urged him to investigate prospects in California and Chicago on his way home from the Northwest.[22]

Faculty discontent came to a head in the university's third year as Hall's compromising politics became ever more difficult. Almost everyone had his own catalogue of discontents, and Boas was further enraged at Hall's resistance to granting him leave the next year to conduct anthropological work for the Chicago World's Fair. "I had to say that I would not allow him to hinder opportunities for scientific work and that I would pack up and go if he put obstacles in my way." Then came Hall's treatment of Chamberlain and West, who were each docked a month's salary for being a few days late for the beginnning of term. That led to a "scandalous" argument between president and docent, which peaked with Hall's accusation that Boas was neglecting his department and had steadily worked against the interests of the university.[23]

On December 17 Boas caught Hall in a blatant contradiction and read to him notes of their previous conversation. He learned that others were equally concerned over similar experiences. Faculty conferences quickly brought out "a number of instances of trickiness and sharp practice on Hall's part that were distinctly unpleasant." At about the same time, word spread that C. O. Whitman and Franklin Mall had offers from the new University of Chicago and that others "were ready to leave as soon as opportunities occurred."[24] After the Christmas holidays, the faculty met to discuss the "great danger" facing the university, with Boas, as a docent, playing an active role but one subordinate to Whitman, Donaldson, Lombard, and others.

What followed was "a bizarre series of encounters between a desperately uncomprehending Hall and an irate faculty goaded to increasingly aggressive action." Hall seemed willing to respond, but he soon relapsed into deviousness. With no reconciliation, nine of the staff, including Boas, signed a joint letter expressing their lack of confidence in the president and tendering their resignations as of September. Hall retreated, but his acceptance of the faculty's demand for more control over appropriations, appointments, discipline, and faculty meetings soon proved shallow.[25] Hall's action was, in any case, too late.

Whitman and Mall, the core of the biology department, had already accepted President William Rainey Harper's offer to join the new University of Chicago. On April 16, Harper, in what Hall characterized as "an act of wreckage," came to Worcester to gather other Clark dissidents for the new university. Whitman and Mall wanted Harper to take seven faculty members, including Boas; he left with eight, but not Boas. Chicago already had an anthropologist and did not need two.[26]

Though passed over by Chicago, Boas had no intention of staying at Clark. Fortunately, he had already agreed to assist Harvard archaeologist F. W. Putnam in the anthropological department of the World's Columbian Exposition. He saw Putnam again on April 30, 1892, and before he could recount the story Putnam told him "you must give us your whole time."[27] He could start in the fall. In the meantime, the Boases would make their summer visit to Germany.

The Clark experiment was over. Begun with great promise, it degenerated to disillusionment, discord, and departure. Two-thirds of the faculty joined Boas in "the hegira" of 1892. With them went some 70 percent of the students, including Gerald West. The university was left only with psychology as a significant department; chemistry was closed entirely. A. F. Chamberlain, who had taken his doctorate in March, was hired as a lecturer for $800 per annum to fill the Boas vacancy. Hall was able to keep the institution alive, but it never regained its former position and, after adding an undergraduate college, lost its unique character.

For Boas, the end was a great disappointment. "After having lived so long there and having had such relationships," he told his father, "I feel a great affection for Worcester. I will, whenever I think about it, always be angry that all our hopes came to such a disgrace."[28] The Clark years had, on the whole, been happy ones. He had found a genuine community of scholars, a group of congenial men devoted to research and discovery. Among them he made several close friendships. Donaldson's was the most important and enduring. The neurologist, a year older than Boas, began at Clark his lifelong study of brain growth, work that complemented and influenced Boas's simultaneously developing interest in the growth of children. His association with Georg Bauer and his family, and with Oskar Bolza, also would be long-lasting.

In this rich and stimulating environment, his own work developed along both old lines and new. He followed his own interests, which now included anthropometrics and biostatistics alongside ethnology, linguistics, and folklore. The anthropology laboratory was as much for his own work as for the handful of students who participated in it, but they became assistants for his child measurements and Indian anthropometrics research. Even when he dropped the laboratory in his third year, his teaching continued to reflect his larger aims. His lectures, "The Application of Statistics to Anthropology," were intended to be published as a book.

His presence at Clark had attracted two students to work under him. Gerald West, who developed a competence in biostatistics, lacked the drive to further himself as a scholar. A. F. Chamberlain, who assisted Boas in measuring in Worcester and Toronto schools and in Kootenay fieldwork for the BAAS committee, became the first Ph.D. in anthropology in North America (Daniel Brinton came up from Philadelphia as external examiner). Boas took pleasure in seeing the thesis, on the Mississauga language of Ontario, through to a successful conclusion, but doubted that Chamberlain would make very much of himself.[29] Chamberlain did have a career as Boas's successor at Clark, but his contributions were neither permanent nor influential.

In mid-June, 1892, the Boases left for Germany on the *Darmstadt*. This was to be Franz's first summer home since 1889, and he welcomed the opportunity to catch up with developments in Europe, especially in physical anthropology. He had chores to do for the Chicago Fair, but mostly he wanted to settle down to his Chinookan material, gathered in his two previous summers' field work.

Chinookan linguistics and ethnology were a diversion that had turned into a preoccupation. He had gone west in 1890 with the intention of spending three months studying the Salish of Oregon and Puget Sound for the Bureau of Ethnology. He needed, incidentally, to determine if the Chinookan languages of the lower Columbia River were Salishan, as Bureau linguists believed, or a separate stock. There was so much to do on the Salish that Boas did not want to spend much time on the problematic Chinookan.[30]

He had undertaken the trip reluctantly. He would have preferred to stay in the East with Helene and Marie ("I'd rather there were no Indians," was her feeling), working on his next year's lectures and his long-postponed geography book. But he needed a summer's income, and fieldwork brought $150 a month. Marie could stay with her mother in New York and then at Lake George with sister Helene. At least on this trip he would be independent of Hale's harassing directives. Powell of the Bureau held a looser, less capricious rein. "The many annoyances I had with Professor Hale . . . have been the cause of my accepting an offer of Major Powell," he confided to E. B. Tylor. "Powell lets me make my own plans." Ironically, Hale now chose to loosen his own reins: "I will not hamper you . . . with any specific instructions. You will consider yourself entirely at liberty to act on your own judgement."[31]

Boas's first destination was the Siletz reservation, a shrunken tract stretching twenty miles along the Pacific coast of central Oregon. A crowded, cosmopolitan agglomeration of Oregon groups brought together under Anson Dart's unratified 1851 and 1855 treaties, it numbered among its 571 Indians at least half a dozen different groups, including the Salish-speaking Tillamook and Siletz. Local officials obliged with good accommodation, and Boas settled immediately to work with Tillamook Hyas John. "The old man I have now is quite good from the ethnological point of view," Boas noted, "but otherwise of not much use." He had little choice: only fourteen Tillamooks lived on the reservation and only three still spoke the language. After ten days he began on the closely related Siletz dialect, working with another old man, one of two brothers who still knew the language. He left Siletz on June 29, feeling it was "lucky accident" to have "pumped" empty the last living Tillamook and Siletz who knew about old things. He had stayed longer than intended and already knew that there was not "the slightest chance" of his doing all he had hoped.[32]

After a short stopover at the Grand Ronde reservation, he went on to Astoria in search of Chinookan-speakers. He learned that there were some Clatsop Chinookans farther south near Seaside, but he was disappointed to find that all spoke Salishan Nehalem, except an old lady, who gave him a vocabulary and a few sentences. He heard of some Chinookans at Bay Center on Shoalwater Bay[33] in Washington State, and here, on July 9, he found Charles Cultee.

In his view, Bay Center was a disgusting place, an "ekelhaftes Nest." It consisted of some twenty houses scattered along the shore of the shallow tidal bay. The people were boring, the locale desolate, and the "hotel" a miserable shack infested with flies in the air and fleas in the bed. The food was awful: no fresh meat was available, so he had only ham, onions, beans, and bad bread. He would have left in a day but for the intelligent Cultee, "brimful of interesting matter" and all the more precious as the last of his tribe. "He is the only person from whom something reasonable is to be learned and so I want to get as much as possible from him."[34]

Cultee's mother had been a Kathlamet, his father a Clatsop, so he knew both Chinookan languages. He conversed with his family in Chehalis, the Salishan language of his wife, and with whites in Chinook Jargon. Collecting grammatical forms through the rudimentary jargon was hard, but Cultee's remarkable intelligence eased the difficulty. "After he had once grasped what I wanted," wrote Boas, "he explained to me the grammatical structure of the sentences by means of examples, and elucidated the sense of difficult periods."[35]

Much as Boas detested Bay Center, he could not let go of this man. "What I now collect," he wrote Toni, "exists now only in the mind of a single man." It was a "curious thought," he added, "to exhaust the *last* of a people and, just as Bastian says, to preserve at the eleventh hour all their tales, customs, etc." He had never expected to give so much time to Chinookan, which certainly was independent from Salish, but "I am afraid that the old fellow may die before someone else gets hold of him." He finally broke away on July 23 for a day's rest in a Portland hotel. "I now feel like a prince: in a clean room, freshly washed, and in clean clothes! without fleas."[36]

The rest of the trip was mostly anticlimatic. By now almost all the Indians were out fishing, and Boas learned little at the Puyallup reservation. The three Chemakum he sought in Port Townsend were fishing, and so he went to Victoria but failed to obtain the Sooke vocabulary he sought. "Everything I want to do fails and I have wasted the whole time."[37] Worst of all, he missed the steamer north for his BAAS work at Bella Bella. He moved over to the New Westminster canneries in search of Indians, but the ones there were too busy to be of use. Only after another week could he quit complaining—when he "struck riches" in Chief George Chehalis,[38] who filled in a great deal of information on the Fraser River Salish. At the Ladner's Landing canneries he got on famously with the Bella Coola working there, aided especially by Nuskelusta, one of his friends from Berlin.

He started back for Portland, hoping to fill in some of his lost Puget Sound work. The Port Townsend Chemakum were now picking hops. He heard of a Chemakum woman at Port Gamble, and there he wasted most of five days in a "stinkige Schnapsbude" of a hotel, before being able to get one day's work with her.[39] The rest of his stay, until he left on September 17, was spent recopying his Chinookan texts, fighting a bout of fever and rheumatism, and cursing the waste of time.

For a trip whose primary purposes were to work on the Puget Sound Salish and the Nishga and Bella Bella, it had a strange outcome. He had his productive Tillamook and Siletz work, but he dealt with the Sound Indians scarcely at all. Among the British Columbia Salishan, he secured more: supplementary material on the Bella Coola and on the lower Fraser River Salish, which he could add to his BAAS reports. Cultee and his Chinookan linguistics and folklore material made up for the loss of the American Salish research.

Boas spent much of the winter of 1890–91 working on his huge collection of Chinookan narratives. In February he sounded out the Bureau about another summer with Cultee. He and Marie had hoped to go to Germany, but they were worried about traveling with baby Ernst and, as usual, their finances were thin, "so I must earn again this summer."[40]

Washington allowed a budget for two months' work, most of which he planned to spend with Cultee in Bay Center. He would do no BAAS work this summer, delegating research on the Kootenay to Chamberlain. He traveled over the Union Pacific with Uncle Kobus, who was off to see Alaska. Cultee, alive and healthy, greeted him on his arrival. (Boas was very worried that something might have happened to his treasure.) Conditions were much the same as the year before: fleas and mosquitos and "ham, ham, ham and beans, beans, beans." But Cultee seemed inexhaustible, now working nine or more hours a day. "The old fellow is so full of legends and customs that I cannot pump him dry."[41] In the first week of August, they shifted to Kathlamet Chinookan. Breaking only for a few days in Portland, Boas spent more than a month with Cultee, leaving Bay Center with five hundred pages of texts.

Despite difficulties, the two summers had been deeply rewarding. "You cannot imagine how much my current activity satisfies me," he wrote from Bay Center.[42] Recording for scientific posterity the dying languages and customs of the dwindling tribes of the West gave personal and scientific satisfaction. On the other hand, he found fieldwork tiring and difficult. He really wanted his summers for his work and family, preferably in Germany, rather than lonely isolation in some "ekelhaftes Nest" or "stinkige Schnapsbude" on the West Coast.

The Cultee texts could help to square the circle. The Chinookan material was complete and self-contained enough to provide work in his study.[43] This was the work that he took with him when he and Marie finally left for Berlin in the summer of 1892. The paucity of letters while with Marie and his parents in Berlin allow few glimpses into the German summer. For the Chicago Fair, he gathered anthropometric instruments and tables in Berlin, Leipzig, Munich, and Vienna and visited the anthropological meetings in Ulm. He saw his old friends at the Berlin Museum and his Baffin Island companion, Wilhelm Weike, now married but still in his parents' service. And he had new brothers-in-law to meet.

Aenne had married Julius Urbach, a Berlin businessman, the previous spring. Toni's engagement to Ludwig Wohlauer in April 1891 had come as a complete surprise. Franz had consigned her, at thirty-six, to permanent spinsterhood. Both sisters presented their husbands with June babies, Walter Ernst Urbach and Elisbeth Wohlauer arriving just as Franz and Marie reached Berlin with their own two youngsters. So many grandchildren in Berlin threw the Grossbeerenstrasse flat into turmoil. "Next time," Franz wrote from the steamer back to America, "you must arrange it that our arrival does not coincide with that of so many babies."[44]

These family affairs, as well as a painful rash that broke out on Ernst's legs, disturbed the anticipated peaceful summer's writing. Boas left for America with the Chinookan texts only about one-third complete. The work would have been further advanced if they had stayed in Europe as long as planned, but a terrible outbreak of cholera had struck Hamburg, and everyone feared its spread. The family departed Berlin abruptly at the end of August, catching the *Weimar* at Bremerhaven on September 2. It was crowded with other refugees, though none, not even cargo, was allowed aboard from Hamburg.[45] They disembarked at Baltimore, and Franz, leaving his family in New York, went immediately to Cambridge to plunge into the business of the Chicago Fair, scheduled to open in less than eight months.

9 "All Our Ships Have Gone Aground"

CHICAGO

B̲OAS ARRIVED IN Cambridge, Massachusetts, in September 1892. Most of the planning and arrangements had already been completed for the Chicago exposition that celebrated the 400th anniversary of Columbus's arrival in the New World. Frederic Ward Putnam, chief of the Archaeology and Ethnology Department at Harvard, had been working since 1890 toward producing "a perfect ethnolographical exhibition of the past and present peoples of America."[1]

Putnam, Harvard professor and director of its Peabody Museum of American Archaeology and Ethnology, stood with J. W. Powell and Daniel G. Brinton as one of the preeminent men of American anthropology. Boas's senior by almost twenty years, Putnam had begun as curator of ornithology at the Essex Institute of his native Salem, then studied under Louis Agassiz at Harvard. He returned in 1866 to the Essex Institute, then the neighboring Peabody Academy, and finally to George Peabody's museum in Cambridge as director in 1875. By then he had established a reputation as a New World archaeologist and began his long service as permanent secretary of the American Association for the Advancement of Science. His relationship with Boas had matured over the years since they first met at the AAAS's conference in Buffalo in 1886. They were thrown into close proximity when the younger man moved to Worcester, near enough to visit the Harvard museum.

At the end of March 1891, Putnam asked Boas to prepare some fall lectures at Harvard and also talked with him about his plans for the Chicago exposition. "He asked me for help with different things," Boas wrote, "and following a happy inspiration I suggested a series of charts which would represent the bodily form of Indians." Putnam immediately fell in with the idea, and within a month Boas was put in charge of a subdepartment of physical anthropology at $50 a month. "This gives me an opportunity that I long have wanted for important work." Boas's idea of a series of charts sounded simple; in fact, as Putnam soon attested, it "proved a vast undertaking, and necessitated an enormous correspondence and much consultation" even to commence the work.[2] Boas intended as complete a survey of Indians and mixed-bloods as possible: the gathering of thousands of individual measurements across the entire continent. That summer, while he continued his work with Cultee at Shoalwater Bay, he had eight Clark and Harvard students and a large number of missionaries, army and navy doctors, Indian agents, and even teachers measuring Indians from Greenland to the Aleutians, and from Nova Scotia to Arizona.

Boas's involvement in the Fair spread from physical anthropology to ethnology, and in 1891–92 he began arranging for large collections of Northwest Coast material to be brought to Chicago. These Boas did not collect himself; he enlisted the aid of experienced people he knew on the coast. He commissioned James Deans of Victoria, who had assisted previous collectors, to make a Haida collection from the Queen Charlotte Islands. Fillip Jacobsen, one of the brothers who had brought the Bella Coolas to Berlin and then stayed on the coast, was to compile a Bella Coola collection. Mrs. O. Morrison, Native wife of a Fort Simpson trader, collected on the Skeena. James G. Swan, who had contributed collections to the Smithsonian, was to collect from Cape Flattery. Myron Eells, a missionary to the Skokomish, was charged with gathering a collection of the Puget Sound Salish, while others were asked to collect at Shoalwater Bay and in the British Columbia interior. Most important, George Hunt would collect among the Kwakiutl.

The Indians at Fort Rupert would be the "standard tribe." The Kwakiutl were made the pivot of the display because, Boas wrote, they were central to the region's culture, much of which had its origin among these Fort Rupert tribes. The evidence of this was in the borrowed Kwakiutl names given to all those winter ceremonies which played so important a part in the culture of their neighbors. Boas arranged with Hunt for a collection to illustrate Kwakiutl life and to bring a troupe of Kwakiutl to live in their big houses along the waterfront of the Jackson Park grounds. The Vancouver Island Indians would demonstrate to Fair visitors "whatever is asked of them in relation to their customs and mode of life, particularly the ceremonies connected with their secret religious societies."[3] All this work had been proceeding while Boas was in Germany. When he arrived in Cambridge in September, the correspondence and anthropometric results awaited his attention.

Short-term housing in the college city proved difficult to find, and by the time he located something half suitable, the children were too sick to move from New York. Helene's tonsillitis passed quickly, but Ernst suffered again from skin sores and a fever. Franz kept his Cambridge room at 768 Main Street, hating the separation. He could scarcely afford the time or money for trips to New York and squeezed in only two short visits.

In November he moved to Chicago, joining Putnam who had gone in advance. Housing was again a problem, with rents near the Jackson Park grounds inflated beyond his means. He looked further south in Engle-wood where Alice Krackowizer, Marie's schoolteacher sister, roomed. By offering five dollars a month more than the existing tenants, he obtained a third floor flat diagonally across the street from her. Marie and the children arrived for moving day, the first day of December, but a mix-up had left their Worcester furniture in storage; after a week in a hotel room, they finally moved into 6636 Stewart Avenue. "I am sick and tired of this vagabonding," wrote Franz as he prepared to settle into this first family home since May. His long commute meant that his time at home was limited and he scarcely saw Ernst awake on work days, but it was nice to be all together again.[4]

The confusion about furniture was nothing compared to the Fair. Everything was in a "sad situation," with no buildings finished, no office, no apparatus, "in short, everything in a jumble and Putnam in despair."[5] The biggest problem was the Anthropology Building. Putnam's Department M was originally planned to form part of the gigantic Manufactures and Liberal Arts Building, but the pressure from exhibitors for additional space pushed it out of that central location and into a special building, belatedly constructed for Putnam's department and a Liberal Arts spillover. Its completion was promised for March, then April, but construction continually lagged. Chicago's "Great White City" opened on May 1 with the carpenters still working on Putnam's building. "The construction department," Boas cursed at the end of the month, "*always* leaves us in the lurch."[6] Only by June 9 could they begin to install their collections, stored until then in a dairy barn. The building opened to the public, still incomplete, on Independence Day. Boas inaugurated his physical anthropology laboratory in the last week of July.

The building was only one concern. Boas's seventy-odd fieldworkers had accumulated such an enormous quantity of anthropometric material that the tabulation of the 17,000 observation slips was "*collosal*." Compilation was necessarily slow and, though the results were interesting, he had "cold sweat on my brow" from fear that he would not be done with them in time for the opening.[7]

The Northwest Coast exhibits were almost on schedule, with the collections beginning to arrive in Chicago even before Boas moved there. From Deans came three carloads of Haida material. Ceremonial and shamanistic material was included, along with an entire Skidegate house and its forty-two-foot pole and models that reconstructed Skidegate village at its 1864 prime. Jacobsen sent a Bella Coola collection particularly strong in clan and secret society material. From Mrs. Morrison came almost $500 worth of Nass and Skeena pieces, including two large poles. Swan sent a small collection from Neah Bay, and Eells a good sampling of everyday articles from Puget Sound as well as a collection of models illustrating canoe types from the Columbia River to Cape Flattery. Last to arrive—delayed by storms at Fort Rupert and Alert Bay—was Hunt's collection. It was easily the largest: in addition to a whole house, it had some 365 pieces heavily emphasizing the winter ceremonials. Boas claimed that his collaborators' efforts had resulted in the most systematic collection ever presented.[8]

The department's outdoor exhibits were less hampered by building problems and were ready for the opening. Putnam had arranged reproductions of Yucatan ruins in front of the building. The portal from Labna and the Serpent House of Uxmal shared pride of place with a Southwest cliff dwelling replicated to natural size. On the ethnographic grounds north of the building, along the shores of South Pond, were the habitations of the Native groups, most particularly two Northwest Coast houses to be occupied by the Kwakiutl.

Led by Hunt and totalling fifteen adults and two children, the visiting Kwakiutl were housed temporarily in three small rooms in the stock pavilion, with mattresses, bedclothing, chairs, and two stoves requisitioned for their comfort until they moved into one of the traditional beam-and-plank houses on the ethnological grounds. The occupation of the houses in May became the occasion for "the first of a series of ceremonials." The dance, Boas noted, was exactly what he had seen seven years ago in Newitti, even with the same people.[9]

Despite the efforts at systematic and authentic representation, the expeditions to Mexico and South America, and Boas's indefatigable anthropometrics and Northwest Coast work, the Fair's anthropology exhibit was something of a failure. The exhibitions were significant in their own right, though the broad appeal for donations, the necessity of assembling a comprehensive collection in two short years, and the chaos of installing everything within weeks created an exhibition that was often more quaint than coherent. Worst of all, Putnam's building, pushed to the remote edge of Jackson Park, literally at the end of the railway track, had become marginal to the exposition. The sorrowful fact was that Putnam had been squeezed out—"buffeted about by more worldly and self-assertive chiefs of departments" and disliked by Director Harlow N. Higginbotham, who never bothered to visit the building.[10] Moreover, the sheer size and diversity of the Fair overwhelmed the department.

Even the Kwakiutl made very little impression. The official ethnological exhibition with its handful of Kwakiutl, Navajo, and Arawak simply could not match the enormous color and panache of the ethnological exhibition "run riot" on the Midway Plaisance. This mile-long "open mart and caravansary of nations" was a free-wheeling entrepreneurial sideshow that almost overshadowed the exposition itself. Crowded under G. W. G. Ferris's 250-foot-high wheel were Egyptians and Sudanese, Indonesians in a Javanese village, fifty-eight Eskimos from Labrador, a party of bare-breasted Dahomans in a West African setting, as well as Malays, Samoans, Fijians, Japanese, and Chinese.[11]

The construction delays of the building had also meant that Boas was kept busy with installation, allowing only a little time for work with the Kwakiutl visitors. "Scientifically, the summer has been extremely unsuccessful," he wrote, but it would be a shame if he let them leave before getting something out of them. "I can get information that perhaps may never again be secured and so I consider this more important than anything else." By September he was able to direct time and energy to the Indians, but he was happy when the Fair's closure would bring the departure of "the damned fellows" back to British Columbia. Nothing had ever caused him more worry and unpleasantness (there were drinking problems), and he swore "never again to play circus impresario."[12] Yet the effort had been worth it: he gathered an impressive amount of information that would form the basis of his 1897 report on the social organization and secret societies of the Kwakiutl. At least as important, he was able to teach Hunt to record Kwakiutl language texts in phonetic script, the preliminary to the thousands of pages of myths, descriptions, and other material that Hunt would send him in the following years.

At dusk on the evening of the last day of October the gates closed on "the greatest of all world expositions." Now began the process of winding down. Boas's immediate task was to help Putnam transfer the mass of material in the Anthropology Building to the Palace of Fine Arts, the structure chosen to house the new Columbian Museum that was to be the Fair's legacy to Chicago.

Putnam originally suggested the idea that the great collections for the exposition would make a "grand beginning for a permanent ethnological museum." His tireless persistence won converts among Fair and civic leaders. Edward Ayer, made rich from railway tie contracts and an exhibitor of Northwest Coast poles for the Anthropological Department, became a major promoter. The depression made pledges difficult, but Ayer captured the interest of department store magnate Marshall Field. Field's million-dollar gift, made after a guided tour of Putnam's building and two others a week before the Fair's closing, insured the foundation of the museum. But the new museum's trustees were not interested in Putnam's paternity, and his own ambitions, which included directorship of the new institution, crossed with some of theirs. He had never been popular with Higginbotham, director of the Fair and now a leading member (eventually chairman) of the board. The University of Chicago, represented by geologist T. C. Chamberlin, disliked Putnam's influence. He was frozen out. "The people here treat Putnam, who has worked two years on behalf of the museum, unspeakably rudely," Boas reported in December, "and make their final arrangements completely behind his back."[13]

Those arrangements included the question of a curator of anthropology. Almost from the beginning Putnam's intention had been that Boas occupy the place. When, in the April 1892 aftermath of the Clark crisis, Putnam had offered to take on Boas full time, he proposed to his new assistant that he might stay in Chicago to "take the ethnological division" of the resulting museum. That had become Boas's ambition.[14] The Field Columbian Museum was Boas's best hope for the future, but the slow process of its organization left him uncertain.

He turned a confident face to his parents' everlasting concern ("I am all right. After the Fair I will not be out of a job."),[15] but even his letters home could not mask the difficulty. The Panic of '93, which hit the country that summer, threw a pall over every institution's budget. He was not without possibilities. He was in close touch with President Harper at the University of Chicago, but Frederick Starr remained in his way there, and even its rich endowment was devastated by the Wall Street collapse. The Bureau of Ethnology had again put out a feeler, this time almost officially, but its appropriation had been cut. Unexpectedly, the University of Pennsylvania invited him to interview for a position to be shared between the University Museum and the Wistar Institute, but that offer collapsed when it was decided that the deed of trust prevented joint appointments. Putnam seemed to want him at Harvard, but had no money for a new position. Without excluding eventualities in Washington, Philadelphia, Cambridge, or even Ottawa, Boas's hopes rode on the embryonic Field Columbian Museum.

Putnam did his best for his protégé. Though he was thoroughly disgusted with the "great disrespect," the "dirty politics," and the "base ingratitude" shown him, he was loyal to his people. "Dr. Boas is the only person besides myself who is qualified to take charge of the anthropological material," he wrote Ayer, and the only one left in Chicago who could bring order from the chaos of boxes stacked in the former Fine Arts Building. Boas was "the best man the museum can get to take charge of it."[16] The museum did need someone to carry on the installation of the anthropological materials it had inherited and agreed Boas could stay, at least temporarily. This decision, just days before his Fair contract ended, was a relief, a stone lifted from Boas's heart. The immediate uncertainty was over. "It is not that I fear not finding a position somewhere," he told his parents, "but that I have none now and no money that I can fall back on." Though he thought the prospects of permanency were good, he knew better than to build Luftschlösser.[17]

"I do not have very good remembrances of 1893," he wrote on New Year's Eve. "A rushing rat-race, great uneasiness, and unsatisfactory work have been its watchwords."[18] Although he could look back with satisfaction at some of the results of his work at the Fair, it had been a bad year professionally, and even more so personally.

The rush of the exposition work had meant little family or social life. The city's downtown was distant—an evening concert or play meant returning home after midnight—and life never seemed to settle down on Stewart Avenue. The flat was small yet hard to heat. Chicago was dirty compared to Worcester and that meant three times more laundry. Sophie, their German maid, was caught with a man in her room and had to be let go. Worst of all were sickness and doctors' bills.

One bill was no surprise. Marie was pregnant, expecting in early April. The baby, a girl, came a week early, hastened by a noisy musicale in the flat below. The nurse did not arrive, so Franz and the doctor brought Hedwig into the world on the morning of March 24, 1893. Mother Krakowizer, delayed by a broken wrist, came five days later. She and Alice were an enormous help, with Franz busy with the catalogue and the Kwakiutl for the Fair's opening in less than a month.

Marie was scarcely out of bed when Helene got measles, then passed them on to Ernst. The next month the baby, nicknamed Hete, suffered from diarrhea and vomiting so severe that they doubted for a time that she would survive. She improved, but slowly; by July, at four months, she was still about three pounds underweight. In August all three children had fevers; in December it was flu, followed by whooping cough. This was serious, and Franz and Marie took turns sitting up the night with them. Little Hete's cough turned to fever and bronchitis and then worsened. She developed a lung infection and a high fever. Complications followed. Her bowels so filled with gas that her breathing became cramped and brought on painful pleurisy. Enemas gave only temporary relief. The doctors thought that her lungs were better and the worst had passed when, on the night of January 11, she suffered a horrifying spasm from the pressure on her diaphragm. Her temperature that night rose to 41.5°C, and she had another attack. At eight in the morning, just as the doctor arrived, came yet another, even worse spasm. "I lifted her up," Franz wrote, "and then the blood spurted from her nose and mouth. She collapsed and it was all over."[19]

Though he went out to dispatch a dutiful telegram to the museum, asking that he be relieved until Monday and for an assistant to be sent around for instructions about carrying on the work, he and Marie could scratch only a few lines to Berlin. "Oh, dear parents, you have yourselves lost a child and know what spirits we are in." Franz asked his Clark friend Georg Bauer, now at Chicago, to make the arrangements. In the afternoon a tiny coffin arrived, and the next day Franz and Marie rode in a wagon, Franz bearing on his knees the little coffin that was to be buried in a plot in Oakwood Cemetery. Bauer and Donaldson, family men themselves, accompanied them, and bachelor Bolza, to Boas's great appreciation, came unasked. The cemetery was detestable—a barren, treeless field bordered by swamps and manure fields. The grave site was too small for plantings, so they bought a new, family-size grave and themselves moved the baby to it on Saturday. On January 14, Boas wrote a long letter home, despairing that "we must now get used to a life without baby things." But they could not forget.[20] In the spring they planted flowers on the grave. Every trip Franz ever made to Chicago included a pilgrimage to the grave site, marked by a small granite block inscribed simply "Hedwig."

All this had cost him more than he could afford. Already by October, before the worst had come, medical bills had used up all his income. There was nothing to pare from the budget except the maids, and Marie could scarcely do without them. Now, with the extra bills—they had two doctors during the last week of Hedwig's illness—and the burial costs, Boas was over his head. He was already in debt to Putnam, who sent him, unasked, another hundred dollars on receiving the tragic news. He preferred, however, to owe his father, from whom he asked for a $2,000 loan to tide them over.

He had scarcely buried his baby when things at the museum began to unravel. Frederick J. V. Skiff, chief of the mines department of the exposition, had been named director of the museum. He impressed Boas as an energetic businessman, though with a doubtful understanding of either science or museums. Boas thought he could get along with Skiff, who seemed willing to allow him a free hand in his own department.[21]

Skiff journeyed to Washington, D.C., in late January and, despite an assurance that he would be discussing the appointment of a geologist not an ethnologist, Boas was nervous about the visit. The press reported that he was searching for both, and Boas was aware that "certain people were agitating strongly for a man from Washington" for the permanent anthropological post. To lose out now "would be the culmination of all my Chicago experiences." On February 14, the day after the director's return to Chicago, Boas bluntly told Skiff that he desired a settlement of his relationship with the museum. Skiff refused to comment, and so Boas, who until now had been waiting for things to take their course, began to delve into the substance of the rumors. He quickly confirmed that an approach had been made to William Henry Holmes, an anthropologist at the Bureau of American Ethnology and formerly with both the Geological Survey and National Museum. Indeed, Holmes, noted Boas "has practically been appointed director of the anthropological department."[22]

Boas was, of course, outraged at this "unsurpassed insult." He wrote Holmes that it seemed "hardly credible that you should not have informed me, if you were offered a position which you are aware I hold." He asked Skiff for an assurance "that since I had the temporary charge of the Anthropological Department, nobody besides myself has been or is being considered in connection with the position." Skiff again refused to reply: "I am not in a position to give you the assurance you request, either one way or the other." Back went Boas's response: "I decline to work further for the Museum under the present terms."[23]

The language was calculated. He was willing to strike a bargain, even with the man who had stabbed him in the back. The museum, he knew, needed the temporary installation finished for its June opening, and he could hardly bear a sudden cessation of his income. "I *must,*" he had told Putnam the day before, "try to make money."[24] Skiff asked for terms, and Boas set $1,100 as his price through the end of April (his initial reaction had been to ask for $1,700). The figure, equivalent to about $500 a month, was accepted.

As Boas pieced together the story, largely from Donaldson, Bauer, and others at the university, it appeared to be a political tangle between the museum, university, and government science.[25] Harper at the University of Chicago had viewed the new Field Museum as a potential rival that might "affect us very severely" unless aligned with the university. T. C. Chamberlin, the distinguished geologist who had left a successful presidency at the University of Wisconsin to chair his discipline at Chicago, recognized the possibilities afforded by the museum and became a trustee, with Harper's blessing. Chamberlain, an accomplished organizational politician, "abounding in plans and push," hoped to elevate Chicago's standing and his own by attracting distinguished friends to the ambitious city.[26] He had worked for Powell's Geological Survey and was a close friend of Charles D. Walcott, invertebrate paleontologist and a senior survey officer.

Times were hard at the U.S. Geological Survey. Powell, taking an impolitic tack on western irrigation, had lost his legendary control over Congress. All the accumulated grievances of a decade were gathered in the Democratic majority's assault on expensive scientific bureaucracies and Powell's survey in particular. The Geological Survey suffered a cut of almost a third of its appropriations. Powell was the real target, and rumors came of his imminent retirement from the survey, which he had largely created but to which he was now a political liability.[27] He would stay at the Bureau of Ethnology, but his salary had always been charged to the Geological Survey. The Bureau's payroll, already cut in the assault against governmental science, would need to be trimmed to make room for Powell.

Chamberlin and his Washington friends saw the new Chicago museum as a way to solve several problems. According to Boas's sources, Chamberlin proposed Walcott, whose Washington paleontological division was under particular attack, as director of the Columbian Museum. At the same time, he tried to divide Bauer's university department of paleontology between vertebrate paleontology, which would go to zoology, and invertebrate paleontology, which was to come to his own geology department. This maneuver would provide room for Walcott in the university as well as the museum.[28] He had already secured an honorary appointment for Holmes in his own department as a non-resident professor of "archaeologic and graphic geology." Holmes's transition to Chicago would help solve the Bureau's budget crisis. Holmes was attracted to the joint position as curator and professor of anthropology at the two institutions.[29]

Stymied in his choice of directors, Chamberlin, it appeared to Boas, switched to supporting Skiff's candidacy in exchange for Skiff's support for Walcott and Holmes as curators of anthropology.[30] Boas's claims to the latter position could be discounted on the grounds of his administrative weakness; he was, after all, tarnished with the same brush that blamed Putnam for the tardiness of the Anthropological Building's opening. Boas's entire association with Putnam was no help. "I am a thorn in Chamberlin's eye," he wrote, "because he regards me as one of Putnam's men."[31] At least as damaging, perhaps, he was a close friend of Donaldson and Bauer, professors who opposed Chamberlin in university politics.

Boas's version of the affair is substantially confirmed by Holmes. Chamberlin was instrumental in bringing his friend Holmes to Chicago, and Walcott was also a key player in the crucial negotiations, though he remained in D.C. The appointment may have been related to the shake-up in Washington science, a consequence of the crises at the Geological Survey and the Bureau of Ethnology, though the Bureau was reluctant to lose Holmes. Certainly Chamberlin had set his heart on having the museum directed by his friends Walcott and Holmes. No such opportunity had ever before presented itself in America; they would make a "glorious team" and lead Chicago science to "the highest and best things." Walcott stuck to his Washington position, "awaiting developments" at the Chicago museum before "my having anything to do with it." Holmes accepted Chicago's prospects.[32]

Just when the contract was closed is unclear, though Boas was correct in assuming it was settled by the time of his demands for clarification from Skiff and the director's prevarications. Holmes's appointment was intended to be secret—secret, Boas thought, only from him.[33] "I am really grieved by this matter," he wrote Putnam, "because I thought a good deal of Mr. Holmes and should have expected him to act differently." His letter to Holmes asking about the rumors brought an ambiguous response, at once a plea of ignorance at Boas's official connection to the Chicago museum, a regret that Boas had not let him know the situation earlier, and an insistence that "as presented to me the proposition contemplated no interference with anyone but the establishment of an entirely new position."[34]

Holmes's ignorance *seemed* genuine, and he was forced, by the confidentiality imposed with the offer, to be circumspect. He had no desire, a colleague assured Boas, "to take any stand inimical to you." Holmes, in his discussions with the New York Natural History Museum, had been very careful in not wanting to appear to be ousting anyone. He was doubtless embarrassed at the appearance his coming to Chicago would make, continuing to insist that he had accepted a "new position" with the assurance that Boas would be retained "in an important capacity at an advance in salary." Boas's "antagonistic position with respect to my coming has given me a good deal of discomfort," he told Skiff; Boas's departure would be a calamity, and he would do everything he could to keep Boas there.[35]

Holmes's embarrassment opened the possibility for a compromise. Boas, whose decision to stay on temporarily had been prompted by financial desperation, quickly realized that his incumbency offered a foothold from which to fight against the "complete scoundrels" opposing him. In fact he achieved little through his own efforts or that of his friends, but his continued presence certainly made it more difficult for Holmes to come. Director Skiff, at Holmes's instigation, suggested a division of the department.[36] The idea was discussed when Holmes arrived in Chicago on May 7. Skiff asked Boas how much he would want for the direction of such a department. Boas responded that he would expect the same salary as any other curator. Skiff then took Holmes uptown to a meeting of the executive committee of the trustees. On Skiff's return, he told Boas that the committee had decided not to divide the department. They did not, he said, feel able to pay $8,000 in salaries. Boas immediately began clearing his office. As he put it "in good German" to his parents, "ich würde herausgeschmissen"—"I was chucked out."[37]

Boas believed that the division might have been achieved "if the Trustees had not been seized by a financial panic" due to escalating costs of installation and building maintenance.[38] This is doubtful, if only because Boas had weakened his position by not accepting Skiff's offer to renew his temporary contract beyond May 1. He lost his foothold, and with it went the moral difficulty of ousting an incumbent. Moreover, his insistence on equality with Holmes made a compromise difficult. While most museum departments were under a curator, Holmes ranked as a director, one of only two such positions under Skiff's general directorship. Holmes's and Skiff's compromise would have given Boas a curatorship under Holmes's directorship, a position Boas was unwilling to consider.

He felt betrayed by Holmes, whom he had regarded since 1884 as an honorable man, but struggled against his bitterness, thinking that he should not judge the man too harshly. "He probably at first did not know the situation and was then led into it step by step." Nor could he contest the Washingtonian's qualification. He doubtless would have agreed with Putnam that he was himself "a far broader man for the place than Holmes," that Holmes's work was "all on the artistic side of Ethnology," but there was no disputing that the man was "first rate."[39]

Holmes, coming to archaeology from a background in art and geology, had a reputation for careful, critical, and meticulous study of material artifacts. Detailed and cautious, his writings were nevertheless suggestive of wide-ranging generalizations on the historical development of art and technology. He had worked throughout the eastern United States, in Mexico, and on the mounds of the Midwest, had closely studied collections in the National Museum in Washington, and had been involved in organizing exhibits there and the impressive life-size groups created by Smithsonian for the Chicago exposition. Personally reserved, even shy, yet "a very human and very lovable companion" to his close friends, Holmes, with his impressive scholarship and Washington network, "was indeed formidable by the early nineties." The American Museum of Natural History in New York was soliciting him for its anthropology department at the same time as Chamberlin succeeded in moving him to Chicago.[40]

Boas, with the collapse of all his possibilities, was now "adrift." He could only appeal to Putnam, who knew he had "nothing to fall back upon" after all the expenses of the past year, for "whatever you may be able to do for me." He had a slender, desperate hope that the university might find a way to take him on. Although President Harper felt that Boas did not "take direction" well, he did seem to want him. It might be possible to sidestep Starr's opposition by an appointment in anthropometrics or American linguistics, and certainly his old Clark colleagues— Donaldson, Whitman, and Bauer—as well as his new friends there— Maaske, E. G. Hirsch, and Albion Small—did their best, but the depression lingered on, and Harper, believably, had no money. Dawson in Ottawa was anxious that he pick up his interrupted BAAS work. Boas lingered a few more days in Chicago. The Stewart Avenue lease had expired, and he stayed on with Donaldson while Marie and the children went to New York. He almost headed west, but Marie would not hear of it. "How much richer does it make us?" she queried. If he had no job in the fall, "a few hundred from Canada is nothing," and he would have another report to write that would hinder him earning elsewhere. "Don't go west," she pleaded, "I can't let you go."[41]

He put off the trip until the fall, deciding instead to spend the summer in New York writing up some of his previously untouched work and preparing his AAAS vice-presidential address. He needed some peace. For the past two years his life had been "an eternal rush and a battle against opposing powers," first Putnam's enemies and then his own. He would spend a month in the city and two at Lake George, there to rest his nerves and "await the future in peace."[42] After a last visit to Hedwig's grave where their pansies were in beautiful bloom, he left Chicago. Nothing, save temporary contract work, was on the horizon. He was exhausted and bitter. The affair had caused him "more anger, bad temper, and stress" than he had ever experienced, "Clark University not excluded." Whenever he thought of it, "my bile overflows."[43]

The year 1894 was the nadir of Boas's early career. For a decade, since his return from Baffin Island, he had been seeking a position that would give scientific satisfaction and an opportunity to employ his industry and enthusiasm. He had been constantly disappointed, and his salaried positions had dissolved like Luftschlösser. *Science* had turned sour and had to let him go, Clark's promise had been betrayed. Chicago was an even more bitter betrayal. Now, at thirty-five and the father of two children, he was unemployed. "All our Chicago ships have gone aground."[44]

Boas's loss of the anthropology department at the Field Columbian Museum was a cruel blow. He had been working in America for almost a decade and seen his reputation, based on productive research in ethnology, linguistics, folklore, and physical anthropology grow to a point where he could, without braggadocio, number himself as "one of the first in my field, here and abroad."[45] Just when he should have gained a position commensurate with his rising place in American anthropology, he had lost the one to which he was most naturally entitled. What had gone wrong?

In one respect, nothing. In 1894, W. H. Holmes was a more established, more distinguished anthropologist whose stature could justly rank second to none in the country. The trustees of the American Museum had been told that he was "at the head of his profession,"[46] an estimate with which few would have quarreled. Chicago's preference was entirely justifiable on scientific and museum grounds. Boas's claim rested more on incumbency than on any superiority to Holmes.

That there was no other place for a runner-up is also understandable. Only a half-dozen institutions—the Bureau in Washington, Chicago, Clark, Pennsylvania, and Harvard universities, as well as museums at Washington, New York, and now Chicago—employed anthropologists in 1894, and some of these were retrenching. Boas had faced the shortage of vacancies as a geographer in Germany, and it had continued for him as an anthropologist in America.

In a sense, Boas was, as has been pointed out, "excluded from the network of personal and institutional loyalties that largely controlled entrance and advancement in American anthropology in the last years of the century."[47] In another sense, however, he was not so much excluded as not yet fully incorporated. In Putnam, Boas certainly had an active and loyal promoter of his career, but Putnam's influence was still limited to Harvard's Peabody Museum, an important but circumscribed and under-funded base, often at odds with the dominant Smithsonian anthropologists. Boas stood outside this Washington scientific establishment, though his relations there had been cordial and supportive. The Bureau of Ethnology had paid for his summer work in the American West, purchased his manuscripts, and published his work since 1884. It had, moreover, made him at least tentative offers for permanent employment in 1890 and 1891 and had renewed them through Holmes as recently as August 1893. None had come to fruition, but the responsibility for that seems to have rested as much with Boas as with the Bureau. A Washington, D.C., job meant a very low, if secure, salary and a curtailment of his scholarly freedom.[48] Holmes, in declining the American Museum job, endorsed Boas as "probably the best man in the country who is not already definitely placed," and McGee recommended him to Mrs. Cornelius Stevenson at Pennsylvania.[49]

Boas was a loose fish because he had, in part, willed it. He was unaccustomed to subordination and disliked the idea of restraints upon his scholarly choices. Though long possessing, as George Stocking has pointed out, "a sense of the importance of institutional power to promote his anthropological viewpoint," he had been unsuccessful in converting any of his positions—his *Science*, Clark, or Chicago roles—into a base for creating his influence. And now he was without any position.[50]

10 "I Have Looked into Hell"

TEMPORARY WORK

B Y THE SUMMER OF 1894, Boas was exhausted and near nervous collapse. "After all the stress and excitement," Marie testified, "poor Franz is completely kaput." His intention to make a quick visit to Germany, built on a desperate wish to visit his ailing father, was shelved. Marie was adamantly opposed; Jacobi, more authoritatively, ordered a rest. Boas conceded: "I will let my nerves run down and await my future in peace." Complying with Jacobi's instructions, he restricted his work to six hours a day, sleeping nights from ten until eight and napping after lunch. He put in three hours writing in the morning and three more in the afternoon at the park. He enjoyed the diversion of attending to his own neglected projects. "I feel really happy at being able to do some scientific work again," he wrote. There was other satisfaction to the work. After the Chicago insult, he wanted to prove a point. "When all my things in press appear," he wrote in June, "enough people will see and understand that no one here has accomplished as much as I have." He made no claims to genius, but recognized his industriousness and the breadth that distinguished him out from almost all of his American colleagues. His reputation would withstand the shabby Chicago treatment: it should be remembered, he had told Skiff, "that I am, both here and abroad, one of the first in my field and that in about two years I will be uncontestably the first."[1] After a month in the city, he went with the family to Lake George for the summer.

Lake George was at its pleasant best in the summer of 1894. The lake, a long, southward-trending sheet on the eastern edge of the Adirondacks, occupying a portion of the Hudson River–Lake Champlain trench, remained wild and romantic. Francis Parkman had rhapsodized it as a spot where wild scenery was tinged with "tranquility and mild repose."[2] Jacobi and his friend Carl Schurz had built houses on the western shore near Bolton. Marie's sister Helene and her husband, attorney Theodore Meyer, had later adopted Alma Farm as their summer home. Marie had been there tending the three young Meyers when Franz came back from

Baffin Island, and it had served as her refuge in Franz's absence in the field. Now Mother Krackowizer had a new cottage, near Helene and Theodore's. Here Franz settled down to work on a final report for Department M of the Chicago Fair and his vice-presidental address for the AAAS meetings in Brooklyn.

He finished as much as he could do of Putnam's report and by the end of July had sent his AAAS address to the printers. He dabbled a little with his backlog of research, but spent most of his time playing tennis, taking walks in the woods and hills, and chasing frogs among the waterlilies with Ernst and Helene. He would have willingly continued his laziness, but he had the Brooklyn meetings and another western trip before him. Hanging over everything was the concern for his future.

The AAAS address went well. He had worked hard at it, all the more because the broad themes appropriate to such an address were not natural to him. He had, he complained, written nothing like it for a long time, disliked handling such general themes, and lacked any "special gift for popular presentation." Yet he was pleased by the reception. Marie and many other friends and relatives were in the audience; he was particularly gratified when Mrs. Jacobi complimented his English.[3]

"Human Faculty as Determined by Race" was a major statement, the first of many which Boas would devote to that intriguing and emotional subject. It challenged easy assumptions that civilization was synonymous with the white race. "Historical events," he suggested, "appear to have been much more potent in leading races to civilization than faculty, and it follows that achievements of races do not warrant us to assume that one race is more highly gifted than the other." Boas granted that because physical differences existed between races so, too, probably did mental differences, but the evidence had not yet brought any conclusive demonstration of the superiority of any particular race. While brain size suggested that whites were superior, there were difficulties with that measurement. The average cranial capacity of women, for example, was smaller than that of men, and "the faculty of women is undoubtedly just as high as that of men." Even if brain size correlated with mental ability, there was such an overlap between races that no clear racial distinction was possible. "We might, therefore, anticipate a lack of men of high genius, but should not anticipate any great lack of faculty among the great mass of negroes living among whites and enjoying the advantages of leadership of the best men of that race."[4]

Mental qualities usually ascribed to primitive groups—impulsiveness, improvidence, fickleness, lack of originality—could all be explained within the context of their own values. In such complicated psychological phenomena, "no specific differences between lower and higher races can be found." Boas's conclusion, simply stated, was that, while differences probably existed among races, "no unquestionable fact" had yet been found "which would prove beyond a doubt that it will be impossible for certain races to attain a higher civilization."[5] This was a liberal pronouncement, almost as much a confession of faith as a statement of science. Bold perhaps for its time, it was a cautious and tepid beginning for his later crusade against racism.[6]

Boas left for the Pacific Coast almost immediately after the Brooklyn meeting. This would be a long trip, both because he had gathered a number of commissions and because he did not know when he would be able to go west again. He planned to work for the BAAS in the British Columbia interior and on the upper coast, for the Bureau of American Ethnology on Chinook, for the American Museum and National Museum gathering casts, photographs, and collections for Northwest Coast life groups, and for the AAAS to remeasure southern California tribes that had been badly measured for the Fair. The National Museum and American Museum had tentatively agreed to employ him temporarily on his return, each for two months to prepare their groups. Short-term contract work ("doing 'jobs,'" he called it) was not very satisfying, but would tide him over and provide him with deskwork he could do in Germany in the summer. The sale of his collection of skulls and skeletons, concluded in September with Chicago museum authorities after lengthy and unpleasant negotiation, gave him enough money to go to Europe after finishing his "job" with the National Museum.[7]

The British Columbia work was largely to fill gaps in his previous BAAS reports. He wanted, for example, to better establish the relative position of the Interior Salish. Here he was aided by James Teit, a Spences Bridge Scot whom he met in September. He recognized in Teit an intelligent, well-read man, knowledgeable on Indians. He delegated him to investigate a virtually extinct Nicola Valley Athapaskan group, hoping that the man would become—as he did—an able colleague.[8]

Boas's coastal work meant a trip to the Nass River on the most northerly part of the British Columbia coast. He had never been in Tsimshian territory before, and he wanted to learn more of the Nishga, but especially something of the Tsetsaut, an isolated Athapaskan group on

Observatory Inlet. Steaming north on the *Boskowitz*, he passed the familiar Kwakiutl villages of Alert Bay, Fort Rupert, and Newitti; reaching Tsimshian territory, he stopped briefly at Kitkatla, the first Indian village that he had ever seen with abundant totem poles. (Kwakiutl villages had fewer poles.) At Kincolith, where he spent almost a month—far longer than intended because the *Boskowitz* was delayed on its return—he was able to gather myths, measurements, and new information on the Tsetsaut (now reduced to about twelve, only two of whom still spoke their language correctly) and much more about the Nishga.

From Kincolith he went back to Fort Rupert, arriving on November 13 in the midst of the winter ceremonial season. Boas's stay, which lasted three weeks, was the most intensive and richest of any period of his Northwest Coast fieldwork. At Fort Rupert he was among old friends—from earlier trips and from Chicago. He was met by George Hunt, who advised him to announce his arrival with a feast on the first day. About 250 listened and watched as Boas gave a speech and presented photographs of the Chicago Kwakiutl to those who were present. Then Boas handed out pilot bread and molasses. After this odd intrusion, the normal cycle of Kwakiutl dances, feasts, potlatches, and secret society initiations recommenced. There was a new feast every day, and Boas reveled in all that he was learning about his favorite Northwest Coast people. Seeing so many feasts, he received a very different idea of their nature than he had gathered from hearing about them or seeing the demonstrations given in Chicago by Hunt's little group the year before. He was up all hours of the day and night, sitting with a cedar bark head ring, his shoulders covered by a blanket (because he was cold and did not want to soil his overcoat as much as in imitation of the Kwakiutl), and eating what he could of the feast food (he could stomach neither the seal blubber nor the rancid eulachon oil). "You should see me," he wrote home, "using a wooden spoon to eat from a platter with 4 Indians."[9]

The situation was near perfect, better than Alert Bay where the presence of Whites, especially the Anglican missionary and Indian agent, would have hampered the ceremonies just at the height of the season. Moreover, one of the Hamatsa initiates that winter was David Hunt, with his father, George, acting as host of several feasts in his name and his maternal uncle serving as master of ceremonies. Boas took shorthand notes during the feasts and dances, transcribing them the next day with Hunt, who explained what Boas had not understood. In addition, he took measurements, scavenged a few skulls and skeletons, bought a few garments and carvings for the two museum life groups, and then, with the arrival of O. C. Hastings, a Victoria photographer he had arranged to meet, took photographs of everything from type portraits to pictures of the apple feast he hosted on November 28. Some of the photos were intended to help with the casting of the group: he posed one woman spinning cedar-bark thread while rocking a baby with string hooked to her toe, another woman making mats and baskets. One incident provided a laugh. He and Hastings were about to photograph a Kwakiutl woman when another, curious to see the subject through the rear of the camera, "noticed that she stood on her head" and went running away telling everyone "that her clothes had fallen over her head."[10]

Much of Boas's work was accomplished with the help of Hunt, who put up the visitor in his new house. The relationship was not entirely agreeable. Hunt was invaluable for securing the cooperation of the Kwakiutl for measurements, but he was not always cooperative himself. After ten days Boas found Hunt "hard to deal with," "too lazy to think," and sometimes deserting him without explanation. "That makes all work so unpleasant," Boas wrote, "but I cannot change things and so I must go on as well as it goes." He knew he had no choice: "I am absolutely dependent upon him here and he knows it."[11]

He left Fort Rupert on December 6 with the return of the *Boskowitz*. The irregular hours, unusual food, and the cold and rainy weather had made the stay less than pleasant, but he had learned a great deal about the winter ceremonials of the Kwakiutl. After a few days in Victoria and Vancouver he returned to the Fraser and Thompson regions to complete some unfinished measurements. He closed his Northwest tribes work on December 18 and headed for Shoalwater Bay where Charlie Cultee was again awaiting him. This too was a clean-up operation, largely to solve some doubtful points of the 1891 Kathlamet texts, but also to add about eighty new pages to them. He was now inured to the unpleasantness of Bay Center, though it was little comfort to have to spend Christmas Eve eating popcorn among people with whom he had nothing in common. "I would rather be anywhere else than here," he lamented. The consolation was that Cultee, a fervent enthusiast of the Indian Shaker religion who refused to work on Sundays, had no compunction about dictating on Christmas Day.[12]

This left Boas with one last duty: to conduct measurements on the southern California Indians. He traveled to Los Angeles and then rapidly touched the major Indian missions in the region, where he took measurements, collected some vocabularies, and clarified tribal relationships.[13]

Returning to San Francisco on January 13, he fulfilled one more responsibility which, he hoped, would lead to opportunity. President David Starr Jordan of Stanford University had recruited assistants for Boas to help with his Indian measurements for the Fair, and Boas had promised, in return, a lecture on the results. There was more to the visit than that. Boas had to scout every possibility. He wanted to make contact with people at both Stanford and the University of California. "With the uncertainty of my future," he wrote, "I must make myself personally known as widely as I can."[14]

This uncertain future was now weighing very heavily upon Boas. He had been able to ignore it in the remoteness of Kincolith, Fort Rupert, and Spences Bridge, but once he crossed into the United States his concern increased. "As long as so much time lay between, in which I had so much to do, I deliberately avoided thinking about it," he wrote Marie. "Now the question lies closer day by day." The burden increased during the holiday season at Bay Center: "What good is the consciousness that I am among the best in my field here in America if I cannot use my ability, but am forced to work, here and there, to earn our living."[15] An idle day in San Francisco was almost unbearable, and Boas let loose an uncharacteristic cry of despair.

The outburst came half against his will, but why should Marie not know "how in my deepest soul I tremble before the future?" The nearer he was to returning home, the heavier became his suffering. He wanted to be home with Marie and the children, "yet if I were with you, every day would be filled with poison and bile because I would not know how I could provide for you, how I could fulfill my primary duty." Were he with her, he could at least hear an encouraging word; here he could only see mountainous difficulties and oppressive responsibilities. "It is the second time that I have looked into hell." The first had been Baffin Island during the winter of 1884–85, "and I hardly know which is worse." He knew "how to be silent with dignity," but he pleaded to be allowed "for once to cry out before you." Any idle moment could provoke renewed despair, times when he saw "no light" and feared that returning East would bring only "disappointment after disappointment." His loneliness, with no one to turn to for solace on the anniversary of Hedwig's death, meant yet deeper depression. Within a week, his mood was tempered by a whirl of sociability at Berkeley and Palo Alto. A few old acquaintances and people he knew by reputation or correspondence ended a long drought of human contact. "After almost 5 months of loneliness," he confessed, "human contact did me a lot of good."[16]

His return to New York was delayed by flood-endangered bridges and then a three-day snow blockage in the mountains. He arrived only on January 29, almost five months after he had left. "Oh how happy I am finally to be back with my family!"[17] The long separation had been as difficult for Marie as for him. She and the children had spent the first two months at the lake, living in the Hotel Mohican at Bolton after the Krackowizers had left at summer's end. She then moved into a boarding house on East 58th Street, a difficult place with the children. The homeless existence was not over with Franz's return. On February 11 they moved to Washington, D.C., where he began his preparation of a Kwakiutl life group for the National Museum. Their boarding house rooms on 14th Street NW became impossible when the landlady proved a drunk, so they quickly removed to new quarters at 1531 "I" Street NW. The board was neither ample nor good, but the rooms were satisfactory, and the landlady was kind enough to watch over the children when he and Marie went out evenings. Transitory and homeless as they might be, they were happy to be together again.

Their relationship had matured since the courtship and marriage almost eight years earlier. Boas wrote of it in a letter while sailing up the British Columbia coast. In his forced leisure, he had been reading Tolstoy's "The Romance of Marriage," and it set him thinking of how their fiery, passionate desire had been replaced by a peaceful trust. "We are not strangers any longer, and a new day does not reveal new qualities in us, but we know each other perhaps better than we know ourselves." Ardent reactions had given way to a quieter feeling which created a less intense but more satisfying happiness. "Passion leaves, love remains; the flower wilts, the fruit comes forth."[18] His thoughts turned to guilt as he remembered some dreadful words he had uttered at the end of the summer, words that had made Marie cry. He never would be so horrible again. Perhaps the long period of separation would give time for reflection and an increased happiness when back together. "For we are happy together, Marie. Our inner and outer life bring us only closer."[19]

Boas's position was not as hopeless as his December glimpse into hell had appeared. His "jobs," with the money from his somatological collection, would allow a trip to Germany and carry him through the end of

1895. "I do not lack for work," he told his parents on his return from California. He had picked up yet another contract, this time from the U.S. Commissioner of Education for statistics on growth.[20] Such contracts did not perfectly ensure his "primary duty" as a husband and father, but he did have two important factors working on his behalf.

For one thing, he found the Washington anthropologists surprisingly sympathetic. He had some suspicion of them after the Holmes-Chicago imbroglio, but he found the Washingtonians embarrassed about his departure from Chicago. "The Washington people," he reported, "felt uncomfortable." They had "participated in the performance," but did not anticipate the final outcome. "Therefore, I know, they will be willing to do for me a good deal that they might otherwise not do."[21] Otis T. Mason's offer of work on a descriptive catalogue of the National Museum's Northwest Coast collections and the preparation of a life group illustrating the region may have been prompted by this feeling. More certainly, W J McGee at the Bureau of American Ethnology (BAE) felt a responsibility toward the man who had been ousted by his close friend and colleague, W. H. Holmes.

McGee was a new man to anthropology, and Boas had not known him well. He had been a geologist with Powell's U.S. Geological Survey since 1883, for which he had done important work in glacial history, and this had eventually associated him with the contentious question of Paleolithic man. When Powell founded the Bureau, he brought McGee along as his chief assistant. Boas knew of McGee largely as a collaborator with Holmes and Chamberlin in the debate with Putnam and others over glacial man, and thus as one of Putnam's adversaries and a co-conspirator in his own "insult" at the Field Columbian Museum. At their May 1894 meeting McGee had seemed eager to make amends. McGee, as Boas later wrote, "gained my esteem and friendship" because he was willing "to shoulder his part of the responsibility" in the intrigues that lay behind Holmes's Field Museum appointment. Alone among the Washingtonians he "had the courage to speak the truth" about "my troubles in Chicago."[22] The May reconciliation was jeopardized, however, by anthropological politics at the August AAAS meetings over which Boas presided as head of Section H.

At the Brooklyn meetings the Washingtonians had put McGee forward for the vice-presidency. This move was resented by many who, like Boas, saw it as a push by the Washington clique to elevate an unestablished newcomer to an undeserved honor. An attempt was made to find harmony through the nomination of Frank Hamilton Cushing, a Bureau anthropologist who had been doing brilliant—if erratic and largely unpublished—work in the Southwest for over a decade. The result was a tie, leaving Boas, as chair, to cast the deciding ballot. He opted for Cushing, a vote he feared would make him enemies, but he could not take McGee seriously as an anthropologist. "He is a slick administrator, and will certainly do good work, but he is really a geologist and he has done little anthropological work."[23]

The months in the capital gave Boas a chance to revise his opinion of McGee and solidify the friendship. McGee, increasingly assuming responsibility for BAE decisions from the failing Major Powell, was in a position to help Boas. They had already discussed the BAE taking up Indian anthropometrics. McGee now seemed all the more willing, and it was soon settled that he would publish some of the results of Boas's Indian surveys. Moreover, McGee contemplated that the Bureau's venture into this field, something avoided earlier because of Powell's dislike of physical anthropology, would eventually result in an opening for Boas.[24] Boas would have first call on the next available BAE opening; in the meantime, McGee agreed to purchase Boas's soon-to-be-completed Kathlamet texts whenever $500 was available. The Bureau, then, was a very good possibility: once its budget and staffing settled down, McGee would be in a position to offer him something.

If the Washingtonians suffered some discomfort over Boas's unemployment, Putnam was plainly outraged. The actions of the Chicago museum toward "poor Boas" had been "disgusting!" and "contemptible!" On the other hand, Putnam's own circumstances had improved to the point that he could contemplate, even before Boas had left Chicago, "doing something for you by and by." In April 1894, three weeks before Boas had been "herausgeschmissen," Putnam had accepted the curatorship of the American Museum of Natural History's department of anthropology, a position declined by Holmes in favor of Chicago. Putnam could hold out a hope "to have you with me in New York for some special work which may lead to something more." Nothing was open at present, "but I think it will come by and by, and of course I shall do all I can for you."[25]

Here something needs to be said about Putnam and his relationship with Boas. Putnam had supported him in the 1887 *Science* debate with Mason, and they had collaborated continually from September 1892 until

December 1893. Neither left much comment on the relationship, and one suspects, from the record, but as much from the temperament of the two, that it was friendly but formal, a matter more of mutual respect than of personal intimacy. The scientific interests of the two scarcely overlapped. Putnam was interested in the archaeological record and in American prehistory, whether Mesoamerican cultures, the nature of mound builders in the Ohio valley, or the presence of Paleolithic man in America. He respected but did not compete in Boas's areas of ethnology, folklore, linguistics, and physical anthropology. Nevertheless, they shared a basic assumption about the nature of anthropological study.

Putnam represented to Boas the "sane and sober scientist who values facts higher than fancies." While Powell's research was directed by fixed philosophical ideas of man's development, Putnam, though "not without ideas as to their interpretation," was concerned with the "steady, painstaking methods of field research" and the careful accumulation of data. "Taught in the Agassiz school of independent search for facts," Boas wrote in memoriam, "he took up anthropological studies with that enthusiastic worship of material data as the indispensable basis for inductive studies that has dominated his life."[26] Putnam, to Boas, was the careful scientist, working upward from his data rather than imposing a theory downward upon it.

In one respect, then, Putnam and Boas stood as colleagues, working on parallel paths with similar aims and methods. At Chicago, Putnam had always been the chief, the man responsible and out in front, but he accepted the initiatives of his younger colleague—in physical anthropology and anthropometrics, in neurological and pyschological laboratories, for a Northwest Coast emphasis in the North American section of the museum, and for the Kwakiutl troupe. While the relationship was collegial, it contained a strong paternal element.

Such a role was natural to Putnam. He had encouraged Harlan I. Smith, an enthusiastic but unschooled archaeologist who had dug with him on Ohio mounds, and hired him for the Fair and later for the American Museum. He assumed a similar fatherly relation toward others, often people without formal training in anthropology or archaeology. C. C. Abbot, Ernst Volk, Marshall H. Saville, C. L. Metz, W. K. Moorehouse, and Alice Fletcher benefited from his support. Putnam was as concerned with the personal welfare of his protégés as with their scientific work. Alfred L. Kroeber, who served under Putnam later in California, paid tribute to "Putnam's helpful influence on men, especially young men, at the outset of their scientific careers. . . . Their existence for him did not end with their departure from the university or exploring camp."[27]

This friendly, fatherly aspect of Putnam's relationship with Boas is hard to capture from the surviving record. A Chicago newspaper did write of how Putnam "refers affectionately to the great and efficient service of his first assistant." He lent money to Boas (as to others) during his extremity. Boas, for his part, jumped to his chief's defense when his mother assumed that her son did all the work while Putnam received all the glory, and he resisted Marie's outbursts over Putnam's vain and dilatory character. These are hints, but Boas's letters do grant one significant revelation. In January 1894, just days after Putnam had left Chicago, Boas wrote a note to acknowledge again that it had been a pleasure working with him. This, from the reticent but correct Boas, might mean little had he not ended it with the quite uncharacteristic, "Your orphan boy, Franz Boas." Again, when the younger man had lost all hope at Chicago and was adrift, he looked to Putnam for whatever help he could provide.[28]

While Boas was penning those plaintive notes, Putnam was hatching his plans for his new institutional base in New York. The American Museum was undergoing a major revitalization under the leadership of Morris K. Jesup, a financier who was devoting his considerable abilities to rescuing it from drift and debt. Anthropology had never been the museum's strength. The department had been initiated by Director Albert Bickmore, but it was neglected because of his other duties. In 1891 it was given over temporarily to Frederick Starr, who soon left for the University of Chicago. James Terry, who followed Starr, seemed more interested in questioning his predecessor's competence than in proving his own. His charges brought about bitter recriminations that led to an investigation, an arbitration of the dispute by Holmes, and the dismissal of Terry. This unhappy sequence led President Jesup to secure for the much-abused department the best man available. After Holmes declined, he settled on Putnam, whose low Harvard salary and unquenchable desire to organize something new kept him restless but never quite uncomfortable enough to abandon Cambridge. Putnam agreed to give Jesup as much time as he could spare in the summer and one week a month during the Harvard term. Doubtless Putnam wanted, as he professed, to give anthropology its proper place within the nation's largest city, but he was also determined to go an ungrateful Chicago museum one better. In the process he could help some of his old associates—Smith, Volk, and especially Boas.

Boas may well have been a little resentful of his old chief's accession to the New York job. Why should Putnam have two curatorships when he could find none? It was a position he had sought in 1886 and, less hopefully, only a month before, when Jacobi's inquiry had brought a response that the museum did not need a curator. But Putnam (and Holmes) commanded a status which he did not yet have, and Jesup wanted absolutely the best available man, even if he could secure Putnam's services only one or two weeks a month. The position at least had gone to a close associate, one who offered "great hopes of some time or another of getting you connected with the museum." Putnam told Boas in May, "I cannot say more than that you must always think of me as your sincere friend, and one who will help you in any way in his power, and that with the many things I am connected with, something may turn up for your benefit."[29] Already Putnam's secretaryship of the AAAS had provided a "job" in California and his New York curatorship a "job" in British Columbia. Now, in July, with those completed, the preparation of life group exhibits began.

Life groups were all the rage after the Paris Exposition of 1889 and the Smithsonian's adoption of them for the Chicago Fair. The idea had been pioneered in Europe, and those constructed by E. T. Hamy and Jules Hebert for the Paris Liberal Arts Building inspired widespread imitation. Like Putnam and the Smithsonian anthropologists who saw them in 1889, Jesup was impressed with the display at the Trocadero during his visit to Paris in the summer of 1894. He wanted life groups for his museum and Putnam was happy to oblige, especially since it allowed him to suggest that they begin with Boas's Northwest Coast, a region where its collections were strong. Moreover, since Boas was visiting the coast in the fall, they might commission him to procure photographs, casts, and a few additional artifacts for the preparation of two such groups as a beginning of a series. This would be a "wedge," Putnam told Boas, "a good opening for the future" and one that offered a possibility to prepare other groups and, ultimately, secure the permanent direction of the ethnological and physical anthropological sections of the New York museum. Such a position might be held jointly with a teaching post at Columbia College. "So I do not see, my dear fellow," exclaimed Putnam, "but what things look bright for you ahead, and that after the cloudy days the sunshine is coming."[30]

Putnam's efforts were appreciated, but his optimism had little effect. It was agonizing to wait helplessly while he wrote of plans and wedges, but seemed unable to offer anything more definite than $300 for expenses in

British Columbia and the possibility of two months' salary to prepare groups. Putnam seemed terribly slow; Marie judged him much more harshly as "lackadaisical and unreliable." She wrote Boas that, on his return from the West, he should see the presidents of the American Museum and Columbia College himself: "You cannot leave it to Putnam." Franz should not be so dependent upon the man, should not accept that Putnam had everything under control. "What do you owe him! For all the friendship which he harbors for you, he has always thought of himself first."[31] Boas, however, had little choice but to wait for Putnam to work things out at his own speed with Jesup and President Seth Low at Columbia. He could only hope that Putnam's wedging tactic would work according to the professor's sanguine expectations.

Jesup was not a man to be rushed, but Putnam had reason to be patiently confident. Jesup had become committed to anthropology. By the fall of 1894, while Boas was feasting among the Kwakiutl at Fort Rupert, Jesup was telling his trustees that the time had arrived for the museum to develop the great subjects of anthropology and mammalian paleontology. The growth of the museum should be in those two departments, "the two great subjects now before the country."[32] He asked Putnam and Henry Fairfield Osborn, curator of vertebrate paleontology, to prepare reports on their departments.

Putnam's report outlined an ambitious scheme for realizing Jesup's desire "to give this department of the Museum the prominence which the subject demands." The museum would concentrate on the archaeology of Peru, Mexico, and Central America, already supported by the Lumholtz, Bandelier, and Honduras expeditions in the field, and on the ethnology of North America. Life groups, representing families or tribal members in some characteristic work, would illustrate the ethnology of living peoples and eventually be extended into the prehistoric past. To achieve these results, he asked for an additional $10,000 over current expenditures for a decade. Jesup reduced the figure to $5,000, but committed himself and the museum to fulfilling the obligation. As token of his conviction, he donated $1,000 himself. But, with the museum in debt and the burden of fund-raising falling on Jesup's own shoulders and pocketbook, he was wary of new payroll obligations. Boas could prepare the Northwest Coast groups but, despite Putnam's plea that he needed assistance if he was to realize the great scheme, Jesup made no further commitment.

While the Boases waited for Putnam's plans to unfold or for McGee to get the BAE in order, they sailed on the *Dania* in early April for Franz's postponed visit to Germany. He had long wanted some scientific "freshening up" among European scholars, and he took along a pile of notes and unfinished manuscripts.[33] The principal reason for the trip, however, was personal. Family matters weighed heavily on his mind.

One concern was Julius Urbach. Aenne's husband was now in the brewery business, proprietor of the H. Schulz Company which was not prospering. Toni, in a different way, was another great worry: her tiny Lisbeth had been diagnosed as hydrocephalic with little hope for survival. These circumstances, unmitigated by Franz's continued professional insecurity, placed a severe burden upon his parents, a burden which did nothing to improve his father's health.

Meier Boas, now seventy-one, had long been plagued by heart trouble. His first attack had come eleven years earlier in Hamburg, the result of the excitement of Franz's departure for Baffin Island. His health had worsened considerably since Franz's previous visit in 1892, his son's concern made all the worse because the letters from Berlin were so vague. ("I am no little kid to whom one can say nothing!", he had scolded Toni.)[34] His anxiety "about all that could happen" had made him want to leave for Germany the previous June. Jacobi's medical authority had put a halt to that, but not to his anxiety about his father.

The *Dania* arrived too late for Boas to attend geographical meetings in Bremen, so they went directly to Berlin. His father was outwardly his old self and full of his usual enthusiasms. Franz delved fruitlessly into Urbach's brewery accounts and gave what comfort he could to poor Toni. Then he settled to work on his backlog of writing, using a room that Bastian lent him at the Museum für Völkerkunde. Finishing the BAAS report on his fall fieldwork, he set to work on the Kathlamet texts, using the new material Cultee had provided at Christmas. Then he planned to work on a monograph dealing with the secret societies and social organization of the Kwakiutl, material gathered over several years, but especially from his recent stay in Fort Rupert. The book would be published by the National Museum as a description to complement the Hamatsa initiation life group he had just completed in Washington, D.C. A very satisfying task was the preparation of an introduction to *Indianische Sagen von der Nord-Pacifischen Küste Amerikas,* his collection of myths that would finally appear as a book published by Asher of Berlin.

He broke away from his desk in June for a trip to England, primarily to see the British Museum's collection of early Northwest Coast material and talk with E. B. Tylor in Oxford. He then met Marie in Cologne to enjoy a holiday on the Rhine and Moselle, visit Gerland in Strassburg and Fischer in Marburg. The trip was no doubt pleasant, but it could not have been relaxed. In London Boas received a letter from W J McGee offering a BAE position beginning July 1. McGee knew it was not an attractive offer in itself, though it would eventually lead to a regular scientific position. For the present, however, it meant editing the backlog of manuscripts for the government printer, with any remaining time free for Boas's scientific research. McGee, moreover, could offer no more than $1,800 for the 1895–96 budget year. He made such an offer hesitantly, "yet it has seemed to me only just, in view of your circumstances, that you should have the refusal of the position."[35]

The BAE offer placed him in a difficult position. Here was an example of McGee's desire to do what he could for him. It was an unsatisfactory position, but would doubtless lead to something much better. Boas had always respected the BAE for its dedication to ethnological and linguistic research unimpeded by museum ties. On the other hand, the work did not pay well and would always be subordinated to BAE priorities. Boas was not attracted to the job, but, with nothing else in hand, he could not turn it down. He did, however, immediately write to President Jordan of Stanford, expressing his interest in relocating on the Pacific coast, his need for "helpers" who could only be obtained by training students, and his conviction that he had "something tangible" to offer the university. But he really needed to know how things were in New York. At the same time he wired Putnam immediately and wrote McGee that he could not consider leaving his current commitments—the Kwakiutl monograph, the Chinook report, and the U.S. Education contract—until the end of the summer.[36]

Boas's cable lit a fire under Putnam, though he had not been entirely idle. He had spoken with faculty at Columbia College, especially Livingston Farrand, a young psychologist who was interested in anthropology. Farrand assured him that he and his colleagues, notably Dean Nicolas Murray Butler, would welcome Boas's joint appointment by the college and the museum. On the strength of this and a conference with Jesup, Putnam wrote President Low suggesting common action that "will secure Dr. Boas to New York." Low's reply was very positive, but he was departing for Europe and could not say more until his return.[37]

Low's response impressed Jesup, but he remained unwilling to commit the museum until a joint arrangement was fully confirmed. This left Putnam paralyzed until Low's return. He could only offer his most optimistic tones in urging Boas to keep his options open. Putnam considered that Columbia, with Farrand and William Z. Ripley, could have a very strong team, once bolstered by Boas, and he planned to "build up a great anthropological institution" at the museum. He was certain that two months' work on the groups would "show the necessity of your being in New York." But, in the end, he had to admit that he could hardly ask Boas to give up a Washington certainty for only a strong New York possibility.[38]

Putnam's plans were enticing, something that Boas felt "suits me in every respect." New York had a number of advantages. The salary would doubtless be higher and more proportionate to his worth than the BAE's. A joint position with Columbia would give an opportunity to recruit students to assist with his work. While it would be a subordinate position, he knew and appreciated the freedom that Putnam allowed. And New York had family and personal attractions for both him and Marie. He thought less of the Columbia prospects. Farrand and Ripley, though without reputations as anthropologists, were already there. He would simply have to await developments.[39]

In early July Putnam visited President Jesup at the latter's Lenox, Massachusetts, summer home. On the strength of Jesup's response to his "great scheme" for anthropology in New York and the president's confidence that an arrangement could be made for a joint appointment with Columbia, he sent Boas a cable of calculated exaggeration. "jesup joins columbia to secure you hold Washington off." Equally calculated, surely, was Putnam's delay in writing details. A full six weeks elapsed, while Boas sat impatiently pondering the cable's meaning, before a letter reached Berlin. Marie diagnosed the situation fairly accurately. "Putnam is a beast!" she wrote, "I know what the delay means—that he has nothing definite and thinks he can regularize things when you go back."[40]

Putnam's August letter was lengthy, but it told only of Jesup's confidence that something would be arranged. Putnam iterated the splendid prospects that New York held for anthropology. A new museum wing, devoted exclusively to the department and including a physical anthropology lab, was to be built. With Marshall Saville already an archaeological assistant and Harlan Smith probably coming, "we would make the strongest team in anthropology in the country." Boas would make a "great mistake" if he bound himself to Washington when prospects were so much better in New York. Putnam could make no definite promises, but "you must have faith enough in me to believe that I will probably succeed in what I have undertaken to do."[41]

Boas wound things up in Berlin as rapidly as possible, calculating that if he returned in mid-October something might have been decided between Columbia and the American Museum and yet not too late for Washington. He left with Marie and the children on October 6, arriving only to find that a definite New York arrangement had foundered. President Low had proposed a joint appointment to the Columbia trustees, but they had balked at so late an appointment when students had already selected their fall courses. Low himself had doubts about Boas's ability as a lecturer, but he offered, as a substitute arrangement and likely a trial, a series of four or five public lectures over the winter at $50 each.[42]

McGee saved the situation. Boas let him in on the entire picture and received a kindly forbearance. The BAE would hold off as long as it could and, if they were forced to close the offer, McGee would let Boas know in time so he could "act accordingly."[43] But Putnam could still find no solution. Jesup had promised Boas's appointment only if Columbia came along, and it would not decide until the new budget was planned in the spring, a time too distant for either Boas or the BAE. Putnam put Boas to work on the Northwest Coast groups at the museum in November and December, but Washington might close its offer at any time.

The Boas family again moved into the boarding house on East 58th, awaiting events as patiently as possible. With Putnam in the city only a week or two a month, things moved slowly, much too slowly for Boas. "If Putnam was not such a dawdler," he complained, "things might have been arranged long ago."[44] But Putnam was keeping up his efforts. He was joined by Jacobi whose secret participation made the difference.

"A friend of the Museum, of the College & of the Doctor's," Putnam had written Jesup on November 7, was prepared to donate $1,500 toward Boas's salary, until Columbia could commit itself. The mutual friend was Jacobi, probably acting in concert with Kobus Meyer.[45] Another month passed before all the pieces fell into place, but Jesup accepted Jacobi's confidential guarantee as a bridge to Columbia's share. Boas had no inkling of this beyond knowing that Jacobi was lobbying on his behalf. Indeed, he never learned that, without Jacobi's guarantee, he might have missed the offer. By December 6 everything was in place and Putnam came forward with a definite proposal of an assistant curatorship for ethnology and somatology. Boas refused.

The problem was rank and authority. Mesoamericanist Marshall Saville had been assistant curator since 1893, and Jesup thought highly of him. Boas would not accept the possibility that, during Putnam's absence in Cambridge, he would be subordinate to Saville. "Again Putnam did not have the courage to make clear to old Jessup [*sic*] that Franz must stand first behind him," Marie commented. "As I had always feared little Saville thinks himself as important as anyone else and will let no one be placed above him." Boas would serve willingly under Putnam, but would not accept the offer "because I consider that my place among American Anthropologists entitles me to more than a third class position." He was willing to accept charge of the department of ethnology and somatology for a year as a special assistant, working under Putnam's direct supervision. Putnam accepted the counter offer.[46]

Boas was not happy. He had been offered an appropriate salary, but "I am sick to death of being put in places of second or third rank," so he had contracted only for one year. "How the thing develops will have to wait," he told his parents. By then the Columbia situation might be clear. "I will not go along with things when they do not give me what I want."[47]

Boas was testy about such matters. He knew how the museum was run and had a firm conception of his role within it. He refused to be a subordinate functionary. If he was charged with responsibility for the ethnology section, then he demanded the right to take initiatives and make plans, not simply to make suggestions and take orders. He would, of course, remain subordinate to Putnam, but he required, in Putnam's absence, direct access to Jesup with no interference from Saville or anyone else. "If you want me to take charge of the Ethnographical Section," he wrote Putnam, "I must have full swing of it inside the limits set by you." This was "the fundamental point on which the future hangs," and Putnam must make it clear to Jesup "that my position in science is such that I can demand *that* much as a simple matter of courtesy." Any other way would so restrict his usefulness that "I should not care for the place, no matter what the salary might be." Putnam allayed Boas's concerns. Saville would remain assistant curator in charge of Mexican and Central American archaeology, while Boas would be special assistant in charge of ethnology and somatology. This settled, and with Jacobi's check in the president's office, Boas was appointed Assistant Curator from January 1, 1896, subject only to the pleasure of the board.[48]

Putnam was ebullient. "I'll have a big thing in New York," he wrote his daughter. "I regard getting Boas as a grand thing for Boas and myself make a pretty strong team and with Saville, Smith and Pepper to help, you see I have the best equipment of any anthropological museum in the country and I'll show Chicago I can go them one better."[49]

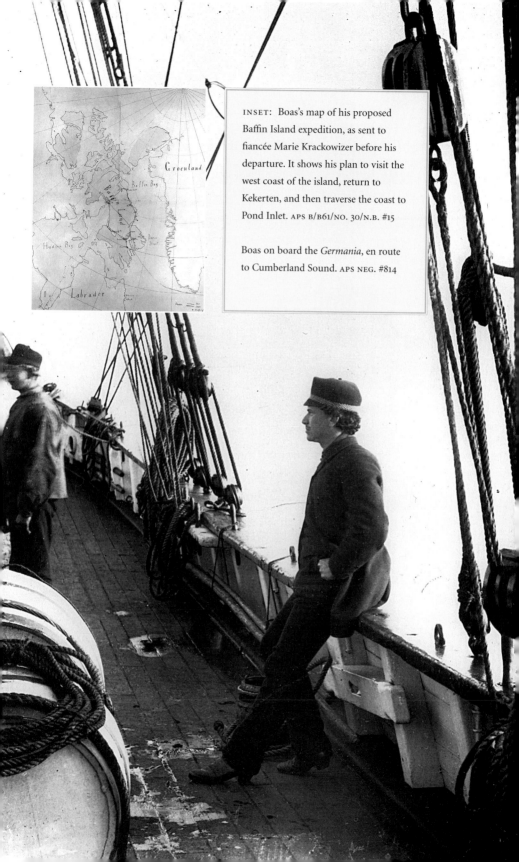

INSET: Boas's map of his proposed Baffin Island expedition, as sent to fiancée Marie Krackowizer before his departure. It shows his plan to visit the west coast of the island, return to Kekerten, and then traverse the coast to Pond Inlet. APS B/B61/NO. 30/N.B. #15

Boas on board the *Germania*, en route to Cumberland Sound. APS NEG. #814

FAR LEFT: Heinrich Kiepert, the Berlin geography professor who so frustrated Boas's habilitation at the university. Photo by Ernst Milster, Berlin, about 1880. BILDARCHIV PREUSSISCHER KULTURBESITZ, BERLIN #34/573

LEFT: Wilhelm Weike posing as an Eskimo sealer. Photographed in Minden by J. Hülsenbeck. APS B/B61/NO. 7/N.B. #58

ABOVE: The Friedrich-Wilhelms University, Berlin, from Unter den Linden. LANDESBILDSTELLE BERLIN #12 466

BELOW: The Royal Museum für Völkerkunde, on Prinz-Albrecht-Strasse at Königgratzerstrasse, where Boas worked as an assistant while preparing for his habilitation at the university. LANDESBILDSTELLE BERLIN #28 404

BELOW: Adolf Bastian, in a portrait taken in 1880, a few years before Boas served under him at the museum. Photo by A. Halwas.
BILDARCHIV PREUSSISCHER KULTURBESITZ, BERLIN #389/6591

RIGHT: Boas in 1884–85. Photo by Naegeli, New York. APS B/B61/ NO. 22/N.B. #74

FAR RIGHT: Marie and Franz Boas at the time of their wedding in 1887. APS B/B61/N.B. #49

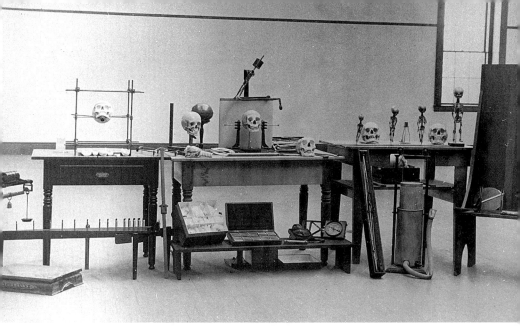

TOP: Boas's anthropometrics laboratory at Clark University. CLARK UNIVERSITY
ARCHIVES #172

BOTTOM: The Psychology Department at Clark University, 1891–92. Boas is seated
second from the left, with Henry Donaldson and G. Stanley Hall to his left. CLARK
UNIVERSITY ARCHIVES #133

11 "The Greatest Thing Undertaken
by Any Museum" AT THE AMERICAN
MUSEUM OF NATURAL HISTORY

F RANZ AND MARIE found a three-story brownstone at 123 West 82nd Street, just minutes from the American Museum and Central Park. The rent was high, $1,300 a year, but Mother Krackowizer occupied the second floor and paid $600 toward the cost. New roomers forced them out of the boarding house and a second one before they could get their furniture and occupy their new house on the last day of January. The children would stay, at least for the time being, in Mrs. Hervey's school.[1] They were now settled in New York, perhaps permanently.

Boas was scarcely a stranger to the New York museum.[2] He had dreamed of a curatorship there in 1886, while his familiarity with its collections went back to his cataloguing of the Powell-Bishop Northwest Coast collection in 1887. He had now been working on the life groups for two months. The most pressing concern during January and February was not museum matters, but his five Saturday evening lectures for Columbia. With these out of the way by March, he threw himself into work on a temporary exhibition on the progress of science and on rearranging the anthropological collections on the ground floor of the old section of the building in preparation for expansion into the new West Wing still under construction.

The American Museum of Natural History was just beginning to be a major player in American anthropology. Boas, even more than the part-time Putnam, would be the driving force over the next decade in raising it to eminence. Behind both stood museum President Morris K. Jesup.

Jesup was one of America's remarkable Gilded Age men. Born in 1830, he began his business career as a twelve-year-old office employee in a New Jersey locomotive and machine works. At twenty-four he entered into a partnership as a railway supplier, then moved into banking and rail investments where he made his fortune over the next twenty years. At the same time he participated in civic and philanthropic activities which so consumed his interests that, by 1884, at the age of fifty-three, he retired from business to devote himself to them. He was involved in forest preservation, the Audubon Society, Beirut's Syrian Protestant College (forerunner of the American University), the YMCA, the Peary Club, and a number of other endeavors. But his primary interest remained the Museum of Natural History where he had been a trustee since 1869. When he became its president in 1881, Jesup's mastery of detail and financial management gained him the confidence of the trustees, and his authority became paramount. He was an established member of the city's financial community and unstinting in his own generosity, and therefore able to tap the immense wealth of New York to museum purposes. He worked successfully with city and state governments to increase the museum's building and maintenance budgets. Between 1889 and 1901, five more wings were constructed to complete the entire 77th Street facade.

By 1896 Morris Jesup was the heart, brain, and soul of the American Museum of Natural History. The success of Putnam's department and Boas's ambitions largely depended upon the president's pleasure, his pocketbook, and his influence among trustees and friends. Fortunately, Jesup was particularly interested in two museum departments: anthropology and paleontology. Donors and trustees had been dazzled by the pre-Columbian civilizations of Latin America and supported expeditions by Alphonse Bandelier in Bolivia and Peru, Carl Lumholtz and Marshall Saville in Mexico, and one in Honduras jointly sponsored with the Peabody Museum. This southern archaeological strength made Putnam, whose Cambridge museum had strong interests in the area, a natural as curator, but North America remained a gap that Boas could fill as naturally. Jesup was anxious to further Putnam's anthropological plans. Public interest in the subject had developed rapidly in the previous five years, and he told Putnam, "that if I can bring before the people of the city of New York what this great Department is now, and what it can be made under your care, and what it will cost to do it, I may be able to enlist outside support."[3]

Putnam's first year as curator had already proved promising. The Hyde brothers, who made their fortune in soap, agreed to spend $2,000 annually for five years to explore the Pueblo region, with Putnam's protégé George H. Pepper as assistant. Harlan I. Smith, another youthful protégé, had been hired for North American archaeology, with Putnam himself initially paying a portion of Smith's salary. Most important, he had secured Boas in ethnology. "We have started out with a grand plan," he told Jesup, "and we have certainly had a success during the year that is most gratifying, and prophetic of our future." This was "only the beginning of what we will attain."[4]

Boas's first year at the American Museum was less auspicious. The city was gripped by depression, with capitalists all the more nervous at the growth of popular discontent symbolized by William Jennings Bryan, free silver, and the single tax. The anthropology department received no acquisition budget for 1896. "The financial outlook, together with the present unsettled condition of business generally," said Jesup, made it unwise to solicit the trustees.[5] Times were bad, cuts had to come from somewhere, and Jesup was now "a little sorry" that he had planned so much for Putnam's department. "Dr Boaz for instance & his work perhaps could have waited another year."[6]

An accidental event, the arrival of a damaged collection of British Columbia artifacts in New York, allowed Boas to break Jesup's ban on purchases. After a good deal of haggling, Boas bought all but ten pieces for $800, rather a bargain, he thought, for 180 items, some of which, notably a Chilkat blanket and a fine Nootka rattle, had entirely escaped damage. Boas's pride in the acquisition was quickly tempered when Jesup made it clear that he should have been consulted at the conclusion of the purchase. Boas, though at the museum for a year, had not yet learned the ways of Morris Jesup. "I did not understand quite clearly that Mr. Jesup desires to have in these matters the final decision of the detail," he wrote Putnam. "I am sure I shall next time be more cautious."[7]

At the same time Jesup expressed surprise that the museum's Northwest Coast collections, among its strongest from North America, should need such supplementing. Boas assured him that "it would be the easiest matter in the world to spend $3000 on that region."[8] Indeed, Boas had already reported to Putnam on the incompleteness of the American Museum's ethnological collections. Alaska, the South Seas, northern Mexico, and Smith Sound Eskimo were best represented, and Alaskan Tlingit and the South Pacific were "very good in their way." The museum held nothing from the Plains or Pueblo Indians, and virtually nothing from Africa, Asia, or South America. Even on the Northwest Coast, where the Powell-Bishop and Emmons collections gave the museum enviable materials, the entire region from southern Alaska to Vancouver Island was unrepresented.[9] Since the Kwakiutl, Bella Coola, and Salish was his special area of interest, Boas was anxious to fill the gap. The salvage purchase was a mere tidbit. He had his eyes on much more.

Boas had realized from the first how much research and collecting depended upon the wealth of the American Museum's trustees and friends. Late in 1896 he drafted a letter to Henry Villard, proprietor of the *Evening Post* and sponsor of the museum's Peru and Bolivia expeditions, proposing that he contribute toward filling the central and south coast collections gap. With several thousand dollars over the next two years, Boas wrote, "we should have the most thorough and I may say a complete collection from the region between Columbia River and Mt. St. Elias."[10] The letter proved unnecessary. Jesup was already considering Boas's much more extensive proposal for an elaborate exploration of the anthropological affinities between Asia and North America.[11]

Boas put his idea, maturing for well over a year, before Jesup on January 19, 1897. Describing the question of the influence between Old and New World cultures as one of the most important problems of American anthropology, he proposed a systematic ethnological and archaeological investigation on both sides of the North Pacific. Fragmentary study, he wrote, had demonstrated the commonality of certain cultural elements in the two regions. Bows, armor, and canoes, for example, had common features. The great diversity of language along both coasts was striking, though, since those on the Asian side were practically unknown, and it was unclear if there were any actual linguistic similarities. Particular points of mythological coincidence suggested early communication. Northwest Coast Indians physically resembled Asians more than any other American stock. "In short," Boas concluded, "there are so many points of similarity between the tribes of this whole region that we are justified in expecting that here a mutual influence between the cultures of the Old and of the New has existed. Thus a foundation for the solution of this important problem with all its important bearings upon the ancient civilization of America may be laid in this region." Conveying his ingrained sense of urgency, Boas noted that everywhere, but especially on the Asian side, the culture of the people was rapidly disappearing, "and the whole work is becoming more difficult from year to year."[12]

Jesup's imagination was struck by the great problem of Asian-American contacts. He became "very much interested in that question"[13] and, in his annual report later in January, wrote that "the theory that America was originally peopled by migrating tribes from the Asian continent" was a subject of great interest to scientists. Opportunities for solving this problem were rapidly disappearing, he wrote, and then he asked the friends of the museum to contribute toward a systematic investigation of the problem.[14]

Before there was an opportunity for a response to his appeal, Jesup jumped in himself. On February 9 he told Boas that he wanted personally to take up the plan and asked for a detailed scheme for carrying it out. Boas was overwhelmed. "Mr. Jesup looks at this proposed expedition in the light that it will be the greatest thing ever undertaken by any Museum either here or abroad and that it will give the Institution an unequalled standing in scientific circles."[15] Thus began the Jesup North Pacific Expedition to investigate affinities between the peoples of Asia and Northwest America.

Jesup's move was not uncharacteristic. He had always been sympathetic to grand designs and large-scale ideas. He had underwritten the Jesup Collection of North American Woods, the Jesup Collection of Economic Entomology, and was currently supporting the polar aspirations of Commander Robert E. Peary. Boas had put before him a vast project dressed in the tempting guise of research on the fundamental question of the relationship between Asia and aboriginal America. He accepted the challenge.

Jesup's decision launched Boas into frenzied action. He visited Leonhard Stejneger, a well-traveled Smithsonian naturalist, in Washington and wrote to Orientalists to ask about young men suitable for Siberian work. The matter was made more urgent because Jesup had seized on the expedition as a lever to secure another museum wing from the New York state legislature. The public announcement, made a little too hastily for Boas's taste, but dictated by the state assembly's calendar, was released for the March 12 editions. (Boas had to provide details—and corrections—to reporters over the next two days.) "The main object of the expedition is to investigate and establish the ethnological relations between the races of America and Asia, and is intended as a contribution to the solution of that question." Field parties would work on the American west coast, along the coast of Okhotsk Sea, and in the northern portion of the Bering Sea. "The expedition will be the greatest, it is said, in point of time spent and territory traversed ever backed by private individuals in this line of research."[16]

Boas was a little unhappy with the press notices, some of which made the project into a touring expedition up the entire coast of British Columbia and Alaska, down the Asian side, and around the Indian Ocean to Egypt.[17] He was intent that it be a systematic scientific examination using only specialists. The results would be of general ethnological interest, but of special importance on the question of the geographical spread of ethnological phenomena.

The roots of Boas's intercontinental project, now Jesup's, reached back to well before Boas's employment in the American Museum. In 1895 he had sounded out Berlin people about a prospective fieldworker and then investigated, through Stejneger, transportation routes to Siberia's Amur River region. An expedition, he told Berlin sinologist Wilhelm Grube, "had in the last year almost come to fruition twice."[18] What Boas meant, at a time when he was without a position, is unclear, but he certainly foresaw an investigation of the connection between Asian groups and Northwest Coast Natives.

He had raised, during that same Berlin summer, more explicitly than ever the probable connections between Asian and American peoples. A number of complicated British Columbia myths, he told the Berlin Geographical Society, showed such similarity with Old World myths that a cultural connection between the two continents was very likely. The distribution of other phenomena, including physical type, pressed toward the same conclusion and "made it probable that firm connecting links between the two cultural areas of both worlds would be found."[19]

Part of the impetus came from Boas's completion for publication of his *Indianische Sagen* that summer. Breaking up myths into "elements," he showed the mixture of these among the coastal and interior groups of the Northwest and traced some far beyond to the Mackenzie and Mississippi basins, the North Atlantic coast, and across the north to Greenland. The mythologies of the Northwest tribes incorporated foreign elements not only from elsewhere in America, but from the Old World too.[20]

He had long collected collaborating data for the mutual influences of the coastal inhabitants of these areas, he wrote a German editor in 1897. His reading of Georg Stellar's eighteenth-century description of Kamchatka "transposes me almost directly into familiar Northwest American surroundings,"[21] but he had been especially struck by Grube's recent *Globus* article on shamanism among the Gold (Nanai) of Siberia's lower Amur River. Some legends recounted there coincided almost exactly with those of the Northwest Coast, which, more importantly, were limited in North America solely to those coastal groups. Other data argued emphatically for an early influence on Northwest Coast cultures.

The Jesup Expedition would be pursued within the research program that Boas had developed. It was to be an explicit demonstration of the efficacy of the historical method of anthropological research. "I believe," he wrote *Globus* editor Richard Andree, "that our science urgently requires an investigation of the historical development of the cultures of primitive peoples in order to obtain a clear understanding of the laws of cultural development." The expedition would cover an area "unusually favorable" for such a method since "the major influences have occurred along a direct coastline."²² This would be an opportunity, he told E. B. Tylor, for a rigid adherence to the historical method, whose superiority over the comparative method he had recently asserted in a paper to the AAAS in Buffalo. "I want to investigate the geographical distribution of certain customs and characteristics over continuous areas." The application of the historical method meant that "we shall not obtain dazzling results, but I hope such as will stand the criticism of later times."²³

The Buffalo paper, "The Limitations of the Comparative Method of Anthropology," had been a reassertion of his decade-old point that generalization must come from careful investigation and induction, not from a priori assumptions. In a sense, this was a continuation of the Boas-Mason controversy of his first winter in the U.S. and, fittingly, it was published in *Science*. The method required a limitation to a restricted and well-defined territory, with comparisons that did not extend beyond the boundaries of the cultural area itself.²⁴ This was an extension of his previous research, notably in *Indianische Sagen.*²⁵

At Buffalo, Boas had spoken strongly. "A detailed study of customs in their relation to the total culture of the tribe practicing them, in connection with an investigation of their geographical distribution among neighboring tribes, affords us almost always a means of determining with considerable accuracy the historical causes that led to the formation of the customs in question and to the psychological processes that were at work in their development." While his general point was methodological, Boas cited the research area already clear in his mind. Though no one believed that slight similarities between Central American and East Asian cultures, for example, were satisfactory proof of a historical connection, "no unbiased observer will deny that there are very strong reasons for believing that a limited number of cultural elements found in Alaska and in Siberia have a common origin."²⁶

The first season's work of the Jesup Expedition would be confined to British Columbia in order to give Boas time to organize the Siberian work for the following year. He had already been planning a summer trip to the coast, partly in the museum's interest, partly to prepare a final report of the BAAS's Northwest Tribes committee. He had originally arranged for only a two-month trip, one month of which would be without museum pay, though with BAAS assistance. Now it became a four-month, first field season of the Jesup North Pacific Expedition.[27]

"I go west better equipped than ever before," he wrote prior to his May departure. More money was part of it, so too was his new intimacy with the American Museum's collection.[28] Equally satisfying was the presence of collaborators and companions who, though often pursuing their own assigned work, would be with him much of the summer.

He was mostly with Harlan Smith, the taciturn young man from East Saginaw whom he had known since the Chicago Fair. Smith was just twenty-five. A boyhood interest in Indian remains had led him to Putnam, who in 1891 had arranged for him to work under Charles Metz at the Madisonville excavations in Ohio. He continued working intermittently under Putnam's supervision while pursuing erratic study at the University of Michigan. In 1895 Putnam had Smith digging in Kentucky with the American Museum's explorations there. In New York he had become Boas's close friend, coming to West 82nd for weekly sessions on anthropological method. Smith's visits soon became casual: "we talk mostly shop," wrote Boas, "until Marie comes in, and then we chat about everything possible." Franz liked the bachelor archaeologist—"his heart is in the right place and he is absolutely reliable"—but doubted that he would ever amount to much in archaeology. While resourceful and good with his hands, Smith lagged behind in anything to do with real scholarship. The "many gaps" in his knowledge were obvious, his questions "unbelievably simple," and he was unable to "see the connection between his work and the general broad questions of anthropology."[29]

A second companion was thirty-year old Columbia psychologist Livingston Farrand, who lectured in ethnology as well. Farrand, totally inexperienced in fieldwork, wanted to apprentice with Boas and volunteered to go west at his own expense. That had not gone well with Jesup who, taking a "narrow-minded" view, wanted no outsiders on his great expedition. A long letter from Boas turned the situation and, though Farrand's field assignments were largely separate from his own, Boas found that Farrand's gaiety, unassuming naturalness, and good manners made him a pleasant companion.[30]

The two offered Boas more than companionship. "I hope that the work will so develop that they can carry on my field investigations and I can gradually withdraw." It seemed pointless to keep researching only to pile up more and more unfinished material.[31] He was "fed up with these trips into the wilderness," with every departure from his family harder.[32]

The trip took Boas through Chicago where he saw his sister-in-law Alice and his Clark University friends. He was worried about Donaldson. In 1896 he had fallen gravely ill from a disease first thought to be cancer. The news that "my best friend in America, whom I treasure more than I can say," was without hope struck Boas very hard. "My heart," he wrote, "turns within me."[33] The disease proved to be tuberculosis of the bone, severe and long debilitating, but not fatal. Boas was pleased to see that Donaldson could get out of bed occasionally and make some movements without pain.[34] He visited Oakwood cemetery, where the trees were now growing and the grounds well kept. Their pansies were in bloom, and he picked one to send to Marie.[35]

The last duty was to visit his "Liebfeinde," his "favorite enemies," at the Field Museum. The museum looked miserable and he was glad he was no longer a part of it. "I really have to thank the noble gentlemen who tossed me out." The major reason for the call was Boas's concern at the news, announced in May, of Chicago's own anthropological expedition to the Northwest Coast. Boas had been outraged at the effrontery, and Jesup had sent a letter to try to keep them out of the area for a year. The request seemed partially to have worked: Skiff told Boas that his anthropologist, George Dorsey, would not be in British Columbia at the same time as Boas's party. Boas also had a meeting with Holmes that, while not entirely satisfactory, at least meant "no more enmity exists between us." Holmes did not let on, but he too was unhappy. In August Boas would learn that he had left Chicago to return to Washington.[36]

The three New Yorkers arrived in British Columbia at the beginning of June. They traveled immediately to Spences Bridge in the southern interior, where they rendezvoused with James Teit, the Scot whom Boas had first met in 1894. Teit had prepared things well, securing local Thompson (Nlaka'pamux) Indians for the physical measurements Boas wished to take. While Smith went on to dig in Kamloops and Lytton, Boas and Farrand, guided by Teit, began a long horseback trip northwestward along the Fraser River, across the Chilcotin plateau, and over the Coast range to Bella Coola on the Pacific. Farrand detached himself at Puntzi Lake when Boas decided that the Chilcotin Indians were so interesting that they deserved a month of Farrand's time. The overland journey took thirty-eight often unpleasant days. Rain poured over the ten-horse pack train in the usually dry interior, the horses became bogged in swampy mountain ground, and rations seldom strayed from beans and bacon. Indians along the way were not keen to allow themselves to be measured. Bella Coola, remote as it was, came as a relief. There Boas found a welcome bed at storekeeper John Clayton's and enjoyed the dietary change to fresh salmon. More important, the waiting George Hunt had done his advance work well. The two collaborated every morning, going over the texts that Hunt had been sending east, with the balance of the day spent investigating Bella Coola religious ideas.

Boas then went north to Port Essington on the Skeena to measure, make casts, and identify museum pieces. He met Charles Edenshaw there and hired the Haida artist to identify items from the museum's collection, to show him something of northern art, and the basics of Haida ethnology. After the Skeena, Boas spent two weeks with Hunt among the Kwakiutl of Rivers Inlet. That concluded Boas's fieldwork. He met up with Farrand, and the two left for New York while Smith stayed on with his excavations in the south until autumn rains drove him home in mid-November.

Boas was pleased with the season. They had made over a hundred plaster-of-Paris facial casts and many more body measurements. Boas had enough information from Edenshaw to write the first publication in the Jesup Expedition series, "Facial Paintings of the Indians of Northern British Columbia," which elaborated upon the place of geometrical design in Northwest Coast decorative art. He had a chance to correct and revise over 300 pages of Hunt's texts and gathered material, published as "The Mythology of the Bella Coola Indians," on the peculiar cosmology of that group. Farrand, unfortunately, "had not done *very* much." The Chilcotin had been less than cordial and he had not been able to find a good interpreter. His collection of legends, however incomplete, did show "a not very rich independent mythology, but a surprising receptivity to foreign influences."[37]

Smith's archaeological results seemed very important. The older shell mounds of the coast region revealed a skull type resembling that of the interior, while even older ones contained deformed skulls related to those of the Koskimo. This seemed to indicate that at an earlier time a rather uniform population had prevailed along the coast from the Columbia River to northern British Columbia and that the various types currently found on the coast were due to migration of Indians from the interior, with the earlier population prevailing now only on the Columbia River and northern Vancouver Island.[38]

An infuriating aspect of the trip had been his encounter, while en route to Port Essington, with George Dorsey of the Field Museum. Dorsey exchanged "very friendly" greetings with Boas, but Boas's friendly response was forced. He resented the incursion into his own territory without the slightest courtesy of consultation. He was sure he would have informed J. W. Fewkes or Frank Cushing, for example, of his plans were he to invade their Southwest field. "This trip of Dorsey's annoys me more than I can say," he told Marie: "this Chicago crowd simply adopt our plan and try to beat us to it." The Northwest Coast was his beat and anyone seriously intending to study the area "should seek and take my advice and not just run out here at random." Dorsey even had the effrontery to speak of going to Fort Rupert, and his companion, James Deans of Victoria, capped it by asking the whereabouts of George Hunt. "I was mean enough," he admitted, "not to tell them where he was, and I have written George Hunt that he should not do anything for Dorsey." The affair made Boas furious, particularly with himself for being so bothered by it and then resorting to deception. He wanted to think of himself as unselfish, but he had to do some things "for my own protection." He found consolation in the suspicion that Dorsey had been to so many places in so short a period that "half of his time must have been spent traveling" and with the conviction that, in any case, "little Dorsey won't have achieved much with the help of the old ass Deans." He considered Dorsey, Holmes's successor to Boas's once-coveted Chicago position, a tenth-rate man.[39]

Boas did not participate in the next two Jesup Expedition field seasons. Farrand returned to the Northwest Coast in 1898 to investigate two Olympic Peninsula groups, the Quinault and the Quileute. Despite considerable disappointment, he collected enough to show a myth transition from Northwest Coast toward Chinook, as well as gathered a number of songs. In the same season Smith did excavations in Puget Sound and Lillooet, then continued his archeological work in 1899 on Vancouver Island. The results seemed to confirm an early migration from the interior to the coast and Vancouver Island that carried with it the art of stone chipping and geometric decorations.[40]

The Siberian side of the Expedition was more difficult to organize. Boas had had, since 1895, one man in mind for the southern portion of the work. Grube had raised Berthold Laufer's name to him as a promising young scholar. Laufer, son of a Cologne confectioner, was nearly finished with his degree and possessed strong recommendations from Leipzig and Berlin, where he had studied Asian languages and cultures.

He had, moreover, sat in on lectures by the Berlin anthropologists, Bastian, Luschan, and Seler. Unfortunately, Laufer still had before him his military obligation. Boas, even though he still had no expedition arranged, recommended that Laufer complete his service as soon as possible so that he would be available should a Siberian worker be required. Laufer did so, receiving his degree, magna cum laude, while in the army. Formally appointed in May of 1897, he came early the next year to New York to prepare for his Siberian work. In March, just as he was scheduled to depart, the museum received word that his visa had been refused by the Russian interior ministry. Laufer was a Jew and Jews were not allowed into Siberia.

It was all very difficult and embarrassing. Boas had just arranged a large farewell reception for the traveler, and Laufer might never be able to leave. Working with urgency, Boas went to Washington, D.C., to meet with officials at the State Department where, in Jesup's name, he pulled all possible strings. He touched base with Andrew White, the United States's representative in Berlin, but first reliance was put on the American minister to St. Petersburg, Ethan A. Hitchcock, who spoke with the interior minister. Ivan Goremykin remained immovable, replying in every instance "simply that it was against the law—to grant such request—Dr. Laufer being a German Jew—who were prohibited from entering Siberia." Vladimir Radlov of the Imperial Academy of Science accomplished what diplomats could not. He called on Grand Duke Constantine, who served as president of the Academy, and on the governor of Siberia, then in the capital. Suddenly, word reached New York that Laufer, by special permission of the Tzar, had been authorized to visit Sakhalin and the Amur River.[41] Laufer, waiting in Victoria where he had been sent should permission be granted, was aboard the next steamer. He arrived in Yokohama on May 23.

Laufer worked from July 1898 to March 1899 on the east coast of Sakhalin Island among the Gilyak (Nivkh), Tungus, and Ainu peoples. Field conditions were difficult. Travel was by horseback, reindeer sledge, and dog sled. For two and a half months he was ill with influenza that turned to pneumonia. He could find no interpreter for his ethnological work: no Gilyak knew more than the most common Russian phrases and the Ainu were not very familiar with Japanese. Having traveled down the east coast of the island, he returned north in time to cross the ice to the mainland before the spring breakup. Here he settled at Khabaravsk on the Amur to study Grube's Gold (Nanai). With the spring thaw, he journeyed downstream, stopping at various Gold and Gilyak villages until he reached the river mouth in August. By October he had finished the season, traveling over Valdivostok to Yokohama, where he spent the remaining weeks of 1899 packing his collection before sailing for New York.[42] Boas found his huge assemblage of art and artifacts exceptionally interesting. So too was Laufer himself. "I take a great interest in the young fellow," he wrote, looking forward to Laufer's February arrival "as if he were my own young brother." Once in the city, he became the Boases' frequent guest, often for dinner twice a week. "It is amusing," Boas commented, "to see how my earlier feelings return with this young fellow. He told me today that he wanted to tear up all his Siberian work and begin it all over again." That, Boas observed, was just the same as he had been with the Baffin Island research.[43]

Laufer's Siberian difficulties paled before those of the Jesup Expedition's northern researchers. Boas had problems even finding someone for the job. He had initially been in touch with Freiherr Erwin von Zach, an Austrian studying in Leiden. Boas was impressed by his credentials and engaged him in May 1897, only to have the arrangement collapse in August. There were doubts about von Zach's ability to endure Siberian hardships, but Boas blamed Leiden museum director J. D. E. Schmeltz for the Austrian's withdrawal.[44] Boas then sought advice from V. V. Radlov, who later helped in Laufer's visa problem. Radlov recommended two experienced Siberian field workers, Waldemar Jochelson and Waldemar Bogoras.[45] In Germany in the summer of 1898, he met with Radlov and Jochelson and confirmed arrangements for the two Russians, who, after making equipment purchases, sailed to New York to receive Boas's instructions and tutoring in anthropometrics. Boas found them "very curious" men, "so different" in personality from western Europeans. Marie did not particularly like either, in part because they kept Franz up late in the evenings, and everything was put on hold at home "until the Russians go."[46] They left late in March 1900 for San Francisco, Nagasaki, and Vladivostok.

Siberia was familiar territory to both men. Their experience there was initially as political exiles, their friendship cemented in a common attachment to the *Narodnaya Volya* or Peoples' Will, a radical populist group that did not shirk from violence. Both used their exile to study the local indigenes, avocations that became a profession. Jochelson, the older of the two, had spent three years in isolated confinement before being transferred to Yakutsk, and later the mouth of the Kolyma on the Arctic

Ocean.[47] He subsequently worked with Yukaghirs on the Imperial Geographical Society's expedition. Bogoras, with the Sibiryakov expedition, did research on the Chukchi and Lamut (Even) that he was now seeing through the press. At the time of his engagement, Jochelson was registered for a doctoral program in Switzerland where his wife was studying medicine, but was willing to interrupt their work.[48]

The Jochelson-Bogoras expedition can only be described as heroic. Arriving in Vladivostok in May 1900, the party split with the Bogorases going to Marinsky Post on the Anadyr River, the most remote Russian settlement in northeast Asia. After studying the Reindeer and Maritime Chukchi and the Asiatic Eskimo Ai'wan group, Bogoras traveled in midwinter to work among the Kamchatka Koryak, to the west coast of the Kamchatka peninsula to collect material from the Kamchadal, then after more study of Koryak and Chukchi, to St. Lawrence Island in the Bering Strait. He returned to Anadyr by Native boat, a voyage of twenty-eight days, to meet his wife, who had remained there to make collections between Marinsky Point and Markova. They left in August for Vladivostok by steamer and, after shipping their collections to New York, returned to St. Petersburg by rail. Illness delayed their departure to New York, the couple arriving only in April 1902.

Jochelson and his wife, Dina Jochelson-Brodskya, had an even more difficult trip. Half of the winter was spent among the Maritime Koryak in underground dwellings filled with smoke, stench, and lice. The other half was among the interior camps of the Reindeer Koryak in bitter cold. They had to search out the Koryak, who had fled to the mountains to escape a measles epidemic. That necessitated a difficult trek by horse across the boggy tundra. Summer boat trips to Tungus and Maritime Koryak groups were accompanied by privation. The Jochelsons stayed on, as planned, for another year to study the Yukaghir of the Kolyma region. That required a difficult fifty-six-day trip across unmapped mountains to famine-plagued villages, then on to Yakutsk, before returning to St. Petersburg via Irkutsk in the summer of 1902. They had traveled some 8,000 miles by foot, sled, boat, and horse.[49]

Boas himself went west in 1900, the fourth year of the Jesup Expedition. As usual, he stopped in Chicago, where he was greeted in the street by Donaldson supported on two canes. Trees now shaded Hedwig's pansy-covered grave.[50] His field season in British Columbia was relatively simple: six days with Teit in the Nicola Valley and then two full months in Alert Bay.

Teit had proven the treasure that Boas had anticipated at their first meeting in 1894. At that time Teit, age thirty, had been in British Columbia for twelve years. Raised in Lerwick on the Shetland Islands, he had left school at sixteen, then two years later joined an uncle who ran a store in Spences Bridge. Teit was soon drawn into the Native world: within three years of his arrival he was living with Lucy Antko, a Thompson woman, whom he officially married in 1892. He made his living by a variety of frontier occupations: packing, guiding, freighting, and as a big-game hunting guide. By the time Boas met him, Teit was already seriously studying the Indians around him. By 1900, he had finished, in addition to several small pieces, a volume of texts on the Thompson and manuscript ethnologies of the Upper and Lower Thompson Indians, which were now in press as a Jesup Expedition publication.[51]

Boas's purpose in meeting Teit on this trip was largely to take physical measurements of the Indians south of Spences Bridge. Boas, soon stiff and sore, rode with Teit from village to village on the horse familiar from the Bella Coola trek, then survived the eight-hour, forty-one mile return to Teit's home. Furnished with only a table, two chairs, and a bed, the one-room cabin was filled with books about Indians and the Shetlands. "Mr. Teit can give us all an example of great industry and of the unassuming fulfillment of duty," Boas wrote his children.[52] After looking through Teit's notes, Boas boarded the train for Vancouver and then the boat to Alert Bay.

At Alert Bay he enjoyed comfortable accommodation with the Spencers and had the daytime use of a small cabin where he could work with the Kwakiutl. He found a good interpreter for the language in William Brotchie and a painter to explain details of the art. Older men came by to tell him stories, and he sought out recipes and information on food preparation and medicines from the women. The sole difficulty was that Hunt was kept busy in Spencer's cannery and so, for most of the time, he could help Boas only evenings and Sundays.

It was during this Jesup Expedition period that the collaboration between Boas and Hunt solidified. Although Boas had worked with Hunt since 1888, most particularly for the World's Fair and then at Fort Rupert in the winter of 1894–95, and Hunt had been sending him Kwakiutl stories, Boas never had full confidence in him. At both Chicago and Fort Rupert he had found Hunt "hard to deal with" and "too lazy to use his brain." In 1897, however, Hunt had come to Bella Coola and prepared things well for Boas's arrival. He did find Hunt "unbelievably clumsy" with the Rivers Inlet dialect of Kwakwala, but he had time to improve Hunt's general orthography.[53]

At this time Hunt was forty-three years old and had been assisting government officials, missionaries, and anthropological collectors since interpreting for the Royal Navy in 1877. The son of an English-born Hudson's Bay Company employee and his high-born Tlingit wife, he grew up in Fort Rupert, where his father was normally the only white man. Although he could not consider himself Kwakiutl, he was raised virtually as one. There was little question of his knowledge of the Fort Rupert language. He was an initiate in the Hamatsa, the highest Kwakiutl dance society, even acquired shaman credentials, and certainly suffered a penalty for participating in a cannibal ceremony. (He was acquitted of the charge, but the trial cost him more than $400.)[54] He twice married high-born Kwakiutl and raised his large family within Indian society. His occupations in fishing and canning were those usual to an Indian, though often at a more responsible level. On the other hand, he was the son of a European father (though one who had gone rather native), and several of his sisters married Whites, one to S. A. Spencer, the trader and cannery owner in Alert Bay. Hunt may have been more "lazy" intellectually than Boas would have liked, but what distinguished him, as much as anything else, from the Kwakiutl around him was his literacy. His spelling was uncertain, but his writing was clear and his style plain. He was never a comfortable writer, but he did not avoid it.

The collaboration was not always easy. The Kwakiutl were among the most conservative of Northwest Coast groups and became easily suspicious of what Boas and his Fort Rupert collaborator were doing. At the very beginning of the Jesup Expedition Boas gave Hunt money for a feast and sent a letter for him to read to the assembled Kwakiutl of Fort Rupert. In it he flattered the people and praised his own efforts on their behalf, especially in trying to show "to the white men in Victoria that your feasts and your potlatches are good . . . that your ways are not bad ways." It was a shame, he went on, that the old laws were not obeyed by the children and that many young men did not know the history and stories of their people. He himself knew more than did the Kwakiutl children for he kept their laws and stories in a box where they would not be forgotten. "Friends, it would be good if my friend, George Hunt, would become the storage box of your laws and your stories."[55]

The feast and flattery seem to have worked, but misunderstandings were easily created. Hunt was in difficulty the next year, for example, with the Alert Bay Kwakiutl, who, Hunt reported, said of him, "here is he Who is finding out all our Dances then gos and tell it to Dr. Boas." Hunt's detractors claimed that Boas wrote that the Hamatsa still ate human flesh. Even in Spencer's store Hunt was attacked for a picture of a Hamatsa mask that Boas had published to explain the dances and rites. The same year Harlan Smith and his new wife, Helena, gave interviews to the Victoria press after having been guests of Hunt's sisters in Fort Rupert. Mrs. Smith reportedly said some quite unflattering things about Sarah and Jane Hunt: "the names she called them there I am shame to talk about." Hunt was no longer being spoken to by his sisters, who retaliated further by informing the Indians that Smith had also collected skulls: they had told "the Indians What Mr. Smith Done to there Daid, and that I was Helping them." Smith would never be allowed to come to Fort Rupert again. If all this was not enough, Chief Hamasaka had heard during a visit to Victoria that Boas had said that everything around the world was changing for the better except for the Kwakiutl, who were "still living on the Daid People." Poor Hunt had been summoned to a feast and there flatly informed that "they Dont want you or me to see the Dance of any kind again." Things were quite desperate: "I have know friend Even Mr Spencer and sisters are against me now. . . . the only thing I am wishing for is for my life Be spared."[56]

Boas acted immediately to quell the discontent and to protect his sources and his own reputation. He sent another letter to Hunt to read to the chiefs at a feast he would pay for and enclosed portions of his writing which refuted the calumny spread against him. Boas could not understand what could be said against the Smiths unless it came from meddlesome newsmen twisting things for excitement. He wrote Chief Hamasaka to deny that he had ever said the Kwakiutl still lived on the dead. "I do not say what is not true." The Kwakiutl, Boas insisted, "have no better friend than I," adding, "wherever I can, I speak for you." He had many times told the chiefs in Ottawa and in England that the potlatches and dances were not bad.[57] The affair seems to have blown over.

Boas occasionally felt obliged to keep his collaborator up to the mark. "I thought you were going to send me a lot of stuff before the close of December," he wrote early in 1901. "I suppose that you are doing your work all right, only you must keep me informed more fully as to what you are doing." He could not get money to continue Hunt's work "unless I can show results of your labors." The irritation continued when no word arrived. Boas suspected lethargy and curtly informed Hunt that "I beg to remind you that under our present arrangement you must continue to collect." Hunt's next shipment of artifacts reassured him since it contained what Boas regarded as the best old pieces yet obtained. Nevertheless, he insisted "you must do your level best to send to the Museum material enough to justify our continued expenses in this direction." The pressures were fierce if Hunt were to keep his $75 a month salary. He accepted the challenge: "I am going to try to get all I can to Pleas you and the Museum this year."[58]

By 1900, Boas was satisfied with Hunt and his command of language and tradition. His experience with him that summer, when he was able to check Hunt's versions against Brotchie's, confirmed Hunt's ability. "I find him quite dependable, more than I had thought."[59] While retaining minor reservations about Hunt's linguistic idiosyncrasies, his tendency toward an older, more formal style, even his command of Kwakwala grammar, Boas felt confident of Hunt's material. Boas would employ Hunt in "epistolary ethnography" for the rest of the man's life.[60]

Boas left Alert Bay and British Columbia satisfied. He had a much clearer understanding of the "terribly difficult" Kwakwala language and was now, after working with Hunt in 1897 and this summer, in a position to publish many of the texts he had been collecting for six years. He thought he also had enough material for a detailed description of the manners and customs of the Kwakiutl. "That," he wrote, "will make a very peculiar cultural picture."[61] He arrived at Lake George on September 19 for a week with Marie and the children before returning to his teaching and museum work.

Boas's 1900 trip was virtually the last on the American side of the Jesup Expedition. Hunt and Teit would work in their own areas over the next two years, but the only visitor was John R. Swanton, whom Boas had assigned to the Queen Charlotte Islands. Swanton was a Putnam student, not an uneducated protégé, but a well-trained Harvard Ph.D. who had done his linguistic training under Boas at Columbia. Swanton, now working for the Bureau of American Ethnology, which paid his salary on this trip while the American Museum paid expenses, was instructed to study the Haida language, religion, and social organization while he collected specimens for the museum.[62] Swanton left much of the artifact collecting to the Victoria doctor turned museum collector, C. F. Newcombe, while he concentrated on language and ethnology.

The research portion of the Jesup Expedition ended in 1902, though Boas sought to fill in and round out parts of it after that. Hunt continued to work on the coast, gathering texts and other information and collecting objects for the museum, not only from the Kwakiutl but also from the Nootka. Teit labored on among the Interior groups, collecting material for later volumes on the Lillooet and Shuswap ethnologies and Thompson myths. Otherwise, field activities for Mr. Jesup's great expedition were over when the Jochelsons arrived in Irkutsk late in the summer of 1902.[63]

12 "A Certain Work Lies Before Me Here"

ORGANIZING ANTHROPOLOGY

IN NEW YORK

Jesup's support of the North Pacific Expedition had settled Boas's mind about his future. The same year the expedition was launched, 1897, the Bureau of American Ethnology had asked him to take charge of its language division at a salary matching his New York one. He was uninterested. The five years of projected Jesup fieldwork and the anticipated publications meant that he could not leave New York. "I told Mr. Jesup," he wrote Putnam, "that this expedition practically tied me to the Museum . . . and I consider that a certain work lies before me here, that I want to do."[1] Moreover, the immensity of the plan confirmed the potential of Jesup's museum as a vehicle for Boas's research ambitions and whetted his appetite for more.

The great North Pacific Expedition was but one project incubating in Boas's fertile mind. His ambition did not stop with the North Pacific, even when extended to Siberia. North Pacific groups were not the only ones threatened by railways and settlement. Everywhere in western North America the inexorable process of Euro-American expansion was threatening the native Indians, destroying their cultures, their languages, and their physical existence. California, with a variety of linguistic groups that exceeded in complexity even his own area, the Northwest Coast, was a region of particular concern, but so too was Oregon, the Indian Territory, indeed, the whole of the western plains and plateau. He discussed the problem of the "vanishing tribes" of the West with Putnam and now, in March 1897, just at the time Jesup had taken up the North Pacific project, raised it with the museum president, promising a proposal in the fall. It was a start. Together with the Jesup Expedition, his projected "Vanishing Tribes of North America" meant that Boas would discard any Washington temptation, any dissatisfaction he had with New York. If this proposed research on the vanishing tribes was carried out, "it would be another thing that would hold me to NY because I was heart and soul in for it."[2]

Boas's formal proposal for western American work came almost a year later, in March 1898. His emphasis was on the urgency of work, on the duty of the present generation to collect information before it passed away. "It is only a question of a few years, when every thing reminding us of America as it was at the time of its discovery will have perished," he wrote. "Our generation is the last that will be able to collect the data which will form the basis of the early history of America." Boas listed eleven western states containing ninety-five tribes that demanded attention. Each tribal investigation would require an expenditure of about $5,000, in work that would continue over twenty-five years. The proposal was, like most of Boas's plans, grandiose in scope. "I am modest," he wrote home, "I want to have $296,000."

With Boas busy preparing his Siberian expedition and then away that summer in Germany, it was almost another year before he renewed the assault. He met in January 1899 with Jesup and Henry Villard, the latter promising to try to raise $50,000. Though Villard could contribute nothing himself that year, he did get western railway magnate C. P. Huntington to give $1,000 toward California work. In May Jesup told Boas that he would give $1,000 (it actually came from Mrs. Jesup). Boas was thus able to despatch Harvard student Roland Dixon to northern California's Maidu Indians and his Columbia student Alfred Kroeber to the Arapaho in the Indian Territory. Dixon's results were so satisfying that he could reasonably count on Huntington to continue the California work. "If that succeeds, the future of anthropology in New York is certain."[3]

At the end of the first season, Boas renewed his proposal to Jesup for a twenty-five-year project, this time devoted exclusively to the diverse tribes of California and projected to cost some $260,883. "I am fully aware of the vastness of this undertaking, but I believe that with due foresight and caution the results obtained will be of such magnitude as to amply justify the great expenditure involved." The salvage imperative remained his most compelling argument: "Later generations will have the most urgent desire to know the beginnings of the history of our country, and they will owe a debt of deep gratitude to him who enables us to preserve this knowledge, which, without a great effort on the part of our own generation, will be lost forever." Huntington's and Mrs. Jesup's money continued in the following year, but the total did not grow, though Villard added $1,000 for work in Oregon, where Boas sent Farrand.[4]

A setback came in 1900 with the deaths of both Huntington and Villard. This was a great loss. Except for Jesup's, theirs was the only help Boas had received. "It won't be easy to replace them," he wrote. The

Huntington family continued support to complete Dixon's work and the publication of his results, but Boas was unsuccessful in securing the same from Mrs. Villard or her son, Oswald Garrison. The Vanishing Tribes work, taken up so energetically two years earlier, he told Jesup in April 1901, was now "sadly lacking." He saw no reason to reiterate the urgency of the undertaking, merely stating that "we shall never be able to present a decent Indian collection if we do not push forward this work." The project was now at a standstill and yet in no other department of the museum, he wrote, "must the work be pushed more energetically on account of the rapid disappearance of the material."[5]

Jesup found no new benefactors, but Boas, now named as honorary philologist to the Bureau of American Ethnology, was able to secure from Washington $2,000 for linguistic work. The person who collected the language material could also collect specimens for the museum, so that summer Boas could send students William Jones to the Sac and Fox of the upper Mississippi and H. H. St. Clair to the Wyoming Shoshone. By then he had found an additional justification. Not only was the material vanishing day by day, but the Field Columbian Museum was spending an enormous amount on North American collecting and the University of Pennsylvania's Wannamaker expeditions were in the field. Though dissatisfied with the stagnation ("everything is going bad with my rich people"), Boas was able to place nine people in the field.[6]

The Huntington heirs continued to support Dixon's California work, now largely on the Shasta. Boas put another student, Clark Wissler, among the South Dakota Sioux (paid for by Jesup) while Jones continued working on the Fox, Ojibwa, and Menominee, St. Clair among the Comanche and Shoshone, with Farrand again in the Northwest to work on the Sahaptian stock, and Constance Goddard DuBois among California's Mission Indians. In 1903 the competition argument became stronger. Private collectors and dealers were buying up ethnological objects and the Brooklyn Institute had initiated a general collecting enterprise, while Chicago continued its western collecting. Boas succeeded in getting $5,000 from the museum, another $1,000 from the Berlin museum (in return for specimens), and BAE money, enough to place Wissler, St. Clair, Jones, and Harvard student Howard B. Wilson in the field and further support the work of Hunt and Teit. In the next year, 1904, Archer M. Huntington decided he had fulfilled the obligations of his dead father. That meant that Boas could spare only $200 for Dixon to round off his California work. On the other hand, Boas used BAE money to send Frank

Speck to the Uchee in Oklahoma. And so it went, a constant struggle to put students in the field to meet the urgent needs of Boas's salvage agenda.[7]

As if the Jesup Expedition and the Vanishing Tribes projects were not enough for Boas, he incubated yet another. Although he disliked the jingoism and imperialism of the Spanish-American War, he was prepared to use the country's new Asian interest to forward his own ambitions. As early as November 1898, he was looking for people qualified to work in the Philippines,[8] but he began pushing an East Asian project earnestly only in the spring of 1900.

He called for the establishment in New York of an Asian studies center based jointly at the American Museum and Columbia University. No such institution existed in the United States, yet "the ever-increasing importance of the relations between America and the countries and peoples of eastern Asia" made it highly desirable that Americans have a better knowledge of Asia. The importance of foreign trade to New York made it the logical place, and it possessed already, in Columbia, one of the best universities in the country. The most practical plan would be to send a young man with good training in Asian ethnology for two or three years to China and Japan to make collections of objects for the museum and literature for the university library. Then he would return to teach in the university. That would cost about $5,000 a year, with another $3,000 for a working library.[9]

Boas met with a number of business leaders in the spring of 1900, but his own western field trip, the illness of Everett Frazar, president of the American Asiatic Society, and Villard's death prevented further pursuit of the scheme until November. By then, the summer's Boxer Uprising had "made the matter even more urgent." Boas renewed his round of correspondence and contacts: Frazar, banker Edward D. Adams, John Foord of the *Journal of Commerce*, and William Barclay Parsons, chief engineer to the transit commission. The first serious interest came from Jacob Schiff of Kuhn, Loeb and Co. The financier was "much taken" with Boas's idea, "for even without being a territorial expansionist, one can readily see that if we wish to expand our commercial and industrial activities, we should know more than we do now of the customs &c. of the people with whom we desire to trade and come into closer contact." Initially Schiff agreed to donate $1,000 a year for three years if another $5,000 were pledged. When Columbia's president, Seth Low, objected to a financial campaign that would compete with his own for covering the university's deficit, Schiff decided to provide the entire $6,000 a year himself. That was enough for Boas to dispatch Laufer the next July to China with instructions to collect industrial and domestic products.[10]

The expedition to China was but stage one. The Jesup Expedition, Boas wrote in a long letter to his acquaintance, Zelia Nuttall, had given him a "first foothold outside our continent." That step was followed by the Chinese enterprise, and he had plans for "successive steps." Boas's Chinese expedition was thus part of a more general plan that moved him from China and the Philippines into Malaya, the East Indies and even Africa. "This is a great undertaking, which will take several years and ample means to accomplish; and I do not believe that work worthy of our people and worthy of this city could be done at an expenditure of less than $100,000." The magnitude of the task "should not deter us from its execution, which may well be said to be a patriotic duty." By August he was writing about developing studies of India, Tibet, Arabia, and Persia as well.[11]

The Jesup Expedition, the Vanishing Tribes project, and the East Asian venture were Boas's major museum preoccupations, but he did not neglect any possibility for increasing the museum's collections. He attempted an arrangement with missionary societies, particularly in the Far East, to obtain African material, especially that which would represent high points of African culture, such as Benin bronzes and ironworking. Nor did Boas neglect opportunities related to his first anthropological love, the Eskimo.

When he joined the museum in late 1896, a family of Labrador Eskimos were in New York, virtually abandoned at the museum by the man who had brought them. Together with Putnam and Smith, Boas raised funds for their passage home, though one, Esther, married a New Yorker and remained, working on display at a Coney Island sideshow. That year, too, he asked Commander Robert Peary, departing for yet another assault on the pole, to try and bring back material from Smith Sound to add to his current collection at the New York museum. Boas renewed the request the following year, again suggesting that the polar adventurer might also return with a middle-aged Eskimo to assist with describing the collection. Peary did more than that. He returned in September 1897 with six Greenlanders. They were domiciled in the museum's basement when Boas returned in October from his British Columbia field season.

Responsibility for the six fell to the museum staff. "Although I am not formally responsible," Boas wrote (it is unclear that anyone was), "the whole thing falls on my shoulders and I feel a stone around my heart."[12] Almost inevitably, the visitors fell victim to colds that turned to pneumonia. Four died before the end of May. One returned to Greenland with Peary in July, but the orphaned, seven-year-old Minik was left in the care of building superintendent William Wallace, who more or less adopted the boy. His life has been compellingly told elsewhere,[13] but the chronicle involved Boas too.

When Qisuk, Minik's father, died on February 17, 1898, the remaining Eskimos were told he was buried according to traditional custom on the museum grounds. Indeed, young Minik was there to witness as the wrapped body of his father was covered with stones, and the boy himself marked the earth to the north of the grave. What none of the Eskimos, not even Minik, knew was that the whole ceremony was faked.

Qisuk's body was not under the stone cairn. It had been left first at the dissecting room at the hospital, where Qisuk's brain was preserved in spirits and his bones sent to the museum for cleaning and mounting. The burial deception had gone without a hitch and the later deaths, which required no mortuary ceremony, brought three more skeletons to the osteological collections of the anthropology department. There would have been no problem had not young Minik remained in New York to grow up as the adopted Mene Wallace. Only in 1906 or so, as a sixteen-year-old, did he learn from friends that his father's body was not where he thought it was. He was understandably shocked and demanded, through his foster father, who had by now been dismissed for misappropriation of funds, the return of his father's body and personal possessions. "Give Me My Father's Body" headlined the New York *World* in January 1907.

Museum Director H. C. Bumpus dodged and procrastinated. No restitution occurred. Boas, by then no longer on the museum staff, made no apologies for the winter twilight's fakery of 1898. The phony ceremony had been held, so he was quoted by the *Evening Mail*, "to appease the boy, and keep him from discovering that his father's body had been chopped up and the bones placed in the collection of the institution." (The words, of course, are not Boas's.) The other Eskimos had not been well and it was only reasonable to spare them and Minik any shock or unease, a purpose that the mock burial accomplished. Boas saw nothing "particularly deserving of severe criticism," and the museum's possession of the body was perfectly legitimate since there was no one to bury the body, Minik being just a boy. The affair fit with an air of ruthlessness in bone collecting that Boas had demonstrated in the field.[14]

Boas otherwise had little to do with the Greenland Eskimo. He had assigned Farrand and Kroeber to work on their myths and language, the latter spending time with the Eskimo over the winter and acquiring enough information for an article. Aleš Hrdlička published an anthropometric article and a somewhat macabre piece on Qisuk's brain.[15] Boas used the opportunity to arrange a museum life group, demonstrating Eskimo home life.

Nonetheless Boas's interest in the Eskimo did not subside, though the museum's future collections from the area would be artifactual and not osteological. In 1903 he secured authorization for his old northern friends, Jimmy Mutch and George Comer, to collect in the Arctic. They obliged with rich and well-documented material, abundant enough for Boas to issue two volumes of descriptive material culture. Linguistic work continued under BAE auspices, with William Thalbitzer, a Danish scholar whom Boas had visited in Copenhagen in 1904, contributing a chapter for the *Handbook of American Indian Languages*.[16]

Boas's plans for the New York museum's anthropological department, though awesome, were consistent with his ambitions since setting foot in America. His role as entrepreneurial fund-raiser, however, was new. Of course, he had scouted for funds for his Baffin Island trip, negotiated free transportation for his first British Columbia trip, and found money from various agencies for his "jobs," but fund-raising from private benefactors on this scale was rather different. He seemed to take to it easily. Many of the contacts came through Villard, but he quickly built on these, in large part within New York's German-American community, of which both Villard and Schiff were members. Raising money became a constant burden, but his ambitions committed him to it. "The eternal plan to dig up money often makes me very sorry," he wrote, but it was necessary and he was tenacious.[17]

Contributors were also essential for the *American Anthropologist*, another venture in which Boas played a leading role. At the AAAS meetings in Ithaca in 1897, he had been appointed chair of a committee to consider a new anthropological journal. Composed of Brinton, McGee, and others, the committee met at Philadelphia in February 1898, where the outline of the proposed journal, a national successor to the Anthropological Society of Washington's existing *American Anthropologist*, was sketched out. The essential details were concluded in December, and a publishing contract signed with G. P. Putnam and Sons. Boas and McGee became partners in the ownership of the new quarterly, equally responsible for financial loss (any profit was to be held in trust). The experienced Frederick Webb Hodge of the BAE was editor, but much of the work fell upon Boas. The first number appeared in March 1899. Handsome in appearance and impressive in content, the beginning was auspicious. Maintaining it was another thing.

Hodge confessed that "to fill 200 pages with first-rate matter each quarter is no child's play."[18] Even more difficult were the finances. Boas had estimated a $300 deficit for the first year; the actual overrun was closer to $1,000. That sent him scrambling for donors. He solicited gifts from Charles P. Bowditch, Joseph F. Loubat, and Augustus Hemenway. The next year George Dorsey scouted out money from Marshall Field and Edward Ayer, and most of the previous year's contributors came along again, but the deficit was kept manageable only by Boas's own donations of $450 and $273. By February 1901, Boas was doubtful of the journal's future. "I do not feel that I want to take the responsibility of the journal any longer than the present year, and unless we can get some support, I am afraid the undertaking will be a failure." He did carry on, obtaining articles, finding new sponsors, and doing whatever else he could to sustain the quarterly (including another $300 personal contribution). By the end of 1902, however, the journal was "in a very precarious condition" with an estimated accumulated debt of $1,369.61.[19] Subscriptions remained at about 400. The new American Anthropological Association, established in 1902, decided to assume full responsibility the next year. The *American Anthropologist*, fragile though its finances were, was immediately successful as a scholarly journal, carrying excellent articles, many of them by Boas's students and associates. Bogoras, Kroeber, Farrand, and Wissler were contributors to the first numbers.

Among the means that Boas used to keep the *American Anthropologist* alive was a revived American Ethnological Society, the New York organization which dated back to 1842 and which he had unsuccessfully tried to co-opt in the winter of 1887–88. His own Anthropology Club, occasionally meeting evenings and composed mostly of Columbia and American Museum people, had been thriving since 1896, and he used this and AES members Bickmore, Saville, and Jesup as vehicles for a friendly takeover of the "almost defunct" society. The resurrected AES provided $230 in subscriptions to the *American Anthropologist*, and a further $125 came through the New York Academy of Science (another Boas initiative).[20]

Boas's first five years in New York were going well: the Jesup Expedition, the Vanishing Tribes project, and the East Asia scheme were all launched. He had reinvented the American Ethnological Society and was prime mover in beginning a national anthropology journal. By then, too, his one dissatisfaction with his New York career, his position at Columbia, had been overcome.

Columbia, under the presidency of Seth Low, had been undergoing an immense transformation at the time of Boas's arrival at the American Museum. In 1897 it abandoned its downtown site for an extensive new campus on Morningside Heights, at the same time becoming a university and introducing a new curriculum. For a private institution dependent on donations and endowments, the up-island move, coming at the end of a general financial depression, put its budget under great strain.

Putnam's 1895 overtures for Boas's joint appointment had been welcomed by college officials, especially by Nicholas Murray Butler, the influential dean of the philosophy faculty. Butler had already received suggestions from faculty to appoint Boas as a professor in anthropology, but the college's financial position had permitted no action. Later that year, however, Butler, describing Boas as "one of the most competent Anthropologists now living" and one whose "reputation is secure," endorsed a joint appointment with the museum.[21] The recommendation, however, came too late for the 1895–96 academic year. The failure of Columbia to appoint Boas brought Jacobi to the secret guarantee of half of Boas's salary and, thus, ensure his museum appointment.

President Low overcame his financial reluctance and agreed to propose Boas's appointment for 1896–97. "The Museum of Natural History is very earnest in its desire to keep Dr. Boas in New York," he wrote Dean Butler, and so his trustees might be willing to make the appointment. "Except for this, I should be sure they would not." The one-year appointment was only as a lecturer, and Low made clear that he could not guarantee it would be continued. Indeed, Low almost dropped the appointment the next winter, telling Jesup that his budget could not sustain it and requesting that the museum pick up the full payment. Jesup refused, partly because Putnam had kept him unaware of the provisional character of the initial Columbia appointment, more persuasively because the museum's budget had already been approved, a deficit budget that required the trustees to cover it by subscription. Under these circumstances, Columbia agreed to continue its share of Boas's salary "as long as we can."[22] Boas's Columbia appointment was never again so precarious. The following year the university even raised its portion of his salary from $1,500 to $2,000.[23] The appointment, however, remained an annual one at the rank of lecturer.

Boas was by now weary of the condition. He had assumed from the first that he soon would have the rank and salary of a professor and became increasingly frustrated at the delay in receiving it. He was more aggravated that, as a lecturer, he was not a member of faculty and thus had no influence on policy and curriculum. He made a major pitch, again through Jacobi, but the result was only the salary increase: "One has to take what one could get." At least his total salary, now $4,000, was equivalent to a professor's, but the whole question had become tiring. That summer of 1898 he received an overture from the University of Vienna. Although Boas did not allow the enquiry to develop into an offer, the Vienna professorship only increased his dissatisfaction with Columbia. "I am sick and tired of this annual bargaining and will try finally to get a secure position." Jesup, impressed by the Austrian invitation, was sympathetic, but Low remained unwilling to assume a permanent commitment of $2,500 a year.[24] Suddenly, however, the situation changed. On February 16 Jesup congratulated Boas on his professorship.

The agent behind the alteration was, once again, Jacobi. He had written to Low with an offer to pay $2,500 toward Boas's professorial salary for two years. His sole condition was "that Dr. Boas should never know of this correspondence." The recipient of the anonymous gift was not entirely in the dark. Boas had heard, accidently, from his niece, Nandi Meyer, that Putnam had called on Jacobi to discuss his professorship. The thought that Jacobi should still be assuming financial responsibility at this time in his life was painful. A direct word with his uncle was inconclusive: Jacobi, "in his redeeming way, declined all responsibility." That had to settle the matter. "I can do nothing about it except to make the most of the opportunity."[25] The professorship, though not in the happiest of circumstances, was at long-last settled. He was just approaching age forty-one.

With the promotion came a raise to $5,000 annually. He had begun in 1896 with $3,000, a sum too little to cover his needs. He was already 6,000 marks in debt to his father and had to borrow from Kobus to cover the initial expenses of settling in New York—school fees, furniture freight, rent, coal—which came simultaneously with his quarterly life insurance premium. His 1897 salary was about $600 less than expenses and so had to be supplemented by lecture and article fees. By 1898 his costs outstripped even his increased salary by about $1,000. He had never expected to have the income of a successful businessman or physician, but he did want enough to live comfortably and without worry.[25] The professorship helped, but his salary was a continuing concern.

Home life in the city had settled into as much a routine as his income and a growing family allowed. The 82nd Street house, shared with Mother Krackowizer, was too small for their needs. They sorely missed a proper parlor and a guestroom, but its convenience to the museum was priceless. In fine weather, Marie and the children often met Boas at the museum for a stroll through Central Park before going home to dinner. They were tempted to look for a bigger house further north, around 145th Street, where rents were more affordable, but kept staying year after year in the narrow three-story brownstone.[27]

They faced a financial crisis in August 1899 when it appeared that Mrs. Krackowizer would move out. The problem was the children. Marie and Franz, but particularly Franz, gave them latitude to play in the living room and to chatter and laugh at the table. The tumult had long been a sore point between the elder Krackowizer and the Boases. The crisis blew over, partly through a reorganization of the quarters with Mrs. Krackowizer moving from the second floor to the front half of the third. She finally left in late 1902, moving to an apartment hotel nearby, but by then Boas's salary had increased so he could manage the loss of rent. The readjustment gave them a little more room, all the more needed after the birth of Gertrude Marianne ("Trudel") in April 1897 and in February 1899 of "Heine," named for Henry Herbert Donaldson. Marie wanted no more children,[28] but a year and a half later, in January 1902, Marie Franziska arrived. Each child prompted Franz to purchase more life insurance, eventually increasing his policy to $18,000, which also raised the premiums to $540 a year.

The demands of a growing household were not always easy. After 1899, they hired an afternoon tutor/sitter for Helene and Ernst, then eleven and eight. One of Miss Patton's duties was to help with the children's English, long neglected because of Franz's concern for their German. He was proud that they spoke only German at home, in contrast to Willy Meyer's boy who could speak almost none. "When we hear them speaking English, they are mercilessly put into separate rooms." Like all children of their generation, the young Boases were victims of frequent illness. Tonsillitis was an almost constant complaint of one or another. The babies were in greatest danger, Heine from bronchitis early in 1899, Trudel from dysentery later the same year. They had a doctor in six times to treat her. "What fright one has with little children!"[29]

Franz saw his children too little with his professional preoccupations. The younger ones were often in bed when he got home, but he did read to the older ones after dinner. In the fall of 1898 they started on the Bible. By December they had reached the Ten Commandments, and when Franz read out "Thou shalt have no other gods but me," Ernst reacted with "Isn't he greedy!" After the children were all in bed, Franz and Marie usually sat together in his study. "Marie and I sit peacefully next to each other at my desk. She usually sews and I scribble."[30] On the couple's thirteenth wedding anniversary in 1900, the two older children put on a skit of events from their parents' lives. These included a dueling scene in which Helene struck Ernst's face precisely where Franz was scarred. "Aren't they fresh brats!" wrote their mother to his.[31]

An October 1900 photograph shows a contented family scene with Franz at the piano watched by a knickerbockered nine-year-old Ernst leaning on the easy chair and Helene, pig-tailed and twelve years old. Above hangs his Beethoven engraving and, just out of the lens's focus, Mozart. Marie sits on the corner sofa, behind the table on which stand photographs of Jacobi, an earlier family portrait, Sophie, Porta Westphalica, and a Northwest Coast model.

The extended family remained close. They saw Jacobi often, but less of Kobus than when they had lived downtown. Jule and Theo Meyer and Dele Meyer Smutney on Franz's side, sister Helene and brother Richard on Marie's, were seen frequently. An old student chum from Bonn lived in Hoboken, and Berthe Krüer, sister of Boas's lost friend Reinhard, worked as a nurse in New York.

These visits were part of a regular lifestyle. During their first years in New York, they typically went out to an opera or a concert. Hetty Damrosch, wife of impresario Frank Damrosch, was a friend of Marie's and passed along free tickets. As the family grew, their outings became more infrequent, though they often entertained family, friends, professional colleagues, and museum visitors.

The normal routine of the Boas household was affected by several events after 1899. Heine's birth had been on February 2, Boas's professorship secured on February 16. Five days later, Jacobi stopped by with a telegram carrying the news of Meier Boas's death. The report, long feared and yet never quite expected, came at the end of an already terrible day. Baby Heine had developed bronchitis, then choking spells so severe that, had the nurse been any less able or the doctor come a minute later, he might have died. He stopped breathing, but the doctor succeeded in putting life back into the boy. Then came the news of Franz's father's death. The exhausted Marie was in bed when Jacobi came, and Franz refused to wake her. He was himself "stiff and dumb" at the news; no words would come from his pen. "Our dear *Alter*, how we will all miss him, but you, dear mother, the worst."[32] The coveted professorship now seemed meaningless; his father would never learn of it.

His father's death was not the only tragedy of these years. Willy and Lilly Meyer lost their eight-year-old daughter in February 1895, and Toni's baby, never well, died that October. Georg Bauer, the German mathematician at Clark and Chicago with whom the Boases had been very close, developed a nervous disorder, took leave to recover in Germany, then died there in 1898. Boas and Donaldson started a fund for Mrs. Bauer and the children, to which Boas contributed annually until her remarriage. "It is terrible to be an academic's widow," Boas wrote about her poverty, and that doubtless reinforced his own emphasis upon life insurance. Another blow was the death that year of Signa, his old friend and guide from Baffin Island. "Poor old Signa!" he wrote after getting Jimmy Mutch's report, "he was a great old fellow."[33]

Another long and sad story ended with the suicide of Gustav Ravenné in November 1900. Boas had met Ravenné, then seventeen, in 1884 while rooming with the youth's mother, who came from Stadthagen, near Minden. Boas thought Gustav a genius and kept in contact with the young man, who enrolled at Clark and house-sat their Worcester home in the summer of 1890. Thereafter, Ravenné's health and career went downhill. He was severely ill in 1892–93, without money or prospects. Boas had Meier find the man's Berlin relatives, who helped him temporarily. He then turned up at the elder Boas's Berlin flat in 1896. Boas wrote his parents of his admiration for the man, strongly endowed with scientific interest and talent, who had never let vicissitudes overtake his ideals. To George Foster, the director of the Berlin Observatory and his acquaintance of 1883, went a long letter of recommendation. But Ravenné neglected Sophie and Meier; worse, he was arrested for selling books stolen from the observatory library. Meier helped with his bond. Even that disgrace did not dampen Boas's loyalty. A few months later he helped Ravenné secure a temporary job at Columbia. When that ended, he was back at Worcester in 1899, taking courses but again penniless. He sought money from Boas, then, after some other irregularities, cashed a check forged on Boas's account. That finished the long relationship. Twenty months later, Boas received word that Ravenné had shot himself in Kansas. It was "a sad story."[34]

Boas's own health was sound. He maintained a steady weight, about 160 pounds, but his receding hairline indicated the end of his youth. He passed his fortieth birthday in 1898. He had some eye trouble in the summer of 1895 and again in March 1896. A muscle was constantly tense and thus became tired. Eyedrops largely solved the problem. At the same time he began to wear glasses, quite weak ones "almost like window glass." More aggravating were hemorrhoids, which caused him almost unbearable irritation during the winter of 1899–1900, disturbing even to his sleep. He went into Mt. Sinai Hospital for surgery in May, remaining there ten days. Putnam found him looking white and weak on leaving the hospital, and Boas, recuperating at Lake George, complained that, even three weeks after the operation, "it takes so long to regain my strength."[35] He recovered well enough to ride a horse for hours in British Columbia's interior a few weeks later.

The summer of 1896 was spent in Mother Krackowizer's Alma Farm cottage in New York. Boas was there through July, mostly relaxing in the hammock and reading French novels. "This time I do absolutely nothing. I do not think about Indians or ethnology." The following summer was taken up with his expeditionary work. Marie and the children went to Lake George, where they lived in a wing of her sister's house rather than staying at her mother's cabin. Boas wanted the children to have their full freedom.[36]

In 1898 he was granted paid leave from the museum to spend the summer in Europe. Leaving in mid-June, they stayed two weeks in Berlin, then Marie and the children went with his parents to Neu Brandenburg while he made a sweeping tour of museums—Dresden, Munich, Amsterdam, Haarlem, Leiden, London, Bremen, Hamburg, Brunswick, and Braunschweig—studying museum exhibition techniques and arranging exchanges and purchases. On the way back he spent two days at Minden and Porta Westfalica, amazed at the changes to his old hometown, how "everywhere, both in and outside the old city, people were building large houses á la Berlin." At the Porta he climbed up the hills, looking for where he had carved his name in a bench twenty-six years earlier and searching for the field of lady slippers he had known as a child. The bench was gone and the new Kaiser Wilhelm monument had obliterated the wildflowers. Such disappointments did not diminish the sweet nostalgia. "You cannot imagine," he wrote Marie, "what pleasure these days gave me." The remaining six weeks of his working holiday were split between Neu Brandenburg and his parents' new Berlin flat at 31 Winterfeldstrasse. They left in late September, the last time Franz would see his father.[37]

They were back at Lake George in 1899, this time at Jacobi's farm near Bolton. The rooms were small, but comfortable, and the house, some 500 feet above the water, had a view down the length of the lake. The next summer Franz was back in the field, the following in Germany where the family managed to fit in a month's stay at the Porta between another of Franz's tours of museum collections. The holiday was for old times' sake and because he wished his children to know this special place of his own childhood.

One mark of Boas's age was the end of his long succession of field trips. His 1900 Jesup Expedition season was, as he had long wished, his last for many years. He seriously contemplated a field summer in 1903, but changed his mind because a hectic winter made him want to "settle down and get some of my old notes worked out." He was "getting to be too old to be accumulating all the time and not work out my stuff." He did not visit the coast for another twenty-two years. He could now leave the basic work to his students. "My own activity in the field will shrink to finishing what I have begun," he wrote, "since I would rather leave further collecting in younger hands."[38] Farrand, Smith, Dixon, Kroeber, Swanton, and others could take to the field. Teit and Hunt would stay there; they could come to New York to help with their collaborations, but Boas was free from the long wilderness trips and isolation from his wife and children. The summers would now be reserved for family, either at Lake George or in Germany.

The field had its rewards and satisfactions, but field conditions were unpleasant, increasingly so to a man past his fortieth year. His first two trips, the year in the Arctic and the 1886 trip to the British Columbia coast, had been made as a young bachelor. Though arduous and lonely, they possessed the thrill of adventure and discovery. The western trips lost some of that thrill and were a great deal more lonely after he became a family man. In the first thirteen years of his marriage, he spent seven field seasons separated from Marie and their children. His 1888 trip kept him absent while Marie was in the sixth and seventh month of her first pregnancy; in 1889 his three-month absence made him miss Helene's first birthday, and in succeeding years he missed her second, third, and sixth. By 1897 he regarded his fieldwork as a "great, great sacrifice," especially as little Trudel, born only a month before he left, would be a stranger when he returned.[39] Little wonder that Boas, who hardly saw his children when he was at home, grew to hate the prolonged absences. Isolation could make the trips torturous.

Marie suffered at least as much, not because she missed the children but because she could not. After 1891 she had to cope with two children while Franz was away; in 1897 her burden became an eight-year-old Helene, a six-year-old Ernst, and a baby only one month old; in 1900, she had Helene (11), Ernst (9), Trudel (3), and Heine, at fourteen months. She was usually with her family, but for months at a time, she lived the life of a single parent—in an age when illnesses were frequent and frightening. After seeing Franz off in 1897, she found it terrible that he would be gone for four long months, and the two oldest realized for the first time that they would be without their father for a long while. "If only we all stay healthy." Fortunately they did, at least as "well and as happy as we can be without a husband and father." But, she said, "I do often wish there never had been an Indian!"[40]

It is not surprising that Boas, as some commentators have noted, did not go more frequently into the field or stay longer, but that, at some neglect to his first responsibility in life, he went so often and so long: eight times in fifteen years, including six of his first twelve as a father.[41]

Despite his growing dislike of these field trips, Boas thrived physically, always gaining weight and returning home tanned and revitalized. The fresh air and physical exercise did him good after the winter's museum routine. "In spite of all the hardships," wrote Marie, "these trips are always a restorative for him."[42]

In most of his fieldwork, he lived in the best available accommodation. This could be a comfortable room with the local storekeeper, though it might be a dirty-sheeted frontier hotel. He seldom stayed with Indians. He worked sometimes as a "participant," most often as an "observer." When he wished to study industries and daily life, he observed them, but he was more concerned with mythology, linguistics, art, and other questions best learned from an informant. When he found a good one, he "pumped him dry" and, when he found one who was reliably literate, he engaged him as an ongoing collaborator. Boas's fieldwork was therefore not just his own: it was as much Hunt's because of his continuing residence among the Kwakiutl, Teit's because of his roving knowledge of the interior groups, and Henry Tate's because of his later recording among the Tsimshian. The use of Natives and local collaborators to write ethnology was (and remains) a seldom-used method.[43]

Almost from the first, Boas had come to regard his New York work as generally "really satisfying." He was accomplishing something, and "that's the main thing."[44] His satisfaction greatly contrasted with the insulting treatment at Chicago and the subsequent despair over a secure position. It emerged after the 1896 AAAS meetings in Buffalo, the site of the same group's gathering during his first summer in America. He was gratified to note that in the intervening decade he had "won an influential position in our scholarly republic." Ten years before he had come as a guest, now he was on all the major committees and stood "right in the middle of official activity." Paul Topinard's praise that "with him American anthropology enters into a new phase" had given him great pleasure.[45] In early 1898 he received a Loubat prize for his monograph, "The Social Organization and the Secret Societies of the Kwakiutl Indians," though that honor was tarnished by being second to a monograph written by his rival, W. H. Holmes.

Boas's successes and satisfactions in these years came much less from his own work than from his ambitious organizational drive. His launch of the Jesup Expedition and other projects made his early years in New York a fulfilling and heady experience, diminished only by the ever inadequate salary and initial uncertainty of his status at Columbia. What kept him in America, he told the University of Vienna, "is a well-defined organizational activity." He hoped "to call into life a thorough investigation of the dying tribes and to build up ethnology to a recognized discipline in the university." In these two tasks he could "actually help our science." He had expended so much energy on these "that I may not step back from them until success is certain."[46]

The active museum acquisitions program combined with the expansion of the department into the west wing meant that cataloguing, fumigating, installing, and labeling—the basic preservation and exhibition functions of a museum—absorbed a large share of Boas's time and effort. Administration, both basic during Putnam's absences and creative in organizing the Jesup Expedition and other field researches, was a major commitment, as were the establishment of the *American Anthropologist* and the reestablishment of the American Ethnological Society. In addition was his teaching, usually six lectures a week. The teaching load

increased to eight or ten hours with the professorship, although the number of students was never large and some of the hours were done at the
museum. All of this meant, however, that he was able to do little of his
own work. "Nowadays Franz never gets to his writing," commented Marie
in 1897.[47]

One thing did lighten his load. That was the presence in his department of the invaluable Miss Andrews. Self-effacing to the point of virtual
invisibility, H. A. Andrews played a role that cannot be undervalued. A
Boston woman with whom he had worked at *Science* in his first years in
America, she came to the museum early in 1897, most likely at Boas's
prompting. A "mere" stenographer, she was his right hand, even his left,
until his death. She was, he put it, a "Schatz." Boas's amazing productivity
increasingly depended upon her efficiency as a typist, stenographer,
proofreader, editor, and office manager. Her obscure role in supporting
his career is inestimable.[48]

Boas's primary focus was the museum, but the Columbia connection
was vital in providing the trained students he needed for his museum
projects. Only Harvard and Columbia had programs that could give adequate professional education for the new generation of fieldworkers, and
the two cooperated in the work. Harvard doctoral students Dixon and
Swanton came to Boas to study linguistics, ethnology, and anthropometrics. Already in the summer of 1899 he had three students in the field, to
him "a resounding success." "If my activity continues to develop," he
wrote that year, "I will soon have an institute as large and as significant as
Washington's Bureau of Ethnology." He could not resist boasting. ("I
don't brag often, but today it just came out of my pen.") If his success continued, "almost all of the American ethnologists of the next generation
entirely or partly will come from my school." The next year, when he had
placed two former students in positions, Kroeber in California with the
Academy of Sciences and Swanton at the Bureau in Washington, he
returned to the theme. "If things go on in the same way, in ten years all
positions will be occupied by my students."[49]

His success was symbolized in 1900 when he was elected to the
National Academy of Science in an almost unanimous vote. "So I am now
officially a *great light.*" The Academy was, he acknowledged, a widely
regarded and enviable honor, though he downplayed his own election to
it. He had been chosen because he was not a member of any clique. Those
elected were, like McKinley to the American presidency, people without
enemies rather than necessarily the most distinguished. He would have

been even more pleased, perhaps, had he known that Holmes, also nominated that year, failed to achieve election. "Don't think me great," he told his mother. "Actually it is very easy to be one of the first among anthropologists over here." There were, just to name Berliners, no Ehrenreich, von den Steinen, or Seler in America and few like Grünwedel or Müller.[50]

His 1901 appointment as philologist to the Bureau was a result of his success and, by giving him $2,000 a year to hire students, consolidated it. "Like the old saying, he who has gets." Now Boas was "among the haves."[51] Yet he was, by his fourth year in New York, deeply dissatisfied.

13 "Nothing Has Worked Out— Or Only a Little" DISSATISFACTION

WITH THE AMERICAN MUSEUM

Boas FELT THINGS in the American Museum were not as they should be. The Jesup publications were a concern, progress on the Vanishing Tribes project was precarious, and the East Asian project seemed stalled at China, with even the Philippines stage uncertain. Lacking assistance in his ethnology division, a disproportionate amount of work fell upon Boas's shoulders. The enormous effort he had to spend on installation, labeling, and cataloguing, in addition to his Columbia responsibilities, meant that he made little progress on his own scholarly work. Farrand volunteered to do some museum tasks and that helped a little, but things remained unsatisfactory. In that summer of 1900 Boas indicated his disgruntlement. He wanted to move little Hedwig's grave from Chicago to New York, but was now uncertain that they would stay in the city. If a good offer came from the Bureau of American Ethnology in Washington, "I believe I would take it."[1]

Part of the difficulty was Putnam and his divided commitments between Harvard and New York. Initially Boas had enjoyed working under the Harvard professor, though the man's "eternal dawdling" and incorrigible tardiness were frustrating. Despite all of Putnam's good qualities, it was hard to get things done.[2] With the growth of the department's projects and its move into the new exhibition halls, the need for full-time direction was increasingly apparent. Moreover, Putnam's incumbency placed Boas in a difficult position: he could not aspire to be chief while Putnam occupied the post. The very growth of the museum, however, offered a possible solution to the dilemma.

Jesup's age (he turned seventy in 1900) and other responsibilities meant that his almost complete administrative control of the museum could not continue for long, especially considering its extraordinary growth. For years Jesup had worked through Secretary Winser, but in May 1899 rumor had it that a director would be appointed to relieve the president of some of his load. Boas feared that H. F. Osborn, who as curator of paleontology was a rival departmental head, might be named to the position. Reacting to the story, Boas wrote urgently to Putnam, advising that he ought to be in New York "in your own interest and in that of the Museum." Putnam, while not modest about his own ability, refused to put himself forward. "I have never asked for a place and could not from my nature say I was a candidate for any place."[3] No director was appointed, though Osborn assumed the role of assistant to the president after resigning his Columbia professorship.

Boas was disappointed. He remained convinced that a director was needed. At least as much, anthropology needed a full-time chief. That was Jesup's view as well. Boas noted that Jesup said he could manage as well as Putnam, "that if Putnam would not come full time, then he wants me." This was an alternative that Boas could neither consider nor condone. He and Putnam, he explained to Jesup, "have been more or less intimately associated for eight years and our relationship is that of fast friends." He still hoped that Putnam would take the directorship and in his letter to Jesup he praised the chief for his firm grasp of museum administration, inspiring example to assistants, and subordinating his personal ambition to the interests of the institution and his younger assistants.[4]

Putnam's absences, however, remained a problem. Boas tried to convince him to come full time, but he just would not. That frustrated, even infuriated, Boas. By October, he had lost patience. He judged that Putnam's position was "impossible." The man either had to become director or give up entirely his New York position. Nevertheless, "I will remain loyal and decent," he wrote, "and will watch Putnam's back."[5] The directorship alternative was closed off in January 1901 when Hermon C. Bumpus, a marine zoologist from Brown University and Woods Hole Laboratory, replaced Osborn as assistant to the president and, a year later, became museum director. Putnam went on in his lackadaisical and dawdling way, giving Boas free rein to his various ambitions.

There was little Boas could do about Putnam, but he could insist upon the position and salary to which he felt entitled by reputation and accomplishment. He was tired of his "assistant" title and told Jesup so.[6] The president agreed and made him a full curator in January 1901, but the question of a corresponding increase in salary was left vague. After three months nothing had happened, so Boas seized the initiative in a long letter of discontent.

He expected, he wrote President Jesup, "fair compensation" for his services. At the present time "you value my work not more than one fourth the value of the work of Professors Osborn and Putnam, an estimate which I decline to accept." He wanted a raise, retroactive to his January curatorship, to $4,000. "In throwing myself into administrative work as vigorously as I have done, I have forgone most of my purely scientific aspirations." He could easily give up administration for the quieter life of research, "but I believe that I have a work to do in my present sphere which I can and which I want to accomplish." But there were limits. He had been humiliated by the lack of a raise with his curatorship. Moreover, he wanted Farrand appointed as his assistant and an improvement in the positions of Smith and sculptor Caspar Mayer.[7]

Jesup was both hurt and regretful. "If you knew the trying position which has encompassed me since January 1st," he replied, "you would not have written that letter." He had expected to advance salaries with the promotions, but difficulties had prevented it. He would, however, do what ought to be done as soon as the way was clear.[8] But Jesup and the museum were facing troubles. He had discovered that Superintendent of Buildings William Wallace, Minik's guardian and a man Jesup had implicitly trusted for twenty years, was dishonest. The scam entailed claims running to six figures against the museum from contractors and left him "un-nerved," and "not strong in body or mind just now." He personally paid about $71,000 to settle matters as quietly as possible.[9]

Boas did get his raise, though only to $3,500, and Smith's salary was increased to $1,600. While given no assistant, Boas received, as he had also requested, paid leave to go to Europe to study Philippine, Malay, African, and Indian collections. The response appeased Boas and a sudden burst of publications—"a rain after two years of drought"—brought personal satisfaction. The summer in Germany, where he hatched winter plans for developing studies of the Malay region, India, Tibet, Arabia, and Persia, revealed the old expansionistic and enthusiastic Boas.[10] But the return to New York at the beginning of October was disillusioning.

Boas was greeted with the shocking news that, in his absence, Putnam had taken charge of a new museum and department of anthropology at the University of California. That "hurt me to the quick."[11] The "California story" shattered the long bond between Boas and his older colleague. Putnam had simply stolen California from him. "I cannot convince myself," he wrote, "that you were right in it." To Boas, it was an incredible betrayal of "all that I had tried to build up for years."[12]

California was an important piece of Boas's Vanishing Tribes fieldwork and part of his plans for anthropology in America. He had begun to solicit research support as early as 1897, succeeding in 1899 in securing the Huntington funds that put Dixon into his fieldwork there. He had helped place Constance Goddard DuBois among the Mission Indians and then Kroeber, at least temporarily, as anthropologist at the California Academy of Sciences. Putnam had known all this. Indeed, just before his European leave, Boas discussed the prospects for California anthropology with Putnam and Phoebe Apperson Hearst, the benefactor of the Berkeley museum and department. Boas had followed up the discussion with a letter to Hearst describing his Vanishing Tribes project, with the hope that she might deliver her own suggested contribution of $1,000 toward it. Putnam also followed up the meeting, raising the work that "Dr. Boas mentioned to you," but then added a "strictly confidential" postscript, proposing to "give a good part of my time to bringing about the further development of the Department at the University." He would, he said, "like to be instrumental in the work of another great centre of anthropology and California is the place for it."[13]

Boas, unaware of his chief's move, continued to pursue the matter in his own way. He had discussed it a year earlier with Zelia Nuttall, a distinguished Mesoamericanist and, as one of Hearst's close friends, a principal advisor on her University of California project. He had written a long letter on May 18, 1901, which outlined his own plans and deep interest in California ethnology. "For the next four or five years, and not longer," he concluded, "give me the opportunity to direct the operations, in order to establish them on a definite systematic basis." The plan, involving training several men at Columbia and Harvard for California work, was consistent with an apprenticeship program for all his projects, but it did not appeal to university president Benjamin I. Wheeler or to Hearst. Instead, they acted on Putnam's confidential initiative. Putnam was to become directing chair of the Berkeley museum and department, employing Kroeber. Boas, in Berlin where he had succeeded in raising money from the Berlin Museum to continue Kroeber's Arapaho work, learned of his former student's California prospects, but little more. He returned from Europe to learn the outrageous details.[14]

The California story is a little hard to judge. On one side was Putnam, everlastingly involving himself in everything. He was an overachieving promoter, taking on more positions than he could responsibly fill. On the other hand, he too had a claim on California that reached back to his research for the 1879 report of the George Wheeler Expedition. He had first initiated contact with Hearst and brought her to the New York museum. There, however, they had talked of cooperation between Berkeley and New York, even of Hearst contributing to the American Museum's work in California ethnology. Boas had followed up with a plan that involved his personal control over California anthropology, but from a New York base that included Putnam both as a Harvard professor and American Museum curator. Putnam simply intervened to take full control, independently of New York, Harvard, and Boas. Perhaps only an independent California department would have satisfied Hearst and the university, but Putnam was instrumental, not merely complicit, in seizing control. Boas was left on the sidelines, his own ambitions thwarted by, of all people, Putnam. Moreover, Putnam's "scheme" sounded to him like "a most heterogeneous mass," which was "thrown together without method or plan."[15]

Boas could probably have moved to California himself to assume direction of the department there. Nuttall had asked if he would, but he outlined to her all his ambitions for a "well-organized school of anthropology" based on the cooperation of the American Museum and Columbia, with a connection to the BAE. "I am committed here in many directions which centre in my activity in the Museum and in Columbia; and if I were to sever my connection with these institutions, it would practically mean to begin all over again."[16] Boas had his ambitions, though they were not so peripatetic as Putnam's.

Putnam negotiated a position that Boas had refused, though without severing his ties to Harvard or the New York museum. Boas's hurt involved both the apparent betrayal and the dent it put in his own ambitions for the development of Californian and American anthropology. The men were acting out opposing ambitions which neither articulated to the other.

The Berkeley program emerged as the brainchild of Putnam and Boas. Its leading members—Nuttall, Fletcher, and Kroeber—were all protégés, friends, or associates of one or the other—usually both. The parents, however, had become rivals, and this disputed child was as much a symptom of their differences as a cause of it. Boas's earlier concern at the invidious disproportion of his salary to Putnam's indicated rivalry, and Putnam's secret usurpation of Berkeley's reins confirmed it.

Boas could not forget the "California story." It "rankled in my mind for weeks." A long discussion with Putnam about the matter settled nothing; relations between the two men remained "forced and unnatural,"[17] with mutual suspicion and distrust breeding upon itself. Putnam's position at the American Museum, an intermittent role that brought him to New York for, at most, two weeks a month, did not help to heal the wound.

The 1901–2 year had started out badly and never got better. Boas was pleased with his "little piece" on the variability of form that came out in January, and he looked forward to his candidate filling the newly endowed chair in Chinese studies at Columbia, but otherwise "nothing goes ahead." Seth Low, elected mayor of New York in the autumn, had resigned from the university presidency, and Boas did not trust successor Nicholas Murray Butler. It was turning into the worst year in a long time, and, with "everything bad in the museum,"[18] he took up his pen to write Jesup another long letter of discontent.

This time his disgruntlement concentrated on the lack of research support. He was unable to interest Jesup in any projects to supplement the North Pacific Expedition. Support for the Vanishing Tribes project had declined in 1901. Things had been going backward for the last two years, yet the material was disappearing "day by day."[19] In the early period, the department had received financial commitments over several years for its projects, but now it had to wait until the last minute for an annual appropriation. "I do my best to interest outsiders," he continued, but he needed museum support. "I have capacity for work, but am dissatisfied at frittering away my energies in vain attempts to reach a settled policy of work to be pressed. If the Museum cannot assist me in these plans, my interest lags."[20] While his dissatisfaction included the lack of support and planning in the museum, the Jesup Expedition publications lay "especially on my heart."[21]

The Jesup Expedition memoirs had been ambitiously projected at some thirty contributions within twelve volumes. Many of those from the American side were prepared quickly. For the Asian side, Laufer had completed his slender volume on Amur decorative art, but Jochelson and Bogoras were, after their arrival in New York in 1902, only beginning their writing.

Publication costs had never been included in the Expedition budget, though Jesup agreed to finance the first set of publications at a cost of $2,000. Boas feared that, without a special appropriation, the museum's publication budget, which had to cover all departments' competing requests, would hopelessly delay the dissemination of his valued results. In February 1902 he pleaded with Director Bumpus for extraordinary money. "The danger is again imminent that the whole enterprise, the appreciation of which has constantly increased as its publications progressed, will fall flat." He found it unbearable to think that the Jesup Expedition should be another example of an enterprise started with great vigor but ending in disappointment. He wanted a decision, once and for all. His estimate of costs was $20,000.[22]

Boas got some of what he demanded. Jesup agreed to publish urgent Expedition work; that represented "finally some progress." He was given $5,000 for the Vanishing Tribes; that, with BAE money and Huntington's support, allowed him to place Clark Wissler among the South Dakota Sioux and Montgomery Schuyler among the Witchita and continue the work of Dixon, Jones, St. Clair, Farrand, and DuBois. In all, he had, including Mutch and Comer collecting in the Arctic, nine fieldworkers in the summer of 1902. Nevertheless, his discontent lingered. The museum work was now just cataloguing, no longer science.[23] Moreover, relations with Putnam had worsened in the months since the explosion over California.

Boas made one attempt to repair the relationship. Early in April 1902 he wrote a long letter, an appeal "to regain our old harmonious relations." The essential difficulties arose, Boas wrote, from Putnam's absences. For himself, he had no intention of interfering or withholding plans, and "I have always told you of what I intended to do." The North American plan, the California work, the Chinese project, the cooperation with the BAE, and other endeavors had been discussed. His procedures had always been the same, "and you never felt this as a neglect on my part until now, when somehow, the old confidence seems to be gone." The California matter had, of course, hurt, "but you must have noticed that I got over it, and that I look at it simply as a point in regard to which our judgment was at variance." He suggested a monthly department meeting that would keep Putnam informed on all matters and be an expression of harmonious unity. Putnam should feel free to use Miss Andrews fully when he was in New York. These changes, "with good will on our part," might remedy the difficulties. "We have worked so many years together successfully," Boas concluded, "that we should be able to continue to do so." This carefully worded letter was sealed in an envelope for mailing, but Boas, for reasons unknown—perhaps not perfectly clear to himself—never posted it. Instead, two days later, he posted another one, shorter and less heartfelt. Putnam's reply, a mere acknowledgment with thanks, was a rebuff.[24] There was no reconciliation, no regaining of the old confidence.

One thing was brighter. In May Jesup agreed to finance the Expedition publications, then in preparation, at an estimated cost of $4,425 should museum funds be insufficient. This was a relief but, all in all, Boas wrote in July 1902, it had been a bad year: "nothing has worked out—or only a little."[25]

He joined the family at the lake at the beginning of July, ready, after the unhappy winter, for a good rest and some solid work. He had spent the previous week in Pittsburgh at the AAAS meetings where he had lost an aggravating battle over the character of the new American Anthropological Association. He had been bothered there by abdominal pains, but, since he had no fever, had ignored the discomfort. At the lake the pains worsened and, on July 10, Jacobi, diagnosed appendicitis and sent him for immediate surgery. Boas was in the Albany hospital the next day and was operated on early the following morning. Before he went under the knife, he penned Marie a letter "in case something happened." He wanted only to tell her to avoid her widowed mother's error of personal isolation. "Trust all my relatives and friends," he wrote; all his life he had labored for his friends and she had the right to build upon that trust and friendship. "May I also say," he concluded, "that I love you and our children more than I can say and that life at your side is my happiness?"[26]

Recovery was slow and uncomfortable. Ten days passed before he could sit up, another five before he could leave the hospital room. He was bored and alone. Marie could not come until the 23rd, then had to return to the children until she came to take him back to the lake on the 30th. Putnam stopped by on his way to Boston, about the only visitor he had.[27]

He left the hospital with his wound still open, and it did not close for another three weeks. He returned to New York at the beginning of September, but tired so quickly that, after a week, he went back to the lake. He could work only two or three hours a day: "I cannot do more." So he and Ernst collected insects and put them in series according to their order. It was the first time since boyhood that he had done such things, and he enjoyed it immensely. But he was not well. Even more disabling than his fatigue was a nerve or muscle affliction in the left thigh that almost prevented him from walking.[28] He improved very slowly; in mid-October he still tired within hours. He seemed better in November, but even the following May he still could not walk far without pain.

Boas was back to the city in October for the International Congress of Americanists hosted by the museum, largely at his instigation. He was a strong supporter of these biennial international meetings, probably attending more than any other Americanist. He was happy to see so many old European friends in New York, especially von den Steinen and Seler. He and Marie entertained at lunch every day, they hosted a dinner for ten one evening (Jacobi sent Emma over to do the preparations), and on Friday had a gentlemen's smoker for thirty. But Putnam noted that, though Boas was full of activity, "the poor fellow is overworked & is a sick man & suffers much."[29]

The strain was made worse by an upheaval at the BAE. J. W. Powell's death brought a refusal by the Smithsonian's secretary, Samuel P. Langley, to appoint W J McGee as his successor. Instead, he installed W. H. Holmes in the job, a move Boas feared was hostile to the Bureau's purpose. "The story is awful," wrote Boas. "I can't remain a spectator since it touches our whole future."[30] The battle would consume much of Boas's depleted energy over the next year.

Despite the museum's excellent hosting of the Congress, things there were no better for Boas and the Anthropology department. He was not the only one concerned. The president's office noticed that "the relations between Putnam and the Museum became ever more difficult." Boas wrote that Bumpus, now in his second year as director, "naturally saw that the machinery in our department ran very poorly because Putnam came only 14 days a month, did not know what was going on, and disturbed all our work."[31] Jesup and Bumpus must also have been concerned with Putnam's commitments to California and how they affected his existing ones to New York. Putnam's problems with his New York superiors had surfaced clearly that summer when Boas's ill-health kept him absent at a time when preparations for the Americanists Congress were pressing. "I am not at all satisfied with the management of the Anthropology Department," Bumpus wrote in July. Boas was recuperating in the hospital, Saville leaving for Mexico, and Putnam planning to be absent in California until September. That threw the entire responsibility of the department upon Smith, himself just back from sick leave. Bumpus suggested that Jesup should write Putnam and ask him to remain in New York. "I cannot help feeling that if Professor Putnam's interest in the development of his department were genuine he would not absent himself at such a critical time." Putnam responded to the presidential request, postponing his California trip and working "as never before" throughout August and into September. But Boas's enforced absence had made clear the need for full-time direction. There is, Jesup wrote Putnam in September, "no head when you are away," and the department now needed almost constant supervision. The writing was on the wall. In December, Jesup virtually asked for Putnam's resignation: "I feel the time has come for you to give your whole time to the interest of your department," and yet Jesup did not see how the museum could compensate him adequately or take responsibility for asking him to leave Cambridge and cut his connections with California.[32]

From Boas's point of view, the situation was "*disgusting.*" Putnam had become "partly superfluous, partly, when he tried to intervene, a hindrance." He would just as soon leave the museum himself, but Columbia could not give him a full salary and, moreover, it was not he who had created the situation. If Putnam had only taken his advice in 1899 and come to New York full time, then matters would never have developed to this critical stage.[33]

The denouement came with Putnam's return from Berkeley. Bumpus and Jesup were frustrated with Putnam's inattentiveness to their museum. They tried to push him out, but he would not go. On January 15 Jesup confronted him, again asking him to give his whole time and energy to the museum, but Putnam's "other ties and other duties" would not permit this. Instead, Putnam proposed a compromise. He would remain as "advisory curator," with his time and salary halved.[34] Bumpus would deal directly with Boas and Saville on matters regarding the ethnology and archaeology divisions, but with Putnam, "as heretofore," on matters relating to the department as a whole. Boas acquiesced on Saturday, January 31.

Three days later Boas picked up the newspaper to read that the Duke de Loubat[35] had donated $100,000 to Columbia for the creation of a chair in archaeology and that Marshall Saville had been appointed the new Loubat Professor. He exploded. He was, as he put it, "beside myself."[36] His anger was directed partly at Columbia, for the trustees having made such an irregular and insulting appointment without the advice of the department, and partly at Putnam, for having him agree to the revised museum proposal without revealing Saville's radically altered status.

Loubat, Boas learned from Saville, had demanded absolute secrecy about the gift and the condition that Saville occupy the chair, but Putnam had known and approved of it before his Saturday discussion with Boas and Bumpus. That meant that Putnam had "forced me to give my agreement to his plans for a decisive turn of affairs here in NY without my knowledge of the important circumstances which he and Saville knew were in progress." That was unacceptable; he immediately withdrew his consent to the museum agreement.[37]

Jesup and Bumpus had equal cause to be angry. Saville was, after all, their curator, and they were as surprised as Boas to read in the press that he was to occupy Columbia's Loubat chair. They had no idea of what demands his new appointment might make upon his museum obligations, and Bumpus was quick to relay his disapproval. Bumpus's irritation was, like Boas's, directed at Putnam. He thought that he and Putnam had been discussing the anthropology department arrangement with "absolute frankness," but learned instead that unknown factors were involved. Under the circumstances, he sided with Boas. Indeed, he and Boas were "very much together" in the affair, while Putnam sat in Cambridge trying to sustain his position by mail. Boas was no longer prepared to "watch Putnam's back," no longer "loyal and decent." In a discussion with Jesup, "I held no leaf in front of my mouth."[38]

Boas's withdrawal of his consent to the agreement "practically compels" a reversion to the earlier decision to split the department completely in two, judged Bumpus. "I am sure," he told Putnam, "that we both feel that the well-merited position of Professor Boas in the scientific world, and the remarkable energy and efficiency that he has displayed since he came to the Museum, ought to lead to a position of more, rather than less prominence." And so the matter was settled. Boas would be an independent curator of ethnology, with Farrand as his assistant; Putnam would be "advisory curator," but only of archaeology, with Saville as curator of Mexican and Smith of American archaeology.[39]

Putnam had been pushed out. That had been the original intention of Jesup and Bumpus all along. Putnam, however, had saved himself through the compromise, only to cloud it by his deception over the Saville professorship. He would stay on, quarter time, as "advisory curator," but that was understood by both sides as a temporary, face-saving camouflage for Putnam's dismissal.

For Boas there was no ambiguity. "Plain and simple," he said, "between us it is finished."[40] Putnam firmly maintained that he had done nothing wrong in his secretive negotiations with California and that he had been only a little thoughtless about mixing in the Columbia appointment. Boas found this unbelievable. "He seems to have absolutely no understanding of how hard the thing hit me."[41] Putnam's error was "that he regarded me as his curator, one who had toward him no rights, but only duties."[42] The man's actions could only be understood as paternalism. "He regards all the 'young people' (among whom he also includes me) around him as his and demands from them eternal thanks. Everyone for whom he had once done something no longer has individuality, but is in his eyes only his creation."[43] This had some truth. His reaction to Boas's withdrawal of consent to the proposed compromise was partly due to this perception. "I am sure Boas that when you stop & think how I have always done all in my power to help you, how I carefully held my own personality in the background and have let you go ahead and have aided you in every way; that it is owing to the Department of Anth. that both you & Saville got your professorships."[44] Deeply wounded by Boas's aggressive response to the Saville appointment, Putnam asked him to remember "that we have coöperated in the work of making the Dept what it is, and think of many other things during our association, you will realize what an unkind thing your letter is." He was "hurt and disappointed," and hoped that Boas would recant the ungracious letter.[45] Boas did not.

Boas was not without his own concerns. The worst was it would look like he had forced Putnam out, and that people would think him a snake for it. The new curatorship raised Boas's museum salary to $4,000, but he donated the amount of the increase back toward an assistant's salary: he did not want anyone to say that the situation had been turned to his financial advantage.[46] Then there was the Saville problem. Without a university degree and ignorant of German and French, the man should never have been given the professorship, let alone shoved into it by Loubat's money. Columbia was now embarrassed by the situation and agreed, at James Cattell's suggestion, to give the archaeologist extended leave to study in Europe before beginning his professorial duties. That, however, was a Columbia problem, not one for Boas's department of ethnology.

Once the matter had been settled, Putnam put his own gloss on the affair. "The frequent trips to New York have become so wearying to me and so unsatisfactory to Mrs. Putnam," he told Zelia Nuttall, that he had given up half his salary and cut his time in half. "I shall withdraw entirely before long." He cast no aspersions on anyone in New York, acting as if the changes were entirely at his own instigation. President Wheeler in California, catching wind of Putnam's altered situation, invited him to assume in Berkeley at least as much as he was relinquishing in New York. Putnam responded favorably to the suggestion of spending four or five months a year there, and, anticipating that, said he would likely withdraw from New York during the year. He did resign at the end of 1903. "It will be a relief for us all when he is gone," wrote Boas. "I cannot forgive him for the way he betrayed himself in the Saville appointment."[47]

Just when the departmental administration seemed settled, Jesup gave Boas a jolt. The president had again changed his mind on the Jesup Expedition publications. Future work had to come from the museum's general publications fund. Boas was devastated. It was "perhaps a harder blow than all those that I have received in recent years." He pleaded with Jesup to reverse the decision. His whole scientific reputation, he said, was at stake and "I cannot afford to have an enterprise for which I have the responsibility, fail." Jesup remained immovable. Boas had not told him at the beginning about the large sums required for publications. The expedition was over and it was for the museum to publish the results. He would allow enough money in the museum budget to keep the publications in progress, but no more. "All is now being done," wrote Bumpus to Jesup, "that is imperatively necessary." At least, said Boas at year's end, "the publications go."[48] He made things somewhat easier by cutting costs. Instead of the museum acting as its own publisher, he got Bumpus to agree to send it to E. J. Brill in Leiden. Future volumes were published by that house, with G. E. Stechert and Company acting as American agents. The contract cut costs substantially.[49]

Printing was expensive, but it was not the only continuing cost. Bogoras and Jochelson had been contracted to write up their results at a monthly salary of $150 each. For over a year, they worked at the museum. An attempt to get them fellowships with the Carnegie Institute that autumn failed and both returned to Europe in 1904, their contracts altered to $150 per chapter. Jochelson settled in Zurich, where his wife was completing her medical training, and Bogoras went to St. Petersburg.

Jochelson's writing was slow but regular. Bogoras, caught up in revolutionary 1905 St. Petersburg, stopped his entirely. For long periods, he ceased even to write letters. "I have had nothing from Bogoras for a month," Jochelson wrote Boas, and "that concerns us very much." Boas finally received a letter from Bogoras apologizing for his neglect, "but you will understand that an epoch like this happens only once in many centuries for every state and nation and we feel ourselves torn away with the current even against our will." Boas lectured him about priorities. "If events like the present happen only once in a century, an investigation by Mr. Bogoras of the Chukchee happens only once in eternity, and I think you owe it to science to give us the results of your studies." A letter from Bogoras in November brought renewed regrets at the lack of progress but no change of mind. He would have to be forgiven: "my mind and soul have no free place to let in science." Arrested in December, then released, Bogoras eventually went to Finland where he gradually returned to his scholarship. Jochelson, too, was affected by the revolution and, lacking "the necessary calm," his writing slowed. Even from afar, Russia's internal turmoil had an upsetting influence. "You know, of course," Jochelson told Boas, "that next to the researcher stands in me a citizen."[50]

Outside the museum, Boas had other battles. One was over the character of a new anthropology organization, the American Anthropological Association (AAA). The idea had been floating around since the mid-1890s and became increasingly attractive with the growth and sophistication of anthropological activity in universities and museums. W J McGee became the moving spirit in promoting a society and, after brief discussions at the Chicago AAAS meeting in December 1901 and further consultation with Boas, he circulated a draft proposal.

McGee and Boas each had strong views on the character of a national organization. McGee was convinced that it ought to be open to all those interested in the subject. Boas, who had doubts about the need for yet another organization in addition to the Washington and New York ones and the AAAS's Section H, was equally convinced that, if there were to be a new organization, it should be a society of professional anthropologists from which "the amateur element is rigidly excluded." McGee's circular sought a compromise by having an open membership policy with a council restricted to working anthropologists, an arrangement which Boas did not accept. McGee, confident in his conviction and in his ability to command a majority of anthropologists to his view, pushed ahead. Boas resisted, urging that the matter was too important for hasty action. McGee ignored the warning and, pursuing his own agenda, quickly incorporated the association.

Boas was outraged. "The Washingtonians, or rather a few people there, have founded a society in complete secrecy in order to force the situation."[51] He bluntly told McGee, "You have not treated me with that openness to which I am accustomed from you." After all that had transpired between them on the matter, Boas claimed a right to have seen the draft incorporation and to have been advised of the Washington meeting that arranged it. Nor had McGee's handling of the circular correspondence allowed a fair expression of opinion by all concerned. Despite McGee's highhanded methods, Boas would not provoke "a most disastrous clash"; if McGee went no further until a meeting was held, he would cooperate "to try to make the best even of the undesirable situation." McGee apologized for inadvertence and oversight, but excused his actions as consistent with majority opinion and subject to alteration at the foundation meeting in June. He had, moreover, been moved by an urgent consideration which he would reveal only personally to Boas and which thus does not appear in the correspondence. He arranged, as Boas demanded, for the dissident to speak before the Washington Anthropological Society, where Boas could, as he himself put it, "carry the war into the land of the enemy."[52]

His Washington paper had no significant effect. There were further discussions, further compromises, but little else. The AAA was formally established at the meeting in Pittsburgh at the end of June. Its organization was essentially that favored by McGee. Boas, supported by Putnam, Dixon, Farrand, and Smith, tried to move the meeting to his exclusionist position, but was outnumbered.[53] McGee was elected first president and Putnam, Boas, Holmes, and Powell as vice-presidents.

Boas left the Pittsburgh meetings "very much disgusted." The affair left him especially wounded by McGee's double-dealing, actions born most likely from an aggressive ambition for anthropological leadership. In fact, as George W. Stocking, Jr., has pointed out, the AAA, despite its adoption of McGee's open-door membership, was founded and remained dominated by professionals in almost every way. The professionalization process, in which Boas was a major factor, went on pretty much unhindered by amateur memberships.[54]

The AAA battle, even McGee's part in it, faded into insignificance when, less than four months later, McGee was passed over for the BAE directorship. McGee had been acting in that capacity for years as Powell's health declined, but succeeded only in convincing Smithsonian Secretary Langley of his administrative incapacity. As Powell neared death in 1902, Langley laid his plans to bring the agency, whose autonomy had been protected by Powell's enormous prestige, under his own conception of administrative subordination and scientific usefulness. Determined that McGee, whom he distrusted and despised, would not succeed Powell, Langley offered the expected opening in February to W. H. Holmes, a long and close friend of McGee's. Holmes declined, wishing neither the position nor to displace McGee's claim. Langley made it clear, however, that McGee was unacceptable and it was either Holmes or someone else. Thus, when Powell died in September, the decision had been made. Holmes, reluctant but pliant, would, while retaining his museum position, succeed

Powell, but within a relationship that placed the BAE directly under the charge of the Smithsonian secretary.[55] It was a decision that some, including Boas, could not take quietly.

In taking up the battle of BAE succession, Boas was prompted by personal, professional, and scientific considerations. First of all, despite Boas's disgust with McGee's "rotten politics" over the AAA, he regarded him as "one of my best friends." The basis of that "lasting friendship" had been established during Boas's hour in 1894, when McGee had, "with courageous frankness," dealt squarely with him over Holmes's appointment to the Chicago museum. On the other hand, Holmes's actions then had left a deep residue of distrust, and Boas now sympathized with yet another who was being ousted by the perfidious Holmes. It was a "shocking injustice." "Holmes had always portrayed himself as an intimate friend of McGee's, yet now let himself be named over him as the Bureau's director." McGee saw it the same way. "You saw Holmes' cloven foot at Chicago," he wrote Boas, "but I see both of them and the forked tail as well."[56] Boas could not idly sit by as his old enemy denied his old friend his rightful place.

From 1894 the Boas-McGee friendship had become a supportive professional collaboration. McGee had made outright offers of employment, then generously fostered Boas's linguistic and mythological work and that of his students. From 1893 until 1903, Boas received $4,527 in BAE funds for his language and mythology research, and that did not include the indirect support for such projects as Swanton's work among the Haida. The collaboration had brought Boas's appointment as BAE philologist, charged with preparing a handbook of American Indian languages and carrying a guarantee of support for Boas's student fieldworkers. Recently the two had concluded an agreement that would bring the BAE at long last into the fields of anthropometrics and a study of racial differences in the American population, with special attention to Blacks. This was Boas's program, now adopted by McGee as the Bureau's own. The two had joined in ownership of the *American Anthropologist* and, just weeks before the succession crisis, McGee, moved by a concern for Boas's health after the appendicitis operation, had offered to assume full financial responsibility for the journal. By 1902, with research support at the American Museum going badly, Boas was increasingly dependent upon the BAE. McGee's fate was intertwined with his own. He could not remain a mere observer "since it touches so closely our whole future."[57]

Boas reacted to the threat as best he could. The first strategy was to work on Langley. Cooperating with Columbia colleagues Cattell and R. S. Woodward, he wrote Smithsonian regents, especially Alexander Graham Bell who was no strong supporter of the secretary, and to the Carnegie Institution president, David C. Gilman. Such protests had no effect, and so the battle went public, with Boas publishing an open letter in *Science,* accompanied by an editorial prepared by Woodward, with Cattell also editorializing in his *Popular Science.* Boas realized that his *Science* letter "will probably make a lot of bad blood" and likely would not help at all, but what else could he do? At least it served to get the matter off his chest. Above all, "if no one has the courage to speak his opinion, our situation will never get better."[58]

There was discussion of a round-robin letter, but it never materialized. McGee had the support of Fletcher, Putnam, Dorsey, Frank Russell of Harvard, and Stewart Culin of the University Museum in Philadelphia, but others were silent and their views divided. The AAA/AAAS meetings in Washington, D.C., that December were tense. Marie noted that Franz was "so alone among the ethnologists." The AAA elections saw Holmes and McGee factions form against each other, with the preponderance on the Holmes side. "Since I have personally taken up the battle for McGee," Boas wrote, "I naturally received relatively the fewest vote."[59]

Boas publicly expressed his opposition to the Holmes appointment in administrative and methodological terms. The BAE had been hampered by Powell's mental decline when its activity ought to have expanded into practical questions of Indian education, and research on the physical and social effects of racial mixtures of White and Indian and Indian and Negro. It should have become an anthropological survey, but Langley took no action during the years of its decline, seeming to think the BAE as Powell's, with its life to end with his, and not as a public institution capable of expanding its usefulness. The choice of Holmes was unfortunate, partly because it meant that either the National Museum or the Bureau, both of which required the full attention of the best man available, would lose by it. Moreover, it was fundamentally wrong to combine the two agencies because they were, in method and outlook, entirely distinct. The museum necessarily concerned itself with material objects which scarcely touched on the ideas behind them. Language, law, religion, and mythology were outside its domain. Holmes's natural gifts gave him a thorough appreciation of visual objects, "but his interest in that part of anthropology which deals with ideas alone is slight."[60]

Boas's BAE battle never had a chance of success. There was no recourse from Langley's determination. The Smithsonian's regents were a nominal body, meeting for a few hours once or twice a year. Congress had power, but McGee had enemies as well as friends on the Hill. Indeed, Langley was able to turn the affair to his favor by instituting an internal investigation into the administration of the BAE that became a means of discrediting McGee and even tarnishing Boas. (There were questions of how Boas handled the salary of those like Jones working under him, of McGee's purchase of his manuscripts, and of the casual to-and-fro of manuscripts between the Bureau's vault and Boas's study.) "The whole story," Boas wrote of the committee investigation, "is a Schweinerei to stain the old administration." McGee, who had remained in the BAE in order, he said, to protect its scientific work, resigned in August 1903, "really tired and sick," in order to take up work for the St. Louis Fair. The McGee battle was now over.[61]

The winter of 1902–3 had been another difficult one, taken up with the Saville and Putnam affair, the Jesup publications crisis, and the Holmes-McGee imbroglio. Boas's health was still not entirely restored and he looked forward to the summer. Unable to touch any of his own material all winter, he canceled plans for a field trip. The Boases arrived at Lake George early in June, to stay again at Jacobi's house at Bolton Landing. His uncle had enlarged the cottage and they could more easily have visitors. Jochelson, the Bogorases, Dixon, and Miss Andrews all came up for working holidays, Berthe Krüer and a school friend of Ernst's for pleasure. Boas first had to fulfill Jesup's request for a popular treatment of the Expedition for the museum's journal, then, just as he was settling down to some Kwakiutl work, Ernst suffered an appendix attack that required an urgent return to New York for surgery. It was serious business—"what fearful hours those were." Cousin Willy Meyer performed the operation at German Hospital. The twelve-year-old came through it wonderfully. "I am," wrote his father, "proud of my brave youngster, of the way he held out, doing all that was asked of him without hesitation and with a smile." The episode brought Franz closer to his son: "I was always fond of him, but now I am a thousand times more." The crisis also brought a renewal of old ties to Willy. They had scarcely spoken for years, and now he hoped that Willy's surgery, followed by an invitation to dinner at Bolton, would renew the bonds.[62]

Ernst's hospitalization, of course, took a great deal out of Franz's summer expectations. Another interruption was the committee investigating the BAE, which required his testimony in late July. He managed to get in some relaxing labor moving rocks and sawing wood. He felt much better, rejuvenated in his "courage for aggressive activity," and the leg pain was practically gone.[63]

The new working year went a little better. Holmes, after some difficulty, suppressed animosity enough to let the *Handbook of American Languages* project proceed. At the university Boas was now teaching only graduate courses, leaving the college courses to Farrand and assistants. At the museum he still lacked money to get his Philippines project off the ground. He had raised $8,000, but needed another $7,000 to begin. The East Asian Committee seemed to be slipping, and Schiff, his mainstay, was going abroad. On the other hand, Laufer's Chinese expedition was concluded and he had found enough money, between the museum and Columbia, to keep Laufer in New York for at least a year. His mother would not believe, he told her, "how one has to fight here for everything, how much petty, personal affairs play in all scientific matters."[64]

These projects continued, but the museum situation remained unsettled. Putnam's departure in December would bring up the "very difficult" question of whether Boas should take over the whole, recombined department. If he did, it would take his entire time. "I would have to leave to Farrand all the work that is so dear to me and for which I have fought for years, and throw myself for a few years into the administration of archaeology." His own choice would have been the reverse—to minimize his museum activity and work largely in the university—though that seemed impossible. "I now very much wish I could leave the museum," he wrote in February 1904. "It claims so much energy that I simply get to nothing else. I would very gladly get back again to scientific work and not concern myself with the work of others."[65]

Spring was freshened with the visit of his sister Hete, who came with Rudolf for six weeks in April and May. He was glad that some of his friends could "see our lives with their own eyes." Two weeks after the Lehmanns left, the Boases, accompanied by Miss Andrews, followed them across the Atlantic. Germany would, he hoped, bring a respite from the strains of American battlefields and give him a perspective from which to reappraise his position and career.

14 "Fundamental
Differences of Opinion"

LEAVING THE AMERICAN MUSEUM

B OAS'S TRIP TO Europe in 1904 included business: to Brill in Leiden with Miss Andrews for the Jesup publications, to Cologne to arrange with Laufer his year in New York, and a stay in Stuttgart for the Congress of Americanists and meetings with Jochelson, Bogoras, and others. But he also took time off for holidays. The Cologne trip was combined with a visit to nearby Bonn for the sixtieth anniversary celebrations of the Alemannen. A number of "altere Brüder" from his time were there, including Willy Meyer, Alf Vogeler, and Franz Richarz. He made the Stuttgart visit with Marie and Helene, and they stopped off in Hildesheim as a guest of Vogeler, the Minden and Bonn friend who now taught in the city's Gymnasium. They stayed over at Marburg to see Fischer and Richarz, then at Heidelberg where Boas took Marie and Helene on a tour of the castle and the Neckar Valley, showing them the Kirschgasse, scene of his first duel.[1] Stuttgart was, of course, where he and Marie had met in 1883 to discuss everything except what they really thought, and so the nostalgia continued. At the end of the Congress they went on to Bavaria to see some of Franz's Reichenbach cousins and across the Austrian border to visit some of Marie's Krackowizer kin. Remembrances of things past continued when they stayed with his mother, who was summering in the Harz, a place of great sentimental attachment.

The Brill publication agreement was working well and the Congress had been a success, especially the last day which was largely taken up with papers on the Jesup Expedition from Boas and Jochelson and a complementary one from Leo Shternberg. "I presided that day," he wrote Bumpus, "and feel very well satisfied with the reception that the works of the Expedition received."[2]

Boas had to leave a few days early on board the *Blücher* in order to reach St. Louis in time for an anthropological congress at the World's Fair. Marie and the children followed days later on the *Phonicia*. He took advantage of his single passage to write his St. Louis lecture, an unap-

pealing task because of bad weather that abetted his usual seasickness and
the difficult theme, the history of ethnology, a broad subject which he was
"not completely comfortable in handling."[3]

Back in New York, Boas had to face a mounting load of museum and
university responsibilities. His desire was to shift his primary concern
away from the museum and to the university. Immediately on his mind
was the thought of being able to see his mother more often. She was not
well, bothered by a cough that took her to Weimar's air. The autumn registration at Columbia added urgency. Anthropology had become a fashionable subject, and the department's enrollment had taken a huge jump
from 44 to 186 students. The spread of his work over both university and
museum, which had long been bothering him, now seemed impossible: "I
simply can no longer fill both posts."[4]

Much as he was attached to his museum projects, no matter how integral the museum was to his teaching program, the institution had lost its
allure. He was convinced, after so many struggles, that the prospect of
meaningful activity there was hopeless. He had a painful conversation
with Bumpus in which "I had to tell him that the museum, as it now is,
had lost for me its attraction." There was little point in having yet another
conversation with Jesup. "I have no faith in his promises; what he
promises today, he takes back tomorrow." Besides, Jesup was up to his ears
with Peary's latest polar expedition, "sport" that impressed the president
"much more than our solid work." Boas's goal, then, was to reduce to a
minimum his museum responsibilities. He wanted freer summers, found
the burden of two positions too heavy, and was fed up with the way
Bumpus and Jesup treated his department.[5]

In a letter to President Butler, Boas sought to clarify his shift toward
Columbia. The department, now with some 140 undergraduate and 18
graduate students, required reorganization. The benefit of a close association between museum and university had been proven, but the double
responsibility could no longer be met. "I am compelled to state definitely
that I feel unable to carry on the duties of administration and instruction
in the University and the responsibility for administration in the Museum
and that the time has come when these two must be separated." That
meant he and Farrand required a larger salary from Columbia. They
would not then feel compelled to devote the greater part of their time to
the museum, though they would continue with duties that were of
mutual advantage. He asked President Butler that his salary and Farrand's

be doubled to $5,000 and $4,000 a year, respectively, that Clark Wissler be given an instructorship, and that Adolf Bandelier, now teaching a single course on Mexico, be given a second.[6]

Butler accepted the main items of Boas's proposition in January 1905, but this led to a complicated set of negotiations and decisions. The university, in raising his salary to $4,000 and providing for additional teaching by Wissler, assumed that Boas would reduce his museum obligations and salary. Boas immediately notified Bumpus of his intention to readjust his museum work. That, however, was not going to be "quite easy."[7]

Unforeseen in Boas's plans was Farrand's decision to accept a position as secretary with the National Tuberculosis Association. No one was now available to step in to fill the museum gap left by his partial withdrawal. Wissler, whose teaching would be vital to Columbia, could not entirely replace Farrand at the museum. Boas tried to bring Kroeber from California, but he absolutely refused. Swanton was a possibility, but he was better off at the BAE. This left Boas's plan in a tangle, all the more so because Jesup would not hear of it. Under these altered circumstances, Boas chose to use the leverage given him by Columbia's increased salary to negotiate better terms at the museum. He would, he decided, continue there if he could secure some fundamental commitments.[8]

On January 20 Boas gave Bumpus his requirements: consolidate the department under his direction, a salary of $5,000, and a guarantee of $7,000 a year over seven years for North American ethnology. With adequate assistance, he could manage both university and museum responsibilities and be in a much stronger position to realize his goals. It meant that he would be even more tied to the museum, "which is not my wish," but conditions would be infinitely better. The stakes were high: "If I succeed, I will have the best anthropology institute anywhere; if not, my many years of work will be lost."[9]

At the end of February an agreement was struck along Boas's lines. The department would be combined under Boas, with Saville as associate curator. Boas's salary would remain at $4,000, but his summers would be entirely free. An assistant would be appointed to gradually take charge of American ethnology, and the museum promised $6,000 a year for two years for fieldwork. Boas would reduce his Columbia salary to $3,200, with the difference going toward an assistant there, and would halve his teaching load to seven hours a week.[10] There were problems. No museum assistant was available, but that might eventually take care of itself. Boas's second thoughts about the agreement stemmed more from a concern about Bumpus.

He had long worried about the director's growing power and intrusions. During the negotiations he had felt that Bumpus would have been happy to see him go because the director "would like more influence in the department." At one point Bumpus suggested that Boas become the head of the consolidated department, but with a new curator taking charge of the exhibition halls. Boas declined the proposal because he did not want to share control of the department, especially with one who might be under Bumpus's influence in exhibition procedures.[11]

Boas had probably known Hermon C. Bumpus since the winter of 1889–90 when the zoologist had been a doctoral fellow at Clark University. After earning a degree there (Clark's first), Bumpus had taught at Brown, where he gained rapid promotion to professor and was entrusted with the directorship of the United States Fish Commission's biological laboratory. He left those posts to come to the American Museum in 1901 as Jesup's presidential assistant and curator of invertebrates. He and Boas had gotten along well at first; they had worked in tandem during the Putnam-Saville crisis, and Boas later wrote of how he kicked himself "for having allowed myself to be duped by him so long."[12] When the cleavage began is uncertain, but it was probably caused by Bumpus's interventions in departmental concerns.

Bumpus's administrative style included active involvment in the running of the museum, especially in its educational role. Where he saw deficiencies, he stepped in. In 1903 Saville had feared that, were he to go on leave for a year, Harlan Smith would not be "strong enough to hold out against Bumpus' ideas." The director, he wrote, wanted "to install the whole Mexican Hall according to his own ideas."[13] Bumpus never went that far, but he did install the Peruvian collection. That material, collected by the scholarly Bandelier, had lain neglected until Bumpus, prompted by Jesup, seized the opportunity to arrange the cases himself. The result, categorized by function (e.g., household and adornment) or material (e.g., wood and stone), pleased Jesup but certainly not Boas. The Peruvian cases were only a prelude. Late in 1904 Bumpus traveled to St. Louis to negotiate the purchase of the Philippines's World's Fair exhibit, an acquisition in which Boas, despite his concern with the region, had remained entirely detached. The strained relationship between Boas and Bumpus, whatever its origin, was clear by the time of Boas's negotiations in early 1905, and Boas had sought, among his conditions, a commitment to retain in the consolidated department full authority over both research and exhibition. He thought he had secured it.

Things did not work out that way. Difficulties appeared almost immediately and accelerated as Boas took hold of the reorganized department. By April the two men were in almost open conflict. "My view and the director's are so different that things don't go," he wrote, and he now feared that he had been mistaken in deciding to cast his lot with the museum. There were difficulties over Bumpus's commandeering of departmental assistants and laborers, of interfering with Boas's subordinates, trouble over a case left unlocked, and over a reception in the Philippines Hall about which Boas had not been informed. In April the two had a furious exchange over the department's exhibits. Bumpus, according to Boas's account, said that the ethnological displays were "indecent," criticized what Boas considered to be his best cases, and then asked what Boas thought of the Peruvian Hall. Boas replied that he thought it bad, after which Bumpus shrugged and told him to change it according to his own ideas. At this same time, Boas submitted his quarterly report, which included mention of the installation of Wissler's new Blackfoot collections, a case illustrating the general culture of the Plains, and a special featherwork exhibit in the South American Hall.[14] Three days later twin bombshells landed on his desk.

One was a letter from Jesup, written on the basis of a recent tour of the halls, and complaining that he simply could not make head or tail of the American Indian exhibit. For years, he said, he had tried to get labels and arrangements "which would enable a person like myself of ordinary capacity to go through these collections and understand by the study of them what they were supposed to represent and get some idea from the collections, of the life, habits, and customs of the people." Boas's cases failed in that "and I am not satisfied." The Peruvian collections, on the other hand, were arranged according to his ideas "of what I have wanted to see done for a long time." Why could not the rest? "Why cannot my ideas be considered as furnishing the educational part of our exhibition coupled with the science part[?]" He was writing frankly, he said, asking that the matter be considered calmly and courteously, yet wishing Boas to remember "the patron I have been to the Museum, the time, thought and money I have given, and it is for that I ask that at least an attempt may be made to please me."[15] The letter, while respecting Boas's professionalism, forcefully questioned his displays.

The other bombshell was Bumpus's letter, also frank but with a much harsher tone. It emphasized that, with the knowledge and sympathy of the president, he had for years striven "to correct a fundamental error" in the treatment of the anthropology exhibits, but had received "practically nothing but evasion, indifference, and opposition." He had hoped that under Boas's curatorship things might go better, but after seeing Boas's report, his new installations, and observing the tone of their recent conversations, he was now forced "to deliberately request that certain alterations be made." The Blackfoot exhibition cases were entirely unworthy of science or education and should be corrected according to an outline to be approved by himself. Though the letter focused on exhibition matters, Bumpus opened it with a complaint about Boas's "attitude toward the work of the Museum as a whole that to me seems most unhealthful and dangerous."[16]

Curator Boas conformed to Director Bumpus's orders while he tried to bring Jesup on his side. He wrote the president a seven-page essay on his methods of exhibition, a separate protest at Bumpus's preemptive manner, and appealed for an opportunity to personally explain what his exhibits were trying to show. Jesup's response, while conciliatory in tone, confessed his inability to understand Boas's explanation of his exhibition method. He backed the director's authority and, since he was pressed with outside business, asked that a meeting be postponed and then held between himself, Bumpus, and Boas. Boas feared just such a meeting; there would be, he wrote, "an unavoidable clash" between him and the director.[17] On May 17 the three protagonists came together at Jesup's home.

Boas began with a statement about his exhibition policy, which Bumpus scorned. Then the conference broke down into argument that revealed fundamental differences over the aim of a museum and, even more, a deep-seated animosity between curator and director. Jesup intervened to ask what might be done under the circumstances. Boas responded that the only solution, considering the spirit and views of Bumpus, was that he himself withdraw from all administrative work and attempt to find a way to continue the work presently at hand. Jesup accepted that solution. He and Boas met three days later to work out arrangements. Boas would continue to be responsible for the work of the Jesup Expedition publications, the East Asiatic committee, and the rounding off of fieldwork and publications in progress. He would retain the full services of Miss Andrews and his salary and vacation would remain as before. His formal resignation as curator, which cited the "fundamental differences of opinion relating to administration between the director and myself," was accepted. On May 24, Boas called the department together and announced his leave.[18]

And so ended, with generous terms and an equally generous letter of appreciation from Jesup, Boas's curatorship of almost ten years with the American Museum. He would remain, with an office and Miss Andrews, to do what he described as "winding up the enterprises that I have in hand."[19] Putnam wrote a note to say it was "sad that the end has come as it has," but not surprising "under the circumstances and conditions." In Washington, D.C., Boas's resignation came as a surprise, but elicited little comment. "It is curious," wrote Aleš Hrdlička, but "that is about the general sentiment."[20]

Boas placed the blame entirely on Bumpus, on the director's interference, intrigues, and dictatorial manner. He had anticipated the difficulty earlier in the year, but had, he believed, secured Bumpus's agreement on the principles of exhibit installation and the necessary freedom of action. Then the director had reneged and, "by means of dictorial interference, to which he knew I would not submit," had made his position untenable. Bumpus did not need scientists as curators, but merely persons to do his bidding. He treated the museum "as a military organization, in which the first purpose is subordination."[21]

Boas scarcely mentioned Jesup's role. "When I look back," he wrote his mother, "the whole thing appears to me so idiotic that I cannot understand how Jesup could have let it happen." That was a mild reproach, but not blame. Yet Jesup had himself pressed for a revised anthropological exhibition, even accepted responsibility "for any friction that may have arisen between you and the Director, for the reason that my ideas and wishes as to how I would like to have the installation of the collections made, have been so pronounced and continued that he has tried to carry out my wishes." Moreover, Bumpus's letter, so offensive to Boas, received the president's express approval as merely exercising the rights and performing the duties he held as director. Boas felt that Bumpus deliberately forced him out, probably because he wanted to free money for other purposes. Jesup simply took a strictly business point of view: there was a director, employees have to obey the director, and it was Boas's business to find a way of doing so.[22]

One fact is beyond dispute. The anthropological halls were disliked by Jesup and had been for some time. The one display that he did like, the Peruvian Hall, was an exhibit which Boas held in contempt. That such a disagreement over exhibition should have come to a head only in 1905 does seem strange. The preceding years had, of course, been a time of construction and reconstruction, of perpetual installation and re-installation, as new wings went on the museum and new halls were added to the exhibition space. Yet Jesup, long before 1905, had expressed his discontent with the anthropology halls. Particularly in 1902, he had voiced dissatisfaction at how little he could find out about the displayed collections. He was "not satisfied" and urged that a "rigorous effort should be made to get into shape the collections we have been getting now for so long a time."[23]

The criticism contained the implication that exhibition was being subordinated to research, something which Boas strongly rejected. Successful installation was dependent upon fieldwork, and the three halls where labeling was most complete and satisfactory were those in which fieldwork had been most systematic. Labeling was least satisfactory for the Terry, Emmons, and Sturgis collections, where little or no field research had been done. This defense had not persuaded Bumpus. A year later he wrote, "I cannot help feeling that I may have made a fundamental mistake in yielding to the urgent appeals for purchases and continued field work and the general enlargement of our collections, rather than to have first cared for the proper installation of the material actually on hand." The clash of priorities was clear. According to Boas's notes of the final rupture, Bumpus felt that "field expeditions of the Museum must not be carried out for scientific purposes, but only to fill gaps in the exhibitions" and that "the acquisition of new collections in the Department had to stop."[24] This was Boas's version of the director's statement and must be read as such, yet it reveals a fundamental disagreement that placed Jesup and Bumpus on one side and Boas on the other.

Boas accepted the twin mission of large museums for both education and research, but he gave a decided priority to research as the motor that drove the educational side. Bumpus and Jesup accepted research, but made it subordinate to the educational display that museums were designated to perform. Moreover, Jesup made it clear that, while he deferred to Boas's scientific professionalism, he was every bit as competent in judging the educational side of museum work. In science, he was a layman; in public displays, he need defer to no one. Boas thought he could accommodate Jesup's view by arranging one series of collections for the general visitor that would be separated from collections that dealt with special questions. Jesup could not understand that. From his experience, an exhibit that was capable of interesting children would capture and retain the interest and attention of adults. Boas claimed that his scheme was comprehensible if the president merely gave him an opportunity to explain it. Jesup felt that displays should be self-explanatory.[25]

With Bumpus, on the other hand, the difference was over authority. Boas refused to be a mere subordinate, was "absolutely unwilling . . . to have no other function than to carry out the instructions of the director." He might compromise with Jesup over exhibitions, but he could not compromise his curatorial independence. This was to be expected. As early as December 1895, when Boas had been at the museum for less than a month, he was insistent that he was not prepared "to take a position in which I am simply to carry out orders, that is, to be a tool without an initiative of my own."[26] Now, almost ten years later, when Bumpus had the authority, chose to use it, and was backed by President Jesup, Boas's only out was resignation. That was easier because he no longer really wanted the job.

If Farrand had not left at just the key time (and Boas regarded his departure as prompted in part by Bumpus), he would never have taken on the combined department. He had yielded to the circumstances and accepted. He was now free, but "with unwholesome hard feeling." Those hard feelings became all too clear over the following months. Boas had continuing charge of half a dozen museum projects. There were difficulties over his role in preparing manuscripts by Kroeber and Emmons for publication, his Kwakiutl texts in the Jesup series, an unauthorized *Cosmopolitan* article on the Jesup Expedition, the handling of the museum's response to Bogoras's arrest, exchanges of specimens with the St. Petersburg museum, and even with office arrangements. None would have been difficult under ordinary circumstances, but each was embittered by the personal enmity between Bumpus and his former curator.[27]

By 1906 it was clear that new terms had to be reached to more precisely describe the areas of Boas's responsibility and define more explicitly his editorial role in the Jesup publications. The Kroeber, Emmons, and Eskimo bulletins were settled quickly, but the Jesup publications were more difficult and brought a breach in the strained cordiality between Boas and Jesup. Boas insisted that payment to him, irrespective of the published amount, should never fall below the $4,000 he had counted upon as his museum remuneration. This insistence touched a sensitive nerve in Jesup. All Boas's previous appeals had been expressed, the museum president wrote, as concerns for the means to sustain his scientific work and for funds to support his scientific reputation. The tone had altered, and Jesup, who felt he had always acted with "the utmost liberality and fairness," now thought that Boas was not living up to his commitment.[28]

The final agreement, mediated by Osborn, contracted Boas to complete the series by 1911 for a stipulated payment per published signature, the total cost not to exceed $25,000. Boas, for his part, was scornful of the whole business. The contract, he wrote, "is like that for building a house; goods to be paid on delivery, and the shoddier my work, the better financially for me! True Bumpus-Jesup style."[29]

The mutual respect between Boas and Jesup was one casualty of Boas's departure. A second was the relationship between Boas and his assistant Clark Wissler. Boas had left New York for the lake on June 16, almost a month after his resignation as curator. That same day, Bumpus approached Assistant Curator Wissler and asked him to become Boas's acting successor. Wissler was inclined to accept the offer. Boas was not pleased.

Wissler, a Hoosier, had taken his first degrees at Indiana before entering Columbia's doctoral program under Cattell in psychology. He had brought with him an interest in anthropology and, with psychology's close association with anthropology at the university (Cattell chaired the joint department and Farrand lectured in both subjects), he pursued it. In his last year his interests shifted entirely to anthropology. Boas, impressed with "his very good training and considerable ability," asked him to do fieldwork in 1902 among the South Dakota Sioux and the following winter used him at the museum where he proved "very adaptable and highly efficient." He was, Boas wrote, "among the young men, the man best adapted, next to A. L. Kroeber, for museum work."[30] By 1903 he was Boas's assistant in both the museum and the university and continuing his work among the Plains Indians, especially the Blackfoot. By 1905 Boas, who had come to value him "very highly," depended upon his background in anthropometric statistics and ethnology for the future development of anthropology at Columbia. Those university plans, together with Boas's now jaundiced view of the museum, determined his reaction to Wissler's report of Bumpus's offer.

He told Wissler that he could not possibly be the museum's curator and also fill his university responsibilities. It was, of course, entirely up to Wissler to decide whether he wished to devote himself to the university or the museum. This cool reaction got Wissler's back up. He was not a young doctorate insecure in his abilities, but a mature man approaching thirty-five who had worked in the museum for two years and taught longer. Much as he might respect Boas, he was not his automaton. The museum, he said, was prepared "to make an experiment" that seemed reasonable to him, and he would accept it. It was up to Boas to take the next move regarding his university appointment: "It is for you to say whether you desire my resignation in whole or in part." Boas, though he hoped that Wissler could come up to the lake for a conversation, replied in the same unbending tone. The younger man was free to do as he pleased, so long as it did not interfere with his university obligations. But the curatorship would. Boas could not, he insisted, delay Columbia's plans in anthropology for an experimental year. He would have to act "as though you were going to take up the Museum work as your principal occupation" and so would be "looking for new men and for a new adjustment of the work."[31]

Boas's threat did not deter Wissler. He accepted the acting curatorship and was prepared, he told Boas, to withdraw completely from Columbia in order to give Boas a free hand to appoint someone else. He felt he could fulfill both obligations, but was quite willing to meet Boas's wishes at the university, suggesting that his obligations be reduced to one course and assistance in the seminar.[32]

Boas returned to the city on July 14 to speak with Wissler, hoping for "a friendly readjustment." While continuing to insist that the museum would require all of Wissler's time, he also did not want Wissler to lose his connection with the university entirely. The two agreed, according to Boas, that it would be best for Wissler to teach only an extension course at Columbia, "the one for which he is best fitted, and which will give him the least amount of work for preparation." Wissler was unhappy with that, but, "because of the attitude Professor Boas has taken with respect to my relations to the Museum," he was willing to take any assignment that would be satisfactory to all concerned.[33] The final resolution awaited the return of Boas's university colleagues.

Farrand emphatically took Wissler's side, forcing Boas to back down. "This whole thing is painful," wrote Boas, "because it shows such complete misunderstanding of university work." Retreating to his usual general principles, he felt that every university teacher should be an authority in his field but found his colleagues thinking that a little general knowledge was enough for students. The university should be responsible for educating sound researchers and "a Wissler and a Farrand do not do that." It was all very aggravating. For three years he had been trying to separate professors from major museum positions. He himself could not perform both duties, so "how should a beginner now be able to undertake both?"[34]

President Butler also sided with Wissler. Wissler would not only conduct the extension course but the new undergraduate ethnology course, teaching for four hours at $800, instead of Boas's proposed two hours for $300. Wissler's scheduled statistics course would be taken by Professor H. E. Crampton of biology, and Laufer would be hired to teach two courses on Asian ethnology for $800.[35]

Wissler had faced Boas and, assisted by Farrand, Saville, and Butler, had won. He emerged with a combined salary of $3,300, a considerable advance over the pay of his two assistantships. Boas thought that remuneration had played a part in Wissler's choice and apologized for his own low offer. Wissler was, after all, six years married and father of two young children. He was also his own man. Though "quiet, reserved, a compromiser,"[36] he was not, in this instance, to be pushed around. He continued to teach at Columbia, under strained conditions, until 1909.

An anonymous note in the *American Anthropologist* wrote of the departure from the museum of Boas, Bandelier, and Laufer, the loss of whom, when added to that of Putnam and Farrand, "cannot fail to cripple seriously the activities of an institution that has done so much during the last few years to advance anthropology in America." In fact, the department under Wissler (he soon became permanent curator) did decline in its activity, but later, especially after 1920, it rose again to became a research center of "immense scientific productivity."[37] In that, Boas would have little part. His museum career was now over.[38]

Boas had always recognized the limitations of anthropology museums. Focused on material objects, whether cultural or physical, museums were able to deal with only a small part of anthropological concerns as he saw them. Specimens, no matter how elaborate, were but a small part of the psychological and historical relations of cultures, "the only objects of anthropological inquiry." What was important, as he expressed it, were "the thoughts that clustered around" the objects, and these could be expressed only inadequately by labels in glass cases.[39] Despite his reservations and personal disillusionment, he had enjoyed the challenges and accomplishments of his decade with the American Museum and dropped them reluctantly. Under his auspices, the institution's North American collections had grown to immense size and, especially in Northwest Coast and Central Eskimo material, developed a comprehensiveness which any museum might envy. He supervised the growth of the museum's important collections of California, Southwest, and Plains material, extended the collections to China and Northeast Siberia, with modest collections in Africa and elsewhere. His one-time rival, George Dorsey from the Chicago museum, gave his own estimate: during the decade between 1895 and 1905, Dorsey wrote in *Science*, American Museum anthropologists made "a systematic attempt to carry on investigations over an ever-increasing large area as fast as means would permit. As a result of this intelligently directed series of field operations there grew up in the American Museum one of the greatest departments of anthropology to be found in any museum in the world." It was doubtful, he continued, "if any institution ever acquired in the same period of time collections of such magnitude or ever accumulated material with such intelligence or exhibited it in an equally sound manner."[40] Dorsey's assessment was not altogether objective (he had just spent several months studying at Columbia under Boas and submitted his article to *Science* through Boas), but it was not inaccurate.

Boas's museum career became increasingly frustrating and disappointing. The generous finances of the earlier years dwindled away, the happy collaboration with Putnam evaporated, the access to Jesup became encumbered by the intervention of Director Bumpus, and administrative duties became increasingly onerous and unsatisfying. He had accomplished much, though nothing seemed complete. The East Asian project never got beyond China, the Vanishing Tribes staggered bit by bit, he lost California entirely, and even the Jesup Expedition, in many ways the showpiece of his American Museum years, turned sour.

That expedition, so much a part of Boas's collaboration with Jesup and the museum, deserves some elaboration. On the American side, the Expedition was a well-endowed continuation of Boas's decade-old research. Museum support and Jesup's money allowed him to add archaeology to his research tools; otherwise they were an extension of his previous method and strategy. "I am going to continue my previous work without practically changing my plans at all," he told McGee, "but since I have ampler funds than heretofore, I shall be able to work to better advantage."[41] The areas touched on lightly by the Expedition were those on which he had done little or nothing before 1897.

In this, the neglect of Alaska was serious. While the Alaska Eskimo and Aleuts had earlier been designated as part of the Expedition, no research appropriation was listed for them and Boas never seriously considered a study of the place of Eskimo and Aleut in intercontinental connections. The Indians of southern Alaska also had been included in the initial plans, with Boas apparently intending to do the work there himself. There were few accounts of the Tlingit, though the museum did have "a mass of manuscript material" on that Southeast Alaska group, but it belonged to G. T. Emmons and was not accessible even to Boas. Yet he did not "feel like spending money in that country as long as this work has been done."[42] A factor in the neglect may simply have been that the museum already had rich artifact collections from both the Tlingit and the Alaska Eskimo.

The American research, then, was uneven. The published results form no coherent corpus. Several deal with decorative art, something that was then a major concern of Boas's, but did not address intercontinental relationships. Farrand's work on the Chilcotin, the only Athapaskan groups at all studied, revealed simply a receptivity to neighbors' traditions. Boas only later realized that more attention needed to be given to the wide-ranging Athapaskans, especially those of the far North.[43]

On the Asian side, no old program disturbed the Expedition's objective. There the Expedition was more productive and suggestive of relationships. Laufer contributed little, but Jochelson's *Koryak* and Bogoras's *Chukchee* were extended ethnographic treatments, and Bogoras went on to do compilations of Chukchi, Asian Eskimo, and other myths. Some of their findings allowed Boas to draw far-reaching conclusions to the great problem that was the Expedition's focus. Both Russians were so struck by the closeness of northwestern American and northeastern Asiatic folklore that they were certain there had to have been either close contact or a kindred origin, and probably both in earlier times.[44] Bogoras found ideas characteristic of the North Pacific Coast prevailing far into Siberia, so much so that he wrote, "from an ethnographical point of view, the line dividing Asia and America lies far southwestward of Bering strait."[45] Boas reached the same conclusion. The Koryak, Chukchi, and Itel'men (Kamchadal) formed one race with Northwest Coast tribes. The unity had been much greater in earlier times, but "enough remains to lead us to think that the tribes of this whole area must be considered as a single race, or at least that their culture is a single culture, which at one time was found in both the northeastern part of the Old World and the northwestern part of the New World." Traditions showed far-reaching conformity between the two regions; the similarity of motifs was beyond doubt. Nor could the languages of the two areas be separated. The speech of the Asian groups inclined more toward America than Central Asia; if a linguistic division was to be made, Eastern Siberian languages were best grouped with those of America. All evidence from physical anthropology tended toward the same conclusion.[46]

Later events had broken the ancient homogeneity. Just as Tungus (Evenk) and Yakut (Sakha) people had reduced the area once occupied by the "Paleo-Asiatic" tribes of Siberia, migrations had broken the continuities on the American side. The Salish along the Fraser River and adjacent coasts were a recent intrusion; so too were the Tsimshian, who seemed originally to have been an interior people more akin to the Shoshone and Kootenay.[47] The Eskimo were the most obvious intrusion—a sharply defined physical type, essentially different from their neighbors.

Some of these conclusions are plausible so far as anthropology and archeology are able to interpret the obscure past. A school of recent scholarship argues for a tripartite division of Americans. Northwest Coast groups, along with neighboring Athapaskans, may be the descendants of a separate migration from Asia. Other American Indians seem to be descended from a Paleo-Indian group, presumably the earliest migrants, who formed the initial, widespread Paleo-Indian Clovis population. The third broad group are the Eskimo and Aleut, descendants of Eskaleut ancestors.[48] This would support the Eskimo as a discontinuity, although the argument is increasingly contested by others using different evidence. The Tsimshian and Coast Salish discontinuities are more dubious.

Within this general schema, however, Boas was led to several dubious subsidiary conclusions. He was persuaded that the commonality of the Northwest Coast and Siberia came from a reverse, America to Asia postglacial migration. Boas seemed convinced that the Siberian groups were an offshoot of American peoples. This "Americanoid" theory receives no current support.[49] He was even more certain that the Eskimo were an American people who had arrived in Alaska and Siberia in recent times, driven northward by the Athapaskan and thus descending to the Arctic coast. "The much discussed theory of the Asiatic origin of the Eskimo," he wrote in 1910, "must be entirely abandoned." Although the dogmatism was sometimes tempered with a wish for archeological confirmation that an earlier, non-Eskimo type had inhabited Alaska, Boas's insistence is curious. He recognized the strongly "mongoloid" physical type of the Eskimo, their very strong maritime cultural similarity with the Koryak and Chukchi, and the possible connection of Yukon pottery with Siberia, but considered their language and physical type quite different. His insistence on a southeastern or central Arctic origin for the Eskimo goes back to his conclusions of the mid-1880s. The view was endorsed by Bogoras and Jochelson, both of whom wrote of the Eskimo as a wedge that split the trunk of the common tree. Eskimo origin was, as a later anthropologist noted, Boas's ideé fixe.[50]

Part of his difficulty was understandable ignorance. The Alaskan Eskimo were imperfectly known. He noted the paucity of knowledge of Eskimo mythology west of the Mackenzie River had prevented "a clear insight into the main characteristics of the folk-lore of the western Eskimo."[51] The uniformity of Eskimo culture was "remarkable," and, though he cited "a certain amount of differentiation" west of the Mackenzie, he attributed it to influence from Indian neighbors. But the case is so complicated, with different data giving quite different results, that relationships seem almost as uncertain as ever.[52]

Another difficulty was that Boas was working without adequate archeology and, had he pursued that in Alaska and northern Siberia, the methods of the time would probably not have revealed the necessary data. A further difficulty was that he was hampered by a shallow temporal view of ethnic relationships. He tended, understandably, to project historical entities back into remote prehistory. He continued, despite his concern with acculturation and diffusion, despite his attempt at historical depth, to lapse into thoughts of migrations of peoples more or less congruent with historical divisions. Although he made salient the idea that tribes were not stable units lacking in any historical development, but cultures in constant flux, each influenced by its nearer and more distant neighbors in space and in time,[53] he did not free himself from that fallacy. While northwestern Indian ancestry reaches back to the Old World, recent archeology has shown the great age of culture in the region and its continuity from its first discernible forms to its appearance at European contact.[54]

The Jesup Expedition did document some of the far-reaching affinities it sought between Siberia and the Northwest Coast and Interior. Similarities of bows, housing, water craft, harpoons, and armor, for example, could be found on each side of the North Pacific. Elements, even structures, of mythologies were so strikingly similar that chance had to be ruled out. That much was true. On the other hand, Boas was blinded by his preconceived idea of Eskimo origin and remained ignorant of the complexities of Alaskan relationships. He (and Jochelson) willfully dismissed any counter–evidence of Eskimo participation in North Pacific culture.[55]

The Expedition's research had ended in 1902, though Boas subsequently tried to fill in and round out parts of it. He requested money from

Jesup for work among the Nootka and for Jochelson to visit the Asian Eskimo and Aleut in order to follow up "fundamental questions" raised by his earlier work. He also sought an appropriation to investigate his theory that the Tsimshian were recent arrivals on the coast.[56] He was unsuccessful in securing funds for any of these projects.

A major difficulty in assessing the Jesup Expedition is that so much was never attempted and so much was never completed. Publications by Bogoras on the Itel'men (Kamchadal), Laufer on the Gold (Nanai), Shternberg on "The Sociology of the Amur Tribes," and Dina Jochelson-Brodskya on the anthropometry of Siberia fell largely by the wayside. Despite Boas's great concern with measurements on both the Asian and American sides, he never correlated the results. Those results, computed a century later, do not support his interpretation of the peopling of North America.[57]

Most tellingly, since no final, summary volume ever appeared, there are only sketchy and fragmentary suggestions of Boas's conclusions. His comparisons drew on similarities of material culture and mythology and on vaguely described physical and linguistic similarities. Even these did not entirely support his conclusions: he was forced to acknowledge—but dismiss—the importance of Chukchi and Eskimo similarities. The conclusions he published in conference papers or journal articles after the Expedition ventured only a little beyond the evidence he had used between 1895 and 1897 to urge it. The material gathered, important as it was (and is) probably could not have sustained much more. That, as much as any other factor, may have been the reason for the absence of the summary volume. The Expedition was never the "systematic" one that Boas claimed to have conceived. With no work at all in Alaska, the results lacked comprehensiveness. Little ever appeared to support Boas's conclusion that Siberian languages should be classified as American—a view he later more or less repudiated.[58] The subject best covered was material culture, and the tangible results lay less in its publications than in the unrivaled collections that were taken from the North Pacific region to the granite buildings on Manhattan's Central Park West.[59]

It had been a very expensive affair. One thing after another contributed to overruns. Boas's initial estimate had projected the Expedition costs at $5,000 a year over six years, a total of $30,000 from Jesup's pocket. In his haste to prepare the proposal, he had not realized that transportation costs and salaries of museum staff when in the field would have to be born by the Expedition's budget and not by the museum's. These costs upset budget projections. Then the hiring of Bogoras and Jochelson brought an embarrassing crisis. He had expected to employ young men, like Laufer, just out of university. The experienced Russians would do the work much better than an untried newcomer, but they were much more expensive: $1,200 a year compared to Laufer's $500. Jesup agreed, despite the overrun his expedition was suddenly facing. Boas expected that work on the Asian side alone would cost $27,667, with the entire Expedition running to almost $50,000, without publication costs. Jesup complained in 1900 that he could not keep the business in his head: "I only know I am advancing a pile of money in this affair & time will prove the success of it." By then Boas was estimating that the cost, including publications, was likely to be $75,000. In June 1906 when Boas contracted to finish the series on a piece-work basis, the additional cost was not to exceed $25,000. By then Jesup had become greatly disturbed with "an enterprise that has involved expense and anxiety out of all proportion to the representations that were originally made" and sorry about "the many disappointments that have come to me in connection with this expedition."[60]

When Jesup died in 1908, his widow expressed a wish to soon see the final volume, but Boas was uninterested. "I have sworn to myself that I will not write the volume until all material is published." Boas had his disappointments, too, and his continuing difficulties with the museum had destroyed his desire to get on with the Jesup publications. Two volumes were about to appear, but there would then be a long pause, since he had done no work for two years. "The fault lies," wrote Boas, "in the obstructionism in the museum." Indeed, "if I could do so in a way consistent with my scientific commitments, I would simply dump the whole Jesup Expedition and concern myself no further with it."[61]

Drop it, he could not. He was too invested and too committed to it. The material from the Russian side came in fitfully, and Boas worked on it, sometimes just as fitfully. Despite delays, some of the Russian material was so extensive that Boas had to find outlets beyond the restricted confines of the Jesup memoirs.

Bogoras was by far the most productive. His Chukchi ethnology had come out in three installments by 1909, the Chukchi mythology in 1910, and the Siberian Eskimo in 1913. His Koryak texts and Chukchi grammar were essentially complete by 1914. Jochelson's Koryak ethnology was in print by 1908, but his Aleutian expedition delayed his work on the Yukaghir. The most remiss was Shternberg, who had been added belatedly to write on the Amur groups he knew from his exile and expedition study.

Then the outbreak of war in Europe made communications between New York and Russia almost impossible and severely interrupted the mail with Brill, the Dutch publishers. The American Museum extended Boas's contract to 1916, then extended it again. The Russian Revolution and its aftermath disrupted things even further. In the meanwhile, the war and post-Armistice conditions in Europe absorbed a great deal of Boas's attention and robbed him of scholarly concentration. Like Bogoras and Jochelson, he could not sever himself from political concerns as a patriotic American filled with German sympathies. The Jesup publications limped along, hampered by war, revolution, and reconstruction. It was squeezed in among Boas's many other concerns, none of which included writing a summary volume.[62]

Such a project went against Boas's temperamental difficulty with making sustained and sweeping generalizations. At least as much, his deep hostility to the American Museum endured beyond Bumpus's departure and Jesup's death. The combination of temperament and hostility was probably enough to prevent the completion of a summary volume, but the delayed Siberian results allowed Boas to eternally procrastinate. The absence of a fitting conclusion was probably inevitable.

15 "Laying Clear the Complex Relations of Each Individual Culture"

RACE, CULTURE, AND METHOD

By 1906, the hallmarks of Boas's anthropology were clear. In the 1880s he had departed from scientific positivism and geographical determinism to embrace historical determinism, while retaining the inductive method central to his conception of science. The aim of anthropology, for Boas, had become the biological and psychological history of mankind: "to trace the history and distribution of every single phenomenon relating to the social life of man and to the physical appearance of tribes." He treated the subject as a historical discipline, concerned with the individual phenomenon in all its complexity. When he had left physics to become a "historian," he left a good deal behind him, but did not depart from a commitment to science.[1]

Anthropology remained a science, and Boas a scientist. He never deviated from this conviction. Science, based on the inductive method, carried with it a professional, even a moral, ethos for him. The value of anthropology, he told a meeting of naturalists in 1898, lies in the potential application of inductive methods to the study of various social phenomena. "Our conclusions," he argued, "must be as truly inductive as those of any other science."[2] His concerns were methodological.

During the two decades surrounding the turn of the century, Boas essentially elaborated on the methodological fundamentals of his writings from the late 1880s. He was an insistent methodologist, attempting to find and propagate the proper method for discovering the physical and psychological aspects of the human past. While his specific findings and conclusions could be as erroneous as those of his contemporaries, his method, even more his concerns for methodology, distinguished him from them. If he attacked the conclusions and theories of others, it was not so much because they were wrong as that they were "speculative," inadequate, and incorrect in their use of method.[3]

Anthropological theory in the previous decades had been dominated by a concern for the origins of human traits—of marriage, kinship, religion, morality, law, language, music, and art.[4] British writers, confronted with the problems presented by Darwin and the discovery of prehistory, had to explain the emergence of human culture in terms of a regular and lawful process, the alternative to divine intervention. Germans, though perhaps less absorbed by Darwinianism, were equally concerned with the remote origins of European civilization. So too were Americans, though the Indians always loomed more immediately in their thought. What concerned this generation of mid- and late-nineteenth-century anthropologists was less the history of any specific group of people than *generic* human nature and development. One of E. B. Tylor's primary aims in *Primitive Culture,* for example, was to arrange, in probable order of evolution, the phenomenon of all human culture. Other writers, hindered by the absence of historical evidence for the origin of inventions and institutions, sought to reconstruct these on the basis of archaeology and language, but when these failed, they were prepared to use data from peoples still living in apparently earlier stages of human evolution. John Lubbock used both "ancient remains" and "the manners and customs of modern savages" to write his *Prehistoric Times,* in the belief that "different races in similar stages of development often present more features of resemblance to one another than the same race does to itself in different stages of its history."[5] This was the comparative method. Tylor, Lubbock, and Hugh McLennan in Britain, Johann Bachofen, S. R. Steinmetz, and A. H. Post on the Continent, and Morgan, Powell, and Daniel G. Brinton in the United States all worked in this way.

Brinton, one of the grand old men of American anthropology, almost caricatured the search for origins and the set of assumptions behind it. To Brinton the most startling discovery of anthropology was that the laws of human thought were inflexible and automatic. The human mind was a machine, wrote the Philadelphia physician: give it the same materials and it will always grind out the same product. This was, for Brinton, the cornerstone of "true anthropology": the discovery of the psychic unity of man and thus the parallelism of his development everywhere, "the nigh absolute uniformity of his thoughts and actions, his aims and methods, when in the same degree of development, no matter where he is, or in what epoch living." Such "ethnographic parallels" between primitive tribes and European ancestors left no doubt that they were controlled by natural laws based on the "one and unvarying psychical nature of man."[6]

Psychic unity underlay the idea of stages of human evolution—classically progressing from savagery to barbarism to civilization. Such an intellectual construction assumed, as succinctly summarized by George Stocking, Jr., that laws, uniform in the past and present, governed social and cultural phenomena; that the growth of society and culture was from the simple to the complex, though at different tempos, resulting in a differential ability to exercise control over external nature in the assumption of a hierarchical ordering of peoples as higher and lower. The differential development meant that living groups of primitive peoples approximated the earlier stages of civilized peoples and thus allowed a comparative reconstruction of the past.[7]

Boas is commonly seen as a critic of such cultural evolutionary ideas. This is true enough, but underplays two important points. First, he was almost equally critical of geographical and environmental determinism, biological and racial determinism, some diffusionist theories, and, later, Freudian interpretation and economic determinism. Moreover, he was not opposed to evolutionary thought. He did not, for example, dispute evolution as development; indeed, he implicitly accepted "the development of civilization" and continued to speak of "stages of culture."[8] His critique of cultural evolutionary theories centered not on evolution itself so much as the methodology employed—especially the misuse of psychic unity and ethnographic parallels.

The "comparative method" bore the brunt of his criticism. He declared it "remarkably barren of definite results."[9] The practitioners whom he targeted were not so much Tylor, Morgan, Spencer, and Bachofen, the great remembered names of evolutionary theory, but his immediate Americanist predecessors, particularly Brinton. In "The Limitations of the Comparative Method of Anthropology," written in 1896, Boas especially had in mind Brinton and his previous year's presidential address to the AAAS on the "Aims of Anthropology."

At this time Brinton commanded great prestige, though Boas regarded him as "very arrogant but not very deep."[10] Boas had already taken a poke at him the previous December at the American Folk-Lore Society. He had outlined some of the results and methodological conclusions of his just-published *Indianische Sagen* and used the occasion to dismiss independent origin as a cause of the similarities of folktales within North America: "We must pause before accepting the sweeping assertion that sameness of ethnical phenomena is *always* due to the sameness of the working of the human mind." He took issue with "modern anthropologists" who dismissed anyone looking for patterns of diffusion as failing to grasp "the true spirit of anthropology," a reference to Brinton and his address. Moreover, since Brinton had used Bastian as an authority on psychic unity, he thought it necessary "to define clearly what Bastian terms the elementary ideas" in an exercise meant as a corrective lecture to the Philadelphian. Boas, as he remembered years later, was fighting "the old speculative theories."[11]

Boas, irritated by Brinton's announced paper at the forthcoming Buffalo AAAS meetings, which he suspected would be critical of his *Indianische Sagen* conclusions, chose a head-on attack of Brinton's extolled comparative method. His paper was written "completely against" Brinton, and he expected it to be the "main dance" at the session.[12]

In "The Limitations of the Comparative Method," Boas criticized the extremes to which the comparative method had been taken and again questioned its "fundamental assumption" that the same phenomenon were always due to the same cause, and thus that "the human mind obeys the same laws everywhere." That a phenomenon was widespread proved nothing if its origins were incomparably different. Even the most cursory review showed that the same phenomenon could develop in a multitude of ways. This was a rematch of the 1887 debate, with Brinton rather than Mason as the antagonist. Boas provided three instances of similar effects from dissimilar causes. One was the existence of totemic clans, those in the Southwest derived by the coalescing of smaller tribes and in the Northwest by the disintegration of larger tribes, distinctly different causes that led "to results which appear identical." Decorative art provided another example: geometric designs had been reached by four different lines of development and from an infinite number of starting points. Finally, in reiteration, he cited masks. Boas's critique rested, again, on the complexity of the origins of superficially similar phenomena. Valid comparisons demanded comparable material; the causes of any phenomenon had to be investigated before the effects of the same causes could be proved.[13]

Such investigation required the historical method. Actual relations of phenomenon were to be sought in slow, careful, and detailed study. It was only after the history of a single culture was clear and an understanding reached on the effects of environment, psychological conditions, and foreign influences upon the complex relationships of that culture and its neighboring tribes that comparisons could be made. Such study afforded a means of "determining with considerable accuracy the historical causes

that led to the formation of the customs in question and to the psychological processes that were at work in their development." The method,
moreover, had to be applied to a small and well-defined territory, with
comparisons limited to the cultural area that formed the basis of the
study. This had been the essence of his own Northwest Coast work,
notably *Indianische Sagen,* and the strategy behind the Jesup Expedition.
"I insist," Boas concluded, "that the application of this method is the
indispensable condition of sound progress."[14] It was the better and safer
method.

Boas's method led him to examine each people in their historical
specificity. The complexity he found undermined the conclusions of
ethnographic parallels and the unity of the human mind as conceived by
Brinton and other comparative evolutionists. The search for the origin of
marriage, religion, or art could be realized only after investigating the origin and development of specific groups in specific cultural areas. "Before
we seek for what is common to all culture, we must analyze each culture."
The quest for *generic* origins could only follow the pursuit of specific
ones. The aims of the comparative method, then, could be achieved only
after "laying clear the complex relations of each individual culture."[15]

Boas returned to these themes whenever he was forced to enunciate
general principles of ethnological methodology. They appeared in his
1902 obituary of Rudolf Virchow, a researcher whose position, Boas
wrote, rested on the scientific principle that it was dangerous to classify
imperfectly known data under general theories and that the sound
progress of science required a clear distinction between hypothetical
assertions and exact observations.[16] In 1904 Boas condemned theories of
evolution based on "observed homologies and supposed similarities," theories that had to be revised again and again as empirical knowledge
proved the fallacy of their foundations. "In place of a simple line of evolution," he wrote, "there appears a multiplicity of converging and diverg-
ing lines which it is difficult to bring under one system." Diversity, not
uniformity, among human cultures was the striking feature revealed by
anthropology. Brilliant theories about a grand scheme of cultural development had collapsed, ushering in a period of "steady empirical work,"
which meant a "complete revision" of old ideas. Anthropology in 1904 was
entering upon the empirical revision, an inductive attack on all theories.
A new science, anthropology was "still struggling with methods," and
Boas believed that localized historical and inductive methods were the
proper ones.[17]

The thrust of all this remained the struggle with methods. Boas, it has often been asserted, was not a generalizer, or a theorist.[18] This is somewhat true, but definitely not the case with method: Boas was an emphatic methodologist. He questioned unilinear evolution, not because he disputed evolutionary processes, but because the assumptions that underlay the conclusions of Brinton and others were hypothetical and deductive rather than empirical and inductive. He was fighting "speculative theories" because they were speculative, not because they were evolutionary. The method determined the results: brilliant and suggestive as they might seem, they were still flawed.

Boas, in a sense, was open to the scientific use of hypothesis and the comparative method when subjected to empirical and inductive constraints, open even to social and cultural evolution. A thorough comparison between cultures was the "indispensable condition" for generalization. Any resulting deductions, however, had to be based on actual history, not upon hypothetical laws of development. Boas declined to speculate on the origin of human language or institutions. In his Columbia course he could accept the idea that civilization resulted from "a long historical evolution that began with cultural forms found among primitive people," and that "the discovery of a system of the evolution of culture" remained a fundamental problem of the discipline, but he left these largely alone. He was uninterested in generic origins.[19]

Boas sometimes envisaged a marriage of the historical and comparative methods, one acting as a restraint upon the other. Seemingly antagonistic, these methods could be used together to check the potentially rash conclusions made by using one alone. Historical analysis could provide data on "the growth of ideas among different people," while general comparisons of "the processes of their growth" could furnish data on the laws governing evolution.[20] But this single example of the usefulness of the two methods together was a hasty and imperfect one.

The Salishan-speaking Bella Coola, he discovered during the Jesup Expedition, possessed a systematic cosmology of deities that was, he wrote, "vastly superior" to their non-Salishan neighbors and Salish speakers elsewhere. Such a sophisticated system could neither have been brought with them nor imported; it must have been developed by the Bella Coola themselves. In moving to their present location, he hypothesized, they had received some foreign ideas from their new neighbors. In assimilating these, they had formulated a different concept of the world, one which coincided in all its main features with those created by men of other zones and of other races. The mind of the Bella Coola philosopher, operating with the class of knowledge common to the earlier strata of culture, has reached conclusions similar to those that have been formed by man the world over, when operating with the same class of knowledge.[21]

This statement was almost Brintonian: the human mind grinding out the same product from the same materials. But Boas's example was itself probably a "rash conclusion" based on "imperfectly known" data. Boas formed his conclusion after spending only ten days in the Bella Coola valley in the summer of 1897, mostly working with a single informant. T. F. McIlwraith, working much more intensely some twenty-five years later, found this an elaboration in the mythology of only two families.[22] The systematic cosmology was largely a chimera, the product of incomplete research and a propensity, unusual for Boas, to grasp at comparative analogy.

Anthropology, as Boas described it in 1904, was "the biological history of mankind in all its varieties; linguistics applied to people without written languages; the ethnology of people without historic records; and prehistoric archeology." This division, eventually to become the fourfold basis of American academic anthropology, was based on different methods for different phenomena. The historical perspective had shaken "the foundations of the old principles of classification." Linguists had tried to classify people by language and biologists by physical features, but these efforts had clashed. "People genetically connected by language, or even by the same language," he wrote, "were found to be diverse in type, and people of the same type proved to be diverse in language." Furthermore, the results of ethnological classifications of people by their customs disagreed with both the linguistic and physical classifications. All such classifications were partial, merely focusing on a specific element to describe the history of peoples. "The attempted classifications were expressions of historical data" that recorded descent, mixture of blood, changes in language, and the development and interchanges of culture. The incongruity among such classifications demonstrated that there was no necessary association between race, language, and culture.[23]

Boas had himself never doubted the distinction. It was virtually a given among many in the German scholarly community during the 1880s, and intrinsic to the distinction between "Anthropologie" and "Ethnologie." As Friedrich Müller had written, the anthropologist did not need to consider Völker (peoples) since the concept of Volk (a people) was completely alien to his science, and the ethnologist did not consider Rasse (race) since that concept was alien to his science. Otto Schräder asserted that a common culture and a shared language were two phenomena that did not necessarily coincide. And, more directly, Virchow had demonstrated that the Indo-European people possessed no uniform physical type and always maintained that language and culture were not congruent. Boas came to the same conclusions: "People who belong to one type may speak different languages and possess different forms of culture."[24]

The differences were, of course, also methodological. Investigations of race revealed the biological history of a people; linguistic study revealed the historical affinities of a people's past which might render different information from research into its customs. Each subject had its own method and constituted a different branch of anthropology. So varied were these subjects and their methods that no single person could be equally proficient in all, and Boas foresaw the separation of physical anthropology and its later attachment to biology. "All the problems relating to the effect of geographical and social environment and those relating to heredity are purely of a biological character." Anthropology might set the problems, but the solutions would come from biologists. Similar reasoning urged the separation of purely linguistic work from ethnology and archaeology.[25] Despite these pronouncements, Boas continued to spread himself over the three, even four, areas, though he remained aware of their dissimilarities.

Most distinctive was physical anthropology. This was one area in which Boas never rejected the physicist's method of establishing orderly rows of facts for generalizations on physical growth, heredity, and differentiation. Physical anthropology was a field in which the methods of the natural sciences, especially statistics, were applicable. Here the individual, whether a single measured Sioux or a solitary Salish skull, lost its significance in the statistics of body and cranial measurements. Since Quetelet, physical anthropology had introduced numerical measurements that could point the way to morphological laws. It sought to discern and classify types, to investigate the influence of social and geographical environment, heredity and population mixtures, and, in the end, to reconstruct the history of human biological groups, even human "types."[26]

These were diverse problems, not all of which directly related to the "primitive" peoples that were the subject of Boas's ethnological and linguistic concerns. In his work on human growth, origin was a variable, but his interest had come in large part from influences at Clark and ran in a separate stream from his other anthropological concerns. His anthropometrics, however, were most often directed toward the usual peoples of his ethnological studies and had their origin with his BAAS work among British Columbia Indians. He had supervised the measurement of some 17,000 Indians and half-bloods for the Chicago Fair, and his quest for bodily statistics occupied many of the Jesup Expedition participants.[27] Boas, with his training, was a fish in statistical waters.[28] Once into anthropometrics and biometrics, he quickly appreciated the advances made by Francis Galton and Karl Pearson and, as a "dabbler" on the frontiers of statistics, made some himself. He had long planned to write a book on statistical method, but never got further than fragments.[29]

It was from this statistical concern, again a methodological one, that he emphasized variation and complexity. In studying the cephalic indices of half-bloods, he stressed two maxima of frequency on the curve, so that an average figure was not just meaningless but misleading. Anthropometric curves were not always probability curves, because half-bloods appeared to revert to one or the other ancestral form, not to a middle type. The effect of intermixture was thus "most complicated," with different curves for different physical features. While the half-bloods were taller than either ancestral group, their faces and noses were intermediate. Some traits worked one way, some another. The Indian type, in breadth of face and darkness of hair and eyes, seemed to have a stronger influence upon the offspring than the White type. Boas's explanation was merely speculative. Dark hair and wide faces might be older, "more primitive characteristics" than light eyes and narrow faces; almost all the half-bloods he measured were offspring of Indian mothers, though there was no proof that children resembled their mothers more than their fathers.[30] The facts were solid, the absurdity of the possible explanations only a mark of the futility that genetic ignorance imposed. His study of half-bloods was filled with frustration.

The complexity of the implications was daunting. So many possible causes for human physical traits existed that they could be combined in various ways to sustain almost any explanation. Social environment, geographical influences, selection, chance variation, or hereditary mixture could be manipulated to explain extremely complex phenomena. All this suggested, as Stocking has written, that physical anthropology was at a crisis, up a "blind alley." The problem was no one understood how traits were passed from parent to child. Heredity, for all its importance, was a mystery. Even after 1900, with the elaboration of mutation theory and the rediscovery of Mendel's forgotten paper, the field was in confusion for years until its basic conclusions and ambiguities could be sorted out into a new synthesis based on genetic transmission.[31]

As a research tool, physical anthropology at the time could contribute little to the solution of significant problems. Boas might explode the prevailing view that half-bloods tended toward infertility and loss of vigor, and reveal instead that they had more children than Indians, were taller, and showed more variation, but he could go no further. His osteological and anthropometric work on the Northwest Coast suggested some historical conclusions, but most of them proved doubtful. His vast anthropometic statistics went largely unprocessed, and probably could not have been by existing means.[32] This was part of the blind alley. Little wonder that Boas was tempted to relinquish solutions to biologists.[33] If he was unable to solve the problems he confronted during these years, only uncovering more as he proceeded, he did become more sophisticated in his scepticism to the prevailing assumptions and solutions.

One key concept underscored by all of his work in physical anthropology and biometrics was variability. The statistical series of his measurements demonstrated the extent of variability within groups. Growth rates varied between boys and girls, and by age, origin, and social classes. Statistics made quite clear that "type" was itself a constructed abstraction, where the average measurements represented merely an ideal.[34] The implications of Boas's stress on variability were spelled out in his infrequent broad-gauged lectures.

His most extended treatment, "Human Faculty as Determined by Race" in 1894, explored the question of racial capabilities. Brain size was the one anatomical feature that seemed to bear most directly on the question. On average, Whites had the largest brains, African Negroes the smallest. There had been problems with using brain size as a determinant of ability, yet it was "more than probable" that a larger brain demonstrated increased mental ability.[35] It seemed a very probable case for White superiority. But Boas questioned this facile conclusion. The grounds, again, were the individual fact and the statistical variation. He asserted that "variations inside any single race are such that they overlap the variations in another race," and that "the overlapping of variations is significant in so far as it shows that the existing differences are not fundamental." Half of all Whites had a skull capacity higher than 1,550 centimeters. More than a quarter of Negroes did too. Thus, while there might be fewer Negroes of high genius, there would not be any great lack of ability among Negroes living in circumstances similar to Whites. Many individuals did not differ in ability, even though the statistic of whole races revealed differences. He concluded that, on the basis of individuality and variation,

> the average faculty of the white race is found to the same degree in a large proportion of individuals of all other races, and although it is probable that some of these races may not produce as large a proportion of great men as our own race, there is no reason to suppose that they are unable to reach the level of civilization represented by the bulk of our own people.[36]

By 1907 his conclusion remained the same, though with a different tone and emphasis. He was still convinced that "there *are* differences in form and size of the brains of different races, but the variability within each race is so great that the small average differences between distinct racial types are almost insignificant as compared to the total range of racial variability." The majority of people constituting two distinct races, it seemed likely, might have approximately the same capacity. Thus "we must guard against the inference that divergence from the European type is synonymous with inferiority." Different they might be, inferior they need not be.[37]

In "Human Faculty" Boas concluded that races might be different in their faculties and character, but it was difficult to discern which manifestations were hereditary and so the cause of a "low stage of culture," and which were a social product of that low stage and so could be "wiped out by civilization." Thus, while there were probably differences in mental characteristics, social factors could not be excluded. Boas remained tentative, however, impressed by the seemingly overwhelming evidence of the inferiority of non-White races. As Stocking emphasizes, he had not yet fully developed cultural determinism as an alternative to racial determinism. He resisted the latter, but only by opting, without proof, for Waitz's formula that mental faculty was determined by the stage of culture rather than the reverse. Boas consequently assumed, as did Brinton and other evolutionists, that "in the main the mental characteristics of man are the same all over the world."[38] To Brinton, this meant that people everywhere, under the same circumstances, would make the same inventions. Thus "psychic unity" enabled the discernment of laws of generic human development. Boas, on the other hand, assumed the similarity of the human mind to seek the laws of mental *processes*.

Anthropology, aside from its biological branch, was essentially psychological. That concept of the discipline, with its emphasis on mental process, was shared with Bastian, Waitz, Gerland, and Wundt. Anthropology, in this sense, was the study of the character, processes, and products of the human mind expressed in the various aspects of ethnology and linguistics. With the assistance of psychology, anthropology might elucidate fundamental problems.

The organization of the human mind, Boas thought, was practically identical among all races, and so mental activity followed the same laws everywhere, but the manifestations of these "depend upon the character of individual experience that is subjected to the actions of these laws." These laws were "a product of the diversity of the cultures that furnish the material with which the mind operates." "Mental manifestations" thus depended upon the individual experience as received through imitation and the association of ideas. Traditional habit, educational precept, as well as how the mind accepted new ideas or experiences by association with old ones, seemed the key elements. Boas considered the primitive mind as characterized by more "emotional" and less logical and rational processes than the civilized mind in making sense of phenomena. Consequently, the primitive was more custom-bound and conservative. While logical forms of association increased with civilization, tradition and habit still affected the civilized mind. Both possessed a mixture of the emotional and rational, but in a decidedly different balance. Though the recipe changed with civilization, the ingredients remained the same.[39]

By 1900 Boas had conceptualized the problem as essentially the distinction between the minds of primitive and civilized man. The primitive mind, "conditioned as it was by its own processes within its own culture," varied from the civilized mind, itself conditioned by its own history. Primitive people might react differently to the same stimulus—or similarly to different stimuli. The processes of the primitive mind were determined and transmitted by imitation, precept, habit, and unconscious associations. These same processes operated upon the civilized mind. All humans were the products of the "character of individual experience" within their culture. It was this psychological process, especially "how people came to their beliefs and how they altered them," that Boas sought to explain.[40] His strategy was to examine the dissemination of ideas and their "acculturation" into existing ones. In that process he might find psychological laws about the workings of the human mind.

The new note here may have been associational psychology. In the past Boas had depended upon Gabriel Tarde's concept of imitation and Otto Stoll's concept of suggestion as great insights into mental processes. While these influences remained, especially Tarde, he was now indebted to the work of his psychologist colleague, Livingston Farrand. Boas explored how the primitive mind associated new and borrowed ideas with old ones; how it constructed the intricate interrelationships of its world view by associations of ideas, habits, and traditions, none of which was usually conscious. While association and acculturation were in a sense new, they were also a reapplication of apperception, used by Boas in his "Alternating Sounds" article of 1889. The concept, dealing with how new ideas are determined by and adapted to those already possessed, went back to J. F. Herbart, but was developed by Steinthal and used by Erdmann. Boas's acculturation was a development of his 1889 article on apperception.[41]

Boas's theory of the mind was a generalizing one, placing all primitive groups into a category and pattern of thought that formed a continuum with civilized—that is, European—groups. It had its elements of evolution, and assumed a uniformity of the human mind that extended from the most primitive to the most civilized. The measure of civilization became an ability to make logical and rational associations between cause and effect. While in some ways as speculative as other theories, it was based in large part on his own empirical study. To that extent, Boas's theory of the mind of primitive man was historical and inductive. It was not, however, very elaborate or penetrating.

Boas, in attempting to explain the difference between the mental processes of primitive and civilized man, came very close to a coherent use of the culture concept. Differences in mental life "may be due almost entirely to the form of individual experience, which is directed by the geographical and social element of the individual," itself "a characteristic of historical development." He still tended to use "social life of the people" or some such phrase for what would later become "culture." Sometimes, in his search for conceptualization, he stretched the meaning of "folklore" toward that end. Folklore, he wrote, was "the total mass of traditional matter present in the mind of a given people at any given time," a phrasing close to anthropological "culture" as it was later known. Folklore, he felt in 1904, had become "the science of all the manifestations of popular life." His phraseology was mixed. The mind of man altered according to "the type of culture of each people" and was "determined largely by the social surroundings of the individuals."[42]

In the decade between 1894 and 1904, Boas had become almost conceptually clear about "culture." A major difficulty, of course, was that "culture" already had a meaning in the singular sense of cultivation and civilization, and it was difficult to unambiguously separate it from that older meaning. Certainly Tylor had used the word "culture" in its widest ethnographic sense, as "that complex whole which includes knowledge, belief, art, morals, law, custom, and any other capability and habits acquired by man as a member of society." But he used it synonymously with "civilization" and in the singular. Culture did not enter into common usage as a plural and conceptual term for decades. Stocking persuasively argues that Boas had much to do with this development. Increasingly Boas used "culture," which could be plural, where he meant "social environment" or where he had been tempted to extend the meaning of "folklore."[43] Folklore, too, had a common meaning, restricted to tales, beliefs, remedies, and other traditions—something difficult to extend to all traditional and habitual elements of a "social environment." Boas was not one to invent new words or compound old ones. He had no taste for neologisms. So he struggled with the ambiguity of language, which made clear conceptualizations difficult.

The concept of culture brought with it yet another rigorous determinism, environmental not geographical. Cultural determinism, the cumulative influence of a historical and social environment, now entered as a dominant theme in Boas's thought.

His cultural determinism, like the historical determinism which formed part of it, was relativistic. During these years, as he was refining his methods and concepts, he noted how difficult it was "to recognize that the value we attribute to our own civilization is due to the fact that we participate in this civilization and that it has been controlling all our actions since the time of our birth." Man was captive to his culture. He could, however, transcend its values through conscious effort and through an examination of contrasting cultures and their values. In order to understand the mind of man in its variety of forms, Boas contended, the anthropologist had to try "to divest himself entirely of opinions and emotions based upon the peculiar social environment into which he is born" and adapt his own mind, as far as possible, to that of the people he was studying. Anthropologists, then, had to free themselves from the bias of their own civilization, remove their own cultural lenses or "Kulturbrille."[44]

Boas's cultural relativism, already enunciated in his debate with Mason in 1887, was a methodological device, directed against a priori judgments. He chastised "the subjective element, emotional in its sources, which leads us to ascribe the highest value to that which is near and dear to us."[45] Such subjective valuations were characteristic of evolutionary theories that made "our own civilization" the standard against which other times and other races should be measured. Anthropology required its students to thoroughly adapt "to the ways of thinking and feeling of foreign tribes and peoples," putting aside, as much as possible, the "opinions and emotions" of their own society. Boas's cultural relativism was to a large extent, as Stocking has noted, "conditioned by considerations of anthropological method."[46]

Boas recognized that it was exceedingly difficult to study the mental thoughts and processes of one's own group because the human mind was "affected by the same influences to which our reasoning is subject." The only corrective was to study the human mind in other historical and geographical environments. The power of the anthropological method, then, lay in its potential to teach "the relative value of all forms of culture," and to check "an exaggerated valuation of the standpoint of our own." Relativism, derived from a study of other times and places, became a methodological tool to foster scientific objectivity.[47]

16 "The Human Mind Has Been Creative Everywhere"

THE CULTURAL VALUES OF FRANZ BOAS

B OAS MADE CULTURAL relativism a methodological tool; it was, of course, more than that. Relativism possessed a redemptive value that touched the core of Boas's own values. Anthropology's usefulness rested in its ability "to impress us with the relative value of all forms of culture." Presented in the right manner, the discipline "broadens the historical point of view, and teaches a greater tolerance towards foreign forms of culture and a higher appreciation of the accomplishments of foreign races." At the American Museum, one of his concerns had been to show the public that "our people are not the only carriers of civilization, but that the human mind has been creative everywhere," and that primitive tribes often had highly developed industries and made objects of rare beauty. At Columbia, too, one of the fundamental aspects of his introductory course had been to bring out "clearly and emphatically" an appreciation of "our old civilization as one of a great many distinct types of human culture." The appreciation of foreign races and cultures thus assumed an "ethical importance."[1] This emphasis upon the redemptive value of cultural relativism in anthropology was most often tagged to the end of a letter, article, or paper. Boas never elaborated upon it, never rationalized or defended it, never even particularly highlighted it. It was a profession of faith, temperament, and ideology.

That anthropology had an ethical importance for Boas was an indication of his personal values. His value system was etched into a great deal of his work, and those grooves became increasingly apparent as the years passed. The acid's bite had begun in his Minden home where the ideals of 1848 were reinforced by his mother, and in the ethical and cultural values of German liberalism and assimilated German Jewry. Such values were also those of his admired German-American friends, Jacobi, Adler, and Schurz.[2]

Most basic of Boas's values, in some ways, was his intellectual commitment to the primacy of reason. He admired the intellectual attributes of Virchow, "a genius for grasping the causal relation of phenomena." Boas believed the history of civilization to be a history of increased rationality, as humanity discarded more and more of its emotional constraints to embrace logical reasoning. Thus the history of civilization—and of science—was one of the increasing triumphs of reason.[3] With the development of civilization, the process of substituting rational for emotional thought had diminished the role of restrictive customs and fostered a general willingness to change. With the increase of rationality came an increase in individualism and the freedom to deviate. But traditions and customs, invariably attached to ethical principles, acted as social constraints and guarded against such deviation, potentially promoting intolerance and persecution. With the advance of civilization and rationality, "the number of thinkers who try to free themselves from the fetters of tradition increases." This represented, as Stocking puts it, "a nineteenth-century belief in a singular human progress in 'civilization' that was based ultimately on the cumulation of rational knowledge."[4] For Boas, it also represented an intellectual self-portrait of how he wished his own mind to work.

The value he placed on rationality was associated with his personal values of liberty and individualism, tolerance for deviation and difference, and a dislike for any restraint that tradition and dogma might impose. These values reflected Boas's version of nineteenth-century liberalism. He was very much the product of what Woodruff D. Smith called the German neoliberal cultural sciences, and his work showed their permanent stamp. "In many ways," declares Marvin Harris, "the Boasian program corresponds rather closely with the fundamental ideological outlook associated with left-of-center political liberalism." The belief in multiracial democracy, relativity of customs, freedom for the individual, and the power of the rational mind, were themes "faithfully mirrored in the work of Boas." Much of Boas's anthropology, to borrow from Carl Degler, was not the result of "disinterested, scientific enquiry," but "derived from an ideological commitment that began in his early life" and continued to shape his professional and personal outlook. They were facets of Boas's own cultural values, which he accepted "as a practical manifestation of social truth."[5]

These facets of his "ideological commitment" were explicit occasionally in his writings before 1906. His thoughts on questions of race, however, were molded by them earlier, and emerged clearly in his "Human Faculty" address, his writings on the primitive mind, his research on racial mixture, and, increasingly, as he turned his attention to the Negro question in his concern for equal rights and opportunities. He was not yet interested in letter-to-the-editor writing, let alone public pamphleteering. His only such ventures were a defense of the outlawed potlatch in a small Canadian newspaper and interventions with government officials to ameliorate the potlatch ban and Native prostitution.[6]

Boas's political views remained personal. His dislike of the German political system, Wilhelm II and Bismarck, German colonial adventurism, chauvinistic "Deutschtum," and the failure to address social questions, were private thoughts, shared with family, friends, and acquaintances. He had come to the United States in part because he felt he could contribute to the social good, but, aside from the classroom and museum hall, he had not done so yet. He continued to be politically passive even as he became disillusioned with America over the Spanish-American War. He opposed the war and the imperial expansion that accompanied it because America had violated the principles that he, along with Schurz and others like him, had felt were at its basis. He had supported McKinley in 1896, hoping the country would be spared from Bryan, but refused to cast a presidential ballot in 1900: McKinley was a hypocrite, but Bryan was useless. He hoped that the Filipinos, Cubans, and Puerto Ricans would be so vexatious that America would be "happy not to want to mix further in their affairs." Roosevelt's Panamanian intervention was a swindle, throwing over all principles of international law.[7] Even then, however, he subordinated his own views given an opportunity to use imperialism for his own purposes. The East Asiatic Committee, composed largely of men with financial interests in Asia, was his most public response.

While Boas remained liberal in his political position, he was not a reformer or a progressive in any meaningful sense. He made no active commitment to reform causes or to political parties. He no doubt had opinions on the events around him, but concerns about poverty, housing, trusts, strikes, Tammany, jobbery and other civic and social concerns of the day are almost entirely absent from his writings, public or private. His recorded reaction to Seth Low's crusade to reform New York City was merely the regret that it took Low away from Columbia's presidency. Because he left few written comments upon social or political issues, a classification of his position is difficult, but, on the little evidence he left, he might better be seen as a mugwump than a progressive. He possessed some of the traits that characterized mugwumpery—a concern for independence, conscience, honor, and a sense of being, by status and intelligence, above the fray.[8]

It is hard to conceive of Boas, the scholarly entrepreneur who counted on Schiff, Harriman, Villard, and Jesup to fulfill his academic ambitions and whose concerns always required the resources of the better classes, as an economic or social radical. Boas's associations with these prosperous businessmen and the professional men of the Germanistic Society leads one to suspect that, while he had reform sympathies, they were those of a patrician. His view of politics had probably not advanced greatly beyond that of a National Liberal in Germany, the mugwump views of Carl Schurz, or the quiet, apolitical professionalism of that former Communist, Abraham Jacobi, who lent his name to New York's fusionist Committee of Seventy. Boas's ethical concerns were almost entirely disciplinary ones, to his own science and his career within it. Broad as his anthropological interests were, he focused narrowly upon them in this period of his life.

The Spanish-American War, coupled with the increasing rivalries of the Great Powers, turned his attention to the phenomena of the nation-state and nationalism. His analysis characteristically attempted a rational and objective examination of an essentially nonrational phenomenon. He had seen the face of nationalism before, notably on his return to Germany in 1885, and he knew it firsthand from the ardent nationalist Fischer. The enthusiasm of so many Americans for war and imperialism in 1898 again brought it to him.

In his 1901 essay, "The Mind of Primitive Man," Boas linked national-ism to tradition and traced its evolution to "the idea of the solidarity of the horde." From this sense of solidarity, the feeling of fellowship gradu-ally broadened. As civilization advanced, it grew into a feeling of tribal unity, then extended to territorial neighbors, and to a fellowship with those who shared the language, customs, and traditions of the commu-nity, culminating in "the belief that it is right to preserve its peculiarities and to impose them upon the rest of the world." The ethical point of view which made it justifiable to increase the well-being of one nation at the cost of another—"the tendency to value one's own civilization as higher than that of the whole race of mankind"—was the same as that which prompted primitive man to consider every stranger as an enemy to be killed. This analysis of nationalism as a sort of primitive atavism was not very profound. More striking is that Boas's own belief in progress sup-ported a social evolutionary diagnosis that implicitly foresaw a progres-sion of the ethical concept of the fellowship of mankind into something transcending its existing limitations.[9] Boas remained a social evolutionist, a believer in the progressive elevation of humanity.

Striking, too, is the note of ethical universalism and the subordination of national values to those of "the whole race of mankind." Boas certainly embraced an "enlightened universalism that transcended ethnic provincialism."[10] And yet he was encumbered by loyalties and identities of which this universalism was a part. His "cosmopolitanism" was not rootless; nor was he alienated from old loyalties or marginal identities.[11]

His early life had been conditioned by "a German home." In becoming American, Boas did not cease to be German. His personal associations were most often German, with his family and Marie's integrated among others of the large German-speaking community of New York. He continued to share in the rich world of advanced German scholarship through university and museum colleagues and his frequent summer visits. His ties to his homeland were not just the tangible ones of family, friends, and scholars, but also of affectionate memory. A deep attachment to Minden and Porta Westfalica, to Bonn and the Alemannen, never left him. In 1904 he was instrumental, with Jacobi, Schurz, and Emil L. Boas of the Hamburg-America Line, in forming the Germanistic Society of America, whose purpose was to promote mutual understanding between the German and American peoples. He became very active as its secretary. He was an "ethnic" German, preserving and promoting German culture and values in America. He possessed, as he wrote many years later, a "starkes Heimatsgefühl," a strong feeling for the homeland.[12] Boas was consciously and ineradicably German.

His Jewishness, as indelible as his Germanness, was a different matter. While sensitive to his Jewishness and to slurs upon it, he conspicuously did not identify himself as a Jew. That others identified him that way, he could not help. Boas did not wish to be set apart; he did not like the feeling that "the term Jew assigns to the bearer an exceptional position"; he did not like the lingering of "the consciousness of the old, sharper divisions which the ages have not been able to efface," divisions strong enough to find "expression as antipathy to the Jewish type."[13] Boas, as Leonard B. Glick has stated, "was in many respects a typical representative of that segment of late 19th-century German Jewry who had in effect abandoned the struggle to integrate Jewish identity with German nationality and had opted for an all-out effort to assimilate themselves out of existence."[14]

Boas was born a Jew. He accepted this fact, never disavowing his ancestry, and, after deliberation, decided against the possible advantages of converting to Christianity. Jewish tradition had a small role in his rearing, and, like most German Jews of his generation, he showed no interest in

ABOVE: A Kwakiutl troupe at the Chicago World's Fair in 1893. George Hunt is absent. AMNH NEG. #337217

BELOW: A portion of the Northwest Coast display at the Chicago World's Fair. AMNH NEG. #102224

ABOVE: Franz, Helene, and Marie Boas. Photo by Rice. APS B/B61/no. 5/N.B. #46

BELOW: The Boases' cottage on Lake George, owned by Abraham Jacobi. APS NEG. #17A

RIGHT: Boas with George Hunt and his family at Fort Rupert. APS NEG. #466.

TOP FAR LEFT: F. W. Putnam, pictured here some years after he had "wedged" Boas into the curator's position at New York's American Museum of Natural History. Photo by Morton-Yourow. AMNH NEG. #2A5220

MIDDLE FAR LEFT: Boas during his Chicago time. Photo by Smith. APS NEG. #715

BOTTOM FAR LEFT: Dr. Abraham Jacobi, Boas's uncle and benefactor. COURTESY OF THE ARCHIVES OF THE MOUNT SINAI SCHOOL OF MEDICINE

TOP LEFT: James Teit with his Thompson wife Lucy Antko, taken in 1897 by Harlan I. Smith. AMNH NEG. #11646

BOTTOM LEFT: Morris K. Jesup, President of the American Museum of Natural History. Photo by Morton-Yourow. AMNH NEG. #2A5200

ABOVE LEFT: Berthold Laufer, Boas's "younger brother." AMNH NEG. #125308

BELOW LEFT: Clark Wissler, Boas's student and colleague who, against Boas's strong wishes, succeeded him at the American Museum. Photo by Morton-Yourow. AMNH NEG. #2A5245

RIGHT: Hermon C. Bumpus, Director of the American Museum, with whom Boas had such "fundamental differences" that he was obliged to resign from his curatorship. Photo by A.J. Rota. AMNH NEG. #319950

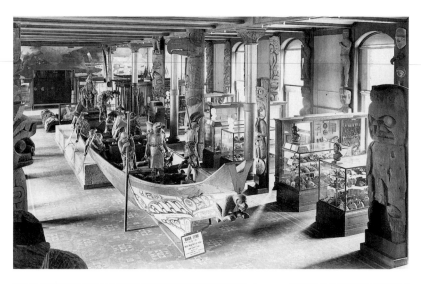

TOP: The North Pacific Hall at the AMNH, about 1902. Photo by Thomas Lunt. AMNH NEG. #33003

BOTTOM: The Boases at home, October 1900. Franz is at the piano with Ernst and Helene as Marie watches. APS NEG. #4

rediscovering it. He was, in virtually every sense, raised within an assimilated milieu and had little to "assimilate out of existence." His childhood and university friends were not Jewish. Although infatuated with a Jewish girl in Bonn, his full love was extended to Marie Krackowizer, an Austrian-American, whose ancestry was Catholic but who seemed, like Boas, a generation removed from that identity. His American associations were often German and so sometimes Jewish, but the ties were more certainly German.

He could, we know, be prickly about his Jewishness and actively hostile to anti-Semitism when he personally encountered it. How this came about, we do not know. Certainly all Jewish youths, no matter what their personal encounters, were aware of the pervasive ambivalence, often hostility, that surrounded them. No doubt Boas heard more rude expressions of prejudice than the ones from Zenker's school and the single recorded childhood incident in a Minden shop. He certainly experienced overt anti-Semitism at Kiel, and cited it as an obstacle to possible careers as a Gymnasium or German university teacher. He avoided any bias since, in both cases, they were careers he did not wish to pursue. Neither in Germany nor America did his Jewishness seem to have hindered him. Disappointments abounded and, while his early career coincided with a rise of anti-Semitism in Germany and America, his difficulties can all be explained by other factors. Significantly, Boas never attributed any of them to prejudice. When Joseph Schiff voiced a suspicion that Columbia was prejudiced in its faculty hiring, Boas protested that he had discerned no such thing. He was "absolutely certain" that there was no anti-Semitic bias among his colleagues. He knew of several Jews recently appointed; there might be others, but he was uncertain "because I never thought about the subject."[15] While attitudes toward him were no doubt filtered through the almost ubiquitous perceptions about Jews, it is impossible to find any evidence of discrimination against him in these years.

He certainly accepted the process of assimilation and anticipated its continuation. The end of the Jewish question (as with the Indian and Negro questions) would be assimilation into the family of man. He never expected ethnic qualities to disappear, but he did not consider Jewishness—certainly his kind of Jewishness—to be an ethnicity. That view was shared by many of his generation and his parents', men and women who considered themselves fully emancipated individuals, discernably Jews at most in their private lives or not at all. Boas's formative years were during the brief golden age of the convergence of Jewish values and aspirations with those of the majority of the German middle class. To many, Jewishness was merely a religious matter, a question of private belief; in all other respects, Jews were Germans. To some, like Boas, it was a matter of family extraction, an incidental feature of "Abstammung." Liberal assimilationism represented the views of the majority of German Jews, even a larger majority of German-American Jews.[16]

As Glick correctly highlights, Boas represents features common to, or typical of, German Jews of his generation. Like many others in the late nineteenth-century, Boas did not convert to Christianity, but "turned instead to a personal philosophy compounded of rationalism, cultural relativism, and ethical humanism, and identified himself as an enlightened universalist who had transcended both ethnic provincialism and supernatural religion." This was, indeed, Boas's personal set of values, held in common with many others of German-Jewish descent. It was, as George L. Mosse insists, a redefined identity based upon the Enlightenment and Bildung, and thus subscribing to individualism, rationalism, humanism, and universalism. German culture, as shaped by the Enlightenment, emancipation, and the concept of Bildung, was an integral part of the "Jewishness" of German Jews. Boas's whole outlook was profoundly determined by that culture, and, more specifically, by the nineteenth-century movement of German Jewry to assimilate to the enlightened culture of that century's "Bildungsbürgertum" and its identity with liberalism. When Boas described his ideals as having developed "because I am what I am and have lived where I have lived,"[17] he was summing up the legacy of his formative years as a German-Jewish liberal. That liberalism, with its stress upon rationality, individualism, liberty, and the cultural determinants of thought and behavior, characterized his outlook and his anthropology.

While Boas's values were common among German–Jewish Americans, it must be said that they were not distinct or unique. Such ideals and values were shared among a large group of European and American liberals, whether followers of Virchow in Germany, Gladstone in Britain, Kossuth in Hungary, or the Jeffersonian tradition in the United States. Boas came to the United States in large part because he admired American attachment to those values.

Important as were Boas's ideas and identity, he owed his successes and some of his failures to his personality and temperament. He recognized that he was not always an easy man to get along with. Cooperation, he diagnosed, was not easy "with one whose work rests essentially on an unfeeling criticism of his own work and that of others." There was more than that, of course. Kroeber noted that he possessed a faculty for build-ing up enmities and sowing antagonism. Lowie indicated a deficiency of empathy and an unwillingness to make allowances for human frailties. Boas had an unswerving loyalty to friends or dependents, but to others he could be "aloof and probably fundamentally indifferent," even coldly hostile.[18]

He had difficulties with Heinrich Kiepert, but attracted the support of almost every other German academic and scholar with whom he dealt. He was aggravated at having to take directions from Horatio Hale, but his problems with President Hall were no more than those of his Clark col-leagues, almost all of whom remained lifelong friends. He enjoyed the strong support of Frederic Putnam, turning against him only when he felt betrayed, but even here, however, he made amends by initiating the Festschrift for Putnam's seventieth birthday. His departmental colleagues in the American Museum, excepting Marshall Saville, were deeply attached to him. He broke bitterly with H. C. Bumpus, less bitterly with Morris Jesup. Outside his own immediate circle he was doubtless more respected than loved. That was true of many anthropologists at Washington, D.C., and a scattering elsewhere. Tact, as Kroeber wrote to Putnam in 1904, was "not Boas' way."

Yet Boas denigrated his own accomplishments: "What I have done is solely and completely the result of my rigorous schooling that would not allow me to participate in all the scientific humbug which reigned in anthropology."[19] As Matti Bunzl has remarked, Boas's orientation "was grounded in a German anthropological tradition extending back through Bastian and Ritter, through Steinthal and Waitz, to the brothers Alexander and Wilhelm von Humboldt."[20] He did possess "unusual intellectual pow-ers" and a many-sided virtuosity. His penetrating and critical mind, per-haps as much the product of his education and training as his personal ability, rejected much of the prevailing "humbug" in the field. The dis-cerning qualities of Boas's intellect came, however, not just from the dis-cipline of a Prussian Gymnasium and the German university system. They rested on his freethinking upbringing, his search for philosophical foundations for his science, and his restless questioning of convention. Boas's very irreligion may have contributed to this. Freud, his close con-temporary, was similarly reared as a nonbeliever. "Because I was a Jew," he wrote in 1926, "I found myself free of many prejudices which restrict oth-ers in the use of the intellect: as a Jew I was prepared to be in opposition and to renounce agreement with the 'compact majority.' "[21]

Boas was also a restless intellect, always seeing new problems and advancing new methods of attacking them.[22] He acknowledge he owed a great deal of his success to sheer industry. He did work very hard. Boas was "endowed with a tremendous physical energy which permitted driving himself ruthlessly," recalled former student Leslie Spier. "No man could have accomplished so much without the physical stamina to sustain brilliant mental powers."[23] At the same time, Boas attributed his success to the newness, indeed rawness, of anthropology in America. As an emerging field, he felt "achievement is easy and the recompense of the industrious." He did not think highly of his American colleagues: "Actually it is very easy to be one of the first among anthropologists over here."[24]

Boas brought with him an intellectual preparation unmatched by his American colleagues. Holmes and Cushing, arguably among the most gifted American anthropologists of Boas's generation, had no scholarly training. Even Putnam was without a university degree. All his contemporaries had apprenticed in other fields: Putnam in zoology, Holmes in art and geology, Powell and McGee in geology, Cushing in nothing in particular. But Boas's preparation was different: his geographical training was partly ethnological, his biological and mathematical background was suitable for anthropometrics, and his apprenticeship was in Bastian's museum, perhaps the most professional of any anthropological institution at the time. From this basis, he was able to master areas such as linguistics, folklore, and art, untouched by his academic training.

If there was a whiff of intellectual, even cultural, arrogance in Boas's regard for American anthropologists, that too was due to his scientific professionalism. Science required disciplined education and training, which he felt was not appreciated enough in North America. Laymen had their role, especially rich laymen, but science was the prerogative of the professionally trained. This attitude formed his position on the membership policy of the American Anthropological Association and his views on other anthropologists.

This opinion was doubtless sensed and resented by those in his field, especially those in Washington, D.C., who had arrived at their anthropological careers in quite a different way and were proud of their own accomplishments. Boas's 1904 "History of Anthropology," for example, disregarded the field's American past, except for a reference to Brinton's extremism on independent origins. Joan Mark notes this omission, and is surely correct in her insistence that Boas "joined—he did not create—an ongoing science of anthropology in the United States."[25] There is truth in Mark's assessment, but also in Boas's evaluation.

Boas had high scientific standards. Kroeber even thought that his introduction of strict standards was perhaps his main service to anthropology.[26] With that went a highly idealized conception of science and scientists. The world of learning formed a special world of intellect, of rational thinkers devoted to ideals that transcended all prejudices. "He seemed to personify," wrote Lowie, "the very spirit of science and with his high seriousness—unsurpassed by any investigator I have ever known in any sphere—he communicated something of that spirit to others."[27] If Boas had any faith, if he deified anything, it was most certainly science.

Through critical thought, organizational drive, the ability to master new and diverse fields, and, as much as anything else, sheer industry, he had commanded the field of American anthropology by 1906, becoming the leading ethnologist, Americanist linguist, folklorist, and physical anthropologist.[28] Moreover, his industry was coupled with a restless ambition that was forever incubating new projects, expeditions, publication series, and institutes. The twelve-year-old who had feared spending his life "unknown and unregarded," the young immigrant who wished "to create a geographical science" in the United States and to turn himself into "the pivot for all geography and related endeavors," retained his will and audacity through disappointments as well as successes. No sooner had he seduced Jesup into funding the North Pacific Expedition, than he sought quadruple the funds for his Vanishing Tribes scheme and thousands for Asian research.

Boas wished to "hold a certain power," to become a fulcrum and establish his students in all the meaningful positions, but he always associated that objective with science. His ambition, even in letters to his parents, was cloaked in the rhetoric of promoting knowledge and advancing science. Boas's ambitions were linked to the secular mission to deepen a rational understanding of the world—to Science.

17 "Searching for Opportunities in Other Fields"

A LEAF IS TURNED

Boas's departure from the American Museum had been marked by Laufer's November 1905 call for scholarly and financial contributions for a Festschrift to honor Boas on the twenty-fifth anniversary of his doctorate in August 1906. Laufer served as secretary and editor and thus was a prime mover, but the idea may also have come from Jacobi, someone with means and influence as well as personal interest. The committee was chaired by President Butler of Columbia. Members included Jesup from the museum, Andrew D. White from the Germanistic Society, Edward D. Adams and Jacob Schiff from the East Asiatic Committee, W J McGee, formerly of the Bureau of American Ethnology, Eduard Seler of Berlin, and Boas's oldest American associates, Jacobi and Schurz.[1] Subscribers included family (Onkel Kobus and Willy Meyer), associates from the German and German-Jewish community (including Felix Adler, Isaac N. Seligman, and Felix M. Warburg), and scientific colleagues. The forty-six contributors were even more varied. Fourteen of them were European, primarily German, eight were former students, and four were field collaborators (Comer, Mutch, Hunt, and Teit). Such close associates mingled with sometime adversaries (Holmes and Dorsey), and two were old German friends (Rudolf Lehmann and Ernst Richard). Theobald Fischer wrote from Marburg with his good wishes, but, off on yet another African trip, he could not contribute. Putnam, forbidden by his doctor from literary work, sent his usual effusive good wishes.

The celebration did not go smoothly. The book, delayed by "manifold typographical and other technical difficulties," was not ready for the anniversary date. Eight months late, Butler presented the freshly printed book to its honoree before a gathering of the University Council. The formal, blue ribbon dinner downtown had to be canceled when Ernst came down with pneumonia, so close to death that Boas would not leave his bedside.[2]

The previous decade had seen an apogee of Boas's career trajectory. With positions in three major institutions—curator of ethnology at the American Museum, professor of anthropology at Columbia, and philologist at the BAE—he had a strong base of training, research, and appointments. At the museum he was directing not only the massive Jesup North Pacific Expedition, but his Vanishing Tribes project with fieldworkers in California and on the Plains. Mutch and Comer were collecting for him in the Eastern Arctic. At the same time, he was initiating the East Asian project that had just despatched Laufer to China and seemed on the verge of sending a fieldworker to the Philippines. At Columbia he headed a growing division that, with Harvard, helped provide trained men for the demands of the museum's expeditions and was beginning to place students into independent positions. This growing cadre of students and ex-students imbibed his methodological insistence upon empirical, field-based experience and embraced most of his fundamental anthropological views.

That phase, marked by the anniversary tributes, was now over. To Laufer the Festschrift was a protest "*in tyrannos,*" and Boas recognized that it was meant as a vindication of his museum work as much as a celebration of his Kiel doctorate.[3] Boas's base was now restricted to Columbia.

Already the Columbia side of his career was impressive—doctorates for Kroeber, Wissler, and William Jones (to whom Dixon and Swanton should be added) and nine more, including Alexander Goldenweiser, R. H. Lowie, Frank Speck, and Edward Sapir in the works—and, almost immediately after leaving the museum, he accepted the chair of the department of psychology, philosophy, and anthropology. He did have some immediate problems there. Farrand's energies were concentrated outside the university, and Wissler, whom he had counted on to take increased responsibilities, had instead chosen to take Boas's place at the museum. On the other hand, Boas had succeeded in securing his choice, Friedrich Hirth, for the new Chinese professorship, depended on Laufer to build up the anthropology side of an East Asian division, and retained Bandelier for South American work.

He now threw his energy into university-based projects: a diplomatic and consular institute shared by Columbia and Yale; an international school of American archaeology in Mexico to be sponsored by Columbia, Harvard, Pennsylvania, Paris, and Berlin; the teaching of the origin and history of civilization at Columbia; and, through his secretaryship of the Germanistic Society of America, the advancing of German culture at

Columbia and other universities. He maintained his philologist position with the BAE and so gained, for his prospective *Handbook of North American Languages* program, support for his students' work and some of his own. To replace the museum as an outlet, he initiated a publication series through the American Ethnological Society.

Boas wrote in early 1906 that he had to find new directions for his activity, "to search for opportunities in other fields." He would continue to push the Yale-Columbia school as a means for studying Latin America, the Far East, and U.S. dependencies, and contemplated directing his administrative and organizational activity toward Spanish America. He spearheaded a joint application by the six major American anthropological and archaeological societies for a large Carnegie grant to solve the problem of anthropology in South America. His own fieldwork might, he thought, be redirected from the Northwest Coast to more southern parts of the continent. He was already working on the collaborative Americanist school in Mexico and inclined to transfer his own work to the south, especially dealing with the languages and cultures of the region. He would perhaps begin with the Pueblos and work systematically southward. Another line of work he increasingly emphasized was the anthropology of the Negro.[4] In May 1906, at the request of Atlanta University's W. E. B. DuBois, he attended the Atlanta Conference and gave a commencement address on "The Negro Race in America," and in 1907 he began teaching a Columbia course on the Negro. The anthropometrics of immigrants had also seized his attention as his research interests increasingly touched upon issues of public policy.

The next few years would be difficult. He was resilient, but the situation was gloomy. "The whole anthropological work in New York is depressing," he wrote at the end of 1907. "While a few years ago we stood at the head of American anthropological work, now everything is dead or nonsense. . . . When I think how the outlook a few years ago was and what they now are, I feel completely discouraged." Laufer's departure to the Field Museum left New York anthropology even more pitiable. "All our former hopes and aspirations have gone to pieces."[5]

In the summer of 1906, Jacob Meyer died. Onkel Kobus, childless and long widowed, left $150,000 in trust to his brother Abraham and his sister Sophie, who, in turn, would distribute the sum to their sons and daughters upon their deaths. In addition, Helene Boas received $5,000 in trust,

Gertrude and Franziska $3,000 each. The legacies left Boas a little more at ease about his family's financial future.[6]

At about the same time, he decided to leave West 82nd Street and build a house across the Hudson River in Grantwood, New Jersey. Borrowing from Jacobi and the development company, he purchased four twenty-five-foot partly wooded lots and hired an architect to design and supervise construction. They moved into the new house in October 1907. This move and his full-time duties at Columbia were paragraphs on the leaf that had turned in his life and career.

Abbreviations

THE FRANZ BOAS papers in the American Philosophical Society, Philadelphia, are in at least two series, which I have called the Professional Papers and the Family Papers. The former are available on microfilm with a published index. The Family Papers are unmicrofilmed. I note the Professional Papers as BPP, leaving the Family Papers without denotation.

AA	*American Anthropologist*
AMNH	American Museum of Natural History, New York
APS	American Philosophical Society Library, Philadelphia
BAE	Bureau of American Ethnology Papers, National Anthropological Archives, Smithsonian Institution, Washington, D.C.
BAAS	British Association for the Advancement of Science
BPP	Boas Professional Papers, American Philosophical Society, Philadelphia
FB	Franz Boas
MB	Marie (Krackowizer) Boas
MK	Marie Krackowizer
NAA	National Anthropological Archives, Smithsonian Institution, Washington, D.C.
RLC	Franz Boas, *Race, Language and Culture.* New York: Macmillan, 1940; New York: Free Press, 1966

Notes

INTRODUCTION

1 Laufer to FB, 1 July 1906, BPP; FB to Mama, 26 April 1907.
2 The literature on Franz Boas is vast. For general discussions of his role in American anthropology, see, among others, Walter Goldschmidt, ed., *The Anthropology of Franz Boas: Essays on the Centennial of His Birth*, AAA memoir 89 (San Francisco: Howard Chandler, 1959); Regna D. Darnell, "The Development of American Anthropology, 1879–1920: From the Bureau of American Ethnology to Franz Boas" (Ph.D. diss., University of Pennsylvania, 1969); George W. Stocking, Jr., *Race, Culture, and Evolution: Essays in the History of Anthropology* (New York: Free Press, 1968); and Joan Mark, *Four Anthropologists: An American Science in its Early Years* (New York: Science History Publications, 1980).
3 Carl N. Degler, *In Search of Human Nature: The Decline and Revival of Darwinism in American Social Thought* (New York: Oxford University Press, 1991). Dinesh D'Souza, *The End of Racism: Principles for a Multiracial Society* (New York: Free Press, 1995).
4 Murray Wax, "The Limitations of Boas' Anthropology," *AA* 58 (1956), 63–74; Marvin Harris, *The Rise of Anthropological Theory: A History of Theories of Culture* (New York: Thomas Crowell Co., 1968), 250, 284–89; Ronald P. Rohner and Evelyn C. Rohner, "Franz Boas and the Development of North American Ethnology and Ethnography," in *The Ethnography of Franz Boas*, ed. Ronald P. Rohner and trans. Hedy Parker (Chicago: University of Chicago Press, 1969); xxiii–xxx; Leslie White, *The Ethnography and Ethnology of Franz Boas*, Texas Memorial Museum Bulletin No. 6 (1963), 59–67; Derek Freeman, *Margaret Mead and Samoa: The Making and Unmaking of an Anthropological Myth* (Cambridge: Harvard University Press, 1983), xvi, 3–61; George W. Stocking, Jr., *After Tylor: British Social Anthropology, 1888–1951* (Madison: University of Wisconsin Press, 1995), 349–66.
5 Melville J. Herskovits, *Franz Boas: The Science of Man in the Making* (New York: Charles Scribner's Sons, 1953); Marshall Hyatt, "The Emergence of a Discipline: Franz Boas and the Study of Man" (Ph.D. diss., University of Delaware, 1979); Marshall Hyatt, *Franz Boas, Social Activist: The Dynamics of Ethnicity* (New York: Greenwood Press, 1990). Muriel Rukeyser, with the Boas family's cooperation, began a biography in the late 1940s. See also Julia Elizabeth Liss, "The Cosmopolitan Imagination: Franz Boas and the Development of American Anthropology" (Ph.D. diss., University of California, Berkeley, 1990).
6 Verne F. Ray, Review of Herskovits, *Franz Boas: The Science of Man in the Making*, *AA* 57 (1955), 138.
7 *Guide to the Microfilm Collection of the Professional Papers of Franz Boas*, 2 vols. (Wilmington: Scholarly Resources with the American Philosophical Society, 1972).

8 See, for instance, George W. Stocking, Jr., ed., *The Shaping of American Anthropology, 1883–1911: A Franz Boas Reader* (New York: Basic Books, 1974); and "The Scientific Reaction Against Cultural Anthropology, 1917–1920," in *Race, Culture, and Evolution*, 270–307.

CHAPTER 1: "MY OLD, GOOD HOMETOWN"

1 There were 44 heads of Jewish households (174 persons) in 1846. Arno Herzig gives the following figures for 1846 heads of household: 30 merchants and bankers (73%); 6 handworkers (15%); 5 professionals/intellectuals (12%). Herzig, "Das Sozialprofil der jüdischen Bürger von Minden im Übergang vom 18. bis 19. Jahrhundert," *Mitteilungen des Mindener Geschichtsvereins* 50 (1978), 60; and *Abraham Jacobi: Die Entwicklung zum sozialistischen und revolutionären Demokraten: Briefe, Dokumente, Presseartikel (1848–1953)* (Minden: Mindener Geschichtsverein, 1980), 23; Hans Nordsiek, *Juden in Minden: Dokumente und Bilder jüdischen Lebens vom Mittelalter bis zum 20. Jahrhundert* (Minden: Kommunalarchiv Minden, 1988).

2 Herzig, "Das Sozialprofil," 56; Staatsarchiv Detmold, Reg. Minden, IL, Nr. 280, Bl. 58, in ibid., 60; ibid., n56.

3 The genealogy here is based in large part on B. Brilling, "Die Vorfahren des Professors Franz Boas," *Mitteilungen des Mindener Geschichts- und Museumsvereins* 38 (1966).

4 English renders it as Boaz, the German as Boas.

5 Universitätsarchiv Münster, Matrikel; Testimonials of Feibes Boas, January 1819.

6 *Mindische Fana*, Beilage zum 37. Stöck des [Mindener] *Sonntagsblatt*, 8 September 1836.

7 Boas Papers, Family Series, American Philosophical Society. All documents otherwise uncited as to location are in this collection. Hete Boas Lehmann, "Reminiscences of Franz Boas."

8 Toni Boas Wohlauer, "Reminiscences," 6.

9 Abraham Jacobi, memorial address to Jacob Meyer, as reported in FB to Mama, 29 July 1906.

10 Kommunalarchiv Minden, E40 and E43.

11 Toni Wohlauer, "Reminiscences"; Hete Boas Lehmann, "Reminiscences."

12 Kommunalarchiv Minden, Inscriptionsbuch der höheren Töchterschule in Minden, I, no. 440; Töchterschule, "Acta scholastica der Töchterschule in Minden," 1842–1844, 1 April 1844; Schulzeugnisse; see Arno Herzig, *"In unsern Herzen glüht der Freiheit Schein": Die Entstehungsphase der bürgerlichen und sozialen Demokratie in Minden (1848–1878)* (Minden: Mindener Geschichtsverein, 1981), 12.

13 Herzig, *Jacobi*, 14.

14 Martin Hundt, *Louis Kugelmann: Eine Biographie des Arztes und Freundes von Karl Marx und Friedrich Engels* (Berlin: Dietz Verlag, 1974), 62.

15 Jacobi to F. Meyer, 27 October 1850, in Herzig, *Jacobi*, 85; Jacobi to F. Meyer, 3 February 1851, ibid., 99; Jacobi to F. Meyer, 10–11 January 1851, ibid., 94.

16 Sophie Meyer to Jacobi, 8–12 March 1851, ibid., 107–8.

17 Quoted in Rhoda Truax, *The Doctors Jacobi* (Boston: Little, Brown and Co., 1952), 155.

18 Kommunalarchiv Minden, F260: Acta betreffend . . . Synagogen-Gemeinde, 1847–78.

CHAPTER 2: "WHAT CLAIM CAN SOMEONE LIKE ME HAVE UPON FAME?"

1 FB reminiscences to Ernst Boas; FB, c.v.

2 Ibid. Hermann Wagner was a Bielefeld teacher and prolific author of nature books

intended especially for children. His name is persistently misspelled as Wagener in the c.v.

3 Kommunalarchiv Minden, F1059, G. Asprion to Oberbergermeister, 30 June 1860; *Mindener-Lübbecker Kreis Blatt,* 1 May 1861, 2; 30 March 1861, 2; Sophie to Dr. A. Braun, 13 March 1862; FB, c.v.

4 Hete's reminiscences spell it as "Pemayer." There is no such name in the Minden city directories or in the municipal file of applications and permissions for private instruction in the Minden archives, F1059.

5 This reference is, admittedly, a little elusive. Hansheinrich Thomas wrote to Muriel Rukeyser in 1947 of an unnamed lady, then living in Göttigen, one year younger than Boas, who had told him of Boas's boyhood intentions to go to the Eskimo.

6 FB to Onkel (Jacobi?), 9 April 1868. Hermann Wagner, who wrote books on Franklin in the Arctic and Vogel in Africa, may also have been an influence.

7 See Marianne Nordsiek, "Siegmund Imanuel (1790–1847) und die Reorganisation des Mindener Gymnasiums," in *Land und Leuten Dienen: Ein Lesebuch zur Geschichte der Schule in Minden,* ed. Friedhelm Sundergeld (Minden: J. C. C. Bruns, 1980), 103–21.

8 Bürger-Zeitung, 30 June 1869, 3.

9 FB to uncle and aunt, 27 December 1867.

10 He studied first at the Meyers' and later from Toni, who had lessons in Jena and then became quite proficient during her 1873–74 year in New York.

11 Cramer had been one of the circle of Minden revolutionaries associated with Jacobi, Herzberg, Kugelmann, and the Meyers in 1848–51.

12 FB, c.v.

13 FB to Jacobi, 9 April 1868, 20 February, 22 September 1869.

14 Hete Boas Lehmann, "Reminiscences."

15 Wilhelm Schroeder, *Chronik der Stadt Minden* (Minden: P. Leonardy, 1883), passim; *Mindener-Lübbecker Kreis Blatt,* 28 September 1870, 3.

16 FB, c.v.

17 FB to Toni, 6 April, 30 June 1871.

18 FB, c.v.

19 Ibid.

20 Meier to Sophie Boas, 14 December 1871, transcribed in Hete Boas Lehmann, "Reminiscences."

21 Meier to Sophie Boas, 14 December 1871.

22 FB to Sophie, 5 January 1872; FB to Toni, 6 January 1872.

23 FB, c.v.

24 Ibid.

25 Ibid.; Willy Meyer to FB, 26 September 1872.

26 FB, c.v.

27 Ibid.

28 Ludwig Uhland (1787–1862) and Adelbert von Chamisso (1781–1838).

29 FB, c.v.

30 Ibid.

31 Meier Boas to Toni, addition to FB to Toni, 27 September 1873; FB to Toni, 6 February 1874. See also Kommunalarchiv Minden, Ratsgymnasium Bestand 179, Conferenz-Protokole, 26 Marz 1874.

32 FB to Mama, 12 and 16 July 1874.

33 FB, C.V.

34 FB to Toni, 8 September 1874.

35 FB to Mama, 2 October 1876; FB, C.V.

36 FB, C.V.

37 FB to Toni, 2 October 1876; FB to Theodor Meyer, 25 February 1877; FB to Toni, 1, 6, 8, 19 October 1876; Sophie Boas to Jacobi, 15 February 1877.

38 FB to Toni, 21 and 27 February 1877.

39 Kommunalarchiv Minden, Bestand 330, "Protokolle über die mündliche und schriftliche Prüfung der Gymnas. Abiturienten," Ostern 1877.

40 "unschön und unausgebildet," Zeugnis der Reife.

41 Sophie Boas to A. Jacobi, 15 February 1877.

42 Sophie to Toni, late February or early March 1877.

43 Meier Boas to Sophie and Toni, 27 November 1877.

44 FB to Toni, 2–4 May 1874.

45 FB to Toni, 3 December 1870; FB to Toni, 22 August, 27 September 1873; FB to Toni, 3–4 May 1874; FB to Toni, 11–12 October 1876; FB to Toni, 5 October 1876.

46 FB to Toni, 5 October 1876.

47 FB, C.V.

48 FB to Toni, 2, 13, 18 March 1877.

49 FB to Toni, 15–26 February 1877; Sophie to Toni, nd; FB to Toni, 2 March 1877; Sophie to Jacobi, 2 March 1877; FB to Toni 13 March 1877.

50 FB to Toni, 18 March 1877.

51 Zeugnis der Reife; FB, C.V.

52 FB, C.V.; FB to Toni, 2 and 8–9 October 1876.

53 FB, C.V.; FB to Toni, 5 September 1875.

54 FB, C.V.; FB to Toni, 11–12 October 1876.

55 FB to Toni, 6 October [1876]; also FB, C.V.

56 FB to Mama, 7 August 1876; FB to Toni, 2 March 1877.

57 FB, "An Anthropologists's Credo," *The Nation* 47 (27 August 1938), 201; also partially reprinted in Stocking, *Shaping,* 41.

58 FB, C.V.

59 FB, "Credo," 201, in Stocking, *Shaping,* 41.

60 FB, C.V.

61 Meier Boas to Toni, in FB to Toni, 27 September 1877; FB, C.V.

62 FB to Mama, 5 August 1876; FB to Toni, 6 October [1876].

63 FB to Toni, 2 October 1876; FB to Sophie, 25 February 1878; FB to MK, 12 July 1890.

64 FB to Toni, 2 October 1876 and 15 August 1876; FB, "Credo," 201.

65 "Confirmieren" is his term; FB, "Credo," 201; FB to Toni, 27 September 1873.

66 FB to Toni, 2 October 1867.

67 FB, C.V.

CHAPTER 3: "ONE LEARNS TO BE CONTENT"

1 Friedrich Meinecke, *Erlebtes, 1862–1901* (Leipzig: Koehler and Amelang, 1941), 85; Geert Seelig, *Ein Heidelberger Bursch vor fünfzig Jahren* (Heidelberg: Johs. Hörning, 1933), 72.

2 FB to Toni, 18 April 1877; FB to Mama, 19 April 1877.

3 FB to Mama, 24 April 1877; FB to Toni, 23 April 1877; FB to Krüer, 22 April 1877; FB to Mama, 24 April 1877.

4 "lauter Juden."

5 FB to Krüer, 22 April 1877; FB to parents, 11 May 1877; FB to Krüer, 22 and 28 April 1877.

6 FB to parents, 26 May 1877; FB to Krüer, 18 May 1877; Konrad H. Jarausch, *Students, Society and Politics in Imperial Germany: The Rise of Academic Illiberalism* (Princeton: Princeton University Press, 1982), 330, 250.

7 FB to parents, 3 June 1877; FB to Mama, 5 June 1877; FB to parents, 30 June 1877.

8 FB to parents, 25 June 1877; FB to Toni, 11 July 1877.

9 FB to Krüer, 27 June 1877.

10 FB to Krüer, 25 and 29 July 1877; FB to parents, 30 July 1877. Custom allowed an unpracticed opponent up to six weeks to prepare and might account for the lapse of time between challenge and combat.

11 FB to parents, 30 July 1877.

12 FB to parents, 21 July 1877.

13 Meier Boas to FB, 31 July 1877.

14 Max Halbe, *Scholle und Schicksal: Geschichte meines Lebens* (München: Verlag Knorr & Hirth, 1933), 273; FB to Mama, 5 June 1877.

15 FB to parents, 3 May 1877; FB to Toni, 4 May 1877. There is no subsequent mention of Fischer; it is possible that Boas did not continue visiting the lectures.

16 FB to parents, 26 May 1877.

17 *Mindener Zeitung,* 25 August 1877, 2; 27 August 1877, 3; *Jahresbericht des Evangelischen Gymnasiums und der Realschule zu Minden,* 1878, 10.

18 FB to Mama, 8 July 1877; FB to parents, 23 July 1877.

19 FB to Toni, 2 November 1877.

20 FB to Toni, 2 November 1877; FB to parents, 5 April 1886.

21 Konventsprotokolle, 10 May–29 July 1879, Verein alter Bonner Alemannen.

22 FB to parents, 19 February 1878.

23 Kevin McAleer, *Dueling: The Cult of Honor in Fin-de-Siècle Germany* (Princeton: Princeton University Press, 1994), 119–58; Ute Frevert, *Ehrenmänner: Das Duell in der bürgerlichen Gesellschaft* (München: C. H. Beck, 1991), 133–59; Otto Oppenheim, *Die Burschenschaft Alemannia zu Bonn und ihre Vorläufer* (Bonn, 1925), 358; R. Fick, ed. *Auf Deutschlands hohen Schulen* (Berlin and Leipzig: Verlag Hans Ludwig Thils, 1900), 233.

24 FB to parents, 14 February 1879.

25 FB to parents, 7 March 1878.

26 Papa to FB, 11 November 1877.

27 FB to parents, 6 December 1877.

28 Ibid.; FB to parents, 1 June 1878.

29 FB to parents, 27 February, 23 July 1879.

30 FB to parents, 15 June 1879, 27 January 1878.

31 FB to Mama, 9 May 1878; FB to parents, 1 June 1878.

32 FB to parents, 10 Feburary 1879.

33 FB to parents, 10 July, 19 August 1879.

34 FB to parents, 19 August 1879.

35 FB to parents, 27 August 1879.

36 FB to Mama, 28 September 1879.

37 FB to parents, 27 October 1879.

38 In July 1881 he moved to Merkenstrasse 8.

39 *Minden-Lübbecker Kreis-Blatt*, 6 May 1882, 5; FB to Bürgermeister, 8 June 1883, Acta betr. berühmte Männer, G1A89, Kommunalarchiv Minden.

40 FB to parents, 30 January 1880. The dissertation's eventual title was "Beiträge zur Erkenntnis der Farbe des Wassers," or "Contributions to the Perception of the Color of Water."

41 FB to parents, 12 June, 12 November 1880, 11 March 1881.

42 I have benefited from comments from physicists Klaus Rieckhoff and Konrad Colbow of Simon Fraser University.

43 FB to parents, 30 May 1881.

44 FB to parents, 12 May 1880, 30 May 1881; Boas, "Ueber eine neue Form des Gesetzes der Unterschiedsschwelle," *Archiv für die gesamte Physiologie des Menschen und der Thiere* 26 (1881), 494. For Erdmann, see Raymond Dodge, "Benno Erdmann," *American Journal of Psychology* 33 (1922), 155–56; Erich Becher, "Benno Erdmann," *Archive für die gesamte Psychologie* 42 (1922), 150–82; Karl Stumpf, "Gedächtnisrede: Benno Erdmann," *Sitzungberichte der Preussischen Akademie der Wissenschaften* 33 (1921), 497–508; Hans Wagner, *Bonner Gelehrte* (Bonn: H. Bonvier und C. L. Röhrscheid, 1968), 55–62.

45 FB to parents, 6 November 1880; FB to Mama, 13 November 1880.

46 Boas, though pursuing psychophysics temporarily, must have been aware that it was "a swampy border region" which could, despite Helmholtz, alienate physicists. So wrote Hertz to H. F. A. Elsas in 1887 and 1888. See Russell McCormmach, *Night Thoughts of a Classical Physicist* (Cambridge: Harvard University Press, 1982), 182*n49*.

47 Geert Seelig, *Eine deutsche Jugend: Erinnerungen an Kiel und der Schwanenweg* (Hamburg: Alster Verlag, 1922) 176; Albert Ladenberg, *Lebens-Erinnerungen* (Breslau: Trewendt & Garnier, 1912), 65; Christa Jungnickel and Russell McCormmach, *Intellectual Mastery of Nature: Theoretical Physics from Ohm to Einstein*, vol. 2: *The Now Mighty Theoretical Physics, 1870–1925* (Chicago: University of Chicago Press, 1986), 50; Hertz to parents, 27 October 1883, Johanna Hertz, *Heinrich Hertz: Memoirs, Letters, Diaries*, 2nd ed.; trans: Lisa Brinner, Mathilde Hertz, and Charles Susskind (San Francisco: San Francisco Press, 1977). See also Charlotte Schrönbeck, "Physik und Astronomie," in *Geschichte der Mathematik, der Naturwissenschaften und der Landwirtschaftswissenschaften, Geschichte der Christian-Albrechts-Universität Kiel, 1665–1965*, ed. Karl Jordan (Neumünster: Karl Wachholtz, 1968), 75.

48 Fischer to Hermann Wagner, 16 January 1880, Nachlass Wagner, Niedersächsische Staats- und Universitäts-Bibliothek, Göttingen.

49 FB to Jacobi, 31 March 1880.

50 See Hermann Wagner, "Theobald Fischer," *Petermanns Mitteilungen* 56, no. 2 (1910), 188–89; Karl Oestreich, "Theobald Fischer," *Geographische Zeitschrift* 18 (1912), 241–54. Fischer's politics were hardly Boas's color: he belonged to the Germanic Colonial Society (he played a role in the second Morocco crisis, 1911) and, the Navy League, and he supported German education in peripheral European areas.

51 FB to Jacobi, 10 April 1882.

52 Friedrich Paulsen, *Aus meinem Leben: Jugenderinnerungen* (Jena: Eugen Diederich, 1910), 147; FB to Jacobi, 10 May 1882. See Klaus Christian Köhnke, *The Rise of Neo-Kantianism: German Academic Philosophy between Idealism and Positivism*, trans.: R. J. Hollingdale

(Cambridge: Cambridge University Press, 1991) for an assessment of the context of Erdmann and Lange's positions.

53 George W. Stocking, Jr., "From Physics to Ethnology," in *Race, Culture, and Evolution: Essays in the History of Anthropology* (New York: Free Press, 1968; reprint, Chicago: University of Chicago Press, 1982), 143. I am much indebted to Stocking's essay. Toni to Herr Doktor [Bertelsmann?], 22 June 1883.

54 "Ja die Judengesichter verwechselt man sehr leicht!" FB to Toni, 6 October 1870. The twelve-year-old records the incident in a very curious way, making interpretation difficult. Certainly, as Julia Liss notes, it demonstrates "his familiarity with prejudice and his own resiliency to it." Liss, "Cosmopolitan Imagination," 81.

55 Adolf Stoecker, the leading anti-Semite after 1879, was elected to the Prussian Landtag from Minden-Ravensberg in September 1879, the same month as he delivered his first speech against "modern Jewry." It is difficult, however, to link Boas's hometown with Stoecker's anti-Semitism. Aside from the peculiarities of the three-role Prussian electoral law, Stoecker's supporters denied any connection between his Berlin anti-Semitic agitation and his electoral success in Minden-Ravensberg or even his 1881 Reichstag election for Siegen, another Westphalian constituency. "It is clear that Minden-Ravensberg did not elect the social agitator but the Christian Stoecker." Walter Frank, *Hofprediger Adolf Stoecker und die christlichsoziale Bewegung* (Berlin: Reimar Hobbing, 1928), 89–91. See also Herzig, "*In unsern Herzen*," 72, who shows that in the 1881 Reichstag election Stoecker received only 3.5% of the Minden vote.

56 This account is drawn from Paul W. Massing, *Rehearsal for Destruction: A Study of Political Anti-Semitism in Imperial Germany* (New York: Howard Fertig, 1967), 21–44; Jehuda Reinharz, *Fatherland or Promised Land: The Dilemma of the German Jew, 1893–1914* (Ann Arbor: University of Michigan Press, 1975), 15–29; Uriel Tal, *Christians and Jews in Germany: Religion, Politics, and Ideology in the Second Reich, 1870–1914*, trans. Noah Jonathan Jacobs (Ithaca: Cornell University Press, 1975), 235–59; Ismar Schorsch, *Jewish Reactions to German Anti-Semitism, 1870–1914* (New York: Columbia University Press, 1972); Wanda Kampmann, "Adolf Stoecker und die Berliner Bewegung," *Geschichte in Wissenschaft und Unterricht* 13 (1962), 558–79; Frank, *Hofprediger Adolf Stoecker*, ch. 3; Hermann von Petersdorff, *Die Vereine deutscher Studenten: Zwölf Jahre akademischer Kampf* (2nd. ed.; Leipzig: Breitkopf und Härtel, 1895), 7–86; Norbert Kampe, *Studenten und "Judenfrage" im deutschen Kaiserreich* (Göttingen: Vandenhoeck & Ruprecht, 1988); Peter Pulzer, *Jews and the German State: The Political History of a Minority, 1848–1933* (Oxford: Blackwell, 1992), esp. 96–105.

57 Landesarchiv Schleswig, Archiv der Universität Kiel, Abt. 47, 673, no. 11/12.

58 FB to parents, 12 November 1880.

59 Meier Boas to FB, 17 November 1880.

60 FB to Papa, 18 November 1880. He had already had a duel in the summer of 1880, but his post-card gives no details except that the cut was scarcely noticeable. FB to Mama, 13 August 1880.

61 FB to parents, 18 January 1881.

62 FB to parents, 6 April 1881, postcard.

63 Kurt-Gerhard Riquarts, "Der Antisemitismus als politische Partei in Schleswig-Holstein und Hamburg, 1871–1914" (Ph.D. diss., Christian-Albrechts-Universität zu Kiel, 1975), 54; Kampe, *Studenten und "Judenfrage*," 31, 40.

64 Fischer to FB, 21 December 1884.

65 Fritz K. Ringer, "Higher Education in Germany in the Nineteenth Century," *Journal of Contemporary History* 2 (1967), 133; R. Fick, ed., *Auf Deutschlands hohen Schulen*, 162; Jarausch, *Students, Society, and Politics*, 41.

66 *Worcester Daily Telegraph*, 6 March 1891.

67 FB, Baffinland letter-diary [23 December 1883], in Douglas Cole, "'The Value of a Person Lies in His *Herzensbildung*': Franz Boas's Baffin Island Letter-Diary, 1883–1884," in *History of Anthropology*, vol. 1: *Observers Observed: Essays on Ethnographic Fieldwork*, ed. George W. Stocking (Madison: University of Wisconsin Press, 1983), 149; FB, *Primitive Art* (Oslo: H. Aschehoug and Co., 1927; reprint New York: Dover, 1955), 3. McAleer, *Dueling*, is a useful treatment on the German and German university dueling culture.

68 FB to parents, 23 June 1878, 15 June 1879.

69 FB, Letter to Committee, excerpted in "The Boas Anniversary," *AA* 9 (1907), 647.

CHAPTER 4: "I BELONG TO THE MEN OF ANARNITUNG"

1 FB to Jacobi, 2 January 1882.

2 Ibid.

3 Documents and a floor plan are in the Minden Bauamt. The building was demolished, over the protests of citizens' groups, in July 1980. An apartment block now occupies the site. FB to parents, 23 June 1878; FB to Mama, 11 July 1881.

4 Sophie Boas to Salomon Meyer, 26 December 1881; Fischer to FB, 31 March and 26 May 1882, BPP.

5 Hete Lehmann to Ernst Boas, 10 February 1947; FB, *Pfluger's Archiv* 28 (1882), 563. Cf. Edward Bradford Titchener, *Experimental Psychology: A Manual of Laboratory Practice* (New York: Macmillan, 1905), II, cxxii, 268; Fischer to FB, 31 March 1882, BPP; FB to Jacobi, 2 January 1882; FB to Jacobi, 10 April 1882; Fisher to FB, 3 April 1882.

6 FB to J. W. Powell, 12 June 1887, BAE; also reprinted in Stocking, *Shaping*, 59–60; FB to Toni Boas, 3 December 1870. See also Hansheinrich Thomas to Muriel Rukeyser, 10 November 1947, BPP; FB, diary, 30 June 1883.

7 FB to Mama, 9 November 1883.

8 FB to parents, 17 November 1883.

9 Boas's father later had to put up a performance bond.

10 FB to parents, 23, 24, 25 January 1883.

11 FB to parents, 4 December 1882.

12 FB to parents, 1 November 1882.

13 FB, "Über die Wohnsitze der Neitchillik-Eskimos," *Zeitschrift der Gesellschaft für Erdkunde zu Berlin*, 18 (1883), 222–33.

14 FB to Jacobi, 26 November 1882, 2 May 1883.

15 FB, "Als Ausgangspunkt . . ."; FB to MK, 27 April 1883.

16 FB, *Baffin-Land: Geographische Ergebnisse einer in den Jahren 1883 und 1884 ausgeführten Forschungsreise* Ergänzungsheft No. 80 zu *Petermanns Mitteilungen* (Gotha: Justus Perthes, 1885), 35.

17 The name Krackowizer has misled some into thinking that she was Jewish. The family, whose documentation dates back to the early seventeenth century, was of Upper Austrian Catholic origin. Ferdinand Krackowizer, "Die Familie Krackowizer" (1890–91), Oberöster-reichisches Landesarchiv, Linz.

18 FB, "Die Reise durch den Harz"; MK to FB, 13 August 1881; FB to Jacobi, 2 May 1883; FB, diary, 24 June 1883; FB to Jacobi, 2 and 9 May 1883.

19 FB to MK, 28 May 1883 (1).

20 FB to MK, 28 May 1883 (2).

21 FB to MK, 6 June 1883.

22 Boas wrote it as "Selig in Lust und Leid, lässt die Liebe nur sein" ("May love be blessed in passion and sorrow"), but no such sentence appears in current Wagner texts. The flag remains among the Boas Papers.

23 FB to MK, 1 and 17 June 1883.

24 MK to FB, 19 June 1883.

25 FB, diary, 17 July 1883. Portions of the diary have been published: see Cole, " 'Value of a Person,' " 13–52.

26 FB, diary, 24 November 1883. Elsewhere his age is given as thirty-five. FB, "Aus dem Eise des Nordens," *Berliner Tageblatt*, 25 November 1883.

27 FB, field journal, 7 October 1883.

28 FB, diary, 5 November 1883; FB, "A Journey in Cumberland Sound and on the West Shore of Davis Strait in 1883 and 1884," *Journal of the American Geographical Society* 16 (1884), 253; Douglas Cole and Lüdger Muller-Wille, "Franz Boas' Expedition to Baffin Island, 1883–1884," *Inuit Studies/Études Inuit* 8, no. 1 (1984), 53–54.

29 The disease closely resembled distemper or the "fox encephalitis" of domestic fox farms. Charles Elton, "Epidemics among Sledge Dogs in the Canadian Arctic and Their Relation to Disease in the Arctic Fox," *Canadian Journal of Research* 5 (1931), 673–92.

30 FB, *Baffin-Land*, 14; FB, diary, 14 February 1884.

31 FB, diary, 7 March 1884.

32 FB, *Baffin-Land*, 14–15.

33 FB, diary, 1 April 1884; FB, *Baffin-Land*, 16–17; FB, diary, 1 April 1884.

34 Wilhelm Weike, diary, 20 December 1883.

35 FB, diary, 21 December 1883.

36 FB to parents, 31 October 1883; FB, diary, 18 November 1883.

37 FB, *Baffin-Land*, 12.

38 FB, diary, 25 January 1884.

39 FB, *Baffin-Land*, 12.

40 Ibid., 19.

41 FB, diary, 11 July 1884.

42 FB to MK, 11 September 1884.

43 FB, diary, 15 February 1884.

44 Ibid.

45 FB, "Die Eskimos des Cumberland Sundes und der Davisstrasse," *Berliner Tageblatt*, 2 November 1884; FB, diary, 23 January 1884. I translate "wilde" as "savage."

46 FB, diary, 23 December 1883.

47 Ibid.

48 FB, diary, 3 January 1884; FB to family and friends, 12 July 1884. It is perhaps within this context that his reading of Kant belongs. "Do you know how I pass the time these long evenings? I have a copy of Kant with me, which I am studying, so that I shall not be completely uneducated when I return. Life here really makes one dull and stupid (only when I get back to Kikkerton (*sic*) I will be sharp again)." FB, diary, 16 December 1883, quoted

in Cole, "Value of a Person," 29. That seems to be his only mention of Kant during the year.

49 FB to parents, 30 April 1884; FB, diary, 5 November 1883; FB, "Journey in Cumberland Sound," 253. Many of the Eskimo-drawn maps are in the Boas collections at the American Philosophical Society, the National Anthropological Archives, and the Museum für Völkerkunde, Berlin.

50 FB, diary, 30 December 1883.

51 Leslie H. Neatby, "Editor's Introduction" to Bernhard Hantzsch, *My Life among the Eskimos: Baffinland Journeys in the Years 1909 to 1911,* Mawdsley Memoir 3 (Saskatoon: University of Saskatchewan, 1977), xviii. The Boas-Hantzsch correspondence is in the Boas Professional Papers.

52 FB, "Der Eskimo-Dialekt des Cumberland-Sundes," *Mitteilungen der Anthropologischen Gesellschaft in Wien* 24 (1894), 97; FB, "History and Science in Anthropology: A Reply" (1936), in FB, *RLC,* 306.

53 FB to parents, 4 June 1884.

54 FB, "Unter dem Polarkreise," *New-Yorker Staats-Zeitung,* 1 February 1885; FB to Bell, 19 March 1886. Robert Bell Papers, vol. 4, National Archives of Canada.

CHAPTER 5: "HOW DEPRESSING IT IS"

1 See Wallace Stegner, *Beyond the Hundredth Meridian: John Wesley Powell and the Second Opening of the West* (Boston: Houghton Mifflin, 1953); Curtis M. Hinsley, Jr., *Savages and Scientists: The Smithsonian Institution and the Development of American Anthropology, 1846–1910* (Washington, D.C.: Smithsonian Institution Press, 1981), esp. 125–44.

2 FB to parents, 11 October 1884.

3 FB to parents, 14 January 1885; Peter Pulzer, *Jews and the German State: The Political History of a Minority, 1848–1933* (Oxford: Blackwell, 1992), 96–105, 327–28.

4 FB to parents, 7 November 1884; FB to Jacobi, 15 October 1884, BPP; Fischer to FB, 21 December 1884, BPP; Fischer to Toni Boas, 30 December 1884.

5 FB to MK, 15 October 1884; FB to Jacobi, 18 January 1885, BPP; FB to Jacobi, 15 October 1884, BPP; FB to Jacobi, 13 January 1885, BPP.

6 FB to parents, 14 January 1885; FB to Jacobi, 18 January 1885, BPP; FB to MK, 14 January 1885.

7 Sophie Boas to Jacobi, transcription, 4 February 1885; FB to parents, 14 January 1885; FB to MK, 13 January 1885.

8 FB to parents, 14 January 1885; FB to MK, 14 January 1885.

9 FB, "Die Eskimo des Baffinlandes," *Verhandlungen des fünften deutschen Geographentages zu Hamburg* (Berlin: Dietrich Reimer, 1885), 1–14.

10 FB to MK, 10–11 April 1885.

11 FB to MK, 2 and 10 April 1885; FB to Jacobi, 20 April 1885.

12 FB to parents, 13 April, 5 June 1885. Fischer was responsible for the Petermanns acceptance. Fischer to H. Wagner, 12 November 1884, Nachlass Wagner, Niedersächsische Staats–und Universitäts–Bibliothek.

13 FB to MK, 3 July 1885.

14 FB to Toni Boas, 29 October 1884; FB to MK, 5 June 1885.

15 FB to MK, 13 July 1885.

16 Max Lenz, *Geschichte der Königlichen Friedrich-Wilhelm Universität zu Berlin* (Halle:

Waisenhausen, 1918), II, 307; J. Partsch, "Heinrich Kiepert: Ein Bild seines Lebens und seiner Arbeit," *Geographische Zeitschrift* 17 (1901), 82–93; FB to Hete and Rudolf, 17 July 1885.

17 FB to MK, 24 July 1885; FB to parents, "Der Besuch bei Kiepert," 21 July 1885.

18 FB to MK, 24 July 1885.

19 FB, *Baffin-Land.*

20 FB to MK, 17 December 1885.

21 *Deutsche Literaturzeitung,* 21 April 1888, 602; FB to MK, 20 December 1885.

22 FB to MK, 14 January, 1 February 1886; Kiepert to FB, 22 January 1886, BPP; FB to parents, 13 February 1886; FB to MK, 23 February 1886.

23 FB to MK, 23 and 28 February, 9 March 1886.

24 FB to MK, 11 April 1886; FB to parents, 13 April 1886; FB to MK, 13 April 1886.

25 Acta Boas, Universitätsarchiv, Humboldt—Universität zu, Berlin; FB to Mama and Toni, 28 May 1886; FB to Papa and Aenne, 28 May 1886; FB to MK, 28 May 1886.

26 FB to MK, 6 June 1886.

27 Hettner (1859–1941), who became the most distinguished German geographer of his generation, did not follow Richthofen to Berlin. He remained at Leipzig for ten years and was called to Tübingen and then Heidelberg where he remained until his retirement in 1928.

28 The term, "Überfüllungskrise," is from Kampe, *Studenten und "Judenfrage,"* 61, who puts it from 1880 to 1900 and relates it to the rise of student anti-Semitism in the competition for positions.

29 FB to MK, 28 February 1886, 12 December 1885; FB to Jacobi, 20 December 1885; FB to MK, 28 February, 27 April 1886.

30 FB to MK, 2 October 1884; FB to parents, 5 April 1886; FB to Ernst Boas, 30 December 1910.

31 FB to Sophie Boas, 13 January 1883.

32 FB to MK, 11 May 1886.

33 Matti Bunzl, "Franz Boas and the Humboldtian Tradition: From *Volksgeist* and *Nationalcharakter* to an Anthropological Concept of Culture," in *History of Anthropology,* vol. 8: *Volksgeist as Method and Ethic: Essays on Boasian Ethnography and the German Anthropological Tradition,* ed. George W. Stocking (Madison: University of Wisconsin Press, 1966), 46–51; Klaus-Peter Koepping, *Adolf Bastian and the Psychic Unity of Mankind* (St. Lucia: University of Queensland Press, 1983); Annamarie Fiedermutz-Laun, *Der kulturhistorische Gedanke bei Adolf Bastian* (Wiesbaden: Franz Sterner Verlag, 1970). Robert H. Lowie's chapter in *The History of Ethnological Theory* (New York: Holt, Rinehart and Winston, 1937), 30–38, remains a useful brief treatment.

34 FB, *The Kwakiutl of Vancouver Island,* Publications of The Jesup North Pacific Expedition, 5, no. 2 (New York, 1909), 307.

35 FB to Powell, 3 October 1885, BAE; FB, *Kwakiutl of Vancouver Island,* 307; FB to Powell, 30 October 1885, BAE.

36 FB, *Kwakiutl of Vancouver Island,* 307; FB, "Capitän Jacobsens Bella-Coola-Indianer," *Berliner Tageblatt,* 25 January 1885. See Douglas Cole, "Franz Boas and the Bella Coola in Berlin," *Northwest Anthropological Research Notes* 16 (1982), 115–24; Wolfgang Haberland, "Nine Bella Coolas in Germany," in *Indians and Europe: An Interdisciplinary Collection of Essays,* ed. Christian F. Feest (Aachen: Rader-Verlag, 1987), 337–74; FB to parents, 25 January 1886; FB to MK, 28 February, 28 January, 1 February 1886. FB, "The Language of the Bilhoola in British Columbia," *Science* 7 (5 March 1886), 218.

37 FB to MK, 23 April 1886.

38 FB to MK, 9 May 1886.

39 FB to Bell, 30 May 1886, Bell Papers, National Archives of Canada.

40 FB to parents, 15 July 1886.

41 FB to parents, 24 August 1886.

42 FB to Bell, 13 June 1886, Robert Bell Papers, APS; Baird to FB, 30 August 1886. Saul Benison has reprinted Boas's appeal to Justice C. P. Daly of the American Geographical Society, 12 August 1886, in *AA* 51 (1949), 524–25; FB to parents, 2 September; FB to Toni, 2 September 1886.

43 FB, diary, 18 September 1886, in *The Ethnography of Franz Boas*, ed. Ronald P. Rohner; trans. Hedy Parker (Chicago: University of Chicago Press, 1969), 20. The 1886 diary was translated by Helene Boas Yampolsky.

44 FB, "The Indians of British Columbia," *Popular Science Monthly* 32 (1888), 628; FB, "Chinook Songs," *Journal of American Folk-Lore* 1 (1888), 221; FB, diary, 19, 22 September 1886; FB to Carl Schurz, 27 October 1886, Schurz Papers, Library of Congress.

45 FB, diary, 30 September 1886; FB to parents, 23 September 1886; FB to Vorsitzender, 17 November 1886, *Verhandlungen der Berliner Gesellschaft für Anthropologie, Ethnologie, und Urgeschichte* 19 (1887), 65; FB, "The Use of Masks and Head Ornaments on the North-West Coast of America," *Internationales Archiv für Ethnographie* 3 (1890), 7.

46 FB to MK, 16 December 1886.

47 Boas to parents, 19 September, 7 October 1886.

48 FB to parents, letter diary, 9–15 October 1886, in Rohner, *Ethnography*, 37–40; FB to Carl Schurz, draft, 27 October 1886, BPP; FB to parents, 23(?) [sic] November, 9 November 1886, in Rohner, *Ethnography*, 57, 60.

49 FB to MK, 21 September, 7 and 30 October; 25 November, 8 December 1886.

50 FB to Putnam, 29 December 1886, Putnam Papers, Harvard University Archives; FB to D. C. Gilman, 5 January 1887, Special Collections, Milton S. Eisenhower Library, Johns Hopkins University; FB to MK, 17 December 1886 (I translate "zerstreute Arbeitskräfte" as "scattered manpower" and "Brennpunkt" as "focal point"); FB to Toni Boas, 10 December 1886.

51 FB to parents, cable, 24 January 1886. The *Entlassungs Urkunde* is dated almost a year later, 31 January 1887. Boas took his naturalization oath while at Clark University, 23 February 1892.

52 FB to Toni Wohlauer, 8 December 1930, in Rohner, *Ethnography*, 295–96.

CHAPTER 6: "THE WHOLE FIELD LIES BEFORE ME"

1 FB to parents, 4 January 1887; nd [late March 1887].

2 FB to parents, [4] January, 12 February, 7 March 1887.

3 FB to parents, 12 February 1887; FB to Papa, 19 February 1887; FB to parents, 28 June 1887.

4 FB to parents, 28 April 1887.

5 FB to parents, 25 November 1887.

6 FB to parents, 14 October 1887.

7 FB to Bastian, nd [received 30 March 1887], Acta Boas, Berlin Museum für Völkerkunde.

8 FB to parents, 20 December 1887.

9 FB to parents, 15 March, 21 October, 15 March, 12 June, 27 January 1887; MK to parents, 12 May 1887.

10 Stanley Nadel deals with the differentiations and particularisms in *Little Germany: Ethnicity, Religion, and Class in New York City, 1845–80* (Urbana: University of Illinois Press,

1990). A breezy treatment of wealthy Jewish circles can be found in Stephen Birmingham, *"Our Crowd": The Great Jewish Families of New York* (New York: Harper and Row, 1967).

11 FB to Papa, 6 February 1888. They decided together on the names: "I in memory of my sister and brother, Marie in memory of her father and after her sister." FB, diary, 7 July 1888. Helene was, of course, also the name of Boas's eldest sister, who had died in 1857 before his birth. His first son was named after his dead brother Ernst. It was Jewish custom, certainly in Germany, to pass the names of departed relatives to children born later. Dietz Bering, *The Stigma of Names: Antisemitism in German Daily Life, 1812–1933*, trans. Neville Plaice (Ann Arbor: University of Michigan Press, 1992), 62.

12 The full title was the committee "appointed for the purpose of investigating and publicly reporting on the physical characters, languages, and industrial and social condition of the North-western Tribes of the Dominion of Canada"; "Circular of Inquiry," Third Report, Committee on North-western Tribes, *British Association for the Advancement of Science*, 1887, 173.

13 Hale to FB, nd [30 January 1888].

14 FB to parents, 26 May 1888.

15 FB, diary, 18 July 1888, in Rohner, *Ethnography*, 102.

16 FB, diary, 6 and 12 June 1888, in Rohner, *Ethnography*, 88, 90; FB, diary 12 June, quoted differently in Rohner, ibid., 90.

17 FB, diary, 24 July 1888, in Rohner, *Ethnography*, 103; 9 June 1888, ibid., 89. Boas later came to doubt the Haida-Tlingit affinity. It remains controversial.

18 FB to MB, 29 June 1888; FB to parents, 28 July 1888; N. D. C. Hodges to FB, 1 August 1888 [microfilmed as 1885], BPP; FB to Robert Bell, 20 March 1888, Bell Papers, APS. Herskovits's description of this job as "scientific hack work" may be harsh but not really wrong (*Franz Boas*, 12).

19 FB to parents, 24 August 1888.

20 FB to E. B. Tylor, draft, 17 August 1888, BPP; BAAS, 4th Report (1888), 234–35.

21 Hale to FB, 8 and 27 June, 3 April 1889, BPP.

22 FB to Hodges and Hodges to FB, 30 January 1889, BPP; Powell to FB, 21 December 1888, BPP; H. W. Henshaw to Boas, 3 January 1889, BPP.

23 FB to parents, 15 January 1889.

24 FB to Papa, 30 October 1888. The report, he wrote, "promises much for my future, since it is very fundamental and comprehensive, if also superficial." FB to parents, 15 January 1889.

25 FB to parents, 11 September, and cable, 10 September 1888.

26 "Wurm," "Pikinini," and "kleine Affe."

27 FB to MB, 28 June 1889. Because Boas had no reason to write letters in this period, the above account is based largely on reports in the *New York Times*, 13 May 1889, and *The Times* (London), 13 May 1889.

28 Hale to FB, 21, 22, 27 May 1888, BPP; FB to MB, 3 June 1888; FB to parents, 27 June 1889; FB to MB, 26 June 1889.

29 Dawson to FB, 14 July 1889, BPP; Hale to FB, 13–14 July 1889, BPP.

30 FB, diary, 18 July 1889; FB to MB, 23 July 1889, in Rohner, *Ethnography*, 106–7.

31 FB, diary, 28 May 1888; Hale to FB, 13–14 July 1889, BPP.

32 Hale to FB, 12, 13–14 July 1889, BPP; FB to parents, 15 January 1891.

33 Jacob W. Gruber, "Horatio Hale and the Development of American Anthropology," *Proceedings of the American Philosophical Society* 111 (February 1967), 26, 29.

34 For a survey of Hale's ideas and context, see Douglas Cole, "The Origins of Canadian Anthropology, 1850–1910," *Journal of Canadian Studies* 8 (February 1973), 33–45.

35 FB to MB, 23 July 1889, in Rohner, *Ethnography,* 106–7; FB, diary, 10, 6, 12 August 1889.

36 FB, diary, 2 September 1889.

37 FB to MB, nd [16? August 1888].

38 FB to parents, 20 August; FB to MB, 21 August 1889.

39 FB to parents, 15 January 1889.

CHAPTER 7: "AN ARDENT DESIRE TO REMOVE OBSCURITY"

1 Fischer to FB, 31 March 1882, BPP; FB, "Credo," 202 (also reprinted in Stocking, *Shaping,* 42); FB, "History and Science," in *RLC,* 305; FB, *Baffin-Land,* 66–89. The quotations are from p. 87. FB, "Credo," 202, in Stocking, *Shaping,* 42.

2 FB to MK, 2 October 1885; "Tortured" is his word in FB to MK, 12 December 1885; "severe mental struggles," he applied generally, but it sounds like a personal reference. FB, "The Study of Geography" (1887), in *RLC,* 643.

3 FB, "Study of Geography," 642.

4 Ibid., 644.

5 FB to MK, 12 December 1885.

6 Benno Erdmann, "Gliederung der Wissenschaften," *Vierteljahresschrift für wissenschaftliche Philosophie* 2 (1878), 72–105; see also Erich Becher's comment on it in "Benno Erdmann," *Archiv für die gesamte Psychologie* 42 (1922), 163; Wilhelm Windelband, "Kritische oder genetische Methode?" (1883), in *Präluden: Aufsätze und Reden zur Philosophie und ihre Geschichte* (Tübingen: J. C. B. Mohr, 1924), vol. II, 99–135; Wilhelm Dilthey, *Introduction to the Human Sciences: An Attempt to Lay a Foundation for the Study of Society and History* (1883); trans. and intro. by Raymon J. Betanzos (Detroit: Wayne State University Press, 1988).

7 R. G. Collingwood, "The Philosophy of History" (1930), in *Essays in the Philosophy of History,* ed. William Debbins (Austin: University of Texas press, 1965), 133–34; Guy Oakes, "Introduction," to Heinrich Rickert, *The Limits of Concept Formation in Natural Science: Logical Introduction to the Human Sciences,* ed: Guy Oakes (Cambridge: Cambridge University Press, 1986), ix; Georg G. Iggers, *The German Conception of History: The National Tradition of Historical Thought from Herder to the Present* (Middleton, Conn.: Wesleyan University Press, 1968), 147–59.

8 Wilhelm Windelband, "History and Natural Science" (1894), ed. and trans. Guy Oakes, *History and Theory* 19 (1980), 165–85. There is a large literature on Dilthey, and his collected writings now number many volumes. See especially Michael Ermarth, *Wilhelm Dilthey: The Critique of Historical Reason* (Chicago: University of Chicago Press, 1978); 188–89; Herbert A. Hodges, *The Philosophy of Wilhelm Dilthey* (London: Routledge and Kegan Paul, 1952), 226; Thomas E. Willey, *Back to Kant: The Revival of Kantianism in German Social and Historical Thought, 1860–1914* (Detroit: Wayne State University Press, 1978), 48, 136–39.

9 The influence of Rickert and Windelband on Boas's early students is marked, certainly in the case of Kroeber, Lowie, and Sapir. See Robert H. Lowie, "Reminiscences of Anthropological Currents in America Half a Century Ago," *AA* 58 (1956), 1006–07.

10 FB, "Study of Geography," 639; Conrad Hermann, "Die Geographie und die teleologische Weltansicht," *Das Ausland* 16 (1879), 304–5; Richard Mayr, "Die Stellung der Erdkunde im

Kreise der Wissenschaften und der Schuldisciplinen," *Zeitschrift für Schul-Geographie* 1 (1880), 263. For a contemporary survey of the discussion, see Hermann Wagner, "Der gegenwartige Standpunkt der Methodik der Erdkunde," *Geographisches Jahrbuch* 7 (1878), 563, 599–616 and Wagner, "Bericht über die Entwicklung der Methodik der Erdkunde," *Geographisches Jahrbuch* 8 (1880), 545–49.

11 FB, "Study of Geography," 644, 642, 644.

12 FB, "History of Anthropology" (1904) in Stocking, *Shaping*, 377.

13 Alexander Lesser, "Franz Boas," in *Totems and Teachers: Perspectives on the History of Anthropology*, ed. Sydel Silverman (New York: Columbia University Press, 1981), 7–8. See also Marian Smith, "Boas' 'Natural History' Approach to Field Method," in *The Anthropology of Franz Boas*, ed. Walter Goldschmidt, *AAA* Memoir 89 (San Francisco: Howard Chandler, 1959), 46–60.

14 FB, "Study of Geography," 647.

15 FB, review of "The Teaching of Geography" by Archibald Geikie, *Science* 10 (16 September 1887), 139; review of "How to Study Geography" by Francis W. Parker, *Science* 12 (7 September 1988), 115.

16 Ibid.; FB, "History and Science," 1936, in *RLC*, 305.

17 FB, review of "The Philosophy of Kant" by John Watson, *Science* 12 (17 August 1888), 81; FB, "The Occurrence of Similar Inventions in Areas Widely Apart" (1887), 485–86, in Stocking, *Shaping*, 63. Matti Bunzl's model essay in the history of ideas, "Franz Boas and the Humboldtian Tradition: From *Volksgeist* and *Nationalcharakter* to an Anthropological Concept of Culture," deals with Boas's grounding in the German anthropological tradition. In *History of Anthropology*. Vol. 8: *Volksgeist as Method and Ethic: Essays on Boasian Ethnography and the German Anthropological Tradition*, ed. George W. Stocking, Jr. (Madison: University of Wisconsin, 1996), 17–78.

18 Herbert Schnädelbach, *Philosophy in Germany, 1831–1933*, trans. Eric Matthews (Cambridge: Cambridge University Press, 1984), 34; Georg G. Iggers, "Historicism," in *Dictionary of the History of Ideas*, vol. 2, ed. Philip P. Weiner (New York: Charles Scribner's Sons, 1973), 457–64; Richter, quoted in Ernst Plewe, *Untersuchung über den Begriff der "vergleichenden" Erdkunde und seine Anwendung in der neueren Geographie* (Ergänzungsheft 4; *Zeitschrift der Gesellschaft für Erdkunde zu Berlin*, 1932), 67.

19 FB, "History of Anthropology," in Stocking, *Shaping*, 25. The idea was so generalized it hardly needs specific citation. See, however, Ermarth, *Wilhelm Dilthey*, 25. For ethnology, see Thomas Achelis, "Die Ethik der Gegenwart in ihrer Beziehung zur Naturwissenschaft," *Vierteljahresschrift für wissenschaftliche Philosophie* 7 (1883), 57.

20 FB, "Occurrence of Similar Inventions" and "Museums of Ethnology and Their Classification" (1887), in Stocking, *Shaping*, 64–66; FB, "Aims of Ethnology," in *RLC*, 633.

21 FB to Powell, 3 October 1885, 12 June 1887, BAE; FB, "Aims," in *RLC*, 633. The Boas Papers contain a lecture, undated but apparently his inaugural Clark University anthropology lecture. It is very similar to his "Die Ziele der Ethnologie" of 8 March 1888 and was published the following year. Boas translated that, very retrospectively and so with some changes, as "The Aims of Ethnology," in *RLC*, 626–38. George Stocking provides a much more careful translation of a portion of it in *Shaping*, 67–71. Because of its accessibility, I usually transcribe the *Shaping* version when applicable, but even then sometimes prefer my own translation.

22 FB, "Museums of Ethnology," in Stocking, *Shaping*, 66; "Temporal depth created a completely different position for the world from that at the beginning of the century." Plewe,

"*Vergleichende*" *Erdkunde*, 67.

23 D. D. Runes, *Dictionary of Philosophy* (1942), quoted in Dwight E. Lee and Robert N. Beck, "The Meaning of 'Historicism,'" *American Historical Review* 59 (1954), 568. For a discussion of the various meanings of "historicism," see Iggers, *German Conception of History*, 287–90; FB, "Occurrence of Similar Inventions" and "Museums of Ethnology," in Stocking, *Shaping*, 61, 62, 64.

24 See Stocking, "Basic Assumptions," 1–20; "Dogmatism, Pragmatism, Essentialism, Relativism: The Boas/Mason Debate Revisited," *History of Anthropology Newsletter* 21:1 (1994), 3–12; Douglas Cole, *Captured Heritage: The Scramble for Northwest Coast Artifacts*, corrected ed. (Vancouver, B.C.: Douglas and McIntyre, 1995; reprint, Norman and Vancouver: University of Oklahoma Press and University of British Columbia Press, 1996), 114–16; Curtis M. Hinsley, Jr., *Savages and Scientists: The Smithsonian Institution and the Development of American Anthropology, 1846–1910* (Washington: Smithsonian Institution Press, 1981), 98–100; Ira Jacknis, "Franz Boas and Exhibits: On the Limitations of the Museum Method of Anthropology," *History of Anthropology*. Vol. 5: *Objects and Others: Essays on Museums and Material Culture,* ed. George W. Stocking, Jr. (Madison: University of Wisconsin Press, 1985), 75–111; John Buettner-Janusch, "Boas and Mason: Particularism versus Gerneralization," *AA* 59 (1957), 318–24.

25 Peschel, *Abhandlungen*, I, 421 (1870), quoted in Wagner, "Der gegennärtige Standpunkt," 576; Georg Gerland, *Beiträge zur Geophysik: Abhandlungen aus dem geographischen Seminar der Universität Strassburg,* I (1887), xxix–xxx; FB, review of *Masks, Labrets and Certain Aboriginal Customs* by William Healey Dall (1885), *Verhandlungen der Gesellschaft für Erdkunde zu Berlin* 13 (1886), 380–81; FB, "The Limitations of the Comparative Method of Anthropology" (1886), in *RLC*, 274.

26 FB, "Occurrence of Similar Inventions" and "Museums of Ethnology," in Stocking, *Shaping*, 62, 66.

27 Ibid.; FB to Mason, draft, 26 June 1887, BPP.

28 Schnädelbach, *Philosophy in Germany*, 85; FB, "Museums of Ethnology," in Stocking, *Shaping*, 64.

29 FB to parents, 12, 14, 31 May, 5 June 1887.

30 FB, Clark lecture; FB, "Aims," in Stocking, *Shaping*, 68 ("Aims," *RLC*, 634).

31 FB, "Aims," in Stocking, *Shaping*, 69 (*RLC*, 634–35); FB, "Anthropology in the American and British Associations for the Advancement of Science," *Science* 10 (11 November 1887), 231; FB, "Aims," in Stocking, *Shaping*, 70–71; FB, Clark lecture, 7–8, BPP.

32 FB, "Die Ziele der Ethnologie," *Gemeinverständliche Vorträge gehalten im Deutscher Gesellig-Wissenschaftlichen Verein* (1888/89), 13, 15–16, 26–27 ("Aims," *RLC*, 631, 632, 636).

33 FB, "Die Ziele," 24, 27; "Aims," *RLC*, 636, 637.

34 Mason to FB, 17 November 1888, BPP; Stocking, "From Physics to Ethnology," 159; Sara E. Wiltse, in "Psychological Literature: II: Experimental," *American Journal of Psychology* 1 (1888), 702–5; FB, "On Alternating Sounds" (1889), 47–53, in Stocking, *Shaping*, 72–77; Stocking, "From Physics to Ethnology," 159.

35 Rulon Wells, "Phonemics in the Nineteenth Century, 1876–1900," in *Studies in the History of Linguistics: Traditions and Paradigms,* ed. Dell Hymes (Bloomington: Indiana University Press, 1974), 434–35; Stocking, "From Physics to Ethnology," 159. Hale's article, "On Some Doubtful or Intermediate Articulations: An Experiment in Phonetics," *Journal of the Anthropological Institute of Great Britain and Ireland* (1885), 233–43, quite forcefully makes

the same conclusion: that "uncertainty is due to a lack of clear perception in the listener" (240). There is no indication that Boas knew of Hale's priority (his article appeared while Boas was on Baffin Island), nor did Hale comment to Boas about the latter's article, though they were in frequent correspondence at the time.

36 Hans Peter Rickman, *Dilthey Today: A Critical Appraisal of the Contemporary Relevance of His Work* (New York: Greenwood Press, 1988), 21–22; FB, "Occurrence of Similar Inventions," in Stocking, *Shaping*, 66. The historicist outlook, Georg G. Iggers insists, "has to recognize that all values arise within the concrete setting of an historical situation, . . . that all values are culture-bound" (Iggers, *German Conception of History*, 8). See also Johannes Tennekes, *Anthropology, Relativism and Method: An Inquiry into the Methodological Principles of a Science of Culture* (Assen: Van Gorcum, 1971), esp. 36–37, 111–12. Woodruff D. Smith, citing Bastian, sees it as a tendency within the framework of German neoliberal anthropology. Smith, *Politics and the Sciences of Culture in Germany, 1840–1920* (New York: Oxford University Press, 1991), 111.

37 FB, "Aims," in Stocking, *Shaping*, 71.

38 FB to Toni Boas, 27 September 1873; FB, "Credo," *The Nation*, 201.

39 FB, "The Development of the Culture of Northwest America," *Science* 12 (26 October 1888), 194–96.

40 FB, Clark lecture, 4.

41 FB to Powell, 12 June 1887, reprinted in Stocking, *Shaping*, 60; FB, "Development of Culture," 194. FB, "Die Ziele," 5.

42 FB to Tyler, 4 October 1888, Tylor Papers, reprinted in Stocking, *Shaping*, 131. Stocking relates this to Tylor's method of adhesions, though it is clear that Boas began his card index of myth elements before he read Tylor's paper. FB to Powell, draft, nd [28 November 1888], BPP; FB, "Dissemination of Tales among the Natives of North America" (1891), in *RLC*, 445.

43 FB, "Notes on the Ethnology of British Columbia," *Proceedings of the American Philosophical Society* 24 (1887), 422–29; FB, "Development of Culture," 194–96; FB, "The Indians of British Columbia," *Transactions of the Royal Society of Canada* 6 (1888), 55–56. The extension of the term "Kwakiutl" into more northern areas is anachronistic.

44 By 1896 he had them back to moving from patriarchy to matriarchy. FB, "Development of Culture," 195. See also Adam Kuper, *The Invention of Primitive Society: The Transformation of an Illusion* (London and New York: Routledge, 1988), 135–39, which misses the initial position.

45 FB, "Anthropology in the American and British Associations for the Advancement of Science" (1887), 231; FB, "Occurrence of Similar Inventions" in Stocking, *Shaping*, 66.

46 Darnell, "Development of American Anthropology," xxxvi-xxxxiii, 374–461; Stocking, "Scientific Reaction," 280–87, 300–7; and Regna Darnell, "The Professionalization of American Anthropology: A Case Study in the Sociology of Knowledge," *Social Science Information* 10 (1971), 81–103.

CHAPTER 8: "THE IDEA IS BETTER THAN THE EXECUTION"

1 The best accounts of Clark University's early years are William A. Koelsch, *Clark University, 1887–1987: A Narrative History* (Worcester: Clark University Press, 1987), ch. 1, and Dorothy Ross, *G. Stanley Hall: The Psychologist as Prophet* (Chicago: University of Chicago Press, 1972), 186–230. G. Stanley Hall, *Life and Confessions of a Psychologist* (New York: D. Appleton

& Co., 1923) needs to be treated with caution. I am indebted to William Koelsch for his insights and corrections.

2 Henry Donaldson, "Memories for My Boys," 91, typescript, Henry Donaldson Papers, American Philosophical Society.

3 Clark University, *Register and Second Official Announcement,* May 1890, 14; "First Annual Report of the President to the Board of Trustees, 4 October 1890," Worcester, 1890, 19.

4 FB to parents, 11 October 1889.

5 FB to MK, nd [5 November 1889].

6 FB to Rudolph Lehmann, 26 December 1889.

7 FB to parents, 25 April 1890; FB to Rudolf Lehmann, 26 December 1889; FB to parents, 25 April, 12 May 1890.

8 FB to MB, 3 June 1890; FB to MB, 3 June 1890; FB to parents, 18 July 1890; FB to MB, 5 June 1890.

9 FB to Papa, 31 October 1890.

10 FB to parents, 19 December 1890.

11 FB to MB, 12 July 1890; FB to Toni, 21 December 1890 and 4 January 1891.

12 FB to parents, 6 March 1891.

13 FB to Papa, 23 December 1890; FB to Mama, 19 July 1891. This became FB, *Indianische Sagen von der Nord-Pazifischen Küste Amerikas,* Sonder-Abdruck aus den Verhandlungen der Berliner Gesellschaft für Anthropologie, Ethnologie und Urgeschichte, 1891 bis 1895 (Berlin: A. Asher and Co., 1895).

14 *Worcester Daily Telegraph,* 5 March 1891.

15 Ibid.

16 FB to parents, 19 April 1891.

17 FB to parents, 1 May 1892.

18 Clark to Hall, 4 and 8 March 1891, G. Stanley Hall Papers, Clark University Archives.

19 Koelsch, *Clark University,* 35; Hall, *Life,* 293–4; Hall dictation, 1908, Hall Papers.

20 Clark to Hall, 19 March 1891, Hall Papers; FB to parents, 27 March 1891.

21 FB to Henshaw, 19 March 1891, BAE; Boas to parents, 12 June 1891; Boas to Hall, 4 June 1891, Hall Papers. Boas offered an option that his teaching begin only in December.

22 FB to MB, 2 August 1891; MB to FB, 15 July 1891.

23 FB to parents, 2 May 1891.

24 FB to parents, 1 May 1891; Donaldson, "Memories for My Boys," 95; Henry H. Donaldson, et al., "Condition of Affairs," 1, Hall Papers.

25 Donaldson, et al., "Condition of Affairs," 29; memorandum of 11 April 1892, BPP; Ross, *Hall,* 222; joint letter, Hall Papers (a draft in BPP, 21 January 1892).

26 Hall, *Life,* 296; Whitman proposed Boas (as an associate professor at $2,500 a year) to form one of those "important departments of Biological knowledge" which would give "greater organic unity among kindred sciences." C. O. Whitman to W. R. Harper, 15 January 1892, Harper Papers, University of Chicago. Chicago's anthropologist was Frederick Starr.

27 FB to parents, 1 May 1892.

28 FB to Papa, 30 October 1892.

29 FB to parents, 12 June 1891.

30 FB to Henry W. Henshaw, 3 December 1888, 27 December 1889, BAE.

31 MB, at the end of FB to parents, 1 April 1890; FB to Tylor, 25 April 1889 [read 1890], BPP; Hale to FB, 21 May 1890, BPP.

32 FB to parents, 14 June 1890, in Rohner, 117; FB to Henshaw, 18 June 1890, BAE; FB to parents, 25 June 1890; FB to MB, 27 June 1890; FB to Henshaw, 1 July 1890, BAE.

33 Shoalwater Bay is now Willapa Bay.

34 FB to Henshaw, 24 July 1890, BAE; FB to MB, 12 July 1890; Boas was almost, but not quite, right. Verne F. Ray, in 1931, found three Lower Chinook living on Willapa Bay, two of whom could give useful ethnological information. None, however, could speak Chinook. Verne F. Ray, "Lower Chinook Ethnographic Notes," *University of Washington Publications in Anthropology* 7 (1938), 29–165.

35 FB, *Chinook Texts*. Bureau of Ethnology Bulletin 20. Washington, D.C.: Government Printing Office, 1894.

36 FB to MB, 13 July 1890; FB to Toni, 12 July 1890; FB to Henshaw, 14 July 1890, BAE; FB to MB, 24 July 1890. Cultee was actually only fifty or fifty-five. He died in 1897. FB to Henshaw, 24 July 1890; BAAS, 7th Report (1890), 431; Daniel L. Boxberger and Herbert C. Taylor, Jr., "Charles Cultee and the Father of American Anthropology," *The Sou'wester* 21 (Spring 1986), 3–7.

37 FB to parents, 31 July 1890.

38 Chehalis may also be Tsehalis. The quotation is from FB to parents, 7 August 1890. I am indebted to my colleague Ralph Maud for making the connection of the unnamed chief with Chehalis in his unpublished "Franz Boas: Early Field Work."

39 FB to parents, 29 August 1890; FB to MB, 3 September 1890.

40 FB to parents, 19 April 1891.

41 FB to parents, 9 July 1891; FB to MB, 21 July 1891.

42 FB to Mama and Toni, 29 June 1891.

43 FB to MB, 29 July 1891; FB to parents, 18 August 1891.

44 FB to parents, 13 September 1892.

45 See Richard J. Evans, *Death in Hamburg: Society and Politics in the Cholera Years, 1830–1910* (Oxford: Clarendon Press, 1987). The city's antiquated water supply system, coupled with overcrowding, was the principal cause for this tragedy, which killed as many people as in all other cholera epidemics of the nineteenth century combined.

CHAPTER 9: "ALL OUR SHIPS HAVE GONE AGROUND"

1 *Chicago Daily Tribune,* 31 May 1890, quoted in Ralph W. Dexter, "Putnam's Problems Popularizing Anthropology," *American Scientist* 54 (1966), 316. I have also adapted a few portions from my *Captured Heritage.*

2 FB to parents, 3 April 1891; monthly report for June 1891, Putnam Papers, 35, by permission of the Harvard University Archives.

3 Putnam, monthly report for October 1891, Putnam Papers, box 35; Boas, "The Exhibits from the North Pacific Coast," Putnam Papers, box 36.

4 FB to parents, 29 November, 18 December 1892.

5 FB to parents, 20 November 1892.

6 FB to parents, 28 May 1893.

7 FB to parents, 23 January 1893.

8 FB, "The Exhibitions from the North Pacific Coast," Putnam Papers, box 36.

9 FB to parents, 8 May 1893.

10 See Nancy L. Fagin, "Closed Collections and Open Appeals: The Two Anthropology Exhibits at the Chicago World's Columbian Exposition of 1893," *Curator* 27 (1984), 255–63; "Prof.

Putnam's Hard Luck," *New York Times,* 22 May 1893, 9; Dexter, "Putnam's Problems," 315–32; Putnam to Higginbotham, 7 August 1895 (draft), Putnam Papers, box 32. See also Ira Jacknis, "Northwest Coast Indian Culture and the World's Columbian Exhibition," in David Hurst Thomas, ed., *The Spanish Borderlands in Pan-American Perspective* (Washington: Smithsonian Institution Press, 1991), 91–118; Robert W. Rydell, *All the World's a Fair: Visions of Empire at American International Exposition, 1876–1916* (Chicago: University of Chicago Press, 1984).

11 Rossiter Johnson, ed., *A History of the World's Columbian Exposition,* 4 vols. (New York: D. Appleton, 1897), vol. 1, 503; vol. 3, 433.

12 FB to parents, 17 and 25 September, 21 October 1893.

13 *Chicago Daily Tribune,* 31 May 1890, quoted in Dexter, "Putnam's Problems," 316; FB to parents, 17 December 1893.

14 FB to parents, 1 May 1892, 17 September 1893.

15 FB to parents, 9 October 1893.

16 Putnam to Higginbotham, 7 October 1895 draft, Putnam Papers, box 32; Putnam to C. O. Whitman, 14 March 1894 copy, Putnam Papers, box 33; Putnam to Ayer, 21 December 1893, Boas file, Registrar's Office, Field Museum of Natural History.

17 FB to parents, 25 and 31 December 1893.

18 FB to parents, 31 December 1893.

19 FB to parents, 14 January 1894.

20 Ibid.

21 FB to parents, 6 and 28 January 1894; Boas to Putnam, 4 January 1894, Putnam Papers, box 8.

22 FB to Putnam, 29 and 30 January 1894, Putnam Papers, box 8; FB to parents, 28 January 1894; FB to Putnam, 18 February 1894, Putnam Papers, box 8.

23 FB to McGee, 17 February 1894, BAE; FB to Holmes, 17 February 1894, Field Coumbia Museum (hereafter FCM); FB to Holmes, 19 February 1894, FCM; FB to Skiff, 19 February 1894, draft, BPP; FB to Skiff, 19 February 1894, BPP.

24 FB to Putnam, 18 February 1894, Putnam Papers, box 8.

25 This account is based largely on correspondence between Boas and Putnam from 18 February to 21 July 1894, in the Putnam Papers, boxes 8 and 31, as well as FB to parents, 21 February 1894; FB to Jacobi, 2 September 1909, BPP; and William Henry Holmes, "Random Records of a Lifetime," vol. 7, Library of the National Collection of Fine Arts and the National Portrait Gallery, Washington.

26 Frederick Starr to Harper, 31 March 1892, Starr Papers, in Darnell, "Development of American Anthropology," 159; McGee to FB, 21 March 1894, BPP.

27 See Thomas G. Manning, *Government in Science: The U.S. Geological Survey, 1867–1894* (Lexington: University of Kentucky Press, 1967), 204–14; William Culp Darrah, *Powell of the Colorado* (Princeton: Princeton University Press, 1951), 336–49.

28 FB to Jacobi, 18 February 1894.

29 Holmes, "Random Records," vol. 7.

30 Actually, it seems that Chamberlin sought to secure both Walcott and Holmes as *scientific* directors of the museum, with Skiff remaining as a titulary, administrative general director.

31 FB to parents, 21 February 1894.

32 W J McGee to Chamberlin, 3 January 1894, BAE-LB; Chamberlin to Holmes, 27 January 1894, Holmes, "Random Records of a Lifetime," vol. 7; Curtis M. Hinsley, Jr. and Bill Holm, "A Cannibal in the National Museum: The Early Career of Franz Boas in America," 315; Walcott to Putnam, 16 April 1894, Putnam Papers, box 33.

33 Holmes had communicated his decision to accept the Chicago offer before February 5. Chamberlin to Holmes, 5 February 1894, Holmes, "Random Record."

34 FB to Putnam, 20 February 1894, Putnam Papers, box 8; Holmes to FB, 21 February 1891, BPP. This was sent to Skiff with the direction to pass it on to Boas if Skiff approved its contents. He did. Holmes to Skiff, 21 February 1894, FCM; Skiff to Holmes, 27 February 1894 in Holmes, "Random Record."

35 W J McGee to FB, 19 February 1894, BPP; J. A. Allen to Jesup, 18 March 1894, AMNH Archives; McGee to FB, 21 March 1894, BPP; Holmes to Skiff, 30 March 1895, FCM; FB to Putnam, 4 May 1894, Putnam Papers, box 8; see also Holmes to Jesup, 28 March 1894, AMNH Archives.

36 FB to parents, 21 February 1894; Holmes suggested that Boas be placed in charge of physical anthropology and made "agent of the Museum for all the great northern regions of the globe," his time to be divided "somewhat equally" between the field and the museum. Holmes to Skiff, 31 March 1894, FCM. Boas was willing to accept a curatorship of overseas anthropology, with Holmes having responsibility for the Americas. FB to Putnam, 21 May 1894, Putnam Papers, box 8.

37 FB to MB, 7 May 1894; FB to parents, 11 May 1894.

38 FB to Putnam, 21 May 1894, Putnam Papers, box 8.

39 FB to MB, 11 May 1894; Putnam to C. O. Whitman, 14 March 1894, copy, Putnam Papers, box 33.

40 John R. Swanton, "William Henry Holmes, 1846–1933," National Academy of Sciences, *Biographical Memoirs* 17 (1935–37), 237; Hinsley, *Savages and Scientists,* 107; E. Hobson to Jesup, 13 December [1893]; A. Rogers to Jesup, 22 December 1893 and 12 January 1894; J. A. Allen to Jesup, 18 January 1894, G. F. Kunz to Jesup, 19 January 1894, AMNH, 1894, H file. See also Joan Mark, "William Henry Holmes," in *Four Anthropologists: An American Science in Its Early Years* (New York: Science History Publications, 1980), 131–71.

41 FB to Putnam, 7 May 1894, Putnam Papers, box 8; Harper, quoted in Stocking, *Shaping,* 219; FB to MB, 11, 14, 15, 16 May 1894; MB to FB, 16 May 1894.

42 FB to parents, 3 April, 22 May 1894.

43 FB to parents, 21 February, 22 May 1894.

44 FB to parents, 22 May 1894.

45 FB to parents, 22 June 1894.

46 Archibald Rogers to M. K. Jesup, 12 January 1894, AMNH Archives, 1894: H file.

47 Hinsley and Holm, "Cannibal in the Museum," 311.

48 Holmes was receiving, in 1892, only $2,700 a year.

49 Holmes to Jesup, 28 March 1894, AMNH Archives, 1894: H file; Stevenson to McGee, 7 March 1894, McGee Papers, Library of Congress.

50 Stocking, "Scientific Reaction," 280.

CHAPTER 10: "I HAVE LOOKED INTO HELL"

1 FB to parents, 25, 22, 30 May; 14 and 22 June 1894.

2 Wilbur R. Jacobs, "Francis Parkman's Oration 'Romance in America,' " *American Historical Review* 68 (April 1963), in *Intellectual History in America,* vol. 2: *Contemporary Essays on Puritanism, the Enlightenment, and Romanticism,* ed. Cushing Strout (New York: Harper and Row, 1968), 152–59.

3 FB to parents, 28 June, 5 July, 28 August 1894.

4 FB, "Human Faculty as Determined by Race," AAAS, *Proceedings of the American Association*

for the Advancement of Science 43 (1894), 308, 315, 316, in Stocking, *Shaping*, 221–42.

5 Ibid., 323, 317.

6 Vernon J. Williams, Jr., makes the point very strongly in his *Rethinking Race: Franz Boas and His Contemporaries* (Lexington: University of Kentucky Press, 1996), especially in chapter 1, although his attribution of the reasons is arguable.

7 FB to parents, 20 June 1894. The collection sold for $2,800, but he still owed his uncle Jacob Meyer $700 for it. For an account of the collection's origins and the difficulties over it, see Cole, *Captured Heritage*, 119–21, 168–69.

8 See chapter 11.

9 FB to MB, 19 November 1894, in Rohner, 181.

10 Wayne Suttles, "Streams of Property, Armor of Wealth: The Traditional Kwakiutl Potlatch," in *Chiefly Feasts: The Enduring Kwakiutl Potlatch,* ed. Aldona Jonaitis, Seattle: University of Washington Press, 1991), 119–33; FB to MK, 1 December 1894, in Rohner, *Ethnography,* 187. See Ira Jacknis's excellent "Franz Boas and Photography," *Studies in Visual Communications* 10 (1984), 2–60. See also Douglas Cole and Ira Chaikin, *An Iron Hand Upon the People: The Law Against the Potlatch on the Northwest Coast* (Vancouver: Douglas & McIntyre/ University of Washington Press, 1990), esp. chapters 2 and 3. In 1885 legislation had been passed outlawing potlatches and winter ceremonials, largely at the instigation of mission-aries and Indian officials. Such ceremonies continued despite the law, mostly because Indians were able to avoid the presence of Whites.

11 FB to MB, 22 November 1894, in Rohner, *Ethnography,* 183.

12 FB to MB, 23 and 24 December 1894; FB to parents, 29 December 1894.

13 FB, "Anthropometric Observations on the Mission Indians of Southern California," *Proceedings of the American Association for the Advancement of Science* 44 (1895), 261–69.

14 FB to parents, 13 January 1895.

15 FB to MB, 20 and 23 December 1894.

16 FB to MB, 30 December 1894, 8 January 1895; FB to parents, 24 January 1895.

17 FB to parents, 29 January 1895.

18 "Die Leidenschaft flieht, die Liebe muss bleiben; die Blume verblüht, die Frucht muss treiben," which Boas attributed to Schiller.

19 FB to MB, 3–5 October 1894; in Rohner, *Ethnography,* 148–49.

20 FB to parents, 4 February 1895.

21 FB to Putnam, 21 May 1894, Putnam Papers, box 8.

22 "The courageous frankness with which he took up our previous conflicts" established a lasting friendship. FB to Jacobi, 2 September 1909, BPP; FB "Eulogy for McGee" in Boas Papers, published in *The McGee Memorial Meeting of the Washington Academy of Sciences Held at the Carnegie Institute, December 5, 1913* (Baltimore: William and Wilkins, 1916). On the question of Paleolithic man, see David J. Meltzer, "The Antiquity of Man and the Development of American Archaeology," in *Advances in Archaeological Method and Theory,* vol. 6, ed. Michael B. Schiffer (San Francisco: Academic Press, 1983), 1–51.

23 FB to parents, 28 August 1894. He later recounted the incident to the Adler Committee, attributing the McGee push to Mrs. Matilda Stevenson, who personally lobbied him "to see that Mr. McGee should be elected vice-president of the section, which I refused to do." Records of the 1903 Investigation of the BAE, "Testimony of Mr Franz Boas," 931, NAA.

24 McGee to FB, 11 June 1894, BPP; FB to Putnam, 21 May 1894, Putnam Papers, box 8.

25 Putnam to Edward H. Thompson, 19 May 1894; Putnam to C. O. Whitman, 14 March 1894,

Putnam Papers, box 33; Putnam to FB, 30 April, 14 May 1894, BPP.

26 FB, "Frederic Ward Putnam," *Science* 42 (10 September 1915), 332; FB, quoted in Alfred M. Tozzer, "The Putnam Anniversary," *AA* 11 (1909), 287; FB, "Putnam," 330.

27 A. L. Kroeber, "Frederic Ward Putnam," *AA* 17 (1915), 717.

28 Chicago *Herald*, 8 October 1893, enclosed in the Boas Family Papers, FB to Putnam, 4 January, 7 May 1894, Putnam Papers, box 8.

29 Winser to Jacobi, 5 March 1894, AMNH Archives; Putnam to FB, 14 May, 1894, BPP.

30 Putnam to FB, 16 July, 3 August 1894, BPP.

31 MB to FB, 15 December 1894, 1 January 1895.

32 Trustees minutebooks, 9 November 1894 (Executive Committee), 12 November 1894 (Trustees); Jesup to Oswald Ottendorfer, 24 November 1894, letterbooks, AMNH.

33 FB to Rudolf Lehmann, 4 January 1891.

34 Hete Lehmann to Ernst Boas, 10 February 1947; FB to Toni Wohlauer, 16 November 1893.

35 McGee to FB, 7 June 1895, BPP.

36 FB to Jordan, 19 July 1895, University Archives, Stanford University Library; FB to Powell [McGee], 19 June 1895, BAE; Putnam to FB, 19 June 1895, BPP.

37 Farrand to Putnam, 16 April and 3 May 1895, Putnam Papers; Butler to Low, 5 October 1895, and Putnam to Low, 15 June 1895, Secretary's Correspondence, Columbia University; Low to Putnam, 17 June 1895, Putnam Papers, box 8.

38 Putnam to FB, 19 June, 2 July 1895, BPP.

39 FB to Putnam, 6 July 1895, Putnam Papers, box 8. Ripley, however, did not hold a regular faculty appointment.

40 Putnam to FB, telegram, 8 July 1895, BPP; MB to FB, 26 July 1895.

41 Putnam to FB, 9 August 1895, BPP.

42 Low might well have remembered Boas's earlier lecturing fiasco at the college. See chapter 5. Low to Putnam, 8 October 1895, Putnam Papers, box 10.

43 FB to McGee, 24 October 1895, BAE.

44 FB to parents, 29 November 1895.

45 Putnam to Jesup, 7 November 1895; Winser to Putnam, 27 December 1895; Winser to Jacobi, 13 and 16 January 1896, AMNH.

46 MB to parents, 11 December 1895; FB to Putnam, 9 December 1895, draft, BPP; Putnam to FB, 10 December 1895, BPP.

47 FB to parents, 11 December 1895.

48 FB to Putnam, 18 December 1895, Putnam Papers, and draft in BPP; "Organization of the Department of Anthopology—Officers and Employees of the Department, 1896," Putnam Papers; Jesup to FB, 3 January 1896, AMNH Archives.

49 Putnam to Alice Putnam, 25 December 1895, quoted in Ralph W. Dexter, "The Role of F. W. Putnam in Developing Anthropology at the American Museum of Natural History," *Curator* 19 (1976), 306. George Pepper was attached to the Museum's Hyde Expedition.

CHAPTER 11: "THE GREATEST THING UNDERTAKEN BY ANY MUSEUM"

1 Later Horace Mann. They were not happy with the school and put the children the next year in one newly opened by Laura Jacobi.

2 I am indebted throughout to Jacknis, "Franz Boas and Exhibits" 75–111. Some of the following is adapted from my *Captured Heritage*, esp. 141–64.

3 Jesup memorandum, nd [January 1895]; Jesup to Putnam, 27 November 1894, AMNH, letterbooks.

4 Putnam to Jesup, 7 November 1895, AMNH Archives, 1895, P file.

5 Winser to Putnam, 7 January 1896, AMNH Archives.

6 Jesup to Putnam, nd [December 1895 or January 1896], Putnam Papers.

7 Boas to Putnam, 11 December 1896, Putnam Papers, box 8.

8 Boas to Putnam, 18 December 1896, Putnam Papers, box 8.

9 This was not really true, because of the Powell-Bishop collection. See Aldona Jonaitis, *From
   the Land of the Totem Poles: The Northwest Coast Indian Art Collection at the American
   Museum of Natural History* (Seattle: University of Washington Press, 1988), 72–82; Cole,
   Captured Heritage, 82–84.

10 Boas to Villard, 23 December 1896, AMNH, Acc. 1897–30.

11 I am indebted to previously published work on the Jesup Expedition: Jonaitis, *From the
   Land of the Totem Poles*; Stanley A. Freed, Ruth S. Freed, and Laila Williamson, "Capitalist
   Philanthropy and Russian Revolutionaries: The Jesup North Pacific Expedition
   (1879–1902)," *AA* 90 (1988), 7–24, and their "The American Museum's Jesup North Pacific
   Expedition," in *Crossroads of Continents: Cultures of Siberia and Alaska,* ed. William W.
   Fitzhugh and Aron Crowell (Washington, D.C.: Smithsonian Institution Press, 1988),
   97–103.

12 Boas to Jesup, 19 January 1897, Putnam Papers, box 16.

13 F. W. Putnam, "Synopsis of Peabody and American Museum of Natural History
   Anthropology Departments," *Proceedings of the XIII International Congress of Americanists,*
   New York, 1905, xliii.

14 AMNH, *Annual Report of the President . . . for the Year 1896* (New York: The Museum, 1897),
   24–25.

15 Boas to Putnam, 11 February 1897, Putnam Papers, box 8.

16 *New York Times,* 13 March 1897, 2, 5.

17 *New York Times,* 12 March 1897, 2, 5.

18 FB to Grube, cited in Laufer, 5 May 1896, AMNH, Acc. 1900–12; Stejneger to FB, 26 November
   1895 and 11 December 1895, BPP.

19 FB, "Zur Ethnologie von Britisch-Columbien," *Verhandlungen der Gesellschaft für Erdkunde
   zu Berlin* 22 (1895), esp. 266 and 270.

20 FB, *Indianische Sagen,* conclusion.

21 FB to Andree, 4 May 1897, AMNH, Anthro. dept., Jesup Expedition file. Grube's article is also
   cited in FB, *The Social Organization and Secret Societies of the Kwakiutl Indians,* Report of
   the United States National Museum for 1895 (Washington, 1897), 663n. The Stellar description is also in the conclusion of *Indianische Sagen.*

22 FB to Andree, 4 May 1897, AMNH, Anthro. dept., Jesup Expedition file.

23 FB to Tylor, 13 April 1897, Tylor Papers.

24 FB, "Limitations," in *RLC,* 277. See also chapter 15.

25 See Boas's more forceful conclusion and insistence on research in "contiguous areas" in
   "The Growth of Indian Mythologies: A Study Based upon the Growth of the Mythlogies of
   the North Pacific Coast" (1896), in *RLC,* 425–36.

26 "Limitations," in *RLC,* 276, 277.

27 The BAAS contributed c$480. G. M. Dawson to FB, 14 May 1897, Geological Survey of
   Canada, vol. 94, National Archives of Canada. Dawson, who had succeeded Hale as the

North-Western Committee's director, was no admirer of Boas's work. "Boas was at first very satisfactory & gave us several good reports, but soon established connections with German & U.S. Museums, till eventually we found we were merely being used by him. I was very glad at last when the work of that Committ. was closed & hope not to resume closer relations with Dr Boas than those of ordinary acquaintance." Dawson to D. P. Penhallow, 8 January 1900, ibid.

28 FB to parents, 9 April 1897.

29 FB to parents, 15 August 1897; FB to MB, 21 August 1897; FB to Putnam, 10 April 1900, Putnam Papers.

30 FB to parents, 9 April, 27 May, 15 June 1897, in Rohner, *Ethnography,* 205–6.

31 FB to parents, 27 May 1897.

32 FB to MB, 6 July 1897, in Rohner, *Ethnography,* 208–9; FB to parents, 27 May 1897.

33 FB to parents, 31 August 1896.

34 FB to MB, 27 May 1897.

35 FB to MB, 18 May 1897. Boas forgot, however, to mail it.

36 FB to parents, 29 May 1897; FB to MB, 9 August 1897, in Rohner, *Ethnography,* 220–22, 29 May, 15 August 1897. Holmes's discontent is recorded in his "Random Record," vol. 7.

37 FB to MB, 13 September 1897; Livingston Farrand, *Traditions of the Chilcotin Indians,* Publications of the Jesup North Pacific Expedition 2, no. 1 (New York, 1900), 4.

38 Untitled lecture (February 1898), 17, Boas Papers, lectures. Owen B. Beattie, "A Note on Early Cranial Studies from the Gulf of Georgia Region: Long-heads, Broad-heads, and the Myth of Migration," *BC Studies* 66 (1985), 28–36.

39 FB to MB, 9 August 1897; FB to parents, 10 June 1898. See Cole, *Captured Heritage,* 169–76.

40 Farrand, assisted by W. S. Kahnweiler, *Traditions of the Quinault Indians,* Publications of the Jesup North Pacific Expedition 2, no. 3 (New York, 1902), 79–80; Harlan Ingersoll Smith, *Archaeology of the Gulf of Georgia and Puget Sound,* Publications of the Jesup North Pacific Expedition 2, no. 6 (Leiden, 1907), 439.

41 Zvolianski to Olarovsky, 12 March 1898; Hitchcock to Jesup, 4 and 23 April 1898; G. Dewollant to Jesup, 26 April 1898, AMNH, Anthro. dept., Jesup Expedition file.

42 See FB, "The Jesup North Pacific Expedition," *American Museum Journal* 3 (1903), 93–98, including Laufer's report of 4 March 1899.

43 FB to Mama, 12 January, 20 February 1900.

44 Letter to FB, 21 September 1897, BPP; FB to MB, 21 August 1897. Born in Vienna in 1872, von Zach later served with the Austrian consular service in East Asia, then in the Dutch government in Indonesia. Von Zack published a number of Chinese linguistic studies and translations of Chinese literature before his death in 1942.

45 Radlov to Boas, 23 May 1898, AMNH, Acc. 1901–70.

46 FB to Mama, 6 March 1900; MB to Mama, 23 March 1900.

47 FB to Mama, 27 August 1903.

48 Both men were Jewish, but, as Russian subjects, did not suffer from the same disabilties as the German, Laufer. They did, however, experience some governmental opposition.

49 Freed, Freed, and Williamson, "Capitalist Philanthropy," 15–24.

50 FB to MB, 15 June 1900.

51 On Teit's ethnology, see Wendy Wickwire, "Women in Ethnography: The Research of James A. Teit," *Ethnohistory* 4 (1993), 539–62. See also Peter Campbell, " 'Not as a White Man, Not as a Sojourner': James A. Teit and the Fight for Native Rights in British Columbia,

1884–1922," *Left History* 2 (1994), 37–57. Teit, *Traditions of the Thompson River Indians of British Columbia*, American Folk-Lore Society, Memoirs 6 (New York: Houghton, Mifflin, 1898); *The Thompson Indians of British Columbia*, Publications of the Jesup North Pacific Expedition 1, no. 4 (Leiden, 1900).

52 FB to MB, 21, 25, 27 June 1900; FB to children, 25, 26, 29 June 1900.

53 FB to MB, 22 November 1894, in Rohner, *Ethnography*, 183; FB to MB, 21 and 20 July, 1 September 1897, in Rohner, *Ethnography*, 214, 211, 236. See Judith Berman, "'The Culture as It Appears to the Indian Himself': Boas, George Hunt, and the Methods of Ethnography," in *History of Anthropology.* vol. 8: *Volksgeist as Method and Ethic: Essays on Boasian Ethnography and the German Anthropological Tradition*, ed. George W. Stocking, Jr. (Madison: University of Wisconsin Press, 1996), 215–56; Ira Jacknis, "George Hunt, Collector of Indian Specimens," in *Chiefly Feasts: The Enduring Kwakiutl Potlatch*, ed. Aldona Jonaitis (for the American Museum of Natural History by Seattle: University of Washington Press and Vancouver: Douglas and McIntyre, 1991), 177–224; Jeanne Cannizzo, "George Hunt and the Invention of Kwakiutl Culture," *Canadian Review of Sociology and Anthropology* 20 (1983), 44–58; Judith Berman, "The Seals' Sleeping Cave: The Interpretation of Boas' Kwakw'ala Texts" (Ph.D. diss., University of Pennsylvania, 1991); and Ira Jacknis, "The Ethnographic Object and the Object of Ethnology in the Early Career of Franz Boas," in Stocking, *Volksgeist*, 185–214. ·

54 See Cole and Chaikin, *Iron Hand*, 73–75.

55 Boas to friends, storage box letter, 14 April 1897. The first half of this letter is in AMNH, Acc. 1897–43; the second half is in Jesup Expedition file H.

56 Hunt to Boas, 4 March 1898, 10 January 1899, BPP. I have been unable to find the Smiths' newspaper interview.

57 Boas to Hunt, 3 February 1899, BPP; Boas to Hamasaka, 3 February 1899, BPP. These letters are printed in Stocking, *Shaping*, 125–27. Boas had lobbied against the 1885 anti-potlatch law, both in interviews with officials and legislators in Victoria and in an 1897 letter in the Victoria *Province.*

58 Boas to Hunt, 7 January 1901, 4 April 1901, 1 May 1901, BPP; Hunt to Boas, 1 June 1901, BPP.

59 FB to MB, 16 August 1900.

60 Berman, "Seal's Sleeping Cave," esp. 27–36; Berman, "'Culture as It Appears,'" 235. Boas did have some reservations. See FB, *The Religion of the Kwakiutl*, Part I, Columbia University Contributions to Anthropology 10 (New York: Columbia University Press, 1930), ix–xii.

61 FB to Mama, 16 August 1900.

62 FB to Swanton, 5 June 1900, AMNH, Acc. 1901–31.

63 Their work on the Yukaghir was not originally to be part of the Expedition, but Boas later included that group. FB to Jochelson, 5 December 1898, AMNH, Anthro. dept., Jesup Expedition file; FB to Jochelson, 24 March 1900, AMNH, Acc. 1901–70.

CHAPTER 12: "A CERTAIN WORK LIES BEFORE ME HERE"

1 FB to parents, 26 February, 8 March 1897; FB to Putnam, 10 March 1897, Putnam Papers, box 8.

2 FB to Putnam, 10 March 1897, Putnam Papers, box 8.

3 FB to Jesup, 21 March 1898, AMNH, 1898, B file; FB to parents, 21 March 1898, 2 January 1899; Villard to FB, 13 April, 15 May 1899, AMNH, Anthro dept., Villard file; FB to parents, 8 and 16 May 1899; FB to Mama, 25 August and ca. 30 November 1899.

4   FB to Jesup, 1 December 1899, 6 January 1900, AMNH, Anthro. dept., Jesup file.

5   FB to parents, 27 November 1900; FB to Jesup, 9 April 1901, FB to Bumpus, 28 April 1901, AMNH, Anthro. dept., Jesup file.

6   FB to Jesup, 9 January 1902, AMNH, Anthro. dept., Reports file; FB to Mama, 2 and 10 May 1902.

7   FB to Bumpus, 30 March and 11 April 1903, AMNH, Anthro. dept., Bumpus file; FB to Bumpus, 28 March 1904, AMNH, 13A file; Huntington to Boas, 25 May 1904, AMNH, Anthro. dept., Huntington file.

8   FB to F. J. K. Müller, 11 November 1898, AMNH, Anthro. dept., Müller file.

9   FB to Henry Villard, 11 April 1900, AMNH, Anthro. dept., East Asian files. The same letter was sent to Columbia University President Seth Low.

10 FB to Jesup, 1 December 1900; Schiff to FB, 27 November, 24 December 1900, AMNH, Anthro. dept., East Asian files; FB to Frazer, 28 November 1900, AMNH, Anthro. dept., American Anthropological Association file; FB to Adams, 28 November 1900, FB to Foord, 1 December 1900, FB to Parsons, 4 December 1900, AMNH, Anthro. dept., East Asian files.

11 FB to Zelia Nuttall, 16 May 1901, BPP; FB to Jesup, 12 March 1901, AMNH, file 13; FB to H. A. Andrews, 22 August 1901, AMNH, Anthro. dept., Andrews file.

12 Boas to parents, 1 November 1897.

13 Kenn Harper, *Give Me My Father's Body: The Life of Minik, the New York Eskimo* (Frobisher Bay, NWT and Newmarket, Ont.: Blacklead Books, 1986). I am dependent on Harper's account for much that follows.

14 *Evening Mail*, 21 April 1909, 4, in Harper, *Give Me My Father's Body,* 94. See Cole, *Captured Heritage,* 119–21.

15 A. L. Kroeber, "The Eskimo of Smith Sound," *Bulletin of the American Museum of Natural History* 12 (1899), 265–327; Kroeber, "Animal Tales of the Eskimo," *Journal of American Folk-Lore* 12 (1899), 17–23; and Kroeber, "Tales of the Smith Sound Eskimo," ibid., 12 (1899), 166–82; Aleš Hrdlička, "Contributions to the Anthropology of Cumberland and Smith Sound Eskimo," *Anthropological* Papers of the *American Museum of Natural History* 5 (1910), 177–280; Hrdlička, "An Eskimo Brain," *American Anthropologist* 3 (1901), 454–500.

16 FB, *The Eskimo of Baffin Land and Hudson Bay,* 2 vols. Bulletin of the American Museum of Natural History 15 (New York: American Museum of Natural History, 1901 and 1907). William Thalbitzer, "Eskimo," in FB, ed., *Handbook of American Indian Languages,* vol. 1, BAE Bulletin 40 (Washington, D.C.: Government Printing Office, 1911), 967–1069.

17 FB to Mama, 15 January, 4 December 1900.

18 Hodge to FB, 13 March 1899, BPP.

19 FB to Culin, 23 February 1901, BPP; FB to C. P. Bowditch, 15 December 1902, BPP. "During the first few years I covered the deficit of the journal myself" (FB to Jacobi, 2 September, 1909), but the contributions may have been something of a fudge. McGee, it was later charged, purchased some of Boas's manuscripts for the BAE with an understanding that the money would go to the *AA*. Boas did not deny it. As he told the 1903 Adler Committee, "I made up my mind to make enough money in some way to cover this deficit myself," and "largely for this reason I sold certain manuscripts," but they "were sold to the Bureau as manuscripts, and there was no mention of any sort that that particular money was to be used for any particular purpose." Cyrus Adler, et al., to S. P. Langley, 24 September 1903, 27–28; "Testimony of Mr Franz Boas," 923–25, Hearings before Special Committee of Administrative Affairs of the BAE, SI, NAA. This arrangement had long-term repercussions for Boas's reputation in some circles.

20 FB to Jesup, 12 December 1899, BPP.

21 Butler to Low, 5 October 1895, Secretary's Papers, Columbia University.

22 Low to Butler, 17 December 1895; Low to Putnam, 10 March 1896; Low to Jesup, 1 February 1897; Low to Cattell, 1 February 1897; Jesup to Low, 1 March 1897; Low to Jesup, 2 March 1897, Secretary's Papers, Columbia University.

23 This was, however, paid by gift, the source untraceable in university records, but it probably came from Jesup, who had guaranteed Boas a total salary of $4,000. Columbia University, *Report of Finance Committee to the Board of Trustees,* 31 March 1898; FB to parents, 11 February 1898.

24 FB to parents, 12 May 1896, 15 February, 9 October 1897, 11 January 1897 [read 1898], 20 May 1898. The correspondence on the Vienna offer is thin, only a draft response, which did not give a definite reply, to Baron Ferdinand von Andrian-Werberg. FB to Andrian-Werberg, 8 August 1898, BPP. He had met with Andrian-Werberg and Franz Heger in Braunschweig. See also Karl von den Steinen to Boas, 9 August 1898, BPP; FB to parents, 22 November 1898; Low to Jesup, 21 December 1898, Secretary's Papers, Columbia University.

25 Jacobi to Low, 9 and 11 February 1899, Secretary's Papers, Columbia University; FB to parents, 17 February 1899.

26 FB to parents, 24 January 1896, 15 February 1897, 7 January 1898, 12 May 1896.

27 FB to parents, 21, 26, 29 May 1896, 4 January 1897, 25 October 1898, 18 April 1899.

28 FB to parents, 6 March 1900; MB to Mama, 14 November 1892; FB to parents, 2 March 1900. Trudel was named after a friend of Marie's, Marianne Christian, who had died four years earlier, just at the time of Hedwig's birth. FB to parents, 23 April 1897; MB to FB, 21–22 June 1900.

29 FB to parents, 2 February 1897, 10 November 1899.

30 FB to parents, 22 November 1898.

31 FB to parents, 8 April 1898, 1 April 1902, 6 December 1898; MB to Mama, 16 March 1900.

32 FB to Mama, 21 February; MB and FB to Mama, 24 February 1899.

33 FB to Mama, 1 January 1900; FB to parents, 21 May 1897.

34 FB to Mama, 27 November 1900.

35 FB to parents, 13 March and 14 April 1896; FB to Mama, 18 May and 18 June 1900; Putnam to Esther Putnam, 26 May 1900, Putnam Papers, box 11; FB to Mama, 6 June 1900.

36 FB to parents, 22 July 1896, 9 April 1897.

37 FB to MB, 31 July, 2 August 1898; FB to parents, 2 October 1898.

38 FB to Kroeber, 1 April 1903, AMNH, Anthro. dept.; FB to Toni, 29 June 1900.

39 FB to MB, 6 July 1897.

40 MB to parents, 28 May 1897; MB to Putnam, 28 May 1897, Putnam Papers. "Why," she wrote Franz, "must you always be gone! I don't want to be separated from you any more!" MB to FB, 6 June 1897.

41 See, for instance, White, *Ethnography and Ethnology,* 59–67. Compare with Ronald P. Rohner, "Franz Boas: Ethnographer on the Northwest Coast," in *Pioneers of American Anthropology: The Uses of Biography,* ed. June Helm (Seattle: University of Washington Press, 1966), 149–212.

42 FB to Toni, 29 June 1900; MB to parents, 6 October 1897.

43 Berman, "Seal's Sleeping Cave," 38. For a general statement on the use of collaborators in ethnography, see Janus Clifford, "On Ethnographic Authority," in *The Predicament of Culture: Twentieth-Century Ethnography, Literature, and Art* (Cambridge: Harvard

University Press, 1988), 21–54.

44 FB to Toni, 4 January 1897.

45 FB to parents, 31 August 1896. Topinard, review of "The Indians of British Columbia," 5th BAAS report, *L'Anthropologie* 6 (1895), 714; FB to parents, 19 February 1896.

46 FB to Baron Ferdinand von Andrian-Werberg, 8 August 1898, draft, BPP.

47 MB to parents, 19 January 1897.

48 FB to parents, 29 August 1899; see also 26 March, 2 April 1897.

49 FB to parents, 16 and 25 June 1899; FB to Mama, 30 March 1900.

50 FB to Mama, 20 April 1900. Ira Remsen, Home Secretary, NAS, to Putnam, 13 March 1900, Putnam Papers, box 11. Holmes was elected only in 1905.

51 FB to Mama, 25 January, 24 May 1901.

CHAPTER 13: "NOTHING HAS WORKED OUT—OR ONLY A LITTLE"

1 FB to Mama, 18 June 1900.

2 FB to parents, 4 December 1896.

3 FB to Putnam, 13 May 1899, Putnam Papers, box 14; Putnam to FB, 14 May 1899, draft, Putnam Papers, box 13. The divergence of this statement from his California actions two years later may not have been lost upon Boas.

4 FB to Mama, 16 May 1899; FB to Jesup, 29 May 1899, draft, BPP.

5 FB to Mama, 5 October 1899.

6 FB to Mama, 25 December 1900.

7 FB to Jesup, 30 March 1901, AMNH Archives.

8 Jesup to FB, 1 April [1901], BPP [microfilmed as 1900].

9 Jesup to Osborn and Bumpus, 24 July 1901, AMNH, file 517, in Harper, *Give Me My Father's Body*, 65–73, which covers the embarrassment well.

10 Jesup to Putnam, 15 April 1901, Putnam Papers; Jesup to FB, 20 April 1901, AMNH, Anthro. dept., Jesup file; FB to Mama, 26 February 1901; FB to Andrews, 22 August 1901, AMNH, Anthro. dept., Andrews file.

11 FB to Putnam, 4 April 1902, unsent, BPP. See Timothy H. H. Thoresen, "Paying the Piper and Calling the Tune: The Beginnings of Academic Anthropology in California," *Journal of the History of the Behavioral Sciences* 11 (1975), 257–75.

12 FB to Putnam, 4 April 1902, unsent, BPP.

13 FB to Hearst, 7 May 1902; Putnam to Hearst, 2 May 1902, Hearst Papers, Bancroft Library.

14 FB to Nuttall, 18 May 1901. Nuttall forwarded it to Mrs. Hearst with a strong endorsement, Nuttall to Hearst, 19 May 1901, Hearst Papers, Bancroft Library; Boas to Merriam, 19 November 1901; D'Aquin to Merriam, 21 January 1902, University of California Department of Anthropology, cited in Thoresen, "Paying the Piper," 267.

15 FB to Kroeber, 18 October 1901, Kroeber Papers, Bancroft Library.

16 FB to Nuttall, 18 May 1901, Hearst Papers, Bancroft Library.

17 FB to Mama, 3 March, 13 January 1903.

18 FB, "The Relations between the Variability of Organisms and That of Their Constituent Elements," *Science* 15 (3 January 1902), 1–5; FB to Mama, 14 October 1901, 21 and 28 February, 4 March 1902.

19 FB to Jesup, 9 January 1902, AMNH, Anthro. dept., Reports file.

20 FB to Bumpus, 21 February 1902, AMNH, Anthro. dept., Bumpus file.

21 FB to Mama, 28 February 1902.

22 FB to Bumpus, 21 February 1902, AMNH, Anthro. dept., Bumpus file.

23 FB to Bumpus, 21 February 1902, AMNH, Anthro. dept., Bumpus file; FB to Mama, 2 May 1902.

24 FB to Putnam, 4 April, unsent, and 6 April 1902; Putnam to FB, 14 April 1902, BPP.

25 Bumpus to Jesup, 19 May 1902, and Jesup note on same, AMNH, file 293a; FB to Mama, 2 July 1902.

26 FB to MB, 12 July 1902.

27 The operation had cost about $250, less than it should have because Jacobi had arranged to lower the doctor's fee.

28 FB to Mama, 21 September 1902; FB to Andrews, 19 August 1902, AMNH, Anthro. dept., Andrews file.

29 Putnam to Esther Putnam, 22 October 1902, Putnam Papers, box 15.

30 FB to Mama, 26 October 1902.

31 FB to Mama, 10 February 1903.

32 Bumpus to Jesup, 25 July 1902, 19 September 1902, AMNH Archives, 1902: B file; Jesup to Putnam, 14 September [1902], 1[?] December 1902, Putnam Papers, 1717.10.

33 FB to Mama, 13 January and 13 March 1903.

34 Putnam to Bumpus, 28 January 1903, Putnam Papers, box 13.

35 Joseph Florimond Loubat was a wealthy American with an interest in archaeology. He endowed professorships in American archaeology at Paris and Berlin as well as at Columbia. His ducal title was bestowed upon him by Leo XVIII in 1893.

36 FB to Mama, 10 February 1903.

37 Ibid. The reason he gave Putnam—that it was inadmissible for all the university's teaching staff to be subordinate to Putnam—was a strained side issue. FB to Putnam, 4 February 1903, AMNH, Anthro. dept., Putnam file.

38 Bumpus to Jesup, 19 February 1903, AMNH, J file; Bumpus to Putnam, 10 February 1903, Putnam Papers, box 13; Saville to Putnam, 12 February 1903, ibid., box 18; FB to Mama, 10 February 1903.

39 Bumpus to Putnam, 10 February 1903, Putnam Papers, box 13; Bumpus to FB, 2 March 1903, AMNH Archives.

40 "Kurz und gut, zwischen uns ist es aus." FB to Mama, 10 February 1903.

41 FB to Mama, 23 February and 13 March 1903.

42 FB to Mama, 3 March 1903.

43 FB to Mama, 10 February 1903.

44 Putnam to FB, 6 February 1903, "strictly personal and confidential," BPP.

45 Ibid. See also Putnam to Bumpus, 6 February 1903, Putnam Papers, box 12.

46 FB to Mama, 23 February, 13 March, 1903; FB to Bumpus, 7 October 1904, BPP.

47 Putnam to Nuttall, 26 March 1903, Putnam Papers, box 17; B. I. Wheeler to Putnam, 17 March 1903; Putnam to Wheeler, 7 April 1903, Putnam Papers, box 19; FB to Mama, 11 December 1903.

48 FB to Jesup, reporting conversation of Jesup to Bumpus, 20 February 1903, AMNH, file 293; FB to Jesup, 20 February 1903, AMNH, file 293; Jesup to FB, 24 February [1903], BPP [microfilmed as 1900]; Bumpus to Jesup, 28 April 1903, AMNH, Antho. dept.; FB to Mama, 23 December 1903.

49 FB to Jesup, reporting conversation of Jesup to Bumpus, 20 February 1903, AMNH, file 293; FB to Winser, 28 July 1905, AMNH, file 1905, B file. The first part of Bogoras's *Chukchee,*

which came out in 1904, was the first volume published by Brill. Waldemar Bogoras. *The Chukchee.* Publications of the Jesup North Pacific Expedition 7 (New York, 1904).

50 Jochelson to FB, 7 March 1905; Bogoras to FB, 6 April 1905; FB to Bogoras, 22 April 1905, 23 November 1905; Jochelson to FB, 7 March, 10 June, 8 May, 29 August 1905, AMNH, Anthro. dept.

51 FB to McGee, 25 January, 13 March 1902, BPP; FB to Mama, 1 April 1902.

52 FB to McGee, 26 March 1902; McGee to FB, 28 March 1902, BPP. The "urgent consideration" might well have been the question of who was to replace the declining Major Powell as head of the Bureau, dealt with below. FB to Mama, 1 April 1902.

53 The Washington paper was published in *Science* 15 (23 May 1902), 804–9, as "The Foundation of a National Anthropological Society." His Pittsburgh effort may not have been helped by the discomfort of his unrecognized appendicitis, the reason, probably, that he did not read his paper on "The Growth of Children," which he presented by title only.

54 FB to Cattell, 5 July 1902, James McKeen Cattell Papers, box 5, Library of Congress. See W J McGee, "The American Anthropological Association," *AA* 5 (1903), 178–92, and, especially, George W. Stocking, Jr., "Franz Boas and the Founding of the American Anthropological Association," *AA* 62 (1960), 1–17.

55 Langley to "dear Sir," 13 October 1902, BPP. See Virginia Hull McKimmon Noelke, "The Origin and Early History of the Bureau of American Ethnology, 1879–1910," (Ph.D. diss., University of Texas at Austin, 1974), 219–22, and Hinsley, *Savages and Scientists*, 248–55.

56 FB to Mama, 26 October 1902; McGee Memorial Volume, Boas draft, Boas Papers, "Boas Library." FB to Mama, 26 October 1902; McGee to FB, 16 June 1903, BPP.

57 FB to Mama, 26 October 1902.

58 FB to Mama, 11 November, 25 December 1902. "The Bureau of American Ethnology," *Science* 16 (21 November 1902), 828–31.

59 MB to Mama, 31 December 1902; FB to Mama, 2 January 1903. Boas's meaning is not quite clear.

60 FB, "The Bureau of American Ethnology," *Science* ns (21 November 1902), 828–31; FB to Schurz, 12 August 1903; FB to Bell, 7 August 1903, BPP.

61 FB to Mama, 23 April 1903; Anita N. McGee to FB, 15 March 1903; McGee to FB, 1 August 1903, BPP. See Noelke, "Origin and Early History," 198–228; Hinsley, *Savages and Scientists*, 248–56.

62 FB to Mama, 15 and 17 July, 27 August 1903.

63 FB to Mama, 9 October; FB to Mama, 26 November 1903, 5 February 1905, 11 December 1903.

64 FB to Mama, 10 November 1903, 16 February 1904.

65 FB to Mama, 15 April 1904.

66 Ibid.

CHAPTER 14: "FUNDAMENTAL DIFFERENCES OF OPINION"

1 FB to Mama, 13, 15, and 17 August 1904.

2 FB to Bumpus, 30 August 1904, AMNH, file 293.

3 FB to MB, 17 September 1904. This lecture was later published as "The History of Anthropology" (1904).

4 FB to Mama, 9 September, 4 November, 25 October 1904.

5 FB to Mama, 4, 11 November, 9 and 20 December 1904.

6 FB to Butler, 9 November 1904, BPP.

7   FB to Bumpus, 4 January 1905, AMNH, Anthro. dept., Bumpus file.

8   FB to Butler, 14 February 1905, Secretary's Papers, Columbia University, Boas file; FB to Jacob H. Schiff, 9 February 1906; FB to Butler, 14 February 1906, BPP; FB to Mama, 13 January 1905.

9   FB to Mama, 13 and 29 January, 6 and 11 February, 27 January 1905.

10 FB to Bumpus, 21 February, and Bumpus to FB, 27 February 1905, AMNH, Anthro. dept., Bumpus file; FB to Mama, 25 February 1904.

11 FB to Mama, 13 January, 6 February 1905; FB to Osborn, 6 May 1905, BPP.

12 FB to Putnam, 13 August 1909, Putnam Papers, box 14.

13 Saville to Putnam, 5 March [1903], Putnam Papers, box 18.

14 FB to Mama, 17 April 1905; FB to Bumpus, "Quarterly Report to 31 March," 24 April 1905, BPP.

15 Jesup to FB, 28 April 1905, BPP.

16 Bumpus to FB, 28 April 1905, BPP.

17 FB to Jesup, both 29 April 1905; Jesup to FB, 2 May 1905; FB to H. F. Osborn, 6 May 1905, BPP.

18 FB, Notes on 17 May meeting; FB to Mama, 19 May 1905; FB to Jesup, 23 May 1905; Jesup to FB, 24 May 1905; FB to Jesup, 23 May 1905; Jesup to FB, 24 May 1905, BPP; MK to Mama, 25 May 1905.

19 FB to Bogoras, 25 May 1905, BPP.

20 Putnam to FB, 29 May 1905, BPP; Hrdlicka to Putnam, 1 June 1905, Putnam Papers, box 15.

21 Notes for 17 May; FB to Bumpus, 5 May 1905; FB to Osborn, 6 May 1905; FB to Jesup, 20 May 1905, BPP. Bumpus's mental or emotional state at the time is an unresolvable question. He took three months leave in June. Bandelier, writing in his characteristically ironic German, commented that he was "not canonical in his upper rooms" and was off to Switzerland "to get back what is lost." Harlan Smith wrote that Bumpus had recently conversed in "a rather bewildering manner" and that "his mind did not seem to be under his full control." Bandelier to FB, 20 June 1905; Smith to FB, 5 July 1905, BPP. Boas, too, suffered from strain. His student Robert Lowie recalled Boas as being curt and preoccupied, so much so that Lowie dreaded any meeting with him. Robert H. Lowie, "Franz Boas, 1858–1942" *National Academy of Sciences, Biographical Memoirs* 24, no. 9 (1947), reprinted in Cora du Bois, ed., *Lowie's Selected Papers in Anthropology* (Berkeley: University of California Press, 1960), 314.

22 FB to Mama, 30 May 1905; Jesup to FB, 2 May 1905; FB to Schiff, 9 February 1906; FB to Arthur von Briesen, 15 February 1906, BPP. See also Jacknis, "Franz Boas and Exhibits," 105–11.

23 Jesup to Putnam, 2 August 1902, AMNH, 1902, B file.

24 FB to Bumpus, 21 August 1902, AMNH, Anthro. dept., Bumpus file; Bumpus to FB, 18 December 1903, AMNH, cited in Jacknis "Franz Boas and Exhibits," 86; FB, "Some Principles of Museum Administration," *Science* 25 (14 June 1907), 921–33; FB to Jesup, 23 May 1905; Jesup to FB, 24 May 1905, BPP.

25 FB to Osborn, 6 May 1905, BPP.

26 FB to Osborn, 6 May 1905, BPP; FB to Putnam, 18 December 1895, Putnam Papers, box 8.

27 FB to Jesup, 20 May 1905, BPP. Boas gives a version of part of the problems in "Notes of Museum work, May 24 to December, 1905," BPP.

28 Jesup to Osborn, 30 April 1906, AMNH, file 293b.

29 Agreement of 31 May 1906, signed by FB, 8 June 1906, BPP. Boas seems himself to have recommended the piece-work idea in order to avoid conflicts with Bumpus (Memo by FB,

25–27 April 1906), though this is contradicted in FB to Osborn, 28 April 1906, BPP; FB to Putnam, 23 June 1906, Putnam Papers, box 14.

30 FB to Bumpus, 22 December 1902, AMNH, file 293. See also FB to Carnegie Institute, 9 January 1903, BPP. See Stanley A. Freed and Ruth S. Freed, "Clark Wissler and the Development of Anthropology in the United States," *AA* 85 (1983), especially 802–3, and George W. Stocking, Jr., "Clark Wissler," *Dictionary of American Biography,* Supplement 4 (New York: Scribner's Sons, 1974), 906–09.

31 FB to Wissler, 22 June 1905; Wissler to FB, 27 June 1905; FB to Wissler, 28 June 1905, AMNH, Anthro. dept., Wissler file; FB to Cattell, 30 June 1905, Cattell Papers, box 5, Library of Congress.

32 Wissler to Bumpus, 30 June 1905, AMNH, file 10A; Wissler to FB, 1 July 1905, BPP.

33 FB to Jesup, 20 July 1905, draft, BPP; Wissler to Butler, 5 August 1905 and 15(?) August 1905, Secretary's Papers, Columbia University, Wissler file.

34 Farrand to FB, 10 August 1905, BPP; FB to Butler, 12 August 1905, Secretary's Papers, Columbia University; FB to Mama, 14 August 1905; FB to Cattell, 11 August 1905, Cattell Papers, box 5, Library of Congress.

35 FB to Butler, 28 September 1905, Secretary's Papers, Columbia University.

36 Freed and Freed, "Clark Wissler," 801.

37 See note, *AA* 8 (1906), 431; George Peter Murdock, "Clark Wissler, 1870–1947," *AA* 50 (1948), 295. See also Stocking, "Clark Wissler," 906–9. The fullest appraisal of Wissler's museum career is Freed and Freed, "Clark Wissler," 800–25.

38 Boas did seek further museum cooperation, succeeding later in having a study collection brought to Barnard, assistants for museum teaching, and nonremunerative Columbia lectureships for museum staff.

39 FB, "Some Principles," 928.

40 George Dorsey, "The Anthropological Exhibits at the American Museum of Natural History," *Science* ns 25 (12 April 1907), 584.

41 FB to McGee, 12 April 1897, BAE.

42 FB to Swanton, 4 April 1901, AMNH, Acc. 1901–31; FB to Bumpus, 11 November 1903, AMNH, Anthro. dept., Bumpus file; FB to Farrand, 20 June 1903, AMNH, Anthro. dept., Farrand file. See also FB, "Die Jesup–Nordpacifische Expedition," *Verhandlungen der Gesellschaft für Erdkunde zu Berlin* 28 (1901), 357, and FB, "Jesup North Pacific Expedition," 97, where he writes that, because of Nelson and Emmons, the principal work of the Expedition had to be done in British Columbia and Washington State. Swanton did do four months of work in 1904 in southeastern Alaska, but that was under Bureau of American Ethnology sponsorship. He published a long report for the Bureau's 26th report on Tlingit society, beliefs, and linguistic relationships in 1908 and a collection of Tlingit myths and texts the following year. The Emmons material was published only in 1991 after heroic editorial work by Frederica de Laguna, incidentally a Boas student. George T. Emmons, *The Tlingit Indians,* edited with additions by Frederica de Laguna (Seattle: University of Washington Press, 1991).

43 FB, "Ethnological Problems in Canada," (1910), in *RLC,* 331–43.

44 Waldemar Bogoras, "The Folklore of Northeastern Asia, as Compared with that of Northwestern America," *AA* 4 (1902), 669; Waldemar Jochelson, "Über asiatische und amerikanische Elemente in den Mythen der Koriaken," *Bericht des XIV Internationalen Amerikanisten Kongrësses, Stuttgart, 1904* (Stuttgart, 1905), 125.

45 Bogoras, "Folklore," 579.

46 FB, "Die Nordpazifische Jesup-Expedition," *Internationale Monatschrift für Wissenschaft, Kunst und Technik* 2 (1908), 1291–1306; FB, "Die Resultate der Jesup-Expedition," *Verhandlugen des XVI Internationalen Amerikanisten-Kongrësses, Wien, 1908,* 3–18. A corrected typescript draft for the latter, "The Results of the Jesup Expedition," is in AMNH, Anthro. dept., Jesup Expedition file. These somewhat repetitive reports are perhaps the best summary of his conclusions in the years immediately following the Expedition.

47 Ibid.

48 This remains a difficult and controversial area where new evidence undermines old models while increasing the complexity of the problems. Nevertheless, much of Boas's general conclusion remains plausible.

49 FB, "Ethnological Problems of Canada," (1910) 337; FB, "The History of the American Race" (1912), in *RLC,* 325. The term was in use by at least 1904: Leo Shternberg, "Bemerkungen über Beziehungen zwischen der Morphologie der giljakischen und amerikanischen Sprachen," *Bericht des XIV Internationalen Amerikanisten Kongrësses, Stuttgart, 1904* (Stuttgart, 1905), 138.

50 FB, "Dissemination of Tales," in *RLC,* 443; FB, "Ethnological Problems," 337; FB, "Some Problems in North America Archaeology," (1902), in *RLC,* 529. As late as 1936 in "History and Science," in *RLC,* 308; FB, "Ethnological Problems," 341; "The Folk-Lore of the Eskimo," in *RLC,* 510; FB, "The Eskimo," *Transactions of the Royal Society of Canada* 5 (1888), 35–39; and FB, "Über die Wohnsitze der Neitchillik-Eskimos," *Zeitschrift der Gesellschaft für Erdkunde zu Berlin* 18 (1883): 222–33. See FB, "The Jesup North Pacific Expedition," typescript, nd [1902?], AMNH, Anthro. dept., Jesup Expedition file: "We must infer . . .that the Eskimo are new arrivals on the Pacific side of America, that their original home was somewhere near the Mackenzie or east of the Mackenzie River, and that they interrupted at an early period the communication between the Siberian and Indian tribes." See also FB to Jesup, 25 November 1905. Bogoras, "Folklore," 670; Waldemar Jochelson, *The Koryak,* Publications of the Jesup North Pacific Expedition 6 (New York, 1905–08), 359; Drucker, "Sources," 60.

51 FB, "Folk-lore of the Eskimo," in *RLC,* 503. In "Some Problems," he again attributed the "remarkable differences" of Alaskan Eskimo from Eastern Eskimo to the influence of the Indians of Alaska, in *RLC,* 537.

52 Emöke J. E. Szathmary, "Human Biology of the Arctic," *Handbook of the American Indians,* vol. 5: *Arctic,* ed. David Damas (Washington: Smithsonian Institution, 1984), 71. It is highly probable, writes S. A. Arutiunov, that with the constitution of the ancient Eskaleut population as a group in the Bering Strait region "the cultural links and influences from Asia to America through the Bering Strait, if they did not stop, at least diminished." S. A. Arutiunov, "Chukchi: Warriors and Traders of the Chukotka," in *Crossroads of Continents: Cultures of Siberia and Alaska,* ed. William N. Fitzhugh and Aron Crowell (Washington, D.C.: Smithsonian Institution, 1988), 40; see also S. A. Arutiunov and William W. Fitzhugh, "Prehistory of Siberia and the Bering Sea," in ibid., 129, where the Eskimo cultures are seen as "a relatively impenetrable isolating layer" blocking Asiatic influences from North American Indians. Stephen D. Ousley, "Relationships between Eskimos, Amerindians, and Aleuts: Old Data, New Perspectives," *Human Biology* 67 (June 1995), 435.

53 FB, "Die Norpazifische Jesup-Expedition," 1296–97; FB, "Die Resultate," 8. For the importance of stratigraphic excavation to archaeological methods, see David L. Browman and Douglas R. Givens, "Stratigraphic Excavation: The First 'New Archaeology,'" *AA* 98 (1996): 15–26.

54 Roy L. Carlson, "Cultural Antecedents," *Handbook of North American Indians.* Vol. 7: *Northwest Coast,* ed. Wayne Suttles (Washington, D.C.: Smithsonian Institution, 1990), 69; and Carlson, "History of Research in Archeology," in ibid., 115; Knut R. Fladmark, *British Columbia Prehistory* (Ottawa: National Museum of Man, 1986), 5.

55 A nice summary of affinities is in Ousley, "Relationships Between Eskimos," 432–33; Jochelson did not include Nelson's Alaska Eskimo myths in his evaluation because "a large part of the episodes of the latter cannot be considered as genuine Eskimo elements" and would only "have caused confusion." Yet the Eskimo influence on Koryak culture—myths, religious rites, and material culture—pointed to a direct intercourse between Koryak and Eskimo at some period. When, and under what circumstances, could only remain an open question. Jochelson, *The Koryak,* 359. See Ann Chowning, "Raven Myths in Northwestern North America and Northeastern Asia," *Arctic Anthropology* 1 (1962), 1–5.

56 FB to Bumpus, 22 December 1902, AMNH, file 293; FB to Jesup, 25 November 1905, AMNH, file 293.

57 Jochelson-Brodskya did publish a long paper on women of North East Siberia as "Zur Topographie des weiblichen Körpers nordostsibirischer Völker," *Archeologische Anthropologie* 6 (1906), 1–58. FB and Livingston Farrand, "Physical Characteristics of the Tribes of British Columbia," "The North-Western Tribes of Canada, Twelfth and Final Report of the Committee," *British Association for the Advancement of Science,* 1898, 628–44. A related study, commissioned by Boas using funds from James M. Constable, was a study of 46 Athapaskans and 40 Eskimo done in 1897–99. FB, "A. J. Stone's Measurements of Natives of the Northwest Territories," *Bulletin of the AMNH* 14 (1901), 53–67, that distinguished the two groups. A severely limited single volume of cranial studies came only in 1930: Bruno Oetteking, *Craniology of the North Pacific Coast* (Leiden and New York: G. E. Stechert, 1930). See Ousley, "Relationships Between Eskimos," 446–47.

58 There was, he concluded in 1933, no proof that they derived from the same stock. There were some similarities, especially of Aleut-Eskimo, Chukchi, Koryak, and Itel'men. FB, "Relationships between North-West America and North-East Asia" (1933), in *RLC,* 355. A number of hypothetical connections between Eskimo-Aleut and Asiatic languages have been proposed, but all remain unproved. Anthony C. Woodbury, "Eskimo and Aleut Languages," *Handbook of North American Indians,* vol. 5: *Arctic,* ed. David Dumas (Washington, D.C.: Smithsonian Institution, 1984), 62.

59 See Cole, *Captured Heritage,* esp. 80–89, 141–64; Jonaitis, *From the Land of the Totem Poles;* and Fitzhugh and Crowell, eds., *Crossroads.*

60 FB to Jesup, 2, 18 November 1898; FB to Putnam, 1 December 1898, AMNH, Anthro. dept.; FB to Papa, 31 October 1898; FB to James H. Lamb Co., 9 November 1900; Jesup to Osborn, 30 April 1906, AMNH, file 293b.

61 FB to Mama, 9 July 1909, 23 June 1910, 18 March 1909.

62 The Jochelsons came to the United States in 1922, continuing his work with support gathered by Boas from the American Museum and privately until his death. Mrs. Jochelson also received museum support for her anthropometric work.

CHAPTER 15: "LAYING CLEAR THE COMPLEX RELATIONS OF
EACH INDIVIDUAL CULTURE"

1 FB, "Anthropology in the American and British Associations for the Advancement of

Science," *Science* 10 (11 November 1887), 231.

2   FB, "Advances in Methods of Teaching" (1899), 94, in *RLC,* 622.

3   FB, "History and Science," in *RLC,* 311.

4   George W. Stocking, Jr., *Victorian Anthropology* (New York: Free Press, 1987), 168. My indebtedness to Professor Stocking in these pages is readily apparent. See also Robert L. Carneiro, "Classical Evolution," in Raoul and Frada Naroll, eds., *Main Currents in Cultural Anthropology* (Englewood Cliffs: Prentice-Hall, 1973), 57–122; Joan Leopold, *Culture in Comparative and Evolutionary Perspective: E. B. Tylor and the Making of Primitive Culture* (Berlin: Dieter Reimer, 1980).

5   Lubbock, quoted in Stocking, *Victorian Anthropology,* 155.

6   Daniel G. Brinton, *Religions of Primitive Peoples* (London: G. P. Putnam's Sons, 1897; reprint: Greenwood, N.J.: Negro Universities Press, 1969), 7; Brinton, "The Aims of Anthropology," *Science* 2 (30 August 1895), 243, 246.

7   This is my summary of Stocking and may contain an element of my own interpretation. See Stocking, *Victorian Anthropology,* 170.

8   FB, "Die Ziele," 7; FB, *The Mind of Primitive Man* (New York: Macmillan, 1911), 162–79; FB, "Psychological Problems of Anthropology" (1910), in Stocking, *Shaping,* 251, 249, 253; FB, "Limitations," in *RLC,* 276. See Harris, *Rise of Anthropological Theory,* 295; and Lesser, "Franz Boas," 23–24, who points out Boas's opposition to "orthogenetic" evolution, though Boas seems to have adopted that word only after 1919.

9   FB, "Limitations," in *RLC,* 250.

10 FB to parents, 17 August 1896.

11 FB, "Growth of Indian Mythologies," in *RLC,* 434–35; FB, "History and Science," in *RLC,* 311.

12 FB to parents, 17 August 1896. Indeed, Brinton was critical, though the text of his paper is not available. His opposition is, however, clear elsewhere, again on the grounds that Boas's mythological elements "arise independently, often in the same connection, owing to the uniformity of the action of the human mind under similar conditions and seeking the expression of similar ideas." Brinton, *The Myths of the New World* (3rd ed., rev., 1896; reprint New York: Haskell House, 1968), 55n1.

13 FB, "Limitations," in *RLC,* 275, 273–4.

14 Ibid., 276, 277, 279.

15 FB, *Jesup North Pacific Expedition,* vol. 1, 1898, 3–4, in Stocking, *Shaping,* 108; FB, "Limitations," in *RLC,* 280.

16 FB, "Rudolf Virchow's Anthropological Work" (1902), in Stocking, *Shaping,* 39. See Smith, *Politics and the Sciences of Culture,* 105, 108; Erwin H. Ackerknecht, *Rudolf Virchow: Doctor, Statesman, Anthropologist* (Madison: University of Wisconsin Press, 1953), 235.

17 FB, "History of Anthropology," in Stocking, *Shaping,* 26, 34.

18 See, for instance, Wax, "Limitations of Boas' Anthropology," 63–74; Harris, *Rise of Anthropological Theory,* 284–89; Stocking, "Basic Assumptions," 18–19.

19 FB, "Anthropology," in *RLC,* 275. No longer were the stages of family life, or the view that all patriarchal families developed from earlier matriarchal ones, tenable; FB, "Limitations," in *RLC,* 279; FB, "Virchow's Anthropological Work," in Stocking, *Shaping,* 39; FB to Laura D. Gill, 5 December 1905, BPP; FB, "History of Anthropology," in Stocking, *Shaping,* 32.

20 FB, *The Mythology of the Bella Coola Indians,* Publications of the Jesup North Pacific Expedition 1 (1898), in Stocking, *Shaping,* 154, 155.

21 Ibid., 154.

22 Thomas F. McIlwraith, *The Bella Coola Indians* (Toronto: University of Toronto Press, 1948), based on fieldwork in 1922 and 1923–24, was published only in 1948. Boas's 1891 BAAS report has one heaven and no underworlds. He altered this with his 1897 evidence of five layers. See also Ralph Maud, *A Guide to B.C. Indian Myth and Legend* (Vancouver: Talon Books, 1982), 87–89; Dorothy I. D. Kennedy and Randall T. Bouchard, "Bella Coola," in *Handbook of North American Indians*. Vol. 7: *Northwest Coast*, ed. Wayne Suttles (Washington, D.C.: Smithsonian Institution, 1990), 330.

23 FB, "History of Anthropology," in Stocking, *Shaping*, 26–30.

24 FB, "Review of *Anthropologische Studien ueber die Ureinwohner Brasiliens* by Paul Ehrenreich" (1897), in *RLC*, 153; "Review of William C. Ripley's *Races of Europe*," in *RLC*, 159; Müller, "Die linguistische Ethnographie im Verhältniss zur Anthropologie," *Geographisches Jahrbuch* 3 (1870), 315; Otto Schräder, *Prehistoric Antiquities of the Aryan Peoples* (1883), trans. Frank Byron Jevons (London: Charles Griffin, 1890), 131; FB, "Virchow's Anthropological Work," in Stocking, *Shaping*, 40.

25 FB, "History of Anthropology," in Stocking, *Shaping*, 35.

26 FB, Anthropology: A Lecture Delivered at Columbia University in the Series on Science, Philophy, and Art, December 18, 1907 (1908), in Stocking, *Shaping*, 268; FB, Review of Ehrenreich, in *RLC*, 152; FB, "Anthropology," in Stocking, *Shaping*, 271; FB, "Some Recent Criticisms of Physical Anthropology" (1899), in *RLC*, 171.

27 Though, it seems important to note, Boas did this much less in the Vanishing Tribes project or Laufer's East Asian work, by which time his interests were on other things.

28 As well as his mathematics at Heidelberg and Bonn, Boas first choice of a dissertation topic had been on probability and random error, and he sat in on Seelig's statistics course in Kiel.

29 Yu Xie, "Franz Boas and Statistics," *Annals of Scholarship* 5 (1988), 280. See J. M. Tanner, "Boas' Contributions to Knowledge of Human Growth and Form," and W. W. Howells, "Boas as Statistician," in Walter Goldschmidt, ed., *The Anthropology of Franz Boas*, AAA Memoir 89 (San Francisco: Howard Chandler, 1959), 76–111, 112–15; John S. Allen, "Franz Boas's Physical Anthropology: The Critique of Race Formalism Revisited," *Current Anthropology* 30 (February 1989), 79–84. See also George W. Stocking's "The Critique of Racial Formalism," in *Race, Culture, and Evolution*, 161–94. These remain the most useful assessments.

30 FB, "Anthropology of North American Indians" (1894) in Stocking, *Shaping*, 191–201; FB, "The Half-Blood Indian" (1894), in *RLC*, 143; FB, "Review of Ripley," in *RLC*, 155–56; Stocking, "Racial Formalism," 163; FB, "The Half-Blood Indian," in *RLC*, 145–46.

31 Peter J. Bowler, *The Eclipse of Darwinism: Anti-Darwinian Evolutionary Theories in the Decades around 1900* (Baltimore: Johns Hopkins, 1983); Stocking, "Racial Formalism," 161–94.

32 This is not to deprecate the effort, and it is, a century later, proving useful. Richard L. Jantz of the University of Tennessee, Knoxville, has assembled most of Boas's data and a team of scholars to process and interpret it. In 1992, he, with D. R. Hunt, A. B. Falsetti, and P. J. Key, published the results as "Variation among North Amerindians: Analysis of Boas's Anthropometric Data," *Human Biology* 64 (1992), 435–61. In 1995 he edited the valuable special issue of the same journal dedicated to the *Population Biology of Late Nineteenth-Century Native North Americans and Siberians: Analyses of Boas's Data, Human Biology* 67 (1995).

33 See Tanner, "Boas' Contribution," 76–111; Allen, "Boas's Physical Anthropology," 79–84.

34 FB, "Statistical Study of Anthropometry" (1912), in *RLC*, 131.

35 FB, "Human Faculty," in Stocking, *Shaping*, 233.

36 Ibid., 227, 233–34, 242.

37 FB, "Anthropology," in Stocking, *Shaping*, 273.

38 Stocking, "Racial Capacity and Cultural Determinism," in Stocking, *Shaping*, 219–20. The address remained essentially a defensive argument, an excerise in scepticism about evidence for the inferiority of non-White races and societies. Vernon Williams views it as the initial formulation of what he calls the Boas "paradox," with Boas, instinctively a liberal humanitarian, captive to the assumptions of physical anthropology and his methodological puritanism. Williams, *Rethinking Race*, 9; FB, "The Mind of Primitive Man," *Journal of American Folk-Lore* 14 (1901), 3.

39 FB, "Primitive Man," 2; "Some Traits of Primitive Culture," *Journal of American Folk-Lore* 17 (1904), 243.

40 FB, "Psychological Problems," in Stocking, *Shaping*, 247; FB, "Some Traits," 253.

41 George W. Stocking, Jr., "Franz Boas and the Culture Concept in Historical Perspective," in *Race, Culture, and Evolution*, 219–20. See Michael Mackert, "The Roots of Franz Boas' View of Linguistic Categories as a Window to the Human Mind," *Historiographia Linguistica* 20 (1993), 340–41. Mackert sees the shift as "a strategic intertextual marker which linked Boas to a different psychological discourse" and avoided linkage to hierarchical classifications.

42 FB, "Primitive Man," 11, 2–3; FB, "History of Anthropology," in Stocking, *Shaping*, 31; FB, "Some Traits," 252, 253.

43 Edward Burnett Tylor, *Primitive Culture*, vol. 1 (1871); reprinted, *The Origin of Culture*, with an introduction by Paul Radin (New York: Harper and Row, 1958), 1; Stocking, "Boas and Culture Concept," 202–3. Hamilton Cravens, *The Triumph of Evolution: American Society and the Heredity-Environment Controversy, 1900–1941* (Philadelphia: University of Pennsylvania Press, 1978), 106. For a survey of definitions, see A. L. Kroeber and Clyde Kluckhohn, *Culture: A Critical Review of Concepts and Definitions* (New York: Vintage Books, 1952).

44 FB, "Some Traits," 253; FB, "Mind of Primitive Man," 1; FB, "History of Anthropology," in Stocking, *Shaping*, 28.

45 FB, "History of Anthropology," in Stocking, *Shaping*, 26.

46 FB, "Some Traits," 243; "Mind of Primitive Man," 1; Stocking, "Boas and Culture Concept," 230.

47 FB, Review of A. Bastian, "Die Welt in ihren Spiegelungen unter dem Wandel des Völkergedankens," *Science* 10 (9 December 1887), 284; FB, "History of Anthropology," in Stocking, *Shaping*, 36.

CHAPTER 16: "THE HUMAN MIND HAS BEEN CREATIVE EVERYWHERE"

1 FB to Jesup, 29 April 1905; Notes of interview with Jesup and Bumpus, 17 May 1905; FB to Laura D. Gill, 5 December 1905; Boas to George Foster Peabody, 19 March 1902, BPP; see also FB to N. M. Butler, 23 February 1906, BPP.

2 See George Stocking, Jr., "Anthropology as *Kulturkampf*: Science and Poltics in the Career of Franz Boas," in *The Ethnographer's Magic and Other Essays in the History of Anthropology* (Madison: University of Wisconsin Press, 1992), 92–113.

3 FB, "Virchow's Anthropological Work," in Stocking, *Shaping*, 39, 41.

4 FB, "Mind of Primitive Man," 8–9; "Some Traits," 247, 244–45, 252–53; Stocking, "Anthropology as *Kulturkampf*," 110.

5 Smith, *Politics and the Sciences of Culture*, 113; Harris, *Rise of Anthropological Theory*, 298; Degler, *In Search of Human Nature*, 82; Smith, 113.

6 On prostitution, see Macdonald to Boas, 22 April 1890, responding to Boas to Macdonald, 6 April 1890, BPP; on potlatch, see Boas in the Victoria *Province*, 6 March 1897, xi–xii, arranged through C. F. Newcombe of Victoria. See Newcombe to FB, 23 February, 12 March 1897, Newcombe Papers, British Columbia Archives. Boas also replied to Edward Sapir's appeal for support against wartime enforcement, FB to Sapir, 18 February 1915, BPP.

7 FB to parents [illeg.], October 1896; FB to Mama, 8 November 1900, 20 November 1903.

8 Richard Hofstadter, *The Age of Reform* (New York: Knopf, 1955), 131–73.

9 FB, "Mind of Primitive Man," 10–11.

10 The quotation is from Leonard B. Glick's perceptive essay, "Types Distinct from Our Own: Franz Boas on Jewish Identity and Assimilation," *AA* 84 (1982), 545–65.

11 Pouring Boas into constructed categories of cosmopolitanism, marginality, or alienation is interesting but unpersuasive. See Liss, "Cosmopolitan Imagination," 1–14, 284–369; and also Julia Liss, "Patterns of Strangeness: Franz Boas, Modernism, and the Origins of Anthropology," in *Prehistories of the Future: The Primitivist Project and the Culture of Modernism*, ed. Elazar Barkan and Ronald Bush, 114–30 (Stanford: Stanford University Press, 1995).

12 Liss, "Cosmopolitan Imagination," 201; Boas to Schmitt-Ott, 2 October 1933, BPP. I have written on some aspects of Boas's Germanness in "Franz Boas: Ein Wissenschaftler und Patriot zwischen zwei Ländern," in *Franz Boas, 1858–1942: Ein amerikanischer Anthropologe aus Minden*, ed. Volker Rodekamp (Bielefeld: Verlag für Regionalgeschichte, 1994), 9–23.

13 FB, "Commencement Address at Atlanta University, May 31, 1906," Atlanta University Leaflet, no. 19, B61p.

14 Glick, "Types Distinct From Our Own," 546.

15 FB to Schiff, 19 February 1915, BPP. Schiff really suspected that no Jew—"by which I meant one who had not actually left the Jewish community"—had recently been appointed, and neither of Boas's examples met his meaning. Schiff to FB, 23 February 1915, BPP.

16 Pulzer, *Jews and the German State*, 332.

17 Glick, "Types Distinct From Our Own," 546; George L. Mosse, *German Jews beyond Judaism* (Bloomington: Indiana University Press, 1985), passim; FB, "Credo," *The Nation*, 204.

18 A. L. Kroeber, "The Place of Boas in Anthropology," *AA* 58 (1956), 155–56; Lowie, "Franz Boas," 317–19; Kroeber to Putnam, 4 February 1904, Putnam Papers.

19 FB, Letter to Committee, excerpted in "The Boas Anniversary," *AA* 9 (1907), 647.

20 Bunzl, "Franz Boas and Humboldtian Tradition," 73.

21 Lowie, "Franz Boas," 320, 312; Freud from *Letters of Sigmund Freud, 1873–1939)*, ed. Ernst L. Freud (London: Hogarth, 1961), 367–68, quoted in Pulzer, *Jews and the German State*, 12.

22 Lowie, "Franz Boas," 312.

23 Leslie Spier, "Franz Boas and Some of His Views," *Acta Americana* 1 (1943), 125.

24 FB to Mama, 26 April 1907.

25 Mark, *Four Anthropologists*, 173, 1. See also Darnell, "Professionalization of American Anthropology," 83–101.

26 Kroeber, "Place of Boas," 156.

27 Lowie, "Franz Boas," 316.

28 The claim in physical anthropology might be qualified by consideration of the emergence of Aleš Hrdlička.

CHAPTER 17: "SEARCHING FOR OPPORTUNITIES IN OTHER FIELDS"

1 Schiff insisted on Jesup's membership. Schurz died before the commemoration was complete.
2 Laufer, "Prefatory," xiv; FB to Mama, 6 May 1907.
3 Laufer to FB, 1 July 1906, BPP; FB to Mama, 26 April 1907.
4 FB to Mama, 5 February 1906; FB to Archer M. Huntington, 30 January 1906, 6 April 1907, BPP.
5 FB to Mama, 23 December 1907, 5 January 1908; FB to Kroeber, 6 January 1908, BPP.
6 Jacob Meyer file, Boas Papers (B61p). Franz was to receive $25,000 of the trust after the death of Abraham and Sophie; Aenne Urbach, whose unfortunate marriage had left her financial situation precarious, received the interest on $15,000 during the minority of her children.

Bibliography

ARCHIVAL COLLECTIONS

Akademie der Wissenschaften, Zentral Akademisches Archiv, Berlin, Nachlass Rudolf Virchow

American Museum of Natural History, New York, Department of Anthropology, Museum Archives

American Philosophical Society, Philadelphia, Franz Boas, Robert Bell, Henry Donaldson Papers

Balfour Library, Oxford University, Oxford, E. B. Tylor Papers

Bancroft Library, University of California, Berkeley, Phoebe Apperson Hearst, A. L. Kroeber Papers

British Columbia Archives, Victoria, C. F. Newcombe Papers

Clark University Archives, Worcester, G. Stanley Hall Papers

Columbia University, New York, Secretary's Papers

Deutsches Hydrographisches Institut, Hamburg

Field Museum of Natural History, Chicago, Registrar's Office

Harvard University Archives, Cambridge, Frederic Putnam Papers

Hessisches Staatsarchiv, Marburg, Nachlass Theobald Fischer

Humboldt-Universität zu Berlin, Universitätsarchiv, Acta Boas

Kommunalarchiv Minden, Minden, verschiedene Akten

Landesarchiv Schleswig, Archiv der Universität Kiel, Kiel

Library of Congress, Washington, D.C., James McKeen Cattell, W J McGee, Carl Schurz Papers

Milton S. Eisenhower Library, Johns Hopkins University, Baltimore, D. C. Gilman Papers

Museum für Völkerkunde, Berlin, Acta Boas

National Anthropological Archives, Washington, D.C., Bureau of American Ethnology Papers

National Archives of Canada, Ottawa, Geological Survey of Canada, Robert Bell Papers

National Collection of Fine Arts and the National Portrait Gallery Library, Washington, D.C., William Henry Holmes, "Random Records of a Lifetime"

Niedersächsische Staats- und Universitäts-Bibliothek, Göttingen, Nachlass Wagner

Oberösterreichisches Landesarchiv, Linz, Ferdinand Krackowizer, "Die Familie Krackowizer"

Rheinische Friedrich-Wilhelms-Universität Bonn, Bonn, Archiv

Staats- und Personenstandsarchiv Detmold, Detmold, Reg. Bez. Minden

333

Stanford University, Palo Alto, University Archives
Universitätsarchiv Münster, Münster, Matrikel
Universitätsbibliothek, Marburg
University of Chicago, William Rainey Harper Papers
Verein alter Bonner Alemannen, Bonn, Konventsprotokolle

UNPUBLISHED SOURCES

Berman, Judith. "The Seals' Sleeping Cave: The Interpretation of Boas' Kwakw'ala Texts."
Ph.D. dissertation, University of Pennsylvania, 1991.
Boas, Franz. "Beiträge zur Erkenntnis der Farbe des Wassers." Ph.D dissertation,
Christian-Albrechts-Universität zu Kiel, 1881.
Darnell, Regna D. "The Development of American Anthropology, 1879–1920: From the
Bureau of American Ethnology to Franz Boas." Ph.D. dissertation, University of
Pennsylvania, 1969.
Hyatt, Marshall. "The Emergence of a Discipline: Franz Boas and the Study of Man."
Ph.D. dissertation, University of Delaware, 1979.
Liss, Julia Elizabeth. "The Cosmopolitan Imagination: Franz Boas and the Development
of American Anthropology." Ph.D dissertation, University of California at Berkeley,
1990.
Maud, Ralph. "Franz Boas: Early Field Work." Typescript.
Noelke, Virginia Hull McKimmon. "The Origin and Early History of the Bureau of
American Ethnology, 1879–1910." Ph.D. dissertation, University of Texas at Austin, 1974.
Riquarts, Kurt-Gerhard. "Der Antisemitismus als politische Partei in Schleswig-Holstein
und Hamburg, 1871–1914." Ph.D dissertation, Christian-Albrechts-Universität zu Kiel,
1975.

ARTICLES

Achelis, Thomas. "Der Ethik der Gegenwart in ihrer Beziehung zur Naturwissenschaft."
Vierteljahresschrift für wissenschaftliche Philosophie 7 (1883).
Allen, John S. "Franz Boas's Physical Anthropology: The Critique of Race Formalism
Revisited." *Current Anthropology* 30 (1989): 79–84.
Arutiunov, S. A. "Chukchi: Warriors and Traders of the Chukotka." In *Crossroads of
Continents: Cultures of Siberia and Alaska*, ed. William W. Fitzhugh and Aron Crowell,
39–42. Washington, D.C.: Smithsonian Institution, 1988.
Arutiunov, S. A., and William W. Fitzhugh. "Prehistory of Siberia and the Bering Sea." In
Fitzhugh and Crowell, *Crossroads of Continents: Cultures of Siberia and Alaska*, 117–29.
Beattie, Owen B. "A Note on Early Cranial Studies from the Gulf of Georgia Region:
Long-heads, Broad-heads, and the Myth of Migration." *BC Studies* 66 (1985): 28–36.
Becher, Erich. "Benno Erdmann." *Archive für die gesamte Psychologie* 42 (1922): 150–82.
Benison, Saul. "Boas's Appeal to Justice C. P. Daly of the American Geographical Society,
12 August 1886." *American Anthropologist* 51 (1949): 524–25.
Berman, Judith. " 'The Culture as It Appears to the Indian Himself': Boas, George Hunt,
and the Methods of Ethnography." In *History of Anthropology*. Vol. 8: *Volksgeist as
Method and Ethic: Essays on Boasian Ethnography and the German Anthropological*

Tradition, ed. George W. Stocking, Jr., 215–56. Madison: University of Wisconsin Press, 1996.

Boas, Franz. "Advances in Methods of Teaching." *Science* 9 (20 January 1899): 93–96. Reprinted in Boas, *Race, Language and Culture,* 621–25. New York: Macmillan, 1940; reprint, New York: Free Press, 1966.

—. "The Aims of Ethnology" (orig. "Die Ziele der Ethnologie," 1889). Reprinted in Boas, *Race, Language and Culture,* 626–38. Partially reprinted in *The Shaping of American Anthropology, 1883–1911: A Franz Boas Reader,* ed. George W. Stocking, Jr., 67–71. New York: Basic Books, 1974.

—. "A. J. Stone's Measurements of Natives of the Northwest Territories." *Bulletin of the American Museum of Natural History* 14 (1901): 53–68.

—. "An Anthropologist's Credo." *The Nation* 147 (27 August 1938): 201–4. Partially reprinted in Stocking, *The Shaping of American Anthropology,* 41–42.

—. "Anthropology: A Lecture Delivered at Columbia University in the Series on Science, Philosophy, and Art, December 18, 1907." New York: Columbia University Press, 1908. Reprinted in Stocking, *The Shaping of American Anthropology,* 267–81.

—. "Anthropology in the American and British Associations for the Advancement of Science." *Science* 10 (11 November 1887): 231–32.

—. "The Anthropology of the North American Indians." *Memoirs of the International Congress of Anthropology,* 37–49. Chicago: Schulte, 1894. Reprinted in Stocking, *The Shaping of American Anthropology,* 191–201.

—. "Anthropometrical Observations on the Mission Indians of Southern California." *Proceedings of the American Association for the Advancement of Science* 44 (1895): 261–69.

—. "Aus dem Eise des Nordens." *Berliner Tageblatt,* 25 November 1883.

—. "The Bureau of American Ethnology." *Science* 16 (21 November 1902): 828–31.

—. "Capitän Jacobsens Bella-Coola-Indianer." *Berliner Tageblatt,* 25 January 1885.

—. "Chinook Songs." *Journal of American Folk-Lore* 1 (1888): 220–26.

—. "Commencement Address at Atlanta University, May 31, 1906," Atlanta University Leaflet no. 19.

—. "The Development of the Culture of Northwest America." *Science* 12 (26 October 1888): 194–96.

—. "The Eskimo." *Transactions of the Royal Society of Canada* 5 (1888): 35–39.

—. "Der Eskimo-Dialekt des Cumberland-Sundes." *Mitteilungen der Anthropologischen Gesellschaft in Wien* 24 (1894): 97–114.

—. "Die Bestimmung der Unterschiedsempfindlichkeit nach der Methode der Ubermecklichen Unterschiede." *Archiv für die gestante Physiologie des Menschen und der Thiere [Pfluger's Archiv]* 28 (1882): 562–66.

—. "Die Eskimos des Baffinlandes." *Verhandlungen des fünften deutschen Geographentages zu Hamburg,* 1–14. Berlin: Dietrich Reimer, 1885.

—. "Die Eskimos des Cumberland-Sundes und der Davisstrasse." *Berliner Tageblatt,* 2 November 1884.

—. "Die Jesup-Nordpazifische Expedition." *Verhandlungen der Gesellschaft für Erdkunde zu Berlin* 28 (1901): 356–59.

—. "Die Nordpazifische Jesup-Expedition." *Internationale Monatschrift für Wissenschaft, Kunst und Technik* 2 (1908): 1291–1306.

—. "Die Resultate der Jesup-Expedition." *Verhandlungen des XVI Internationalen Amerikanisten-Kongrësses, Wien, 1908*, 3–18. Vienna, 1910.

—. "Die Ziele der Ethnologie." *Gemeinverständliche Vorträge gehalten im Deutsche Gesellig-Wissenschaftlichen Verein* 16: 3–30. New York: Herman Bartsch, 1889.

—. "Dissemination of Tales among the Natives of North America." *Journal of American Folk-Lore* 4 (1891): 13–20. Reprinted in Boas, *Race, Language and Culture*, 437–45.

—. "Ethnological Problems in Canada." *Journal of the Royal Anthropological Institute of Great Britain and Ireland* 40 (1910): 529–39. Reprinted in Boas, *Race, Language and Culture*, 331–43.

—. "The Folk-Lore of the Eskimo." *Journal of American Folk-Lore* 17 (1904): 1–13. Reprinted in Boas, *Race, Language and Culture*, 505–16.

—. "The Foundation of a National Anthropological Society." *Science* 15 (23 May 1902): 804–09.

—. "Frederic Ward Putnam." *Science* 42 (10 September 1915): 330–32.

—. "The Growth of Indian Mythologies: A Study Based upon the Growth of the Mythologies of the North Pacific Coast." *Journal of American Folk-Lore* 9 (1896): 1–11. Reprinted in Boas, *Race, Language and Culture*, 425–36.

—. "History and Science in Anthropology: A Reply." *American Anthropologist* 38 (1936): 137–41. Reprinted in Boas, *Race, Language and Culture*, 305–11.

—. "The History of the American Race." *Annals of the New York Academy of Sciences* 21 (1912): 177–83. Reprinted in Boas, *Race, Language and Culture*, 324–30.

—. "The History of Anthropology." *Science* 20 (21 October 1904): 513–24. Reprinted in Stocking, *The Shaping of American Anthropology*, 23–36.

—. "Human Faculty as Determined by Race." *Proceedings of the American Association for the Advancement of Science* 43 (1894): 301–27. Reprinted in Stocking, *The Shaping of American Anthropology*, 221–42.

—. "The Indians of British Columbia." *Popular Science Monthly* 32 (1888): 628–36.

—. "The Indians of British Columbia." *Transactions of the Royal Society of Canada* 6 (1888): 47–57.

—. "The Jesup North Pacific Expedition." *American Museum Journal* 3 (1903): 93–98.

—. "A Journey in Cumberland Sound and on the West Shore of Davis Strait in 1883 and 1884." *Journal of the American Geographical Society* 16 (1884): 242–72.

—. "The Language of the Bilhoola in British Columbia. " *Science* 7 (5 March 1886): 218.

—. Letter to Committee. Excerpted in "The Boas Anniversary." *American Anthropologist* 9 (1907): 646–48.

—. "The Limitations of the Comparative Method of Anthropology." *Science* 4 (18 December 1896): 901–8. Reprinted in Boas, *Race, Language and Culture*, 270–80.

—. "The Mind of Primitive Man." *Journal of American Folk-Lore* 14 (1901): 1–11.

—. "Museums of Ethnology and Their Classification." *Science* 9 (17 June 1887): 587–89. Reprinted in Stocking, *The Shaping of American Anthropology*, 63–67.

—. "Notes on the Ethnology of British Columbia." *Proceedings of the American Philosophical Society* 24 (1887): 422–29.

—. "The Occurrence of Similar Inventions in Areas Widely Apart." *Science* 9 (20 May 1887): 485–86. Reprinted in Stocking, *The Shaping of American Anthropology*, 61–63.

—. "On Alternating Sounds." *American Anthropologist* 2 (1889): 47–53. Reprinted in Stocking, *The Shaping of American Anthropology*, 72–77.

—. "Psychological Problems in Anthropology." *American Journal of Psychology* 21 (1910): 371–84. Reprinted in Stocking, *The Shaping of American Anthropology*, 243–54.

—. "The Relations Between the Variability of Organisms and That of Their Constituent Elements." *Science* 15 (3 January 1902): 1–5.

—. "Relationships between North-West America and North-East Asia." In *The American Aborigines, Their Origin and Antiquity*, ed. Diamond Jenness, 357–70. Toronto: University of Toronto Press, 1933. Reprinted in Boas, *Race, Language and Culture*, 344–55.

—. Review of *Anthropologische Studien ueber die Ureinwohner Brasiliens* by Paul Ehrenreich. *Science* 6 (10 December 1897): 880–83. Reprinted in Boas, *Race, Language and Culture*, 149–54.

—. Review of *Die Welt in ihren Spiegelungen unter dem Wandel des Völkergedankens* by A. Bastian. *Science* 10 (9 December 1887): 284.

—. Review of *How to Study Geography* by Francis W. Parker. *Science* 12 (7 September 1888): 114–15.

—. Review of *Masks, Labrets and Certain Aboriginal Customs* by William Healey Dall. *Verhandlungen der Gesellschaft für Erdkunde zu Berlin* 13 (1886): 380–81.

—. Review of *The Philosophy of Kant* by John Watson. *Science* 12 (17 August 1888): 81.

—. Review of *The Races of Europe* by William Z. Ripley. *Science* 10 (1 September 1899): 292–96. Reprinted in Boas, *Race, Language and Culture*, 155–59.

—. Review of *The Teaching of Geography* by Archibald Geikie. *Science* 10 (16 September 1887): 139.

—. "Rudolf Virchow's Anthropological Work." *Science* 16 (19 September 1902): 441–45. Reprinted in Stocking, *The Shaping of American Anthropology*, 36–41.

—. "Some Principles of Museum Administration." *Science* 25 (14 June 1907): 921–33.

—. "Some Problems in North American Archaeology." *American Journal of Archaeology* 6 (1902): 1–6. Reprinted in Boas, *Race, Language and Culture*, 525–29.

—. "Some Recent Criticisms of Physical Anthropology." *American Anthropologist* 1 (1899): 98–106. Reprinted in Boas, *Race, Language and Culture*, 165–71.

—. "Some Traits of Primitive Culture." *Journal of American FolkLore* 17 (1904): 243–54.

—. "Statistical Study of Anthropometry." *American Physical Education Review* 4 (1902): 174–80. Reprinted in Boas, *Race, Language and Culture*, 131–37.

—. "The Study of Geography." *Science* 9 (11 February 1887): 137–41. Reprinted in Boas, *Race, Language, and Culture*, 639–47.

—. "Ueber die verschiedenen Formen des Unterschieds-schwellenwertes." *Archiv für die gesamte Physiologie des Menschen und der Thiere [Pflüger's Archiv]* 27 (1882): 214–22.

—. "Ueber die Wohnsitze der Neitchillik-Eskimos." *Zeitschrift der Gesellschaft für Erdkunde zu Berlin* 18 (1883): 222–33.

—. "Über eine neue Form des Gesetzes der Unterschiedsschwelle." *Archiv für die gesamte Physiologie des Menschen und der Thiere [Pflüger's Archiv]* 26 (1881): 493–500.

—. "Unter dem Polarkreise." *New-Yorker Staats-Zeitung*, 1 February 1885.

—. "The Use of Masks and Head-Ornaments on the North-West Coast of America." *Internationales Archiv für Ethnographie* 3 (1890): 7–15.

—. "W J McGee." The McGee Memorial Meeting of the Washington Academy of Sciences Held at the Carnegie Institute, December 5, 1913. Baltimore: William and Wilkins, 1916.

—. "Zur Ethnologie von Britisch-Columbien." *Verhandlungen der Gesellschaft für Erdkunde zu Berlin* 22 (1895): 265–70.

337

Boas, Franz, and Livingston Farrand. "Physical Characteristics of the Tribes of British Columbia." *The North-Western Tribes of Canada, Twelfth and Final Report of the Committee, British Association for the Advancement of Science* (1898): 628–44.

Bogoras, Waldemar. "The Folklore of Northeastern Asia, as Compared with That of Northwestern America." *American Anthropologist* 4 (1902): 577–683.

Boxberger, Daniel L., and Herbert C. Taylor, Jr. "Charles Cultee and the Father of American Anthropology." *The Sou'wester* 21 (Spring 1986): 3–7.

Brilling, B. "Die Vorfahren des Professors Franz Boas." *Mitteilungen des Mindener Geschichts- und Museumvereins* 38 (1966).

Brinton, Daniel G. "The Aims of Anthropology." *Science* 2 (30 August 1895): 241–52.

Browman, David. L., and Douglas R. Givens. "Stratigraphic Excavation: The First 'New Archaeology.'" *American Anthropologist* 98 (1996): 80–95.

Buettner-Janusch, John. "Boas and Mason: Particularism versus Generalization." *American Anthropologist* 59 (1957): 318–24.

Bunzl, Matti. "Franz Boas and the Humboldtian Tradition: From *Volksgeist* and *Nationalcharakter* to an Anthropological Concept of Culture." In *History of Anthropology*. Vol. 8: *Volksgeist as Method and Ethic: Essays on Boasian Ethnography and the German Anthropological Tradition,* ed. George W. Stocking, Jr., 17–78. Madison: University of Wisconsin Press, 1996.

Campbell, Peter. " 'Not as a White Man, Not as a Sojourner': James A. Teit and the Fight for Native Rights in British Columbia, 1884–1922." *Left History* 2 (1994): 37–57.

Cannizzo, Jeanne. "George Hunt and the Invention of Kwakiutl Culture." *Canadian Review of Sociology and Anthropology* 20 (1983): 44–58.

Carlson, Roy L. "Cultural Antecedents." In *Handbook of North American Indians.* Vol. 7: *Northwest Coast,* ed. Wayne Suttles, 60–69. Washington, D.C.: Smithsonian Institution, 1990.

—. "History of Research in Archaeology." In *Handbook of North American Indians.* Vol. 7: *Northwest Coast,* ed. Wayne Suttles, 107–15. Washington, D.C.: Smithsonian Institution, 1990.

Carneiro, Robert L. "Classical Evolution." In *Main Currents in Cultural Anthropology,* ed. Raoul Naroll and Frada Naroll, 57–121. Englewood Cliffs, NJ: Prentice-Hall, 1973.

Chowning, Ann. "Raven Myths in Northwestern North America and Northeastern Asia." *Arctic Anthropology* 1 (1962): 1–5.

Clifford, James. "On Ethnographic Authority." In *The Predicament of Culture: Twentieth-Century Ethnography, Literature, and Art,* 21–54. Cambridge: Harvard University Press, 1988.

Cole, Douglas. "Franz Boas: Ein Wissenschaftler und Patriot zwischen zwei Ländern." In *Franz Boas, 1858–1942, Ein amerikanischer Anthropologie aus Minden,* ed. Volker Rodekamp, 9–23. Bielefeld: Verlag für Regionalgeschichte, 1994.

—. "Franz Boas and the Bella Coola in Berlin." *Northwest Anthropological Research Notes* 16 (1982): 115–24.

—. "Kindheit und Jugend von Franz Boas: Minden in der zweiten Hälfte des 19. Jahrhunderts." *Mitteilungen des Mindener Geschichtsvereins* 60 (1988): 111–34.

—. "The Origins of Canadian Anthropology, 1850–1910." *Journal of Canadian Studies* 8 (1973): 33–45.

—. " 'The Value of a Person Lies in His *Herzensbildung*': Franz Boas' Baffin Island Letter-

Diary, 1883–1884." In *History of Anthropology.* Vol. 1: *Observers Observed: Essays on Ethnographic Fieldwork,* ed. George W. Stocking, Jr., 13–52. Madison: University of Wisconsin Press, 1983.

Cole, Douglas, and Ludger Müller-Wille. "Franz Boas' Expedition to Baffin Island, 1883–1884." *Inuit Studies/Études Inuit* 8, no. 1 (1984): 37–63.

Collingwood, R. G. "The Philosophy of History." 1930. In *Essays in the Philosophy of History,* ed. William Debbins, 121–39. Austin: University of Texas Press, 1965.

Darnell, Regna. "The Professionalization of American Anthropology: A Case Study in the Sociology of Knowledge." *Social Science Information* 10 (1971): 83–103.

Dexter, Ralph W. "Putnam's Problems Popularizing Anthropology." *American Scientist* 54 (1966): 315–32.

—. "The Role of F. W. Putnam in Developing Anthropology at the American Museum of Natural History." *Curator* 19 (1976): 303–10.

Dodge, Raymond. "Benno Erdmann." *American Journal of Psychology* 33 (1922): 155–56.

Dorsey, George. "The Anthropological Exhibits at the American Museum of Natural History." *Science* 25 (12 April 1907): 584–89.

Drucker, Phillip. "Sources of Northwest Coast Culture." In *New Interpretations of Aboriginal American Culture History,* ed. Betty J. Meggers, 59–81. Washington, D.C.: Anthropological Society of Washington, 1955.

Elton, Charles. "Epidemics among Sledge Dogs in the Canadian Arctic and Their Relation to Disease in the Arctic Fox." *Canadian Journal of Research* 5 (1931): 673–92.

Erdmann, Benno. "Gliederung der Wissenschaften." Vierteljahresschrift für wissenschaftliche Philosophie 2 (1878): 72–105.

Fagin, Nancy L. "Closed Collections and Open Appeals: The Two Anthropology Exhibits at the Chicago World's Columbian Exposition of 1893." *Curator* 27 (1984): 249–64.

Freed, Stanley A., and Ruth S. Freed. "Clark Wissler and the Development of Anthropology in the United States." *American Anthropologist* 85 (1983): 800–825.

Freed, Stanley A., Ruth S. Freed, and Laila Williamson. American Museum's Jesup North Pacific Expedition." In *Crossroads of Continents: Cultures of Siberia and Alaska,* ed. William W. Fitzhugh and Aron Crowell, 97–103. Washington, D.C.: Smithsonian Institution, 1988.

—. Capitalist Philanthropy and Russian Revolutionaries: The Jesup North Pacific Expedition (1897–1902)." *American Anthropologist* 90 (1988): 7–24.

Glick, Leonard B. "Types Distinct from Our Own: Franz Boas on Jewish Identity and Assimilation." *American Anthropologist* 84 (1982): 545–65.

Gruber, Jacob W. "Ethnographic Salvage and the Shaping of American Anthropology." *American Anthropologist* 72 (1970): 1289–99.

—. "Horatio Hale and the Development of American Anthropology." *Proceedings of the American Philosophical Society* 111 (1967): 5–37.

Haberland, Wolfgang. "Nine Bella Coolas in Germany." In *Indians and Europe: An Interdisciplinary Collection of Essays,* ed. Christian F. Feest, 337–74. Aachen: Rader-Verlag, 1987.

Hale, Horatio. "On Some Doubtful or Intermediate Articulations: An Experiment in Phonetics." *Journal of the Anthropological Institute of Great Britain and Ireland.* London (1885) 14: 233–43.

Hermann, Conrad. "Die Geographie und die teliologische Weltansicht." *Das Ausland* 16 (1879): 300.

Herzig, Arno. "Das Sozialprofil der jüdischen Bürger von Minden im Übergang vom 18.– zum 19. Jahrhundert." *Mitteilungen des Mindener Geschichtsvereins* 50 (1978): 45–70.

Hinsley, Curtis M., Jr., and Bill Holm. "A Cannibal in the National Museum: The Early Career of Franz Boas in America." *American Anthropologist* 78 (1976): 306–16.

Howells, W. W. "Boas as Statistician." In *The Anthropology of Franz Boas: Essays on the Centennial of His Birth,* ed. Walter Goldschmidt, 112–16. AAA Memoir 89. San Francisco: Howard Chandler, 1959.

Hrdlička, Aleš. "Contribution to the Anthropology of Cumberland and Smith Sound Eskimo." *Anthropological Papers of the American Museum of Natural History* 5 (1910): 177–280.

——. "An Eskimo Brain." *American Anthropologist* 3 (1901): 454–500.

Iggers, Georg G. "Historicism." In *Dictionary of the History of Ideas,* vol. 2, ed. Philip P. Wiener, 457–64. New York: Charles Scribner's Sons, 1973.

Jacknis, Ira. "The Ethnographic Object and the Object of Ethnology in the Early Career of Franz Boas." In *History of Anthropology. Vol. 8: Volksgeist as Method and Ethic: Essays on Boasian Ethnography and the German Anthropological Tradition,* ed. George W. Stocking, Jr., 185–214. Madison: University of Wisconsin Press, 1996.

——. "Franz Boas and Exhibits: On the Limitations of the Museum Method of Anthropology." In *History of Anthropology. Vol. 3: Objects and Others: Essays on Museums and Material Culture,* ed. George W. Stocking, Jr., 75–111. Madison: University of Wisconsin Press, 1985.

——. "Franz Boas and Photography." *Studies in Visual Communications* 10 (1984): 2–60.

——. "George Hunt, Collector of Indian Specimens." *In Chiefly Feasts: The Enduring Kwakiutl Potlatch,* ed. Aldona Jonaitis, 177–224. Seattle: University of Washington Press, 1991.

——. "Northwest Coast Indian Culture and the World's Columbian Exhibition." In *The Spanish Borderlands in Pan-American Perspective,* ed. David Hurst Thomas, 91–118. Washington, D.C.: Smithsonian Institution Press, 1991.

Jacobs, Wilbur R. "Francis Parkman's Oration 'Romance in America.' " In *Intellectual History in America. Vol. 2: Contemporary Essays on Puritanism, the Enlightenment, and Romanticism,* ed. Cushing Strout, 152–59. New York: Harper and Row, 1968.

Jantz, Richard L., D. R. Hunt, A. B. Falsetti, and P. J. Key. "Variation among North Amerindians: Analysis of Boas's Anthropometric Data." *Human Biology* 64 (1992): 435–61.

Jochelson, Waldemar. "Über asiatische und amerikanische Elemente in den Mythen der Koriaken." *Bericht des XIV Internationalen Amerikanisten Kongrësses, Stuttgart, 1904,* 119–27. Stuttgart, 1905.

Jochelson-Brodsky, Dina. "Zur Topographie des weiblichen Körpers nordostsibirischer Völker." *Archeologische Anthropologie* 6 (1906): 1–58.

Kampmann, Wanda. "Adolf Stoecker und die Berliner Bewegung." *Geschichte in Wissenschaft und Unterricht* 13 (1962): 558–79.

Kennedy, Dorothy I. D., and Randall T. Bouchard. "Bella Coola." In *Handbook of North American Indians. Vol. 7: Northwest Coast,* ed. Wayne Suttles, 323–39. Washington, D.C.: Smithsonian Institution, 1990.

Kroeber, A. L. "Animal Tales of the Eskimo." *Journal of American Folk-Lore* 12 (1899): 17–23.

—. Eskimo of Smith Sound." *Bulletin of the American Museum of Natural History* 12 (1899): 265–327.

—. "Frederic Ward Putnam." *American Anthropologist* 17 (1915): 712–18.

—. "The Place of Boas in Anthropology." *American Anthropologist* 58 (1956): 151–59.

—. "Tales of the Smith Sound Eskimo." *Journal of American Folk-Lore* 12 (1899): 166–82.

Laufer, Berthold. "Prefatory." In *Boas Anniversary Volume: Anthropological Papers Written in Honor of Franz Boas Presented to Him on the Twenty-fifth Anniversary of His Doctorate,* vii–xiv. New York: G. E. Stechert, 1906.

Lee, Dwight E., and Robert N. Beck. "The Meaning of 'Historicism.'" *American Historical Review* 59 (1954): 568–77.

Lesser, Alexander. "Franz Boas." In *Totems and Teachers: Perspectives on the History of Anthropology,* ed. Sydel Silverman, 1–31. New York: Columbia University Press, 1981.

Liss, Julia. "German Culture and German Science in the Bildung of Franz Boas." In *History of Anthropology.* Vol. 8: *Volksgeist as Method and Ethic: Essays on Boasian Ethnography and the German Anthropological Tradition,* ed. George W. Stocking, Jr., 155–84. Madison: University of Wisconsin Press, 1996.

—. "Patterns of Strangeness: Franz Boas, Modernism, and the Origins of Anthropology." In *Prehistories of the Future: The Primitivist Project and the Culture of Modernism,* ed. Elazar Barkan and Ronald Bush, 114–30. Stanford: Stanford University Press, 1995.

Lowie, Robert H. "Franz Boas, 1858–1942." *National Academy of Sciences, Biographical Memoirs* 24, no. 9 (1947): 303–20. Reprinted in *Lowie's Selected Papers in Anthropology,* ed. Cora du Bois, 425–40. Berkeley: University of California Press, 1960.

—. "Reminiscences of Anthropological Currents in America Half a Century Ago." *American Anthropologist* 58 (1956): 995–1016.

Mackert, Michael. "The Roots of Franz Boas' View of Linguistic Categories as a Window to the Human Mind." *Historiographia Linguistica* 20 (1993): 331–51.

Mayr, Richard. "Die Stellung der Erdkunde im Kreise der Wissenschaften und der Schuldisciplinen." *Zeitschrift für Schulgeographie* 1 (1880).

McGee, W J. "The American Anthropological Association." *American Anthropologist* n.s. 5 (1903): 178–92.

Meltzer, David J. "The Antiquity of Man and the Development of American Archaeology." In *Advances in Archaeological Method and Theory,* vol. 6, ed. Michael B. Schiffer, 1–51. San Francisco: Academic Press, 1983.

Müller, Friedrich. "Die linguistiche Ethnographie im Verhältniss zur Anthropologie." *Geographisches Jahrbuch* 3 (1870): 310–18.

Murdock, George Peter. "Clark Wissler, 1870–1947." *American Anthropologist* 50 (1948): 292–304.

Neatby, Leslie H. "Editor's Introduction." In Bernhard Hantzsch, *My Life Among the Eskimos: Baffinland Journeys in the Years 1909 to 1911.* Mawdsley Memoir 3, xii–xx. Saskatoon: University of Saskatchewan, 1977.

Nordsiek, Marianne. "Siegmund Imanuel (1790–1847) und die Reorganisation des Mindener Gymnasiums." *In Land und Leuten Dienen: Ein Lesebuch zur Geschichte der Schule in Minden,* ed. Friedhelm Sundergeld, 103–21. Minden: J. C. C. Bruns, 1980.

Oakes, Guy. "Introduction: Rickert's Theory of Historical Knowledge." In Heinrich Rickert, *The Limits of Concept Formation in Natural Science,* trans. and intro. Guy Oakes, vii–xxx. Cambridge: Cambridge University Press, 1986.

Oestreich, Karl. "Theobald Fischer: Eine Wurdigung seines als Forscher und Lehrer." *Geographische Zeitschrift* 18 (1912): 241–54.

Ousley, Stephen D. "Relationships between Eskimos, Amerindians, and Aleuts: Old Data, New Perspectives." *Human Biology* 67 (1995): 427–58.

Partsch, J. "Heinrich Kiepert: Ein Bild seines Lebens und seiner Arbeit." *Geographische Zeitschrift* 17 (1901): 82–93.

Putnam, Frederic Ward. "Synopsis of Peabody and American Museum of Natural History Anthropology Departments." *Proceedings of the XIII International Congress of Americanists, New York, 1902,* xxxix–xliv. New York, 1905.

Ray, Verne F. "Lower Chinook Ethnographic Notes." *University of Washington Publications in Anthropology* 7 (1938): 29–165.

——. Review of *Franz Boas: The Science of Man in the Making* by Melville J. Herskovits. *American Anthropologist* 57 (1955): 138–41.

Ringer, Fritz K. "Higher Education in Germany in the Nineteenth Century." *Journal of Contemporary History* 2 (1967): 123–38.

Rohner, Ronald P. "Franz Boas: Ethnographer on the Northwest Coast." In *Pioneers of American Anthropology: The Uses of Biography,* ed. June Helm, 149–212. Seattle: University of Washington Press, 1966.

Rohner, Ronald P., and Evelyn C. Rohner. "Franz Boas and the Development of North American Ethnology and Ethnography." In *The Ethnography of Franz Boas,* ed. Ronald P. Rohner and trans. Hedy Parker, xiii–xxx. Chicago: University of Chicago Press, 1969.

Schrönbeck, Charlotte. "Physik und Astronomie." In *Geschichte der Christian-Albrechts-Universität Kiel, 1665–1965,* vol. 6, *Geschichte der Mathematik, der Naturwissenschaften und der Landenschaftwissenschaft,* ed. Karl Jordan, 59–93. Neumünster: Karl Wachholtz, 1968.

Shternberg, Leo. "Bemerkungen über Beziehungen zwischen der Morphologie der gil-jakischen und amerikanischen Sprachen." *Bericht des XIV Internationalen Amerikanisten Kongrësses, Stuttgart, 1904,* 137–40. Stuttgart, 1905.

Smith, Marian. "Boas' 'Natural History' Approach to Field Method." In *The Anthropology of Franz Boas: Essays on the Centennial of His Birth,* ed. Walter Goldschmidt, 46–60. AAA Memoir 89. San Francisco: Howard Chandler, 1959.

Spier, Leslie. "Franz Boas and Some of His Views." *Acta Americana* 1 (1943): 108–27.

Stocking, George W., Jr. "Anthropology as *Kulturkampf:* Science and Politics in the Career of Franz Boas." In *The Ethnographer's Magic and Other Essays in the History of Anthropology,* 92–113. Madison: University of Wisconsin Press, 1992.

——. "The Basic Assumptions of Boasian Anthropology." In Stocking, *The Shaping of American Anthropology,* 1–20.

——. "Clark Wissler." *Dictionary of American Biography,* Supplement 4, 906–09. New York: Scribner's Sons, 1974.

——. "The Critique of Racial Formalism." In *Race, Culture, and Evolution: Essays in the History of Anthropology,* 161–94. New York: Free Press, 1968; reprint, Chicago: University of Chicago Press, 1982.

——. "Dogmatism, Pragmatism, Essentialism, Relativism: The Boas/Mason Debate Revisited." *History of Anthropology Newsletter* 21, no. 1 (1994): 3–12.

——. "Franz Boas and the Culture Concept in Historical Perspective." In *Race, Culture, and Evolution: Essays in the History of Anthropology,* 195–233.

—. "Franz Boas and the Founding of the American Anthropological Association," *American Anthropologist* 62 (1960): 1–17.

—. "From Physics to Ethnology." In *Race, Culture, and Evolution: Essays in the History of Anthropology,* 133–60.

—, "Racial Capacity and Cultural Determinism." In Stocking, *The Shaping of American Anthropology,* 219–21.

—. "The Scientific Reaction Against Cultural Anthropology, 1917–1920." In *Race, Culture, and Evolution: Essays in the History of Anthropology,* 270–307.

Stumpf, Karl. "Gedächtnisrede: Benno Erdmann." *Sitzungsberichte der Preussischen Akademie der Wissenschaften* 33 (1921): 497–508.

Suttles, Wayne. "Streams of Property, Armor of Wealth: The Traditional Kwakiutl Potlatch." In *Chiefly Feasts: The Enduring Kwakiutl Potlatch,* ed. Aldona Jonaitis, 71–133. Seattle: University of Washington Press, 1991.

Swanton, John R. "William Henry Holmes, 1846–1933." *National Academy of Sciences, Biographical Memoirs* 17 (1937): 223–37.

Szathmary, Emöke J. E. "Human Biology of the Arctic." In *Handbook of the American Indians.* Vol. 5: *Arctic,* ed. David Damas, 64–71. Washington, D.C.: Smithsonian Institution, 1984.

Tanner, J. M. "Boas' Contributions to Knowledge of Human Growth and Form." In *The Anthropology of Franz Boas: Essays on the Centennial of His Birth,* ed. Walter Goldschmidt, 76–111. AAA Memoir 89. San Francisco: Howard Chandler, 1959.

Thalbitzer, William. "Eskimo." In *Handbook of American Indian Languages,* Vol. 1, ed. Franz Boas, 967–1069. Bureau of American Ethnology, Bulletin 40. Washington, D.C.: Government Printing Office, 1911.

Thoresen, Timothy H. H. "Paying the Piper and Calling the Tune: The Beginnings of Academic Anthropology in California." *Journal of the History of the Behavioral Sciences* 11 (1975): 257–75.

Topinard, Paul. Review of The Indians of British Columbia by Franz Boas. *L'Anthropologie* 6 (1895): 711–14.

Tozzer, Alfred M. "The Putnam Anniversary." *American Anthropologist* 11 (1909): 285–88.

Wagner, Hans. "Benno Erdmann, 1851–1921." In *Bonner Gelehrte: 150 Jahre Rheinische Friedrich-Wilhelms-Universität zu Bonn, 1818–1968, Philosopie und Altertumswissenschaften.* Bonn: H. Bouvier & L. RÖhrscheid, 1968.

Wagner, Hermann. "Bericht über die Entwicklung der Methodik der Erdkunde." *Geographisches Jahrbuch* 8 (1880): 523–653.

—. "Der gegenwärtige Standpunkt der Methodik der Erdkunde." *Geographisches Jahrbuch* 7 (1878): 550–636.

—. "Theobald Fisher." *Petermanns Mitteilungen* 56, no. 2 (1910): 188–89.

Wax, Murray. "The Limitations of Boas' Anthropology." *American Anthropologist* 58 (1956): 63–74.

Wells, Rulon. "Phonemics in the Nineteenth Century, 1876–1900." In *Studies in the History of Linguistics: Traditions and Paradigms,* ed. Dell Hymes, 434–53. Bloomington: Indiana University Press, 1974.

Wickwire, Wendy. "Women in Ethnography: The Research of James A. Teit." *Ethnohistory* 40 (1993): 539–62.

Wiltse, Sara E. "Psychological Literature: II: Experimental." *American Journal of Psychology* I (1888): 702–5.

Windelband, Wilhelm. "Kritische oder genetische Methode?" (1883). In *Präluden: Ausätze und Reden zur Philosophie und ihrer Geschichte,* vol. 2, 99–135. Tübingen: J. C. B. Mohr, 1924.

—. "History and Natural Science" (1894). Ed. and trans. Guy Oakes. *History and Theory* 19 (1980): 165–85.

Woodbury, Anthony C. "Eskimo and Aleut Languages." In *Handbook of the American Indians.* Vol. 5: *Arctic,* ed. David Damas, 49–63. Washington, D.C.: Smithsonian Institution, 1984.

Xie, Yu. "Franz Boas and Statistics." *Annals of Scholarship* 5 (1988): 269–96.

BOOKS AND MONOGRAPHS

Ackerknecht, Erwin H. *Rudolf Virchow: Doctor, Statesman, Anthropologist.* Madison: University of Wisconsin Press, 1953.

American Museum of Natural History. *Annual Report of the President . . .for the Year 1896.* New York, 1897.

Bering, Dietz. *The Stigma of Names: Antisemitism in German Daily Life, 1812–1933.* Trans. Neville Plaice. Ann Arbor: University of Michigan Press, 1992.

Birmingham, Stephen. *"Our Crowd": The Great Jewish Families of New York.* New York: Harper and Row, 1967.

Boas, Franz. *Baffin-Land: Geographische Ergebnisse einer in den Jahren 1883 und 1884 ausgeführten Forschungsreise.* Ergänzungsheft No. 80 zu *Petermanns Mitteilungen.* Gotha: Justus Perthes, 1885.

—. *Chinook Texts.* Bureau of Ethnology Bulletin 20. Washington, D.C.: Government Printing Office, 1894.

—. *The Eskimo of Baffin Land and Hudson Bay.* 2 vols. *Bulletin of the American Museum of Natural History* 15. New York: American Museum of Natural History, 1901 and 1907.

—. *Indianische Sagen von der Nord-pacifischen Küste Amerikas.* Sonder-abdruck aus den Verhandlungen der Berliner Gesellschaft für Anthropologie, Ethnologie und Urgeschichte, 1891 bis 1895. Berlin: A. Asher and Co., 1895.

—. *The Kwakiutl of Vancouver Island.* Publications of the Jesup North Pacific Expedition 5, no. 2. New York, 1909.

—. *The Mind of Primitive Man.* New York: Macmillan, 1911.

—. *The Mythology of the Bella Coola Indians.* Publications of the Jesup North Pacific Expedition 1, no. 2. New York, 1898.

—. *Primitive Art.* Oslo: H. Aschehoug and Co., 1927; reprint, New York: Dover, 1955.

—. *Race, Language and Culture.* New York: Macmillan, 1940; reprint, New York: Free Press, 1966.

—. *The Religion of the Kwakiutl Indians,* pt. 1. Columbia University Contributions to Anthropology 10. New York: Columbia University Press, 1930.

—. *The Social Organization and Secret Societies of the Kwakiutl Indians.* Report of the United States National Museum for 1895, 311–738. Washington, D.C.: Government Printing Office, 1897.

Bogoras, Walderman. *The Chukchee.* Publications of the Jesup North Pacific Expedition 7. New York, 1904.

Bowler, Peter J. *The Eclipse of Darwinism: Anti-Darwinian Evolutionary Theories in the*

Decade around 1900. Baltimore: Johns Hopkins University Press, 1983.

Brinton, Daniel G. *The Myths of the New World*. 1876. 3d ed., rev., 1896. Reprint, New York: Haskell House, 1968.

—. *Religions of Primitive Peoples*. London: G. P. Putnam's Sons, 1897; reprint, Greenwood: Negro Universities Press, 1969.

Cole, Douglas. *Captured Heritage: The Scramble for Northwest Coast Artifacts*. 1985. Reprint, Norman: University of Oklahoma Press; Vancouver: University of British Columbia Press, 1996.

Cole, Douglas, and Ira Chaikin. *An Iron Hand Upon the People: The Law Against the Potlatch on the Northwest Coast*. Vancouver, B.C.: Douglas and McIntyre; Seattle: University of Washington Press, 1990.

Cravens, Hamilton. *The Triumph of Evolution: American Society and the Heredity-Environment Controversy, 1900–1941*. Philadelphia: University of Pennsylvania Press, 1978.

Darrah, William Culp. *Powell of the Colorado*. Princeton: Princeton University Press, 1951.

Degler, Carl N. In *Search of Human Nature: The Decline and Revival of Darwinism in American Social Thought*. New York: Oxford University Press, 1991.

Dilthey, Wilhelm. *Introduction to the Human Sciences: An Attempt to Lay a Foundation for the Study of Society and History*. 1883. Reprint, trans. and intro. Raymon J. Betanzos, Detroit: Wayne State University Press, 1988.

D'Souza, Dinesh. *The End of Racism: Principles for a Multiracial Society*. New York: Free Press, 1995.

Emmons, George Thornton. *The Tlingit Indians*. Ed. with additions Frederica de Laguna. Seattle: University of Washington Press, 1991.

Ermarth, Michael. *Wilhelm Dilthey: The Critique of Historical Reason*. Chicago: University of Chicago Press, 1978.

Evans, Richard J. *Death in Hamburg: Society and Politics in the Cholera Years, 1830–1910*. Oxford: Clarendon Press, 1987.

Farrand, Livingston. *Traditions of the Chilcotin Indians*. Publications of the Jesup North Pacific Expedition 2, no. 1. New York, 1900.

Farrand, Livingston, assisted by W. S. Kahnweiler. *Traditions of the Quinault Indians*. Publications of the Jesup North Pacific Expedition 2, no. 3. New York, 1902.

Fick, R., ed. *Auf Deutschlands hohen Schulen*. Berlin and Leipzig: Verlag Hans Ludwig Thils, 1900.

Fiedermutz-Laun, Annemarie. *Der kulturhistorische Gedanke bei Adolf Bastian*. Wiesbaden: Franz Sterner Verlag, 1970.

Fitzhugh, William W., and Aron Crowell, eds. *Crossroads of Continents: Cultures of Siberia and Alaska*. Washington, D.C.: Smithsonian Institution, 1988.

Fladmark, Knut R. *British Columbia Prehistory*. Ottawa: National Museum of Man, 1986.

Frank, Walter. *Hofprediger Adolf Stoecker und die christlichsoziale Bewegung*. Berlin: Reimar Hobbing, 1928.

Freeman, Derek. *Margaret Mead and Samoa: The Making and Unmaking of an Anthropological Myth*. Cambridge: Harvard University Press, 1983.

Frevert, Ute. *Ehrenmänner: Das Duell in der bürgerlichen Gesellschaft*. München: C. H. Beck, 1993.

Gerland, Georg. *Beiträge zur Geophysik: Abhandlungen aus dem geographischen Seminar der Universität Strassburg*, vol. 1. 1887.

Goldschmidt, Walter, ed. *The Anthropology of Franz Boas: Essays on the Centennial of His Birth.* AAA Memoir 89. San Francisco: Howard Chandler, 1959.

Guide to Microfilm Collection of the Professional Papers of Franz Boas. 2 vols. Wilmington, Del.: Scholarly Resources with the American Philosophical Society, 1972.

Halbe, Max. *Scholle und Schicksal: Geschichte meines Lebens.* München: Verlag Knorr & Hirth, 1933.

Hall, G. Stanley. *Life and Confessions of a Psychologist.* New York: D. Appleton and Co., 1923.

Harper, Kenn. *Give Me My Father's Body: The Life of Minik, the New York Eskimo.* Frobisher Bay, NWT, and Newmarket: Blacklead Books, 1986.

Harris, Marvin. *The Rise of Anthropological Theory: A History of Theories of Culture.* New York: Thomas Cromwell Co., 1968.

Herskovits, Melville J. *Franz Boas: The Science of Man in the Making.* New York: Charles Scribner's Sons, 1953.

Hertz, Johanna. *Heinrich Hertz: Memoirs, Letters, Diaries.* Trans. Lisa Brinner, Mathilde Hertz, and Charles Susskind. 2d ed. San Francisco: San Francisco Press, 1977.

Herzig, Arno. *Abraham Jacobi: Die Entwicklung zum sozialistischen und revolutionären Demokraten: Briefe, Dokumente, Presseartikel (1848–1953).* Minden: Mindener Geschichtsverein, 1980.

—. *"In unsern Herzen glüht der Freiheit Schein": Die Entstehungsphase der bürgerlichen und sozialen Demokratie in Minden (1848–1878).* Minden: Mindener Geschichtsverein, 1981.

Hinsley, Curtis M., Jr. *Savages and Scientists: The Smithsonian Institution and the Development of American Anthropology, 1846–1910.* Washington, D.C.: Smithsonian Institution Press, 1981.

Hodges, Herbert A. *The Philosophy of Wilhelm Dilthey.* London: Routledge and Kegan Paul, 1952.

Hofstadter, Richard. *The Age of Reform: From Bryan to F.D.R.* New York: Knopf, 1955.

Hundt, Martin. *Louis Kugelmann: Eine Biographie des Arztes und Freundes von Karl Marx und Friedrich Engels.* Berlin: Dietz Verlag, 1974.

Hyatt, Marshall. *Franz Boas, Social Activist: The Dynamics of Ethnicity.* New York: Greenwood Press, 1990.

Iggers, Georg G. *The German Conception of History: The National Tradition of Historical Thought from Herder to the Present.* Middleton, Conn.: Wesleyan University Press, 1968.

Jantz, Richard L., ed. *Population Biology of Late Nineteenth-Century Native North Americans and Siberians: Analyses of Boas's Data.* Special issue of *Human Biology* 67 (1995).

Jarausch, Konrad H. *Students, Society, and Politics in Imperial Germany: The Rise of Academic Illiberalism.* Princeton: Princeton University Press, 1982.

Jochelson, Waldemar. *The Koryak.* Publications of the Jesup North Pacific Expedition 6. New York, 1905–08.

Johnson, Rossiter, ed. *A History of the World's Columbian Exposition.* 4 vols. New York: Appleton, 1897.

Jonaitis, Aldona. *From the Land of the Totem Poles: The Northwest Coast Indian Art Collection at the American Museum of Natural History.* Seattle: University of Washington Press; Vancouver, B.C.: Douglas and McIntyre, 1988.

Jungnickel, Christa, and Russell McCormmach. *Intellectual Mastery of Nature: Theoretical Physics from Ohm to Einstein.* Vol. 2: *The Now Mighty Theoretical Physics, 1870–1925.* Chicago: University of Chicago Press, 1986.

Kampe, Norbert. *Studenten und "Judenfrage" im Deutschen Kaiserreich: Die Entstehung einer akademischen Trägerschicht des Antisemitism.* Göttingen: Vanderhoeck & Ruprecht, 1988.

Koelsch, William A. *Clark University, 1887–1987: A Narrative History.* Worcester, Mass.: Clark University Press, 1987.

Koepping, Klaus-Peter. *Adolf Bastian and the Psychic Unity of Mankind: The Foundations of Anthropology in Nineteenth Century Germany.* St. Lucia: University of Queensland Press, 1983.

Köhnke, Klaus Christian. *The Rise of Neo-Kantianism: German Academic Philosophy between Idealism and Positivism.* Trans. R. J. Hollingdale. Cambridge: Cambridge University Press, 1991.

Kroeber, A. L., and Clyde Kluckhohn. *Culture: A Critical Review of Concepts and Definitions.* New York: Vintage Books, 1952.

Kuper, Adam. *The Invention of Primitive Society: Transformations of an Illusion.* New York: Routledge, 1988.

Ladenberg, Albert. *Lebens-Erinnerungen.* Breslau: Trewendt & Garnier, 1912.

Laufer, Berthold, ed. *Boas Anniversary Volume: Anthropological Papers Written in Honor of Franz Boas Presented to Him on the Twenty-fifth Anniversary of His Doctorate.* New York: G. E. Stechert, 1906.

Lenz, Max. *Geschichte der Königlichen Friedrich-Wilhelms Universität zu Berlin.* Vol. 2. Halle: Waisenhauses, 1918.

Leopold, Joan. *Culture in Comparative and Evolutionary Perspective: E. B. Tylor and the Making of Primitive Culture.* Berlin: Dieter Reimer, 1980.

Lowie, Robert H. *The History of Ethnological Theory.* New York: Holt, Rinehart and Winston, 1937.

Manning, Thomas G. *Government in Science: The U.S. Geological Survey, 1867–1894.* Lexington: University of Kentucky Press, 1967.

Mark, Joan. *Four Anthropologists: An American Science in Its Early Years.* New York: Science History Publications, 1980.

Massing, Paul W. *Rehearsal for Destruction: A Study of Political Anti-Semitism in Imperial Germany.* New York: Howard Fertig, 1967.

Maud, Ralph. *A Guide to B.C. Indian Myth and Legend.* Vancouver, B.C.: Talonbooks, 1982.

McAleer, Kevin. *Dueling: The Cult of Honor in Fin-de-Siècle Germany.* Princeton: Princeton University Press, 1994.

McCormmach, Russell. *Night Thoughts of a Classical Physicist.* Cambridge: Harvard University Press, 1982.

McIlwraith, Thomas F. *The Bella Coola Indians.* 2 vols. Toronto: University of Toronto Press, 1948.

Meinecke, Friedrich. *Erlebtes, 1862–1901.* Leipzig: Koehler & Amelang, 1941.

Mosse, George L. *German Jews Beyond Judaism.* Bloomington: Indiana University Press, 1985.

Nadel, Stanley. *Little Germany: Ethnicity, Religion, and Class in New York City, 1845–80.* Urbana: University of Illinois Press, 1990.

Nordsiek, Hans. *Juden in Minden: Dokumente und Bilder jüdischen Lebens vom Mittelalter bis zum 20. Jahrhundert.* Minden: Kommunalarchiv Minden, 1988.

Oetteking, Bruno. *Craniology of the North Pacific Coast.* New York: G. E. Stechert, 1930.

Oppenheim, Otto. *Die Burschenschaft Alemannia zu Bonn und ihre Vorläufer.* Bonn, 1925.

Paulsen, Friedrich. *Aus meinem Leben: Jugenderinnerungen.* Jena: Eugen Diederich, 1910.

Plewe, Ernst. *Untersuchung über den Begriff der "vergleichenden" Erdkunde und seine Anwendung in der neueren Geographie.* Ergänzungsheft 4. Zeitschrift der Gesellschaft für Erdkunde zu Berlin, 1932.

Pulzer, Peter. *Jews and the German State: The Political History of a Minority, 1848–1933.* Oxford: Blackwell, 1992.

Reinharz, Jehuda. *Fatherland or Promised Land: The Dilemma of the German Jew, 1893–1914.* Ann Arbor: University of Michigan Press, 1975.

Rickert, Heinrich. *The Limits of Concept Formation in Natural Science.* Trans. and intro. Guy Oakes. Cambridge: Cambridge University Press, 1986.

Rickman, Hans Peter. *Dilthey Today: A Critical Appraisal of the Contemporary Relevance of His Work.* New York: Greenwood Press, 1988.

Rohner, Ronald P., ed. *The Ethnography of Franz Boas.* Trans. Hedy Parker. Chicago: University of Chicago Press, 1969.

Ross, Dorothy. *G. Stanley Hall: The Psychologist as Prophet.* Chicago: University of Chicago Press, 1972.

Rydell, Robert W. *All the World's a Fair: Visions of Empire at American International Expositions, 1876–1916.* Chicago: University of Chicago Press, 1984.

Schnädelbach, Herbert. *Philosophy in Germany, 1831–1933.* Trans. Eric Matthews. Cambridge: Cambridge University Press, 1984.

Schräder, Otto. *Prehistoric Antiquities of the Aryan Peoples.* 1883. Trans. Frank Bron. London: Charles Griffin, 1890.

Schroeder, Wilhelm. *Chronik der Stadt Minden.* Minden: P. Leonardy, 1883.

Schorsch, Ismar. *Jewish Reactions to German Anti-Semitism, 1870–1914.* New York: Columbia University Press, 1972.

Seelig, Geert. *Eine deutsche Jugend: Erinnerungen an Kiel und an den Schwanenweg.* Hamburg: Alster Verlag, 1922.

—. *Ein Heidelberger Bursch vor fünfzig Jahren.* Heidelberg: Johs. Hörning, 1933.

Smith, Harlan Ingersoll. *Archaeology of the Gulf of Georgia and Puget Sound.* Publications of the Jesup North Pacific Expedition 2, no. 6. Leiden: E. J. Brill, 1907.

Smith, Woodruff D. *Politics and the Sciences of Culture in Germany, 1840–1920.* New York: Oxford University Press, 1991.

Stegner, Wallace. *Beyond the Hundredth Meridian: John Wesley Powell and the Second Opening of the West.* Boston: Houghton Mifflin, 1953.

Stocking, George W., Jr. *After Tylor: British Social Anthropology, 1888–1951.* Madison: University of Wisconsin Press, 1995.

—. *Race, Culture, and Evolution: Essays in the History of Anthropology.* New York: Free Press, 1968; reprint, Chicago: University of Chicago Press, 1982.

—. *Victorian Anthropology.* New York: Free Press, 1987.

Stocking, George, W., Jr., ed. *The Shaping of American Anthropology, 1883–1911: A Franz Boas Reader.* New York: Basic Books, 1974.

Strout, Cushing, ed. *Intellectual History in America: Contemporary Essays on Puritanism, the Enlightenment, and Romanticism,* ed. Cushing Strout, 152–59. New York: Harper and Row, 1968.

Tal, Uriel. *Christians and Jews in Germany: Religion, Politics, and Ideology in the Second Reich, 1870–1914.* Trans. Noah Jonathan Jacobs. Ithaca: Cornell University Press, 1975.

Teit, James. *The Thompson Indians of British Columbia.* Publications of the Jesup North Pacific Expedition 1, no. 4. New York, 1900.

—. *Traditions of the Thompson River Indians of British Columbia.* American Folk-Lore Society Memoirs 6. New York: Houghton, Mifflin, 1898.

Tennekes, Johannes. *Anthropology, Relativism and Method: An Inquiry into the Methodological Principles of a Science of Culture.* Assen: Van Gorcum, 1971.

Titchener, Edward Bradford. *Experimental Psychology: A Manual of Laboratory Practice.* New York: Macmillan, 1905.

Truax, Rhoda. *The Doctors Jacobi.* Boston: Little Brown and Co., 1952.

Tylor, Edward Burnett. *Primitive Culture.* Vol. 1. 1871. Reprinted, with an introduction by Paul Radin, as *The Origin of Culture.* New York: Harper and Row, 1958.

von Petersdorff, Hermann. *Die Vereine Deutscher Studenten: Zwölf Jahre akademischer Kampf.* 2d. ed. Leipzig: Breikopf & Härtel, 1895.

White, Leslie A. *The Ethnography and Ethnology of Franz Boas.* Bulletin of the Texas Memorial Museum 6. Austin: Texas Memorial Museum, 1963.

Willey, Thomas E. *Back to Kant: The Revival of Kantianism in German Social and Historical Thought, 1860–1914.* Detroit: Wayne State University Press, 1978.

Williams, Jr., Vernon J. *Rethinking Race: Franz Boas and His Contemporaries.* Lexington: University of Kentucky Press, 1996.

Index

ogy, 254, 257; and associational psychology, 273; and biology, 268; and comparative method, 129–30, 262, 263, 264, 265; concern with, 131; as cosmographer, 123; and cultural area, 265; and cultural determinism, 271, 274; and cultural development, 127, 130, 132; and cultural origins, 265–66; and cultural relativism, 3, 131–32, 133, 136, 274–75, 276; and cultural specificity, 264, 265; and culture concept, 273–74; and diffusion vs. independent invention, 130, 135; and empirical induction, 128, 129, 131; and environmental determinism, 122, 125, 127, 128; ethnological, 133–34, 220, 265; and evolutionary theory, 128, 129; and fieldwork, 133–36, 219–20; and geography, 121, 124, 125, 130; and historical determinism, 126; and historical method, 190–91; and historical relativism, 133; and historicism, 126–27, 264–65; and independent invention, 127, 130, 135; and individualism, 128; and mental processes, laws of, 272–73; and museum arrangement, 127–29; and physical anthropology, 133–34, 268–69; and physics, 123, 268; and positivism, 56, 125; and racial determinism, 268–71; and science vs. history, 123–24, 190–91; and scientific materialism, 56, 125; in transition, 135; and use of term "folklore," 273–74. *See also* Anthropology; Geography; History; Physics; Psychophysics; Science(s)

PERSONALITY: and career, 282–83; criticism of, 283; depression, 50, 92, 172 (*see also* Boas: and loneliness); grandiosity, 205; humility, 222, 283, 284; iconoclasm, 133; idealism, 103, 125; independence, 117, 166, 183–84, 250; industry, 167, 284, 285; intellect, 283, 284; and irreligion, 283; loyalty, 283; personal values, 277–78, 282; and physical energy, 284; productivity, 64, 221; and relations with colleagues, 283; and relations with superiors, 117, 250, 283; sentimentality, 7, 50, 74, 217–18, 242, 280; tenacity, 210; and upbringing, 133, 283

Boas, Gertrude Marianne ("Trudel") (daughter), 214, 219

Boas, Hedwig (daughter), 158–59

Boas, Hedwig (sister). *See* Boas, Hete

Boas, Heine (son), 214, 215–16

Boas, Helene (daughter), 114, 141, 154, 214, 215, 242

Boas, Helene (sister), 16

Boas, Hete (Hedwig) (sister), 17, 22, 64, 65; engagement, 88; marriage, 88; in United States, 241

Boas, Marie Franziska (daughter), 214

Boas, Marie (née Krackowizer) (wife), 167–68; birth of children, 110, 114, 141, 154, 158, 214; and FB's career, 144, 164, 179, 182, 184, 219; courtship, 69–70; engagement, 70, 78; in Germany, 70, 242; marriage, 105; and separation from FB, 173; in United States, 78, 99, 119, 214–15

Boas, Max (uncle), 11

Boas, Meier (father): and anti-Semitism, 58; birth, 11; and FB, 23, 24–25, 28, 29, 42, 59, 105; and business, 11, 13, 16, 22; death, 215–16; education, 11; and Franco-Prussian War, 21; health of, 180; personality, 13; and religion, 12–13, 16; residences, 9, 10, 16, 64, 109, 218; on voters list, 12

Boas, Salomon (uncle), 11

Boas, Sophie (née Meyer) (mother): and *Bildung*, 14; and FB, 17–18, 23, 28, 85, 98; education, 12, 13; and Franco-Prussian War, 21; and Froebel Kindergarten, 18; health of, 243; and Jacobi, 14–15, 16; marriage, 11, 16; and parents, death of, 15, 16; personality, 13; and religion, 13; residences, 9, 10, 11, 16, 109, 218; revolutionary sympathies, 14, 15, 16

Boas, Toni (Antonie) (sister): birth, 16; and FB, 17, 23, 30, 35, 39, 50–51, 57, 70, 88, 105–6; child, 150, 180, 216; and depression, 88, 94, 98; engagement, 150; and finishing school, 21; in Germany, 21–22, 43, 50–51; health of, 21–22, 50–51; kindergarten, 18; and Lehmann, 88; in United States, 99, 105

Body measurements. *See* Anthropometry

Bogoras, Waldemar, 240; and *American Anthropologist*, 211; and Jesup North Pacific Expedition, 197, 198; writing/publications, 228, 235–36, 255, 258, 259

Bolza, Oskar, 137, 139, 146, 159

Bonn, Germany, 43; university, 44–51 passim

Botany, 22, 25–26, 32, 47, 48

Bowditch, Charles P., 211

Brill, E. J. (German publisher), 235, 242, 260

Brinton, Daniel G., 107, 131, 146, 210; and FB, 263–64; and cultural evolution, 271–72; stature in American anthropology, 152

British Association for the Advancement of Science (BAAS): and FB's B.C. expeditions, 110–12, 114, 116, 118; and FB's reports, 139–40; and FB's research proposal, 113; committee on northwestern tribes, 110

British Columbia: FB's interest in, 99. *See also* Boas: Fieldwork: British Columbia

Broca, Paul, 134

Brooklyn Institute, 206

Brotchie, William, 199

Bryan, William Jennings, 187

Bumpus, Hermon C.: and American Museum of Natural History, 224, 231, 232, 245–50; background of, 245; and FB, 1, 242, 243, 244, 245–47, 248, 249, 250; and faked burial incident, 209; and fieldwork, 249; and museum exhibits, 245, 246, 247; on museums, role of, 249; and Saville appointment, 233

Bunsen, Robert, 38, 39, 42, 43

Bunzl, Matti, 283

Bureau of American Ethnology (BAE), 1, 2, 157, 166; and FB's appointment, 82, 206, 222; and FB's expedition plans, 81; and FB's Northwest Coast